Communications
in Computer and Information Science 2341

Series Editors

Gang Li⬤, *School of Information Technology, Deakin University, Burwood, VIC,*
Australia
Joaquim Filipe⬤, *Polytechnic Institute of Setúbal, Setúbal, Portugal*
Zhiwei Xu, *Chinese Academy of Sciences, Beijing, China*

Rationale

The CCIS series is devoted to the publication of proceedings of computer science conferences. Its aim is to efficiently disseminate original research results in informatics in printed and electronic form. While the focus is on publication of peer-reviewed full papers presenting mature work, inclusion of reviewed short papers reporting on work in progress is welcome, too. Besides globally relevant meetings with internationally representative program committees guaranteeing a strict peer-reviewing and paper selection process, conferences run by societies or of high regional or national relevance are also considered for publication.

Topics

The topical scope of CCIS spans the entire spectrum of informatics ranging from foundational topics in the theory of computing to information and communications science and technology and a broad variety of interdisciplinary application fields.

Information for Volume Editors and Authors

Publication in CCIS is free of charge. No royalties are paid, however, we offer registered conference participants temporary free access to the online version of the conference proceedings on SpringerLink (http://link.springer.com) by means of an http referrer from the conference website and/or a number of complimentary printed copies, as specified in the official acceptance email of the event.

CCIS proceedings can be published in time for distribution at conferences or as post-proceedings, and delivered in the form of printed books and/or electronically as USBs and/or e-content licenses for accessing proceedings at SpringerLink. Furthermore, CCIS proceedings are included in the CCIS electronic book series hosted in the SpringerLink digital library at http://link.springer.com/bookseries/7899. Conferences publishing in CCIS are allowed to use Online Conference Service (OCS) for managing the whole proceedings lifecycle (from submission and reviewing to preparing for publication) free of charge.

Publication process

The language of publication is exclusively English. Authors publishing in CCIS have to sign the Springer CCIS copyright transfer form, however, they are free to use their material published in CCIS for substantially changed, more elaborate subsequent publications elsewhere. For the preparation of the camera-ready papers/files, authors have to strictly adhere to the Springer CCIS Authors' Instructions and are strongly encouraged to use the CCIS LaTeX style files or templates.

Abstracting/Indexing

CCIS is abstracted/indexed in DBLP, Google Scholar, EI-Compendex, Mathematical Reviews, SCImago, Scopus. CCIS volumes are also submitted for the inclusion in ISI Proceedings.

How to start

To start the evaluation of your proposal for inclusion in the CCIS series, please send an e-mail to ccis@springer.com.

Limin Sun · Yongle Chen

Editors

Wireless Sensor Networks

18th China Conference, CWSN 2024
Taiyuan, China, September 20–22, 2024
Proceedings, Part I

Editors
Limin Sun
Chinese Academy of Sciences
Beijing, China

Yongle Chen
Taiyuan University of Technology
Taiyuan, China

ISSN 1865-0929   ISSN 1865-0937 (electronic)
Communications in Computer and Information Science
ISBN 978-981-96-2185-9   ISBN 978-981-96-2186-6 (eBook)
https://doi.org/10.1007/978-981-96-2186-6

This Springer imprint is published by the registered company Springer Nature Singapore Pte Ltd.
The registered company address is: 152 Beach Road, #21-01/04 Gateway East, Singapore 189721, Singapore

If disposing of this product, please recycle the paper.

Preface

The China Conference on Wireless Sensor Networks (CWSN) is the annual conference on the Internet of Things (IoT) which is sponsored by the China Computer Federation (CCF). The 18th CWSN took place in Taiyuan, China, in September 2024. As a leading conference in the field of IoT, CWSN is the premier forum for IoT researchers and practitioners from academia, industry, and government in China to share their ideas, research results, and experiences, and this strongly promotes research and technical innovation in these fields domestically and internationally. The conference provides a forum for exchange of academic research and a development forum for IoT researchers, developers, enterprises, and users. Exchanging results and experience of research and applications in IoT, and discussing the key challenges and research hotspots, is the main goal of the forum. As a high-level forum for the design, implementation, and application of IoT, the conference promotes the exchange and application of theories and technologies on IoT-related topics. This year, CWSN received 164 submissions, including 75 English-language papers and 89 Chinese-language papers. After a careful double-blind review process, 41 revised and completed papers were selected. The high-quality program would not have been possible without the authors who chose CWSN 2024 as the venue for their publications. We are also very grateful to the members of the Program Committee and Organizing Committee, who put a tremendous amount of effort into soliciting and selecting research papers with a balance of high quality, new ideas, and new applications. We hope that you enjoy reading and benefit from the proceedings of CWSN 2024.

September 2024
Limin Sun
Yongle Chen

Organization

Conference Chairs

Yunhao Liu   Tsinghua University, China
Dengao Li   Taiyuan University of Technology, China

Honorary Conference Chair

Hao Dai   Chinese Academy of Engineering, China

Steering Committee Chairs

Jianzhong Li   Harbin Institute of Technology, China
Huadong Ma   Beijing University of Posts and
      Telecommunications, China

Program Committee Chairs

Limin Sun   Institute of Information Engineering, Chinese
      Academy of Sciences, China
Yongle Chen   Taiyuan University of Technology, China

Program Committee Vice Chairs

Zhibo Wang   Zhejiang University, China
Shuang Xu   Taiyuan University of Technology, China

Best Paper Award Chairman

Hong Gao   Zhejiang Normal University, China

Industry-Education Integration Forum Chairman

Jian Peng   Sichuan University, China

Excellent Young Scholars Forum Chairman

Linghe Kong   Shanghai Jiao Tong University, China

Organization Committee Chairs

Liang Liu	Beijing University of Posts and Telecommunications, China
Jiliang Wang	Tsinghua University, China
Jumin Zhao	Taiyuan University of Technology, China

Organization Committee Vice Chairs

Xiufang Feng	Taiyuan University of Technology, China
Dan Yu	Taiyuan University of Technology, China

Organization Committee Members

Huanhuan Zhang	Beijing University of Posts and Telecommunications, China
Junbing Cheng	Taiyuan University of Technology, China
Yue Li	Taiyuan University of Technology, China
Mingliang Dou	Taiyuan University of Technology, China
Xiaoling Yu	Taiyuan University of Technology, China
Ruiqin Bai	Taiyuan University of Technology, China
Jianfeng Guo	Taiyuan University of Technology, China
Nian Xue	Taiyuan University of Technology, China
Zhihui Zhao	Taiyuan University of Technology, China
Jianhua Wang	Taiyuan University of Technology, China
Biaokai Zhu	Shanxi Police College, China

Program Committee Members

Guangwei Bai	Nanjing Tech University, China
Ming Bao	Institute of Acoustics Chinese Academy of Sciences, China
Yuanguo Bi	Northeastern University, China
Qingsong Cai	Beijing Technology and Business University, China
Shaobin Cai	Huzhou University, China
Bin Cao	Harbin Institute of Technology, Shenzhen, China
An Zeng	Guangdong University of Technology, China
Deze Zeng	China University of Geosciences, Wuhan, China
Fanzai Zeng	Hunan University, China
Shan Chang	Donghua University, China
Haiming Chen	Ningbo University, China
Hong Chen	Renmin University of China, China
Honglong Chen	China University of Petroleum (East China), China
Liangyin Chen	Sichuan University, China
Quan Chen	Guangdong University of Technology, China
Weiwei Chen	Shanghai University, China
Wei Chen	Beijing Jiaotong University, China
Xi Chen	State Grid Corporation of China, China
Xiaojiang Chen	Northwest University, China
Xu Chen	Sun Yat-sen University, China
Yanru Chen	Sichuan University, China
Yihong Chen	China West Normal University, China
Yongle Chen	Taiyuan University of Technology, China
Zhikui Chen	Dalian University of Technology, China
Keyang Cheng	Jiangsu University, China
Xiuzhen Cheng	Shandong University, China
Hongju Cheng	Fuzhou University, China
Lianglun Cheng	Guangdong University of Technology, China
Siyao Cheng	Harbin Institute of Technology, China
Kaikai Chi	Zhejiang University of Technology, China
Li Cui	Institute of Computing Technology, Chinese Academy of Sciences, China
Xunxue Cui	Army Military Academy, China
Haipeng Dai	Nanjing University, China
Feng Shan	Southeast University, China
Xiaochao Dang	Northwest Normal University, China
Qingyong Deng	Guangxi Normal University, China

Xiaoheng Deng	Central South University, China
Fang Dong	Southeast University, China
Wei Dong	Zhejiang University, China
Hongwei Du	Harbin Institute of Technology Shenzhen, China
Junzhao Du	Xidian University, China
Chao Fang	Beijing University of Technology, China
Juan Fang	Beijing University of Technology, China
Xiaolin Fang	Southeast University, China
Dingyi Fang	Northwest University, China
Guangsheng Feng	Harbin Engineering University, China
Xiufang Feng	Taiyuan University of Technology, China
Deyun Gao	Beijing Jiaotong University, China
Guoju Gao	Soochow University, China
Hong Gao	Zhejiang Normal University, China
Ruipeng Gao	Beijing Jiaotong University, China
Xiaofang Gao	Shanghai Jiao Tong University, China
Yi Gao	Zhejiang University, China
Jibing Gong	Yanshan University, China
Chaojie Gu	Zhejiang University, China
Zhitao Guan	North China Electric Power University, China
Songtao Guo	Chongqing University, China
Xiuzhen Guo	Zhejiang University, China
Zhongwen Guo	Ocean University of China, China
Jie Guang	Hohai University, China
Jinsong Han	Zhejiang University, China
Rui Han	Beijing Institute of Technology, China
Zhanjun Hao	Northwest Normal University, China
Daojing He	Harbin Institute of Technology, China
Shiming He	Changsha University of Science and Technology, China
Yuan He	Tsinghua University, China
Shibo He	Zhejiang University, China
Pengfei Hu	Shandong University, China
Qiangsheng Hua	Huazhong University of Science and Technology, China
Zhan Xuan	Changzhou University, China
Haiping Huang	Nanjing University of Posts and Telecommunications, China
He Huang	Soochow University, China
Liusheng Huang	University of Science and Technology of China, China
Longbo Huang	Tsinghua University, China

Qianyi Huang	Sun Yat-sen University, China
Shuqiang Huang	Jinan University, China
Jie Jia	Northeastern University, China
Riheng Jia	Zhejiang Normal University, China
Nan Jiang	East China Jiaotong University, China
Wenchao Jiang	Guangdong University of Technology, China
Hongbo Jiang	Hunan University, China
Xianlong Jiao	Chongqing University, China
Haiming Jin	Shanghai Jiao Tong University, China
Jiahui Jin	Southeast University, China
Qi Jing	Peking University, China
Linghe Kong	Shanghai Jiao Tong University, China
Zhufang Kuang	Central South University of Forestry and Technology, China
Chao Li	Institute of Computing Technology, Chinese Academy of Sciences, China
Deying Li	Renmin University of China, China
Dao Li	Taiyuan University of Technology, China
Fan Li	Beijing Institute of Technology, China
Feng Li	Shandong University, China
Guangshun Li	Jiangnan University, China
Guangshun Li	Qufu Normal University, China
Guirui Li	Northeastern University at Qinhuangdao, China
Hong Li	Institute of Information Engineering, Chinese Academy of Sciences, China
Hongwei Li	University of Electronic Science and Technology of China, China
Jianqiang Li	Shenzhen University, China
Jianbo Li	Qingdao University, China
Jianzhong Li	Harbin Institute of Technology, China
Jie Li	Northeastern University, China
Jinbao Li	Qilu University of Technology, China
Minglu Li	Zhejiang Normal University, China
Peng Li	Wuhan University of Science and Technology, China
Renfa Li	Hunan University, China
Xiangyang Li	University of Science and Technology of China, China
Yanjun Li	Zhejiang University of Technology, China
Zhetao Li	Xiangtan University, China
Zhijun Li	Harbin Institute of Technology, China
Zhiyuan Li	Jiangsu University, China

Zhong Li	Donghua University, China
Zhuo Li	Beijing Information Science and Technology University, China
Hongbin Liang	Southwest Jiaotong University, China
Jiuzhen Liang	Changzhou University, China
Wei Liang	Shenyang Institute of Automation, Chinese Academy of Sciences, China
Chi Lin	Dalian University of Technology, China
Feng Lin	Zhejiang University, China
Chao Liu	Ocean University of China, China
Chi Liu	Beijing Institute of Technology, China
Dongning Liu	Guangdong University of Technology, China
Hongbo Liu	University of Electronic Science and Technology of China, China
Jiaqi Liu	Northwestern Polytechnical University, China
Jiajia Liu	Northwestern Polytechnical University, China
Kai Liu	Chongqing University, China
Liang Liu	Beijing University of Posts and Telecommunications, China
Min Liu	Institute of Computing Technology, Chinese Academy of Sciences, China
Peng Liu	Hangzhou Dianzi University, China
Qin Liu	Wuhan University, China
Tang Liu	Sichuan Normal University, China
Tao Liu	Southwest University for Nationalities, China
Tong Liu	Shanghai University, China
Xiaoying Liu	Zhejiang University of Technology, China
Xingcheng Liu	Sun Yat-sen University, China
Yunhao Liu	Tsinghua University, China
Zhidan Liu	Shenzhen University, China
Zhouzhou Liu	Xi'an Aeronautical Institute, China
Xiang Liu	Peking University, China
Jianfeng Lu	Wuhan University of Science and Technology, China
Chengwen Luo	Shenzhen University, China
Chuanwen Luo	Beijing Forestry University, China
Haibo Luo	Minjiang University, China
Hanjiang Luo	Shandong University of Science and Technology, China
Juan Luo	Hunan University, China
Junzhou Luo	Southeast University, China
Feng Lv	Central South University, China
Jiamei Lv	Zhejiang University, China

Shichao Lv   Institute of Information Engineering, Chinese
                          Academy of Sciences, China
Huadong Ma   Beijing University of Posts and
                          Telecommunications, China
Li Ma   North China University of Technology, China
Lianbo Ma   Northeastern University, China
Qian Ma   Sun Yat-sen University, China
Jianwei Niu   Beihang University, China
Xiaoguang Niu   Wuhan University, China
Hao Peng   Zhejiang Normal University, China
Yuanyuan Pu   Yunnan University, China
Wangdong Qi   PLA University of Science and Technology, China
Kaiguo Qian   Kunming University, China
Jiefan Qiu   Zhejiang University of Technology, China
Tie Qiu   Tianjin University, China
Fengyuan Ren   Tsinghua University, China
Ju Ren   Tsinghua University, China
Qianqian Ren   Heilongjiang University, China
Yanzhi Ren   University of Electronic Science and Technology
                          of China, China
Shikai Shen   Kunming University, China
Yulong Shen   Xidian University, China
Tuo Shi   City University of Hong Kong, China
Jian Shu   Nanchang Hangkong University, China
Xiaoxia Song   Shanxi Datong University, China
Geng Sun   Jilin University, China
Limin Sun   Institute of Information Engineering, Chinese
                          Academy of Sciences, China
Peng Sun   Hunan University, China
Weifeng Sun   Dalian University of Technology, China
Wen Sun   Northwestern Polytechnical University, China
Yan Sun   Beijing University of Posts and
                          Telecommunications, China
Haisheng Tan   University of Science and Technology of China,
                          China
Zhanyong Tang   Northwest University, China
Fengxiao Tang   Central South University, China
Dan Tao   Beijing Jiaotong University, China
Xiaohua Tian   Shanghai Jiao Tong University, China
Xinyu Tong   Tianjin University, China
Shaohua Wan   University of Electronic Science and Technology
                          of China, China

Yang Wang	University of Science and Technology of China, China
Chao Wang	Northwestern Polytechnical University, China
Cong Wang	Tianjin University of Science and Technology, China
En Wang	Jilin University, China
Guoren Wang	Beijing Institute of Technology, China
Jiliang Wang	Tsinghua University, China
Jingjing Wang	Qingdao University of Science and Technology, China
Ku Wang	Nanjing University of Posts and Telecommunications, China
Lei Wang	Dalian University of Technology, China
Li Wang	Beijing University of Posts and Telecommunications, China
Liangmin Wang	Jiangsu University, China
Liang Wang	Northwestern Polytechnical University, China
Lin Wang	Yanshan University, China
Lu Wang	Shenzhen University, China
Pengfei Wang	Dalian University of Technology, China
Ping Wang	Chongqing University of Posts and Telecommunications, China
Qi Wang	Institute of Computing Technology, Chinese Academy of Sciences, China
Qingshan Wang	Hefei University of Technology, China
Rui Wang	University of Science and Technology Beijing, China
Shuai Wang	Southeast University, China
Tian Wang	Beijing Normal University, China
Xiaoming Wang	Shaanxi Normal University, China
Xinbing Wang	Shanghai Jiao Tong University, China
Xiong Wang	Huazhong University of Science and Technology, China
Xue Wang	Tsinghua University, China
Yiding Wang	Northwestern Polytechnical University, China
Yilei Wang	Qufu Normal University, China
Yongcai Wang	Renmin University of China, China
Yuexuan Wang	University of Hong Kong, China
Zhibo Wang	Zhejiang University, China
Zhi Wang	Zhejiang University, China
Zhu Wang	Northwestern Polytechnical University, China
Zhu Wang	Harbin Institute of Technology, Weihai, China
Liansuo Wei	Qiqihar University, China

Zhenchun Wei	Hefei University of Technology, China
Hui Wen	Institute of Information Engineering, Chinese Academy of Sciences, China
Zhongming Weng	Tianjin University, China
Hejun Wu	Sun Yat-sen University, China
Honghai Wu	Henan University of Science and Technology, China
Libing Wu	Wuhan University, China
Liantao Wu	East China Normal University, China
Tao Wu	National University of Defense Technology, China
Weiwei Wu	Southeast University, China
Xiaojun Wu	Shaanxi Normal University, China
Xingjun Wu	Tsinghua University, China
Kaisheng Wu	Hong Kong University of Science and Technology, Guangzhou, China
Chaocan Xiang	Chongqing University, China
Deqin Xiao	South China Agricultural University, China
Fu Xiao	Nanjing University of Posts and Telecommunications, China
Liang Xiao	Xiamen University, China
Ling Xiao	Hunan University, China
Kun Xie	Hunan University, China
Lei Xie	Nanjing University, China
Mande Xie	Zhejiang Gongshang University, China
Pengjin Xie	Beijing University of Posts and Telecommunications, China
Xiaolan Xie	Guilin University of Technology, China
Xin Xie	Tianjin University, China
Yongping Xiong	Beijing University of Posts and Telecommunications, China
Jia Xu	Nanjing University of Posts and Telecommunications, China
Tianyi Xu	Tianjin University, China
Wenzheng Xu	Sichuan University, China
Chenren Xu	Peking University, China
Guangtao Xue	Shanghai Jiao Tong University, China
Yubo Yan	University of Science and Technology of China, China
Bo Yang	Northwestern Polytechnical University, China
Geng Yang	Nanjing University of Posts and Telecommunications, China

Guisong Yang	University of Shanghai for Science and Technology, China
Hao Yang	Yancheng Teachers University, China
Panlong Yang	University of Science and Technology of China, China
Weidong Yang	Xidian University, China
Zheng Yang	Tsinghua University, China
Xin Yao	Central South University, China
Xinwei Yao	Zhejiang University of Technology, China
Weidong Yi	University of Chinese Academy of Sciences, China
Zuwei Yin	Dongxinyuan Chip Microelectronics Co., Ltd., China
Ruiyun Yu	Northeastern University, China
Jiadi Yu	Shanghai Jiao Tong University, China
Jiguo Yu	Qilu University of Technology, China
Peiyan Yuan	Henan Normal University, China
Daqing Zhang	Peking University, China
Deyu Zhang	Central South University, China
Di Zhang	Beijing Jiaotong University, China
Fusang Zhang	Institute of Software, Chinese Academy of Sciences, China
Guanglin Zhang	Donghua University, China
Hao Zhang	Harbin Institute of Technology, China
Jian Zhang	Wuhan University, China
Jiao Zhang	Beijing University of Posts and Telecommunications, China
Jing Zhang	Xi'an University of Science and Technology, China
Lan Zhang	University of Science and Technology of China, China
Lei Zhang	Tianjin University, China
Li Zhang	Hefei University of Technology, China
Lianming Zhang	Hunan Normal University, China
Shigeng Zhang	Central South University, China
Shiwen Zhang	Hunan University of Science and Technology, China
Shuqin Zhang	Zhongyuan University of Technology, China
Xiao Zhang	South-Central University for Nationalities, China
Yanyong Zhang	University of Science and Technology of China, China
Yin Zhang	University of Electronic Science and Technology of China, China

Yongmin Zhang	Central South University, China
Yunzhou Zhang	Northeastern University, China
Dong Zhao	Beijing University of Posts and Telecommunications, China
Jumin Zhao	Taiyuan University of Technology, China
Junhui Zhao	East China Jiaotong University, China
Liang Zhao	Shenyang Aerospace University, China
Xiaoyan Zhao	Henan Normal University, China
Yang Zhao	Harbin Institute of Technology, Shenzhen, China
Zenghua Zhao	Tianjin University, China
Zhiwei Zhao	University of Electronic Science and Technology of China, China
Jiping Zheng	Nanjing University of Aeronautics and Astronautics, China
Kechen Zheng	Zhejiang University of Technology, China
Meng Zheng	Shenyang Institute of Automation, Chinese Academy of Sciences, China
Xiaolong Zheng	Beijing University of Posts and Telecommunications, China
Ping Zhong	Central South University, China
Anfu Zhou	Beijing University of Posts and Telecommunications, China
Huan Zhou	Northwestern Polytechnical University, China
Jian Zhou	Nanjing University of Posts and Telecommunications, China
Juejia Zhou	Xiaomi Technology, China
Pengzhan Zhou	Chongqing University, China
Ruiting Zhou	Southeast University, China
Xiaobo Zhou	Tianjin University, China
Changbing Zhou	China University of Geosciences (Beijing), China
Zhi Zhou	Sun Yat-sen University, China
Hongzi Zhu	Shanghai Jiao Tong University, China
Hongsong Zhu	Institute of Information Engineering, Chinese Academy of Sciences, China
Peidong Zhu	Changsha University, China
Weiping Zhu	Wuhan University, China
Yihua Zhu	Zhejiang University of Technology, China
Liehuang Zhu	Beijing Institute of Technology, China
Shihong Zou	Beijing University of Posts and Telecommunications, China
Yongpan Zou	Shenzhen University, China

Contents – Part I

Cloud Computing and Edge Computing

GL-CrackNet: A Lightweight Network for Crack Segmentation
in Vehicular Systems 3
*Jing Zhang, Nan Jiang, Ziyi Li, Zefeng Zou, Zesheng Yu,
and Yuejing Zhang*

Multi-UAV Distributed Incremental Learning for Frequency-Hopping
Prediction 16
Ruyan Zhang, Yuben Qu, Xiaojun Zhu, Haipeng Dai, and Chao Dong

Task Offloading Scheduling and Privacy Protection Optimization
in Vehicular Edge Computing Based on Double Deep Q-Network 27
Lu Weifeng, Yang Saijun, Xu Jia, Xu Lijie, and Jiang Lingyun

Crowdsourcing Task Recommendation Method Based on Heterogeneous
Graph Feature Anomaly Detection 40
Kai Wei, Qingxian Pan, Song Yu, Zequn Fan, and Jinru Li

Topology Inference of IoT Edge Network Based on Network Flow
Behavior Analysis 52
*Xiaofeng Zhang, Jinfa Wang, Chunyang Zheng, Haiqiang Fei,
Wenhao Li, and HongSong Zhu*

SmartTask: Efficient Dispatching for Low-Latency Tasks on Dynamic
Edge Networks 64
Zhi Ding, Boyu Kong, Jiamei Lv, Yi Gao, and Wei Dong

BM^{2}SS: Blockchain-Aided Multi-authority and Multi-keyword Searchable
Scheme for IoT 76
*Yao Huang, Zhongyuan Yu, Guijuan Wang, Baobao Chai,
Hongliang Zhang, and Jiguo Yu*

Fog-Enabled Network Intrusion Detection Based on Variational
Autoencoder for Internet of Vehicles 92
Shizhao Tian, Haiqiang Fei, Yongji Liu, Hongsong Zhu, and Limin Sun

Enabling Sub-second QoS-Aware Scheduling for Dynamic Serverless
Workloads   104
    Haodong Tian, Tianyu Huang, Mengyang Liu, Fang Dong,
    and Ruiting Zhou

EdgeMeter: Towards Efficient and Accurate Latency Prediction of Neural
Network Model Inference on Edge Devices   118
    Songtao Lu, Weilong Wang, Borui Li, Shuai Wang, Xiaolei Zhou,
    and Zhao-Dong Xu

Enhancing IoT Compliance Checking with Distributed Process Mining:
A Scalable Framework for Log Data Streams   130
    Chao Song, Zheng Ren, Ruilin Hu, and Li Lu

Internet of Things Security and Privacy Protection

EMLogger: Inferring Computer Activities via EM Side-Channel of Disks   143
    Wenfan Song, Jianwei Liu, and Jinsong Han

A Lightweight Authentication Protocol for LAFED   155
    Yuzhao Liu

Generalizable and Robust Log Anomaly Detection Based on Transformer   168
    Zhaoyang Lou, Xiaolin Chai, Ce Shang, and Yan Sun

Internet of Things Service and Application Technology

Research on the Method of Face Recognition Based on Attention
Mechanism   181
    Wenbin Liu, Guoqing Xu, and En Wang

Lightweight and Efficient Top-Down Human Pose Estimation Algorithm
Research   205
    Xiaofang Mu, Minghui Song, Hong Shi, Mingxing Hou, Shuxian Guo,
    and Wu Xiaotong

Research on Transformer Tracking with Temporal Context and Bounding
Box Refinement Module   218
    Xiaofang Mu, Zijian Wang, Hong Shi, Mingxing Hou, Yiming Wu,
    Shuxian Guo, and Xiaotong Wu

VibECG: Non-contact Electrocardiogram Monitoring Based on mmWave
Sensing   234
    Qi Lin, Langcheng Zhao, Anfu Zhou, and Huadong Ma

Human Activity Recognition Based on Fine-Grained Capture
Spatiotemporal Features of Body RFID Skeleton 247
    Meng Liu, Yihong Chen, and Yilin Zhao

ChewSense: Real-Time Detection of Chewing Counts and Food Types
with Reverse Signals from Headphones 258
    Chenyu Bao, Qingbin Li, Fangming Tian, Qiance Zang, and Feng Hong

Simulated Annealing-Based Routing Optimization Algorithm for LEO
Satellite-Assisted UAV Networks 269
    Yang Shen and Xiaojun Zhu

SimilarBP: Leveraging Similar Samples for Few-Shot PPG-Based Blood
Pressure Measurement 280
    Yixuan Song, Dong Zhao, Qi Wang, and Zhou Fang

Author Index 293

Contents – Part II

Smart Internet of Things

Semantic Information Enhancement and Semantic Alignment for Artistic
Cross-Modal Retrieval 3
 Shasha Hao, Muyan Yao, Peng Qi, and Dan Tao

Dynamic Task Scheduling Strategy for Cloud-Edge Collaborative
Environment 14
 Hui Xiang, Hui Liu, Changyuan Liu, and Junzhao Du

Mobility and Physical-Layer-Assisted Routing Protocol for UAV
Networks in Jamming Environments 29
 Jinyao Sun, Chao Dong, Xiaojun Zhu, and Lei Zhang

NNLoc: Enhancing COTS mmWave Localization with Neural Network 40
 Yuxuan Ding, Yu Fan, Pengjin Xie, Liang Liu, and Huadong Ma

Efficient Visual Reinforcement Learning for IoT Control from Pixels 53
 Haitao Wang, Hejun Wu, and Qiang Tu

Dual-Channel Mixed Token Progressing Unit Model for Sign Language
Production with Global Transformer and Local GCN 63
 Yarun Yang, Qingshan Wang, Qi Wang, and Peng Liu

AI-Enhanced Forecasting in Telesurgery: When Machine Learning Meets
Tactile Internet 74
 Ziying Mo, Lianming Zhang, Qian Wang, Pingping Dong, and Jing Zhang

A Distributed Software Framework for Vision-Based Drone Swarm
Applications 96
 Wei Li, Taoying Liu, Qiang Liu, Yuwei Ben, and Yan Jiang

Hybrid Unsupervised Time-Series Anomaly Detection for Industrial IoT
Based on Spatio-Temporal Feature 110
 Yu Dong, Muyan Yao, Peng Qi, and Dan Tao

GAIN: Game-Theoretic Design of Fair Incentive Mechanisms for Multiple
Model Owners in Federated Learning 121
 Gangqiang Hu, Xiaowei Zeng, Jianmin Han, Bing Li, and Jianfeng Lu

Theory and Technology of Wireless Sensor Network

A Synthesis Library Subset Screening Method for High Energy Efficiency
Requirements 135
   Yidi Li, Kairan Zhang, Chenxu Yang, Sizhou Liu, Hao Guo,
   and Hongfei Zhang

An Optimization Strategy for Adaptive Wireless Sensor Networks Based
on Compressed Sensing 147
   ShenWei Shou and Hui Wang

Unmanned Vehicles Based Optimal RFID Inventory 158
   Zhuoying Chen, Yunguo Zou, Weiping Zhu, and Chao Ma

ESC: Energy-Saving Caching Scheme for Underwater Named Data
Networking 170
   Jinhui Liu, Yingjian Liu, Ruoyu Wang, Zonghai Zha, and Zhongwen Guo

Deep Reinforcement Learning-Based Joint Transmission Power
and Channel Selection in UAV-Assisted Wireless Networks 184
   Khalid Ibrahim Qureshi, Lei Wang, Muhammad Ali Lodhi,
   and Muhammad Asim Ejaz

A Novel eLoran Waveform Based on Linear Frequency Modulation 195
   Xinming Huang, Shugan Zhang, Qi Li, Jing Peng, Hang Gong,
   and Ming Ma

A Dynamic Privacy-Awared Incentive Mechanism Based on Deep
Reinforcement Learning for Opportunistic Networks 206
   Yuxiang Gu, Bing Li, Honghai Wu, Ling Xing, and Huahong Ma

TinyML-Based Approach for Dynamic Transmission Power in LoRaWAN
Network 217
   Muhammad Ali Lodhi, Lei Wang, Khalid Ibrahim Qureshi,
   and Khalid Mahmood

Resource Allocation for Reliable Transmission in IRS-Assisted Industrial
Wireless Sensor Networks 228
   Chuqing Wang, Meng Zheng, and Wei Liang
   Author Index

Author Index 239

Cloud Computing and Edge Computing

GL-CrackNet: A Lightweight Network for Crack Segmentation in Vehicular Systems

Jing Zhang⬚, Nan Jiang⁽✉⁾⬚, Ziyi Li⬚, Zefeng Zou⬚, Zesheng Yu⬚, and Yuejing Zhang⬚

School of Information and Software Engineering, East China University of Technology, Nanchang 330013, Jiangxi, China
jiangnan1018@gmail.com
https://xgxy.ecjtu.edu.cn

Abstract. Deep neural networks in IoV must meet stringent requirements for real-time performance, low latency, lightweight design, and low power consumption. However, most existing deep neural networks are challenged by their complex structures, which demand significant time and computational resources for feature extraction. This limitation hinders their application on portable devices, particularly in the context of in-vehicle image and video processing. To address this, we introduce GL-CrackNet, a lightweight deep neural network tailored for crack detection on portable devices. GL-CrackNet is based on DeepLabv3+ and includes an encoder and decoder. The encoder integrates the GhostNet embedded network and two CCAM modules to capture a comprehensive representation of features. The decoder employs RFB and Dense Aggregation modules for focused feature processing and fusion. On a custom dataset, GL-CrackNet achieves a mIoU of 80.93%, surpassing the baseline by 0.9%–1.5%. This demonstrates a significant improvement in crack detection efficiency while maintaining low storage and power consumption.

Keywords: Road crack segmentation · Internet-of-Vehicles · Lightweight neural networks · Deeplabv3+

1 Introduction

The Internet-of-Vehicles (IoV) enhances transportation systems by interconnecting vehicles, road infrastructure, and cloud resources for seamless information exchange [1]. Using communication and sensor technologies, IoV supports real-time navigation, traffic optimization, and remote vehicle management [2]. Road cracks, including linear or irregular fissures, compromise road smoothness, comfort, and safety. Integrating crack detection into IoV systems involves using deep learning models to detect cracks in real-time via onboard vehicle cameras. These images are uploaded to the cloud for analysis, and drivers receive crack detection

4   J. Zhang et al.

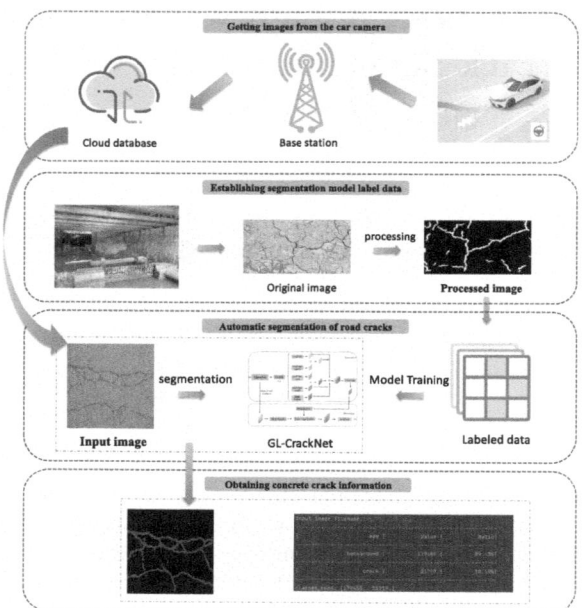

Fig. 1. Framework of IoV crack segmentation.

results, including the area size, through in-vehicle applications or displays [3]. This allows drivers to make informed decisions about route navigation based on crack severity. Figure 1 illustrates the process from data acquisition to detection, showcasing how vehicles with onboard cameras upload images to the cloud for crack detection.

Recently, advancements in DNNs have led to significant breakthroughs in various image-related tasks, such as image classification [4], object detection [5], and semantic segmentation [6–8]. An increasing number of deep learning-based crack detection methods have been implemented on vehicles and UAVs [9,10]. Li et al. [11] proposed a new technique for road crack detection based on UAV pictures, called DenxiDeepCrack. This network introduces an innovative method that combines object detection with image stitching to address issues related to multi-region repetitive images and image occlusion. Furthermore, Chen et al. [12] introduced the Locally Enhanced Cross-shaped Transformer (LECSFrorer) for improved road crack detection, featuring a finely designed encoder-decoder structure. The encoder uses window-based transformer blocks to model long-range dependencies, integrating locally enhanced modules to enrich local context and applying token shuffling to build cross-window connections. The decoder utilizes dense connections to fuse multi-scale information, with a feature fusion module that merges hierarchical features and reweights them through a channel attention mechanism. Despite advancements in road crack detection methods, there are notable deficiencies in lightweight design. Lightweight networks aim to minimize model parameters and size while maintaining acceptable performance levels, making them suitable for deployment on resource-constrained devices. However, many approaches [13] involve complex model architectures that require substantial computational resources. Additionally, efforts to reduce model size often come at the expense of detection accuracy, failing to achieve an optimal balance between lightweight design and performance.

To address these challenges, we propose GL-CrackNet, a lightweight network based on an encoder-decoder architecture, using DeepLabv3+ as the baseline. Our approach employs GhostNet in the encoder for efficient feature extraction, enhanced by CCAM and ASPP modules. The decoder includes the RFB module and Dense Aggregation to effectively restore features to their original dimensions. Designed specifically for crack detection, GL-CrackNet precisely identifies the presence of cracks in images. In summary, our contributions are:

- We propose GL-CrackNet, a lightweight encoder-decoder network architecture that enhances segmentation performance. On a custom dataset, GL-CrackNet achieves an impressive mIoU of 80.93%, surpassing the original model by 0.9% to 1.5% under the same benchmark.
- We propose a new decoder composed of the RFB module and Dense Aggregation. This new decoding architecture aims to enhance feature processing and fusion for improved performance in crack detection tasks.
- The proposed GL-CrackNet network has half the number of parameters compared to MobileNetV2 and one twenty-fourth of those in Xception network. Additionally, the FLOP count of GL-CrackNet is approximately 20% lower than that of MobileNetV2 and about 70% lower than Xception.

2 Related Work

2.1 Based on Traditional Method

Image processing and traditional machine learning techniques are synergistically employed for concrete crack detection, incorporating edge detection algorithms and filters. Nguyen et al. [14] applied PSCEF for non-crack object removal, employed threshold filtering and shape thinning algorithms for image binarization, and used cubic spline curves to connect edge points for continuous crack edges. The work in [15] proposed a robust method for automatic crack detection on noisy concrete surfaces, involving relaxation processing and an enhanced local adaptive threshold method. In [16], integrated channel features were introduced for crack extraction. Simultaneously, the authors employed random forest trees for structured information mining and eliminated noise using two feature histograms, leading to improved detection results. However, these methods may struggle with complex scenes and diverse crack shapes due to their reliance on features like intensity variations, texture, and shape.

2.2   Based on Deep Learning

Deep learning-based crack detection methods can be categorized into patch-based and pixel-based approaches. In 2020, Feng et al. [17] introduced a road crack recognition approach using a hybrid deep convolutional neural network model. They employed the SSD network for crack classification detection and replaced the U-Net feature extraction network with a residual network for crack segmentation, resulting in significant improvements in accuracy and recall rates. BARNet [18], introduced in 2021, is a specialized encoder-decoder network for road crack detection. It comprises a fundamental prediction module, an edge adaptation module, and a refinement module. BARNet outperforms existing methodologies in accurately localizing cracks and adapting to challenging scenarios. Additionally, Liu et al. [19] proposed CrackFormer, a transformer network combining self-attention and scaled attention mechanisms for precise crack detection.

3   Our Methodology

3.1   Framework Overview

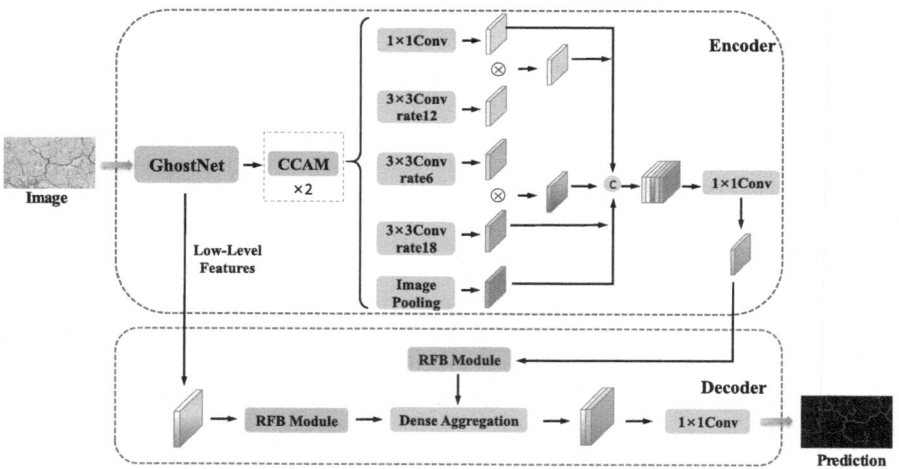

Fig. 2. The architecture of our proposed network. GL-CrackNet, which takes deeplabv3+ as the baseline. The encoder in this model is divided into four key components: 1) the GhostNet backbone network; 2) the CCAM module; 3) the modified ASPP module; and 4) decoder.

Figure 2 illustrates the specific structure of our proposed network. The input image first passes through the encoder, where GhostNet produces a low-level feature, and the entire encoder outputs a high-level feature. These two types of features are then processed through RFB modules and aggregated in Dense Aggregation module. The final step involves mapping the input feature maps to category predictions using a 1 × 1 convolution, resulting in the final segmentation output.

3.2   Encoder-Backbone Architectures

The DeepLabv3+ architecture typically uses the Xception network [20] as its backbone. However, this complexity can lead to a significant computational burden. Thus, we integrated the lightweight GhostNet [21] into the architecture and streamlined its structure. To address Feature map redundancy, we replaced the traditional convolutional layer with a Ghost Module. This involves compressing the input feature map using a 1 × 1 convolution to reduce the number of channels, followed by generating additional feature maps using deep separable convolutions. These feature maps are then concatenated to form a new output feature map. The GhostNet architecture consists of multiple Ghost Bottlenecks. In the original GhostNet, 16 Ghost Bottlenecks are stacked. But we only stack 10 Ghost Bottlenecks and adjust the parameters of each layer.

3.3   Criss-Cross Attention Module

Figure 4 illustrates the Criss-cross Attention module (CCAM). Since a single Criss-Cross Attention module only captures information within the row and column of a specific location, we use two modules to effectively capture global information.

The Criss-cross Attention Module captures contextual information as follows: Given a local feature F, it generates feature maps Q, K, and V through three 1 × 1 convolutions. Q and K have the same dimension, while V retains the original dimensions of F. An affinity operation on Q and K, followed by a softmax function, produces an attention weight matrix A. The aggregation of A and V, with the addition of F as a residual, results in the feature map F'.

Here are some basic definitions. We represent the dimension of the local feature F as (H × W × C), and the dimensions of Q and K as (H × W × C'). The pixels in Q are denoted by q_i, where i∈[1 , H×W]. We use Q_i to represent the one-dimensional vector composed of all pixel points in the channel dimension of q, with dimension (C' × 1 × 1). Since Q and K have the same dimension, the pixel points on Q and K can be one-to-one correspondent. We denote a pixel point in K as k_i, where i∈[1 , H×W]. At the same time, we use K_i to represent the one-dimensional vector composed of each pixel point in K in the channel dimension.

The Affinity operation is detailed as follows: First, take all the pixel points of q' in both horizontal and vertical directions, a total of (H + W − 1), and expand them in the channel dimension to obtain a malformed three-dimensional matrix K(q) with dimensions (H + W − 1) × C'. Then, multiply Q_i (C' × 1 × 1) with K(C') ((H + W − 1) × C') to obtain a three-dimensional matrix Aq with a shape of (H + W − 1) ×1×1. Note that k_i is only one of the H×W instances. We stack

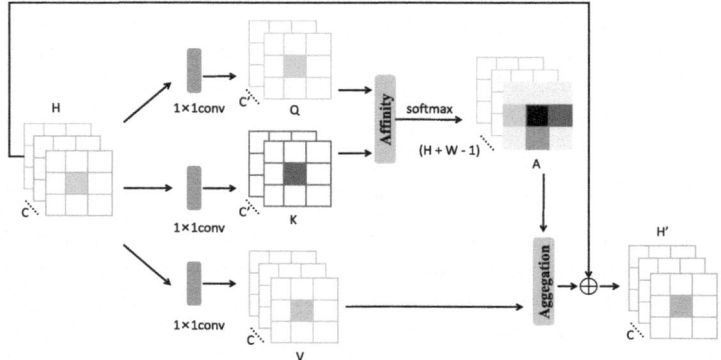

Fig. 3. The architecture of Criss-cross Attention module.

the H×W three-dimensional matrices with a shape of (H + W − 1) ×1×1 to form a feature map S with a dimension of (H + W − 1) ×H×W. Finally, we apply the softmax function to transform the feature map S into an attention-weighted feature matrix A with a shape of (H×W×C). The expressions are as follows:

$$Aq = Q_q K(q)^\mathsf{T} T \tag{1}$$

$$A = \sum_{i=1}^{H \times W} Aq_i \tag{2}$$

The horizontal and vertical features of each pixel point in V are multiplied with the horizontal and vertical features of each pixel point q in A, and then added to the original feature F as a residual to obtain a feature Fq' with stronger representation ability. The expression is as follows:

$$Fq' = V(q)A + F \tag{3}$$

3.4 Decoder Design

In reference to the cascaded section of the decoder, we observed that the shallow features, possessing higher resolution, consume significant computing resources, while the deep features can effectively capture the spatial details of the shallow features. Consequently, we opted to replace the DeepLabv3+ decoder with a novel decoder architecture. Our decoder incorporates the RFB Module and Dense Aggregation. Low-level semantic features from GhostNet and high-level semantic features from the encoder are processed through an RFB module and then sampled within Dense Aggregation for optimal feature fusion.

Figure 4 illustrates the RFB Module. This module integrates multiple convolution branches with varying sizes, similar to the Inception architecture, and includes cavity convolutions. Drawing from ACNet [22], which validates that an n×n convolution is equivalent to two asymmetric convolutions (1 × n and n × 1), we use these asymmetric convolutions to capture larger region information and enhance contextual understanding while minimizing parameters.

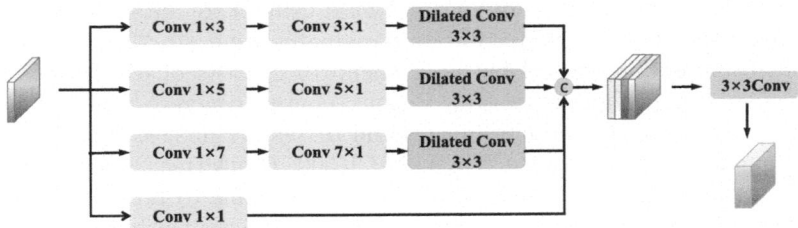

Fig. 4. The architecture of RFB module.

Figure 5 depicts Dense Aggregation, achieved through element-level multiplication. After multi-scale feature extraction with the RFB module, feature maps of varying sizes are obtained. These features are upsampled to the same scale, multiplied, and concatenated with another input feature of corresponding scale. A convolution operation then generates a feature tensor containing informative features.

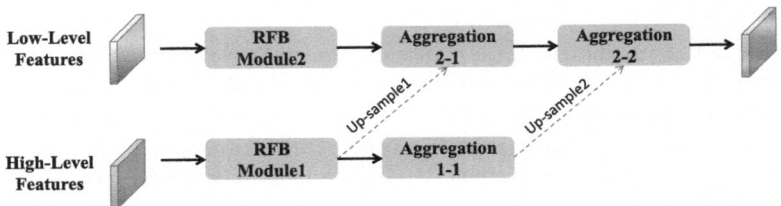

Fig. 5. The architecture of Dense Aggregation module.

The complementary feature representations from deep and shallow semantic branches are merged using a bilateral fusion mechanism. This involves upsampling and downsampling to combine features at corresponding scales, resulting in multiscale representations. This seamless integration enhances the efficiency of information merging between the branches.

4   Experiment and Results

4.1   Implementation Details

We implement our network using the PyTorch framework, and all experiments are conducted on one NVIDIA GeForce RTX A6000.

We evaluate the efficacy of our network using two datasets: CrackMix and Cement610. The CrackMix dataset originates from [16,23,24], while the Cement610 dataset is created by us. Cement610 consists of 610 images, each sized 787 × 522 pixels, showcasing various poured concrete structures. The dataset is split into 549 training images and 61 testing images. The CrackMix dataset includes four datasets-CFD, CRACK500, CrackTree, and DeepCrack-totaling 1,309 images. The creation of this dataset aims to provide richer and more diverse training samples for crack detection tasks. During training, the initial global learning rate is set to 0.007, with the default minimum learning rate being 0.01 times the maximum learning rate. The learning rate adjustment follows the cos policy. For experiments with the SGD optimizer, we set momentum and weight attenuation to 0.9 and 0.0001, respectively. The training process spans a total of 500 epochs.

We use the mIoU as a performance indicator to evaluate the degree of match between the segmented image and the ground truth label. Additionally, we evaluate more comprehensive metrics, namely accuracy, precision, F1_score, and pixel accuracy.

4.2   Abliation Study

As shown in Fig. 6, there is no obvious difference between mPA and Accuracy on the training set, but our network is always slightly higher. Notably, when using mIoU as the evaluation metric, the mIoU curve for GL-CrackNet in our network distinctly separates from the other three curves. The Vanilla model achieves an mIoU of approximately 79.14%, and the introduction of two CCAM modules enhances the mIoU to about 79.41%. Furthermore, the incorporation of the MASPP module alone results in an increased mIoU of approximately 79.37%. We attribute this enhancement to the MASPP module's capability to expand the receptive field, enabling the capture of more global information. The synergistic integration of the GhostNet embedded network, two CCAM modules, and our Decoder module–referred to as the GL-CrackNet network-further elevates performance, yielding an mIoU of about 80.56%. Importantly, the convergence speed of GL-CrackNet surpasses that of the other three curves.

On the test set (shown in Fig. 7), our network demonstrated exceptional performance across all three key performance indicators, mIoU, mPA, and overall Accuracy outperforming other models. This observation underscores the remarkable generalization capability of GL-CrackNet in real-world scenarios, surpassing its performance on the training set. These results affirm the feasibility and effectiveness of our optimization strategy.

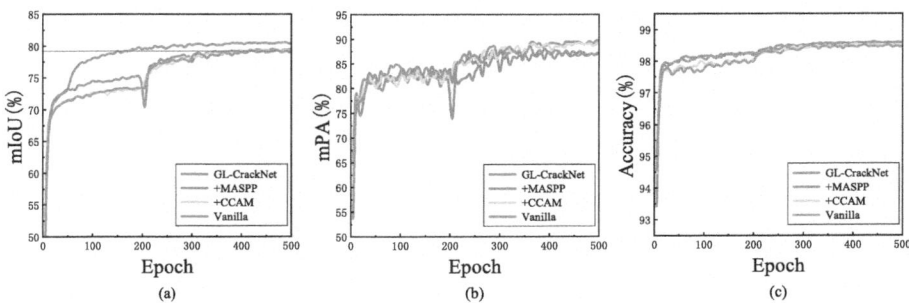

Fig. 6. Ablation experiments of each module.

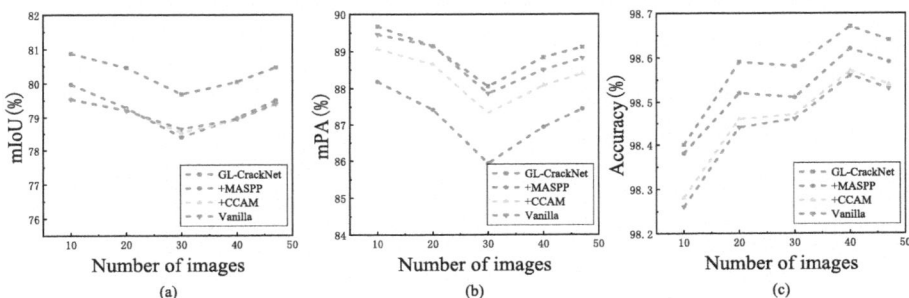

Fig. 7. Ablation experiments of each module.

4.3   Comparative Experiments

Our study presents a comprehensive analysis of various deep learning methods for crack detection and segmentation. The results were obtained from two different datasets: CrackMix and Ours.

On the CrackMix dataset, the performance of different methods was evaluated based on metrics like mIoU, mPA, Overall Accuracy, and F1_Score. The detailed results are shown in Table 1. Our proposed method demonstrated a superior performance with an mIoU of 0.7957, closely followed by DeepLabv3+ (Xception) at 0.7809. The F1_Score of our method was also competitive at 0.8550, indicating a high precision and recall balance. DeepLabv3+ (MobileNetv2) and CrackSeu also showed commendable performance, with DeepLabv3+ (MobileNetv2) achieving the highest mPA of 0.8910. However, U-Net and DeepCrack lagged behind, especially in terms of mIoU and F1_Score, suggesting limitations in handling complex crack patterns.

When tested on our dataset, the methods exhibited a slightly different performance pattern. The detailed results are shown in Table 2. Our method outperformed others with an mIoU of 0.8046 and an F1_Score of 0.8845, reflecting its robustness and adaptability across different datasets. Notably, DeepLabv3+ (Xception) showed a significant improvement on our dataset, achieving an mIoU

Table 1. Results of comparative experiments on the CrackMix dataset

Method	mIoU	mPA	Accuracy	F1_score
DeepLabv3+(Xception)	0.7809	0.8762	0.9796	0.8560
DeepLabv3+(MoblieNetv2)	0.7765	0.8910	0.9780	0.8450
U-Net	0.6210	0.7630	0.9740	0.7750
CrackSeu	0.7234	0.8563	0.9536	0.8017
DeepCrack	0.5813	0.6973	0.9292	0.6904
DAU-Net	0.6857	0.7868	0.9602	0.7195
Ours	0.7957	0.8759	0.9788	0.8550

Table 2. Results of comparative experiments on the Cement610 dataset

Method	mIoU	mPA	Accuracy	F1_score
DeepLabv3+(Xception)	0.7892	0.9068	0.9840	0.8670
DeepLabv3+(MoblieNetv2)	0.7480	0.9176	0.9775	0.8570
U-Net	0.6384	0.7745	0.9855	0.6950
CrackSeu	0.7242	0.8356	0.9640	0.7982
DeepCrack	0.5878	0.6754	0.9328	0.7142
DAU-Net	0.6934	0.7969	0.9645	0.7443
Ours	0.8046	0.8911	0.9864	0.8845

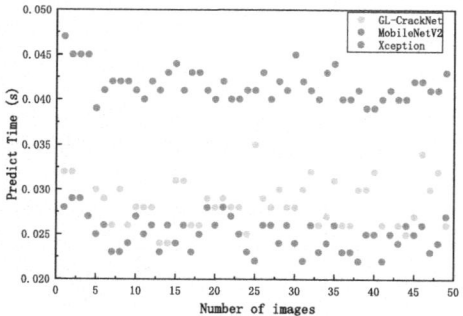

Fig. 8. Predict time of different networks.

Fig. 9. Loss on training and validation sets.

of 0.7892 and the highest mPA of 0.9068. The performance of U-Net and Deep-Crack remained lower than the other methods, although U-Net showed a slight improvement in accuracy on our dataset. This variation in performance across datasets underscores the importance of dataset characteristics in model evaluation.

We compared the processing times of different networks for crack detection, as illustrated in Fig. 8. The results show that our method significantly outperforms the Xception network in terms of speed. Although it is slightly slower than Mobilenetv2, our method demonstrates superior accuracy. Overall, our method ensures real-time performance while maintaining high precision. The graph 9 illustrates that the network's training and validation losses converge closely with minimal variance across epochs, indicating strong generalization ability.

5 Conclusion

In this paper, we propose a lightweight encoder-decoder architecture network named GL-CrackNet, which demonstrates superior performance in crack segmentation tasks. To further enhance network efficiency, we replaced the original Xception backbone with the GhostNet model and introduced two criss-cross attention modules. Addressing the issue of potential information loss due to direct upsampling, we present an innovative solution with a novel decoder composed of the RFB Module and Dense Aggregation. The incorporation of the RFB Module expands the neural network's receptive field, enhancing its understanding of global contextual information. Simultaneously, the use of Dense Aggregation facilitates more efficient feature transmission during the decoding process, mitigating the risk of information loss. In summary, these innovative enhancements have propelled our GL-CrackNet to achieve superior performance in segmentation tasks while maintaining the lightweight nature of the network.

Acknowledgments. This work was supported by National Natural Science Foundation of China under Grant No. 62062034 and 62172160, National Key Research and Development Program of China under Grant No. 2022YFB2602200, Double Thousand Plan of Jiangxi Province under Grant No. JXSQ2023201010 and Jiangxi Province Key Laboratory of Advanced Network Computing under Grant No. 2024SSY03071.

Disclosure of Interests. The authors declare that they have no conflict of interest.

References

1. Elmoiz Alatabani, L., et al.: Deep and reinforcement learning technologies on internet of vehicle (IoV) applications: current issues and future trends. J. Adv. Transp. **2022**, 1–13 (2022)
2. Hemmati, A., Zarei, M., Souri, A.: Blockchain-based internet of vehicles (BIoV): a systematic review of surveys and reviews. Secur. Priv. **6**(6), e317 (2023)
3. Haider, M., Peyal, M. K., Huang, T., Xiang, W.: Road crack avoidance: a convolutional neural network-based smart transportation system for intelligent vehicles. J. Intell. Transp. Syst. 1–13 (2023)
4. Azizi, S., et al.: Big self-supervised models advance medical image classification. In: Proceedings of the IEEE/CVF International Conference on Computer Vision, pp. 3478–3488. IEEE (2021)

5. Tan, M., Pang, R., Le, Q. V.: EfficientDet: scalable and efficient object detection. In: Proceedings of the IEEE/CVF Conference on Computer Vision and Pattern Recognition, pp. 10781–10790. IEEE (2020)

6. Wang, C.-Y., Bochkovskiy, A., Liao, H.-Y. M.: YOLOv7: trainable bag-of-freebies sets new state-of-the-art for real-time object detectors. In: Proceedings of the IEEE/CVF Conference on Computer Vision and Pattern Recognition, pp. 7464–7475. IEEE (2023)

7. Zhang, C., Lu, W., Wu, J., Ni, C., Wang, H.: SegNet network architecture for deep learning image segmentation and its integrated applications and prospects. Acad. J. Sci. Technol. **9**(2), 224–229 (2024)

8. López-González, C.I., Gascó, E., Barrientos-Espillco, F., Besada-Portas, E., Pajares, G.: Filter pruning for convolutional neural networks in semantic image segmentation. Neural Netw. **169**, 713–732 (2024)

9. Shan, J., Jiang, W., Huang, Y., Yuan, D., Liu, Y.: Unmanned aerial vehicle (UAV)-based pavement image stitching without occlusion, crack

10. Kariminejad, N., et al.: Evaluation of various deep learning algorithms for landslide and sinkhole detection from UAV imagery in a semi-arid environment. Earth Syst. Environ. 1–12 (2024)

11. Li, Y., Ma, J., Zhao, Z., Shi, G.: A novel approach for UAV image crack detection. Sensors **22**(9), 3305 (2022)

12. Chen, J., Zhao, N., Zhang, R., Chen, L., Huang, K., Qiu, Z.: Refined crack detection via LECSFormer for autonomous road inspection vehicles. IEEE Trans. Intell. Veh. **8**(3), 2049–2061 (2022)

13. Kheradmandi, N., Mehranfar, V.: A critical review and comparative study on image segmentation-based techniques for pavement crack detection. Constr. Build. Mater. **321**, 126162 (2022)

14. Nguyen, H.-N., Kam, T.-Y., Cheng, P.-Y.: An automatic approach for accurate edge detection of concrete crack utilizing 2D geometric features of crack. J. Sig. Process. Syst. **77**, 221–240 (2014)

15. Fujita, Y., Hamamoto, Y.: A robust automatic crack detection method from noisy concrete surfaces. Mach. Vis. Appl. **22**, 245–254 (2011)

16. Shi, Y., Cui, L., Qi, Z., Meng, F., Chen, Z.: Automatic road crack detection using random structured forests. IEEE Trans. Intell. Transp. Syst. **17**(12), 3434–3445 (2016)

17. Feng, X., Xiao, L., Li, W., Pei, L., Sun, Z., Ma, Z., Shen, H., Ju, H.: Pavement crack detection and segmentation method based on improved deep learning fusion model. Math. Probl. Eng. **2020**, 1–22 (2020)

18. Guo, J.-M., Markoni, H., Lee, J.-D.: BARNet: boundary aware refinement network for crack detection. IEEE Trans. Intell. Transp. Syst. **23**(7), 7343–7358 (2021)

19. Liu, H., Miao, X., Mertz, C., Xu, C., Kong, H.: Crackformer: transformer network for fine-grained crack detection. In: Proceedings of the IEEE/CVF International Conference on Computer Vision, pp. 3783–3792. IEEE (2021)

20. Chollet, F.: Xception: Deep learning with depthwise separable convolutions. In: Proceedings of the IEEE Conference on Computer Vision and Pattern Recognition, pp. 1251–1258. IEEE (2017)

21. Han, K., Wang, Y., Tian, Q., Guo, J., Xu, C., Xu, C.: GhostNet: more features from cheap operations. In: Proceedings of the IEEE/CVF Conference on Computer Vision and Pattern Recognition, pp. 1580–1589. IEEE (2020)

22. Ding, X., Guo, Y., Ding, G., Han, J.: AcNet: strengthening the kernel skeletons for powerful CNN via asymmetric convolution blocks. In: Proceedings of the

IEEE/CVF International Conference on Computer Vision, pp. 1911–1920. IEEE (2019)

23. Zou, Q., Zhang, Z., Li, Q., Qi, X., Wang, Q., Wang, S.: Deepcrack: learning hierarchical convolutional features for crack detection. IEEE Trans. Image Process. **28**(3), 1498–1512 (2018)

24. Yang, F., Zhang, L., Yu, S., Prokhorov, D., Mei, X., Ling, H.: Feature pyramid and hierarchical boosting network for pavement crack detection. IEEE Trans. Intell. Transp. Syst. **21**(4), 1525–1535 (2019)

Multi-UAV Distributed Incremental Learning for Frequency-Hopping Prediction

Ruyan Zhang[1], Yuben Qu[2](✉), Xiaojun Zhu[1], Haipeng Dai[3], and Chao Dong[2]

[1] College of Computer Science and Technology, Nanjing University of Aeronautics and Astronautics, Nangjing 211106, China
{zhangruyan,xzhu}@nuaa.edu.cn
[2] College of Electronic and Information Engineering, Nanjing University of Aeronautics and Astronautics, Nangjing 211106, China
quyuben@nuaa.edu.cn
[3] Department of Computer Science and Technology, Nanjing University, Nanjing 210093, China

Abstract. In military operations, unmanned aerial vehicle (UAV) swarms equipped with electromagnetic sensors and computing devices can easily capture enemy spectrum data, enabling the training of deep neural network models to predict enemy frequency-hopping sequences. Traditional methods typically rely on single nodes for data sensing and model training. However, the limited onboard resources of UAVs lead to extended model training times, and the sense-then-train approach exacerbates the overall task duration, severely impacting real-time requirements on the battlefield. To address these issues, this paper proposes a Multi-UAV Distributed Incremental Learning (MDIL) method. This method establishes parallel sensing and training task flows, continuously collects data, and updates the model. By leveraging the distributed data sensing and incremental learning of UAV swarms and considering the heterogeneity of UAVs, this method optimizes the sensing sequence and workload, enhances real-time responsiveness, and reduces sensing and training times. Experimental results show that this method effectively reduces task training time by 22.13% and overall time by 36.89%, albeit at the expense of some accuracy.

Keywords: multiple UAVs · distributed incremental learning · frequency-hopping(FH)

1 Introduction

Unmanned aerial vehicle (UAV) swarms equipped with sensors such as electromagnetic and synthetic aperture radar can effortlessly acquire three-dimensional data in low-altitude airspace. Furthermore, UAVs with computing devices can replace traditional modes of data backhaul to ground stations or cloud servers, significantly reducing task latency, thus becoming typical mobile edge computing devices [1,2]. By further integrating artificial intelligence (AI), especially deep neural networks, UAV swarms play significant roles in civilian sectors like target detection and resource allocation, as well as in military applications [3, 4].

In military contexts, real-time monitoring and analysis of adversary frequency-hopping (FH) information are crucial for predicting enemy frequency use. Traditional ground stations or fixed-frequency monitoring devices need to transmit monitoring data back to the ground for processing, which consumes significant bandwidth resources and fails to meet the high demands of real-time performance in military environments. In contrast, UAVs equipped with electromagnetic sensors and computing devices can easily collect the FH data of opponents in three-dimensional space and train deep learning models for FH prediction tasks. Long short-term memory networks (LSTM), capable of handling long-term dependencies and overcoming the vanishing gradient problem in deep neural networks, are widely applied in sequence analysis [5]. Therefore, Li et al. [6] proposed using a LSTM model to predict FH sequences. However, due to the temporal nature of FH data, the traditional approach relied on a single UAV for centralized FH data collection instead of utilizing a swarm of UAVs. Subsequently, all data were loaded into memory for batch training. Nevertheless, the embedded computational resources in UAVs are limited, such as constrained memory and processing capabilities [7], which leads to excessively long model training times and potential memory crashes. The traditional sense-then-train approach requires extensive data collection before training can commence, which prolongs the sensing and processing times, thereby increasing the overall task duration. This places higher demands on the UAV's battery life and poses significant challenges to real-time performance and system stability on the battlefield.

To address these issues, this paper proposes a multi-UAV distributed incremental learning (MDIL) approach for FH prediction, leveraging multiple UAVs to reduce training and overall time. Specifically, the core idea of MDIL involves parallelizing the sensing and training processes. Multiple UAVs continuously collect data in a pipeline manner and use their gathered data to iteratively train predictive models for dynamic updates. During this process, each UAV node trains the model using its own FH data, while subsequent UAV nodes continue to collect additional data. Once training is complete, each UAV transfers the model to the next node, which performs incremental updates using its own dataset on the received model. This iterative process continues until the final UAV outputs the ultimate model. Incremental learning helps avoid redundant training and reduces overall training time. Additionally, the parallel operation of sensing and training further shortens the total task execution time. Considering the heterogeneity in computing performance within a multi-UAV system, MDIL also involves sorting UAVs based on their computing performance before commencing core tasks to determine the execution order and task allocation. This sorting helps assess the impact of data proportion on task distribution and overall time, optimizing task allocation strategies. The contributions of our work are summarized as follows:

- To the best of our knowledge, this is the first work to propose the integration of incremental learning with a multi-UAV system for online training of FH prediction models. Considering the characteristics of streaming data, it introduces the MDIL method, which utilizes multiple UAVs in coordination to perform sensing and training tasks concurrently, addressing the issue of prolonged processing time associated with traditional methods.

- Considering the heterogeneity of computing devices on UAVs, MDIL further optimizes the impact of computational heterogeneity on task duration by dividing the execution order and workload according to the computing performance of the UAVs.
- We collected real FH data and conducted extensive experiments on the computational devices onboard UAVs to validate the effectiveness of our algorithm. The results indicate that compared to traditional methods, our algorithm reduces training time by approximately 22.13% and overall time by 36.89%.

2   Related Works

UAV Swarm AI Computing. As artificial intelligence technology expands to unmanned aerial vehicles (UAVs), onboard computing demands are increasing significantly. However, UAVs typically have limited computing resources, making it hard for a single UAV to meet comprehensive airborne intelligent computing needs. Current solutions often involve using UAV swarms to enhance edge AI capabilities collectively [8,9]. For example, Qu et al. [10] proposed the eCoEI architecture for elastic deep neural network inference across multiple UAVs, while Wu et al. [11] used UAV swarms for federated learning. However, the former focuses on model inference and is unsuitable for battlefield scenarios, where UAV swarms need to train models with online data rather than rely on offline models. Similarly, the latter does not fit because FH data typically appears as streaming data, and federated learning does not address the sequential nature of this data.

Incremental Learning. Incremental learning differs from batch training in that it does not require loading all data into memory at once; instead, it continuously learns new knowledge using newly available training data [12]. Recent studies, such as Wang et al. [13], propose a centralized incremental learning LSTM approach suitable for streaming data. This method partitions newly generated data into weak learner subsets and combines them with the old model to form a strong learner. Takele et al. [14] extend this idea to Industrial Internet of Things (IIoT) devices, incrementally processing continuously generated new data. Melgar-García et al. [15] introduce a method for matching new pattern data under incremental learning, focusing more on addressing performance degradation issues caused by new class input or changes in the structure of time-series data. These strategies focus on continuous reception of large amounts of data for incremental learning on a single device, posing challenges for devices with limited computing capabilities like UAVs. Therefore, due to high energy consumption requirements, these strategies become impractical.

As of now, there are few airborne real-time computing efforts dedicated to FH prediction tasks, especially utilizing a multi-UAV collaborative strategy. FH data represents a typical example of streaming data. Inspired by the aforementioned research, we propose a novel approach where multiple UAVs collaborate in a pipeline-style execution of sensing and training tasks, optimizing task allocation considering the computational heterogeneity among UAVs.

3   System Model and Problem Formulation

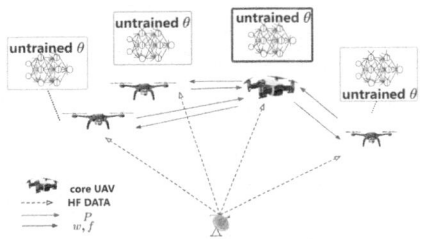

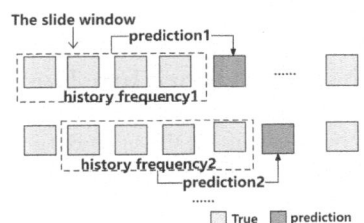

Fig. 1. System design.

Fig. 2. LSTM-based predictive model under time expansion.

Our system, as shown in Fig. 1, consists of a swarm of n UAVs denoted as $U = \{U_1, U_2, \ldots, U_n\}$. These UAVs collectively need to collect S frequency points. Each UAV is equipped with computational devices and radio frequency sensor, storing untrained prediction models $\Theta = \{M_i\}_{i=1}^{m}$, where m denotes the number of layers in the model. The UAVs are capable of transmitting Θ and their own information via communication modules. U_i is denoted as $< p_i, w_i, f_i, \Lambda_i, s_i, D_i >$, where p_i represents the computational capability of U_i, w_i defines its weight in the system as $w_i = \frac{p_i}{\sum_{j=1}^{n} p_j}$, f_i denotes its priority or task execution sequence, and Λ_i is a binary variable indicating whether the UAV is a core UAV ($\Lambda_i \in \{0, 1\}$). The amount of frequency point data U_i needs to collect, s_i, is defined as $s_i = w_i \times S$. The dataset D_i collected by U_i is given by $D_i = (s_i - l + 1)$, where l is the step length used during model training.

During the execution of tasks, except for the first UAV, the sensing duration of each UAV overlaps with the training time of the preceding UAV. Therefore, the total training time for the models is defined as $T_{\text{train}} = \sum_{f=1}^{n} T_f^{\text{train}}$, which sums up the training times for all UAVs. The total task completion time, including both sensing and training durations, is specifically defined as $T_{\text{total}} = T_{f=1}^{\text{sense}} + \sum_{f=1}^{n-1} \max(T_f^{\text{train}}, T_{f+1}^{\text{sense}}) + T_{f=n}^{\text{train}}$, Here, T_f^{train} denotes the training time for UAV with priority f, and T_{f+1}^{sense} denotes the sensing time of UAV with priority $f + 1$. Data transmission time, significantly shorter compared to training and sensing times, is therefore not included in the total time.

Figure 2 illustrates the process by which UAVs construct datasets, sliding a window forward from the initial portion of acquired FH data. Due to the difficulty in accurately predicting actual frequency points, predictions are transformed from point-wise to interval predictions. A prediction is deemed accurate if the forecasted frequency falls within an error range around the actual frequency, consistent with prior research [6]. This error range is defined as error range $= \frac{2 \cdot \Delta f}{F}$, where Δf denotes the error interval between predicted and actual frequency points, and F represents the frequency hopping bandwidth. Furthermore, prediction accuracy is defined as accuracy $= \frac{\text{count}(|y_i - \tilde{y}_i| < \Delta f)}{\text{count}(y_i)}$, where y_i is the actual frequency and $\tilde{y}_i$ is the predicted frequency. For instance, with $\Delta f = 3$ and $F = 100$, a prediction is considered accurate if $\tilde{y}_i$ falls within $y_i \pm 3$, indicating an error range of 6%.

4   MDIL Algorithm Design

The core idea of MDIL is to determine the sensing weights, order, and task volume based on the computing capabilities of individual UAVs within a group. In this framework, multiple UAVs collaborate to perform data sensing and model training simultaneously. Specifically, the training process for a U_i occurs concurrently with the data sensing processes of subsequent UAV nodes. This synchronization ensures that data sensing continues in a pipeline fashion across UAVs, allowing each UAV to incrementally train the model Θ with its newly gathered data. This method facilitates continuous updating of the model parameters, thereby supporting incremental learning.

Algorithm 1 outlines the detailed process of MDIL. The initialization of MDIL primarily involves each UAV U_i determining if it is a core UAV. If it is a core UAV, it collects and stores the computational capabilities of all UAVs in the swarm (lines 2–4), then sorts these UAVs in descending order based on their computational capabilities (line 5). Next, each core UAV computes weights for each UAV based on their computational capabilities (line 7) and determines the priority or perception sequence of each UAV based on the sorting results, returning the weight and order information to each UAV (line 9). When a UAV U_i detects available data, it checks if it has received its weight and priority. If not, it waits until it receives this information and then initiates the core steps of MDIL as shown in Fig. 3. First, UAV U_i checks if it is the initial node, i.e., the UAV with the highest computational capability among all UAVs (line 12). If confirmed, based on its weight w_i, it calculates the amount of data s_i to collect and selects the corresponding frequency channels (line 13). After completing data collection, it constructs its dataset D_i using this data (line 14). Once D_i is constructed, U_i sends a notification signal to successor nodes with the priority or perception sequence $f_i + 1$ and proceeds to train a predictive model Θ using its constructed dataset (line 15). After training the model, U_i transfers the trained model Θ to the next node (line 16). If U_i is not the initial node, it waits until it receives a notification signal from its predecessor node (line 18). Upon receiving the signal, U_i calculates the amount of data s_i to perceive based on its weight w_i and collects the corresponding frequency channels (line 19). It then waits until it receives the pretrained Θ from the predecessor node (line 20). Once Θ is received, U_i constructs its dataset D_i based on perceived s_i (line 21). Subsequently, U_i determines if it is a terminating node, i.e., whether f_i equals n. If U_i is not a terminating node, it sends a notification signal to successor nodes and incrementally trains Θ using its dataset D_i (line 23). After training, U_i sends the trained Θ to the successor node (line 24). If U_i is a terminating node, it directly performs incremental training of Θ using its dataset D_i (line 26) and outputs Θ after training completion (line 27).

Algorithm 1: MDIL: multi-UAV distributed incremental learning

---

    Input: S, n, l
    Output: Trained Θ
0 **Initialization:**
1 **if** $\Lambda_i = 1$ **then**
2   **for** $j \leftarrow 1$ **to** n **do**
3   get (p_j) from U_j;
4   list.append (U_i, p_i);
5   list.descend(p_i);
6   **for** $j \leftarrow 1$ **to** n **do**
7         $w_j \leftarrow \frac{p_j}{p_1 + p_2 + \ldots + p_n}$;
8         $f_j \leftarrow$ list.index$(U_j) + 1$;
9   send (f_j, w_j) to U_j;

10 **When** U_i **detects available data:**
11 Wait until receiving f_i, w_i sent from the core UAV;
12 **if** $f_i = 1$ **then**
13   Collect s_i frequency points according to own weights $(s_i \leftarrow w_i \times S)$;
14   Build the dataset D_i using its own s_i $(D_i \leftarrow (s_i - l + 1))$;
15   Send a notification signal to successor node with priority $f_i + 1$, then train the Θ locally;
16   Send the trained Θ to the successor node with priority $f_i + 1$;
17 **else**
18   Wait until the notification signal sent by the predecessor node is received;
19   Collect s_i frequency points according to own weights $(s_i \leftarrow w_i \times S)$;
20   Wait until the Θ sent by the predecessor node is received;
21   Build the dataset D_i using its own s_i $(D_i \leftarrow (s_i - l + 1))$;
22   **if** $f_i \neq n$ **then**
23   Send a notification signal to successor node with priority $f_i + 1$, then incrementally train the received Θ using D_i;
24   Send the trained Θ to successor node with priority $f_i + 1$;
25   **else**
26   Incrementally train the received Θ using D_i;
27   Output the trained Θ;

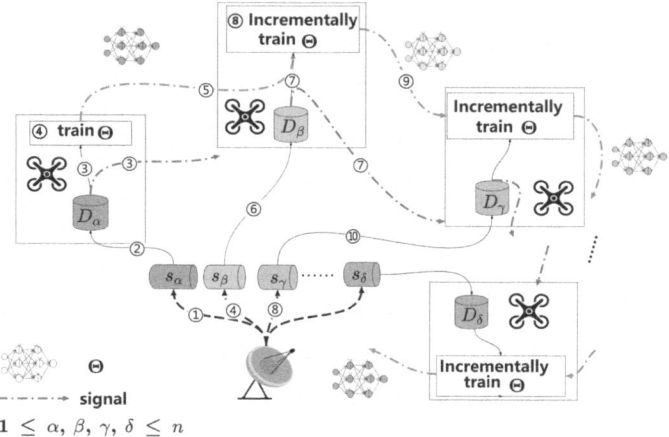

Fig. 3. Core operational processes of MDIL.

5   Evaluation

5.1   Experimental Setup

Implementation. As illustrated in Fig. 4, we utilized the HAROGIC SAE-90 spectrum sensing module mounted on the UAV to collect actual FH data points. The hopping bandwidth was set at 1.40–1.50 GHz. Table 1 provides detailed parameters of the sensing module settings. Furthermore, we evaluated the performance of MDIL on the computing devices onboard the UAV, specifically two Jetson NX units with computational capabilities of 7.2 and 8 GB of memory, and one Jetson Nano unit with a computational capability of 5.3 and 4 GB of memory. The UAV equipped with Jetson NX #1 as core UAV. We constructed a prediction model using Keras, which comprises three hidden LSTM layers followed by a fully connected layer. The model optimizer is Adam, and specific model hyperparameters are detailed in Table 2.

Table 1. Configuration Parameters of the Sensing Module.

Parameter	Value
Total number of sensing frequency points	4048
Bandwidth Range	1.40–1.50 GHz
Resolution Bandwidth	300e3 Hz
Collection interval	200 ms

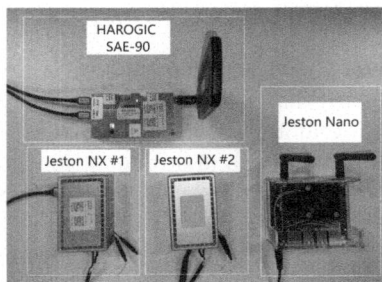

Fig. 4. Experimental Setup of the Proposed MDIL.

Table 2. Model Parameters.

Parameter	Value
Number of LSTM units per hidden layer	64
Time step	15
Batch size	512
Learning rate	0.01

Approaches. Due to the lack of research on distributed incremental learning in the UAV domain, we chose to compare it with the conventional centralized batch learning (CBL) method. Additionally, MDIL addresses the heterogeneity of embedded computing devices carried by UAVs in distributed incremental learning environments by implementing task prioritization and workload allocation strategies. To demonstrate the effectiveness of this approach, we conducted ablation experiments to reflect the importance of computational capability ranking and weighted perception in the designed algorithm. The following section will provide a detailed description of these methods:

- CBL: Centralized batch learning involves centrally sensing FH data at a single node, followed by loading the entire dataset into the model for batch learning.
- MDIL: Multiple UAVs are sorted in descending order according to their computational capabilities, and they perceive corresponding FH data amounts based on their computational weight. Distributed incremental learning is then conducted among these UAVs.
- MDIL-cs: Multiple UAVs are sorted in descending order by computational capability, uniformly sense the same amount of FH data, and perform distributed incremental learning among multiple machines.
- MDIL-ws: Multiple UAVs are sorted in ascending order by computational capability, sense data in proportion to their weights, and engage in distributed incremental learning among multiple machines.
- MDIL-cw: Multiple UAVs are sorted in ascending order by computational capability, uniformly sense the same amount of FH data, and conduct distributed incremental learning among multiple machines.

5.2   Performance Analysis

As shown in Fig. 5, MDIL reduces training time by approximately 22.13% compared to CBL. This indicates that even with minimal perceptual time, the benefits of incremental learning alone allow our algorithm to demonstrate significant superiority. The MDIL approach and its ablation studies also indicate that incremental learning strategies can integrate new data while retaining existing knowledge, thereby significantly reducing the training cost and time of the model. The superior performance of MDIL is primarily attributed to initial nodes with higher computational capabilities collecting more data and accumulating rich prior knowledge. Consequently, subsequent nodes receive more mature models, facilitating the extraction of knowledge from new data and accelerating learning convergence, thereby significantly reducing overall training time.

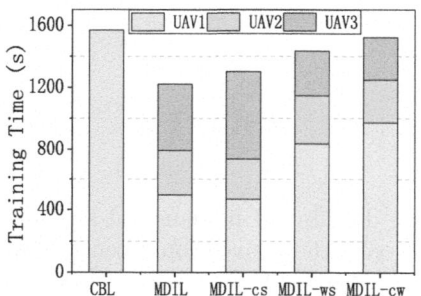 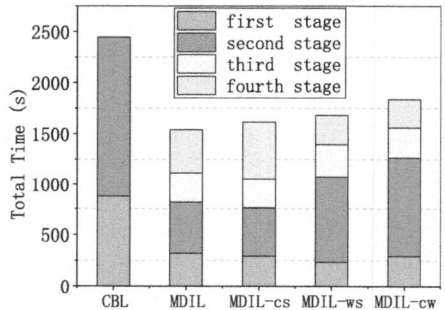

Fig. 5. The training time for each approach to complete the training task.

Fig. 6. The total time for sensing and training under each approach.

As shown in Fig. 6, Compared to CBL, MDIL adopts a dual-task flow parallelization of perception and training, further reducing the total task time by approximately 36.89% beyond the saved training time from incremental learning. Additionally, MDIL utilizes computational capability-based sorting and weighted sensing to optimize waiting times between UAVs, enhancing overall efficiency and significantly shortening the total task duration. Ablation experiments indicate that removing these two characteristics, namely disregarding the heterogeneity of computational performance, results in varying degrees of delay compared to MDIL.

As shown in Fig. 7, in incremental learning mode, the model tends to prioritize learning new data over retaining old data. Therefore, the accuracy of models trained using incremental training may be slightly lower than batch learning. However, compared to several other ablated methods, MDIL mitigates this phenomenon to some extent by allocating more data to pre-sorted UAV nodes, resulting in a relatively minor decrease in accuracy. Additionally, Table 3 provides a comparison of root mean square errors (RMSE) across different methods, indicating that our algorithm sacrifices a small amount of accuracy to save more

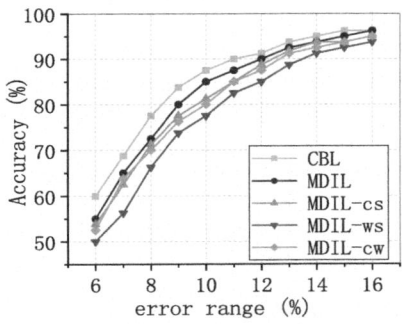
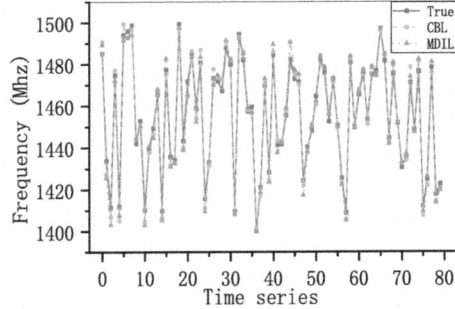

Fig. 7. Accuracy of models trained by different methods.

Fig. 8. The prediction results of FH with different approaches.

time while still maintaining within an acceptable error range. Figure 8 illustrates the comparison of prediction results between MDIL and CBL.

Table 3. Comparison of RMSE for Various Approaches.

Approach	CBL	MDIL	MDIL-cs	MDIL-ws	MDIL-cw
RMSE	3.441	3.615	3.791	3.935	3.798

6   Conclusion

This paper proposes an MDIL method to address the issue of prolonged sensing and training times affecting real-time performance in UAVs during sensing of FH sequence prediction models using traditional methods. MDIL prioritizes and allocates the sequence and task load of sensing based on computational performance weights. Multiple UAVs collaborate in a pipeline fashion for FH data sensing and subsequently engage in distributed incremental learning, thereby reducing training time. Furthermore, by independently parallelizing sensing and training tasks, the overall task execution time is further minimized. It is worth noting that our approach saves significant time while sacrificing only a minor amount of accuracy.

Acknowledgments. This research was supported by the National Natural Science Foundation of China under Grant Nos. 62372230 and 62072303.

References

1. Zhu, X., Han, Z., Tang, S., Lijie, X., Dong, C.: Deploying the minimum number of rechargeable UAVs for a quarantine barrier. ACM Trans. Sens. Netw. **19**(2), 1–28 (2022)
2. Dong, C, Shen, Y, Qu, Y.: A survey of UAV-based edge intelligent computing. Chin. J. Intell. Sci. Technol. 227–239 (2020)
3. Li, J., Ye, D.H., Kolsch, M., Wachs, J.P., Bouman, C.A.: Fast and robust UAV to UAV detection and tracking from video. IEEE Trans. Emerg. Top. Comput. **10**(3), 1519–1531 (2021)
4. Dong, C., et al.: UAVs as an intelligent service: boosting edge intelligence for air-ground integrated networks. IEEE Network **35**(4), 167–175 (2021)
5. Hochreiter, S., Schmidhuber, J.: Long short-term memory. Neural Comput. **9**(8), 1735–1780 (1997)
6. Li, G., Wang, W., Ding, G., Qihui, W., Liu, Z.: Frequency-hopping frequency reconnaissance and prediction for non-cooperative communication network. China Commun. **18**(12), 51–64 (2021)
7. Li, Y., Qu, Y., Dong, C., Zhou, F., Zhang, L., Wu, Q.: Dynamic DNN model switching for collaborative edge intelligence in UAV swarm. In: 2023 International Conference on Wireless Communications and Signal Processing, pp. 923–929 (2023)
8. Ding, Y., Yang, Z., Pham, Q.V., Hu, Y., Zhang, Z., Shikh-Bahaei, M.: Distributed machine learning for UAV swarms: computing, sensing, and semantics. IEEE Internet Things J. (2023)
9. Wu, W., Zhou, F., Wang, B., Wu, Q., Dong, C., Hu, R.Q.: Unmanned aerial vehicle swarm-enabled edge computing: potentials, promising technologies, and challenges. IEEE Wirel. Commun. **29**(4), 78–85 (2022)
10. Qu, Y., Sun, H., Dong, C., Kang, J., Dai, H., Wu, Q., Guo, S.: Elastic collaborative edge intelligence for UAV swarm: architecture, challenges, and opportunities. IEEE Commun. Mag. (2023)
11. Wu, F., et al.: Participant and sample selection for efficient online federated learning in UAV swarms. IEEE Internet Things J. (2024)
12. Ade, R.R., Deshmukh, P.R.: Methods for incremental learning: a survey. Int. J. Data Min. Knowl. Manage. Process **3**(4), 119 (2013)
13. Wang, H., Li, M., Yue, X.: Inclstm: incremental ensemble lstm model towards time series data. Comput. Electr. Eng. **92**, 107156 (2021)
14. Takele, A.K., Villányi, B.: Resource aware long short-term memory model (ralstmm) based on-device incremental learning for industrial internet of things. IEEE Access (2023)
15. Melgar-García, L., Gutiérrez-Avilés, D., Rubio-Escudero, C., Troncoso, A.: A novel distributed forecasting method based on information fusion and incremental learning for streaming time series. Inf. Fusion **95**, 163–173 (2023)

Task Offloading Scheduling and Privacy Protection Optimization in Vehicular Edge Computing Based on Double Deep Q-Network

Lu Weifeng[ID], Yang Saijun, Xu Jia[✉][ID], Xu Lijie, and Jiang Lingyun

Jiangsu Key Laboratory of Big Data Security and Intelligent Processing, Nanjing
University of Posts and Telecommunications, Xianlin Street, Nanjing 210023,
Jiangsu, China
{luwf,xujia,ljxu,jianglingyun}@njupt.edu.cn

Abstract. As the applications and services within vehicular networking systems become increasingly diverse, vehicles with limited computing resources face challenges in handling these computationally intensive and latency-sensitive tasks. In this paper, we propose an improved Task Offloading Scheduling Strategy based on a Double Deep Q-Network (TOSDDQN) for a dynamic multi-vehicle, multi-edge unit task offloading environment in vehicular networking. This strategy designs communication models and computational models aimed at minimizing the total system overhead in processing tasks. To further protect the privacy of vehicle users, a Distributed Training Algorithm based on Federated Learning (DTAFL) is proposed. Comparative experimental results indicate that, compared to three other task offloading schemes, our approach reduces the average system overhead in processing tasks by 11%–36%.

Keywords: vehicle edge computing · task offloading and scheduling · DDQN · FL · DRL

1 Introduction

In recent years, there has been a notable integration of Mobile Edge Computing (MEC) within the context of Vehicular Ad Hoc Networks (VANET), leading to the emergence of Vehicular Edge Computing (VEC) [1]. Within the VEC network, while offloading data to edge computing nodes significantly decreases data processing latency, transmitting data through wireless links imposes a burden on wireless spectrum resources. The substantial increase in communication demands during data offloading presents significant challenges to the existing communication resources in VEC networks [2]. Consequently, there is a necessity for joint optimization of communication, computation, and caching resource allocation during the task offloading scheduling process.

Numerous studies currently utilize Machine Learning (ML) techniques for task offloading and scheduling [3–5]. However, ML necessitates prior knowledge,

L. Sun and Y. Chen (Eds.): CWSN 2024, CCIS 2341, pp. 27–39, 2025.
https://doi.org/10.1007/978-981-96-2186-6_3

and the data generated by vehicles exhibit variability and dynamics. Hence, alternative research suggests that Reinforcement Learning (RL) is a potential solution for task offloading [6]. However, this approach is applicable only to low-dimensional decision problems. To address these limitations, Deep Reinforcement Learning (DRL) was proposed [7,8]. Kumar et al. [9] proposed a Deep Deterministic Policy Gradient method based on Lyapunov optimization for multi-agent systems. This method combines computational task allocation with wireless resource allocation, minimizing energy consumption and latency. He et al. [10] introduced a Deep Q-Network (DQN)-based approach to address the joint optimization problem involving vehicular networking communication, caching, and computational resources.

Past studies typically focused on optimizing computation and caching while seldom considering the holistic aspects of computation, communication, caching, and service charging within the vehicular network. Addressing these gaps, this paper integrates computational models, communication models, and vehicle queue models. For each vehicle, corresponding task priority queues are designed. Leveraging relevant knowledge from Deep Reinforcement Learning (DRL), this study aims to identify effective computational offloading decisions in the dynamic vehicular network environment to minimize the overall system overhead in processing tasks. Additionally, by utilizing the distributed training method of Federated Learning [11], this paper ensures privacy protection for vehicles while maintaining training accuracy. The main research contributions of this paper are as follows.

- This paper presents an improved task offloading scheduling strategy based on Double Deep Q-Network (TOSDDQN), which aims to minimize system latency, energy consumption, and service charges while ensuring the requirements of latency-sensitive tasks.
- This paper leverages a Distributed Training Algorithm based on Federated Learning (DTAFL) for vehicle-edge computing task offloading scheduling. Employing a distributed training approach safeguards the privacy of vehicle users.
- Experimental simulation results verify the convergence and effectiveness of the proposed algorithm. Compared with other task offloading schemes, the proposed scheme can reduce the average system overhead by 11% to 36%.

2 System Model

2.1 System Overview

Consider a section of straight road with N vehicles, denoted as $V = \{v_1, v_2, ..., v_N\}$, where each vehicle $v_i \in V$ travels on the road at speed s_i. Each vehicle has multiple task queues and an energy queue. The task queue store tasks that need to be processed, while the energy queue stores energy units used to power the vehicle for task processing. Let the set of M roadside units be denoted as $G = \{u_1, u_2, ..., u_M\}$. Each roadside unit $u_m \in G$ has a communication range represented by a circle with a diameter d_m. The roadside units are equipped with communication and computing devices that can be viewed as miniature edge servers. For simplicity, we assume that a vehicle can communicate with only one roadside unit at a time. The set of vehicles within the communication range of a roadside unit u_m is denoted as V_m, and these vehicles can communicate with the corresponding roadside unit u_m for V2I communication. The road segment is divided into M segments based on the communication ranges of the M roadside units. Figure 1 shows the schematic diagram of the vehicular network intelligent task offloading system. We divide the total time into multiple time slots of size τ, where τ is a small time interval. It is assumed that the network state and topology of the system remain unchanged within each time slot. All vehicles share K different types of tasks, and each type of task has different generation probabilities on the vehicle. At each time slot, the k-th generation probability of the task on the vehicle is λ_k, $k \in \{1, 2, ..., K\}$. Each type of task is represented by quads: $a_k = (z_k, c_k, b_k, p_k)$, where z_k, c_k, b_k, p_k respectively represent the data size of the task, the number of CPU cycles required for the task, the delay limit of the task and the urgency of the task.

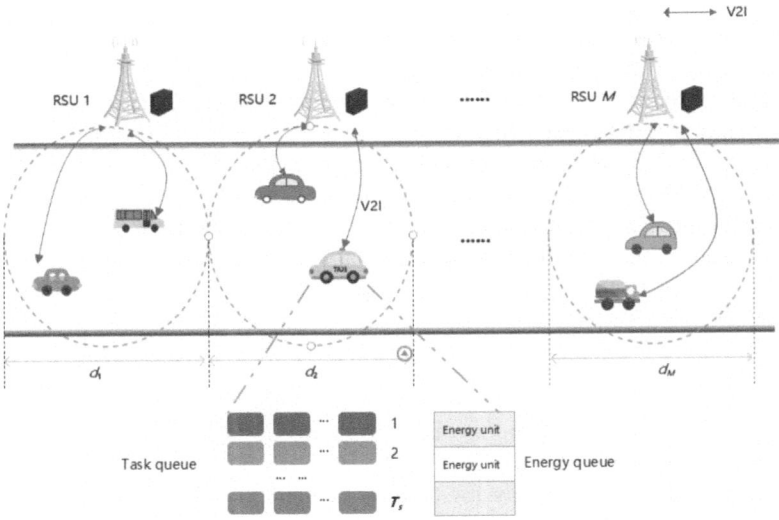

Fig. 1. Intelligent Task Offloading System for Connected Vehicles

2.2   Communication Model

In this paper, the wireless communication between the vehicle and the roadside units is based on orthogonal frequency division multiple access (OFDMA)

[12], and the wireless communication interference between the roadside units is assumed to be negligible. The uplink wireless communication rate from the vehicle v_i to the roadside unit u_m is:

$$r_i^m = B \log \left(1 + \frac{P_i}{L_0 d_{i,m}^\alpha P_w}\right) \qquad (1)$$

where L_0 is the path loss, P_i is the transmission power of the vehicle v_i, P_w is the Gaussian white noise power, α is the path loss index, $d_{i,m}$ denotes the distance between the vehicle v_i and u_m, and B is the channel bandwidth.

The uplink transmission delay of the vehicle v_i to u_m is:

$$\tilde{t_u} = \frac{Z_k}{r_i^m} \qquad (2)$$

The transmission energy consumption of the vehicle for offloading the task to the roadside unit is:

$$E_i^{up} = P_i \tilde{t_u} \qquad (3)$$

2.3   Computational Model

This paper uses two binary decision variables, $x_{i,m}^{k,t}$ and $y_{i,m}^{k,t}$. When $x_{i,m}^{k,t} = 1$, it indicates that the task a_k of the vehicle v_i during time slot t is offloaded to the roadside unit u_m. When $y_{i,m}^{k,t} = 1$, it indicates that the task a_k of vehicle v_i during time slot t, located in section m is processed locally in the vehicle. If $x_{i,m}^{k,t} = y_{i,m}^{k,t} = 0$, it means that the task a_k during time slot t remains in the task queue of the vehicle and has not yet been processed.

(1) Task offloading to the roadside unit for computation:

The computation time for offloading task a_k to a roadside unit u_m is:

$$\tilde{t_m} = \frac{C_k}{\rho_m^i f_m} \qquad (4)$$

where ρ_m^i represents the computational resource ratio assigned to vehicle v_i, and f_m is the CPU frequency of the roadside unit u_m.

(2) Task is calculated locally in the vehicle

The local computation delay for task a_k in vehicle v_i is:

$$\tilde{t_c} = \frac{C_k}{f_i} \qquad (5)$$

where f_i represents the CPU frequency allocated for computing a task in vehicle v_i.

The locally calculated power [13] of vehicle v_i is:

$$P_i^{local} = K_1(f_i)^3 \qquad (6)$$

where K_1 represents the effective capacitance coefficient related to the vehicle chip architecture. Therefore, the local computation energy consumption of vehicle v_i is expressed as:

$$E_i^{local} = P_i^{local}\tilde{t}_c = k_1(f_i)\tilde{t}_c \tag{7}$$

The amount of tasks that vehicle v_i can process locally in a time slot is expressed as:

$$D_i^{local} = \frac{f_i \tau}{c} \tag{8}$$

where $c = \frac{\sum_{k \in K} c_k}{K}$ represents the average processing density of the task a_k. Total time of the vehicle v_i processing task a_k:

$$\tilde{t}(i,k) = y_{i,m}^{k,t}\tilde{t}_c + x_{i,m}^{k,t}(\tilde{t_u} + \tilde{t_m}), x_{i,m}^{k,t} + y_{i,m}^{k,t} = 1 \tag{9}$$

The total time for vehicle v_i to process the task in each time slot must meet the delay limit of task a_k:

$$\tilde{t}(i,k) \le b_k \tag{10}$$

2.4   Task Queue

Assuming that different types of tasks are randomly generated on each vehicle in each time slot. We use pr_k to denote the initial priority of the task k generated in the vehicle for each time slot. The task with a smaller initial priority value is preferred.

$$pr_k = \frac{b_k}{z_k P_k} w \tag{11}$$

where w denotes the weight parameter used to adjust the priority value according to the actual task type. The size of the task priority index is inversely proportional to the amount of data z_k and the urgency of the task P_k, and is proportional to the delay limit of the task.

When a task is generated, it is first placed in the vehicle's task queue. There are T_s task queues in each vehicle. T_s is the ceiling of the maximum initial priority among all types of tasks, i.e. $T_s = max\{[pr_k]^*, k \in \{1, 2, \ldots, K\}\}$, where $[pr_k]^*$ represents the ceiling of pr_k. This ensures that the vehicle's task queue can accommodate any task with an initial priority that can be placed in any time slot. The task queue is numbered $\{1, 2, ..., l, ..., T_s\}$. Tasks in a queue with a lower number are processed preferentially.

2.5   Energy Queue

The energy queue of the vehicle can continuously harvest energy, and each vehicle has an energy queue with a maximum capacity of eq_i^{max} to store energy units. Assuming that the vehicle will automatically charge its energy queue, the energy queue will obtain energy units according to the Poisson distribution. The energy change of the energy queue is formulated as

$$eq_i^{t+1} = min\{eq_i^t - E_i^t + g_i^t, eq_i^{max}\} \tag{12}$$

where eq_i^t represents the existing energy in the energy queue of vehicle v_i at time slot t. g_i^t represents the number of energy units harvested by the vehicle in the time slot t. E_i^t is the energy consumed by vehicle v_i in time slot t, and $E_i^t = y_{i,m}^{k,t} E_i^{local} + x_{i,m}^{k,t} E_i^{up}$ represents the sum of the local computation energy consumption and transmission energy consumption of the vehicle in time slot t. The energy consumed by the vehicle in each time slot cannot exceed the existing energy in the vehicle's energy queue, which is shown as

$$E_i^t \leq eq_i^t \tag{13}$$

2.6 Definition of the Problem

In this paper, a penalty mechanism is introduced to apply a penalty to the amount of tasks exceeding the delay limit, with the penalty factor sets as w_1.let h^t be the amount of tasks that cannot be processed in time slot t.

$$h^t = \sum_{k \in K} \sum_{v_i \in V} (y_{i,m}^{k,t} max(0, uq_{i,1}^t - D_i^{local}) + (1 - y_{i,m}^{k,t})uq_{i,1}^t) \tag{14}$$

where $uq_{i,1}^t$ represents the number of tasks in the queue with subscript 1 in the task queue of vehicle v_i at time slot t.

The service charge for offloading task a_k to the roadside unit u_m is $cs_{k,m} = \tilde{t}_m o_u$, where o_u represents the charge per unit time of the edge server. The calculated cost of task s_k executed locally by vehicle v_i is $cs_{k,i} = \tilde{t}_c o_v$, where O_v represents the cost per unit time of the vehicle processing the task. Therefore, the total cost of vehicle v_i processing task a_k in time slot t is shown as

$$cs_i^{k,t} = x_{i,m}^{k,t} cs_{k,m} + y_{i,m}^{k,t} cs_{k,i} \tag{15}$$

The goal of this paper is to minimize the total overheads of system processing tasks over a long-term period of time slots, subject to delay and energy consumption constraint for vehicle tasks in each time slot. Therefore, the objective function is expressed as

$$\min_{\{x,y\}} Overheads \sum_{t=1}^{\infty} \{(\sum_{u_m \in G} w_1 h^t + \sum_{k \in K} \sum_{v_i \in V} (y_{i,m}^{k,t} w_2 E_i^{local} + x_{i,m}^{k,t} w_2 E_i^{up} + w_3 cs_i^{k,t}))\} \tag{16}$$

$$\text{s.t.} \quad x_{i,m}^{k,t} = \{0,1\}, y_{i,m}^{k,t} = \{0,1\} \tag{17}$$

$$x_{i,m}^{k,t} \cdot y_{i,m}^{k,t} = 0, x_{i,m}^{k,t} + y_{i,m}^{k,t} = 1 \tag{18}$$

$$\tilde{t}(i,k) \leq b_k \tag{19}$$

$$E_i^t \leq eq_i^t \tag{20}$$

where w_2 and w_3 are weight constants, Constraint (17) ensures that the offloading decision variable can only be 0 or 1. Constraint (18) indicates that each vehicle can only select one decision variable per time slot. Constraint (19) indicates that the processing delay of the task in each time slot be less than or equal to the delay limit of the task. Constraint (20) indicates that the task's energy consumption in each time slot must be less than or equal to the existing energy in the vehicle's energy queue.

3 MDP Design

In this section, we model the task offloading scheduling as a Markov chain decision process.

3.1 State Space

The state of the entire system at time slot t includes the state of the vehicle queue and the state of the vehicle position: $S^t \triangleq \{S_1^t, S_2^t, ..., S_M^t, X^t\}$, where $S_m^t (1 \leq m \leq M)$ represents the state of the vehicle queue in the m-th road section in time slot t, and X^t represents the position of the vehicle at time slot t.

3.2 Action Space

$A^t \triangleq \{A_1^t, A_2^t, ..., A_M^t\}$ is used to describe action space of vehicles in each road segment, and further $A_m^t \triangleq \{a_{1,m}^t, a_{2,m}^t, ..., a_{|V_m^t|,m}^t\}(1 \leq m \leq M)$, where $a_{i,m}^t = \{x_{i,m}^{k,t}, y_{i,m}^{k,t}\}(v_i \in V_m^t)$ represents the offloading decision variable.

3.3 State Transition

The energy queue transformation can be obtained from Eq. (12).

State transition equation of task queue is expressed as

$$tq_{i,l}^{t+1} = \begin{cases} \max\{0, uq_{i,2}^t + D_i^{t,local}\}, l = 1 \\ \max\{0, uq_{i,l+1}^t + D_l^{t,new} - D_{i,m}^{t,V2I} - D_i^{t,local}\}, 1<l<T_s \\ \max\{0, D_{T_s}^{t,new} - D_{i,m}^{t,V2I} - D_i^{t,local}, l = T_s \end{cases} \quad (21)$$

3.4 Reward Function

At time slot t, the reward function for the vehicle to take action A^t when the system state is S^t is given by:

$$Reward^t = \sum_{u_m \in G} (w_1 h^t + \sum_{k \in K} \sum_{v_i \in V} (y_{i,m}^{k,t} w_2 E_i^{local} + x_{i,m}^{k,t} w_2 E_i^{up} + w_3 cs_i^{k,t})) \quad (22)$$

This optimal task offloading scheduling policy can be expressed as

$$\pi^* = \arg\min_\pi E(\sum_{t=1}^\infty \eta^t Reward^t) \quad (23)$$

where $0 < \eta < 1$ is a discount factor, used to indicate the impact of future rewards on current operations.

4 Double Depth Q-network Algorithm Based on Federated Learning

4.1 Task Offloading Scheduling Based on Double Depth Q-Network

To obtain the optimal task offloading schedule, this paper uses TOSDDQN to solve it. In the initial state, the Q-network will choose the policy that minimizes the vehicle's overheads, as represented by Eq. 23, and transition to the next state, a batch of $(S^t, A^t, Reward^t, S^{t+1})$ will be added to the experience replay to train the Q-network. Throughout the training process, the network will also perform actions according to the greedy policy to avoid local optima. This approach balances the exploration of unknown actions with the utilization of existing knowledge. As training progresses towards convergence, the target Q-network will be obtained, which can then be uses to find the minimum overheads in this paper's environment. $Y_{DoubleQ}^t$ represents the value of the optimal Q-function updated at time slot t and can be expressed as:

$$Y_{DoubleQ}^t = Reward^t + \eta Q(S^{t+1}, \arg\min_{A^t} Q(S^{t+1}, A^{t+1}; \theta^{t-1}); \theta^t) \tag{24}$$

The purpose of training is to make the updated Q-network approach the target Q-network through continuous iteration, ensuring that the training will eventually converge. To minimize the difference between the estimated value and the target value, this paper defines the loss function of the Q-network as:

$$L(\theta^t) = E[\frac{1}{2}(Y_{DoubleQ}^t - Q(S^t, A^t; \theta^t))^2] \tag{25}$$

The full algorithm for training the TOSDDQN for optimal task scheduling is presented in Algorithm 1.

First, initialize the weights and the experience replay buffer. Steps 5–10 involve selecting a random action A^t with probability ε, or taking the greedy action with the minimum Q-value, using a random probability to avoid local optima. Step 12 calculates the next system state S^{t+1} and the reward. Step 13 stores the current time slot's experience samples in the experience replay buffer. Step 14 selects a batch of experiences randomly from the buffer for training the neural network and calculates the target value. Step 15 calculates the loss function for the current time slot. Step 16 calculates the gradient, and step 17 updates θ^t.

4.2 DRL Training Based on Federated Learning

To further protect the privacy of vehicle users, this paper adopts the distributed federated learning algorithm [14] in the vehicle network. Algorithm 2 shows the federated learning process in a road section m.

Algorithm 2 considers the distributed training process based on federated learning for a set of vehicles within communication range of a roadside unit u_m. Step 4 represents the selection of a random set of vehicles V^t within the coverage range for training. Steps 5–11 detail the local training process for each vehicle, while Steps 12–15 describe the model aggregation process for the roadside unit.

Algorithm 1. Task Offloading Scheduling Strategy based on Double Deep Q-Network

---
1: Given learning rate φ, greedy probability threshold ε, and discount factor η.
2: Initialize TOSDDQN with random initial parameter θ, action Q-function, and experience buffer pool.
3: **for** each given vehicle traffic state **do**
4:     Observe the initial state of the system;
5:     **for** each $t \in \{0, ..., t_{max}\}$ **do**
6:         Choose an action with probability p ;
7:         **if** $p \leq \varepsilon$ **then**
8:             Select a random action A^t;
9:         **else**
10:             Choose action $A^t = \arg\min_{A^t} Q(S^t, A^t; \theta)$;
11:         **end if**
12:         Execute action A^t, calculate $Reward^t$ and derive the next state S^{t+1} according to formulas (21) and (22)
13:         Store the experience $(S^t, A^t, Reward^t, S^{t+1})$ in the experience replay buffer;
14:         Select a training sample randomly from the experience replay buffer, and calculate the value of the target Q-function according to formula (24);
15:         Calculate the loss function $L(\theta^t)$ according to formula (25);
16:         Calculate the gradient of $L(\theta^t)$ with respect to θ^t according to $\nabla_{\theta^t} L(\theta^t) = E[(Q(S^t, A^t; \theta^t) - Y_{DoubleQ}^t)\nabla_{\theta^t} Q(S^t, A^t; \theta^t)]$;
17:         Update θ^t according to $\theta^t \leftarrow \theta^t - \delta\nabla_{\theta^t} L(\theta^t)$;
18:     **end for**
19: **end for**

Algorithm 2. Distributed Training Algorithm based on Federated Learning

---
Initialize the random initial parameters θ^0 of the DRL agent in the roadside unit, initialize the training time C^0 of the loss function for all vehicles; initialize the local DRL model θ_i^0 of the vehicles, download θ^0 from the roadside unit, and set $\theta_i^0 = \theta^0$;
2: Iteration:
    for $t \in \{0, ..., t_{max}\}$ **do**
4:     Select randomly a set $V^t \subseteq V_m^t$ of n vehicles;
        for each $v_i \in V^t$ **do**
6:         Obtain the parameters θ_m^{t-1} of the associated roadside unit u_m;
            Update the local parameters of the vehicle as $\theta_i^{t-1} \subseteq \theta_m^{t-1}$;
8:         Obtain the local data of the vehicle D_i^t;
            Obtain the training parameters and training time as $(\theta_i^t, C_i^t) \Leftarrow Train(\theta_i^{t-1}, D_i^t)$;
10:         Update θ_i^t and C_i^t to the roadside unit u_m ;
        end for
12:     Roadside unit u_m:
            Receive parameter updates from all vehicles $V^t \subseteq V_m^t$;
14:         Perform global aggregation of the model $\theta_m^t \Leftarrow \frac{1}{\sum_{v_i \in V^t} C_i^t} \sum_{v_i \in V^t} C_i^t \theta_m^t$
    end for

5   Simulation Results

5.1   Experimental Parameter Setting

In this paper, we experimentally consider a realistic IoV scenario, The experimental data was obtained from a real dataset [15] of a 25 km long highway section in Austria. We used data from 40 roadside units and 100 vehicle positions. There was a total of 4 types of tasks for vehicles, with data sizes ranging from 1.2 KB to 4.8 KB and latency constraints ranging from 1ms to 4ms. The urgency of tasks was also categorized into 4 types, represented by numerical values, with a larger value indicating a more urgent task. The size of time slot is set to $\tau = 100$ ms, the communication bandwidth is set to B = 1 MHz, the transmission power of the vehicle is $P_i = 40$ dBm, $o_u=1$, $o_v = 0.5$, the greedy probability threshold is set to $\epsilon = 0.99$, and the discount factor is set to 0.9.

5.2   Experimental Results

To analyze the performance of the proposed algorithm, we compared the experimental results of our approach with the following four computation task offloading mechanisms in IoV:

(1) Local computing only: Computing tasks are performed only locally on vehicles, without offloading to roadside units (RSUs).
(2) Offloading computing only: All computing tasks of vehicles are offloaded to connected RSUs, with no local computing on vehicles.
(3) Deep Q Networks (DQN) [16]: A reinforcement learning method combining Q-learning with deep neural networks.
(4) Non-cooperative game: A mobile edge computing framework with multiple-user task offloading and transmission scheduling, proposed in [17], which uses a non-cooperative game among vehicles to find the optimal task offloading decision that maximizes utility.

Figure 2 shows the changes in the average overheads of each scheme under different task data sizes, where "average overheads" refers to the average overheads per time slot. It can be seen that the proposed scheme is significantly better than the other four schemes, especially when the task data size is large. Overall, the proposed scheme reduces the system's average overheads by approximately 11%–36%.

Figure 3 shows the changes in average energy consumption of vehicles under different task data sizes, including both computation and transmission energy consumption. Overall, when dealing with larger volumes of task data, the proposed approach demonstrates superior performance in terms of average vehicle energy consumption, achieving a reduction of approximately 25%.

Figure 4 shows the changes in the handling of vehicle tasks under different task data volumes. Since the vehicle's task queue has a capacity limit, the proportion of tasks retained in the queue will exhibit a trend of initially increasing and then decreasing as the total data volume increases.

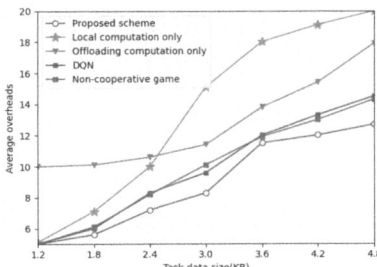

Fig. 2. Average overheads of different schemes

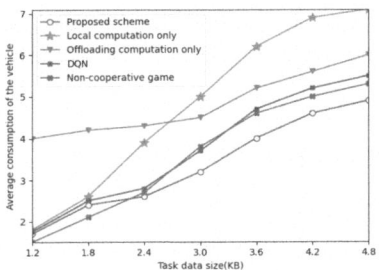

Fig. 3. Average energy consumption of vehicles for different schemes

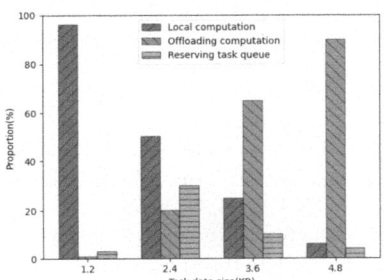

Fig. 4. Task processing modes under different task data sizes

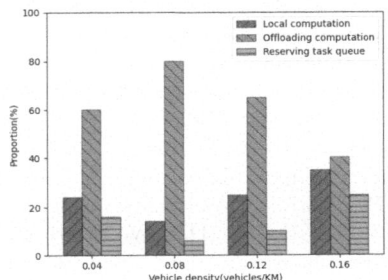

Fig. 5. Task processing modes under different vehicle densities

Figure 5 shows the changes in the handling of vehicle tasks under different vehicle densities when the task data volume is 3.6, The proportion of locally computed and reserved vehicle tasks in the task queue will increase.

6   Conclusion

This paper addresses the task transmission scheduling optimization problem within the context of vehicular edge computing, taking into account both the system's communication and computing resources. To find the optimal scheduling strategy for the dynamic vehicular network environment, this paper employs TOSDDQN. Additionally, the distributed training method of federated learning is used to protect the privacy of terminal vehicle data. Numerous simulation results demonstrate that the proposed scheme effectively reduces the total system overhead.

Acknowledgements. Foundation Items: The National Natural Science Foundation of China (62372249, 62072254, 62272237, 62302236, 62171217, 62372250).

References

1. Qi, B., Kang, L., Banerjee, S.: A vehicle-based edge computing platform for transit and human mobility analytics (2017)
2. Sun, F., Hou, F., Cheng, N.: Cooperative task scheduling for computation offloading in vehicular cloud. IEEE Trans. Veh. Technol. **67**(11), 11049–11061 (2018). https://doi.org/10.1109/TVT.2018.2868013
3. Guo, H., Liu, J., Lv, J.: Toward intelligent task offloading at the edge. IEEE Network **34**(2), 128–134 (2020). https://doi.org/10.1109/MNET.001.1900200
4. Manogaran, G., Srivastava, G., Muthu, B.A.: A response-aware traffic offloading scheme using regression machine learning for user-centric large-scale internet of things. IEEE Internet Things J. **8**(5), 3360–3368 (2021). https://doi.org/10.1109/JIOT.2020.3022322
5. Fan, W., Chen, Z., Hao, Z.: Joint task offloading and resource allocation for quality-aware edge-assisted machine learning task inference. IEEE Trans. Veh. Technol. **72**(5), 6739–6752 (2023). https://doi.org/10.1109/TVT.2023.3235520
6. Binh, T.H., Son, D.B., Vo, H.: Reinforcement learning for optimizing delaysensitive task offloading in vehicular edge-cloud computing. IEEE Internet Things J. 1–1 (2023) https://doi.org/10.1109/JIOT.2023.3292591
7. Lin, N., Tang, H., Zhao, L.: A pddqnlp algorithm for energy efficient computation offloading in UAV-assisted mec. IEEE Trans. Wirel. Commun. 1–1 (2023). https://doi.org/10.1109/TWC.2023.3266497
8. Zhao, L., Zhang, E., Wan, S.: Meson: A mobility-aware dependent task offloading scheme for urban vehicular edge computing. IEEE Trans. Mobile Comput. 1–15 (2023). https://doi.org/10.1109/TMC.2023.3289611
9. Kumar, A.S., Zhao, L., Fernando, X.: Task offloading and resource allocation in vehicular networks: a lyapunov-based deep reinforcement learning approach. IEEE Trans. Veh. Technol. **72**(10), 13360–13373 (2023). https://doi.org/10.1109/TVT.2023.3271613
10. He, Y., Zhao, N., Yin, H.: Integrated networking, caching, and computing for connected vehicles: a deep reinforcement learning approach. IEEE Trans. Veh. Technol. **67**(1), 44–55 (2018). https://doi.org/10.1109/TVT.2017.2760281
11. Lim, W.Y.B., Luong, N.C., Hoang.: federated learning in mobile edge networks: a comprehensive survey. IEEE Commun. Surv. Tutorials **22**(3), 2031–2063 (2020). https://doi.org/10.1109/COMST.2020.2986024
12. Guan, X., Huang, Y., Chen, M.: Exploiting interference for capacity improvement in software-defined vehicular networks. IEEE Access **5**, 10662–10673 (2017). https://doi.org/10.1109/ACCESS.2017.2711003
13. Mao, Y., Zhang, J., Song, S.H.: Power-delay tradeoff in multi-user mobileedge computing systems. In: 2016 IEEE Global Communications Conference (GLOBECOM), pp. 1–6 (2016)
14. AbhishekV, A., Binny, S., JohanT., R.: Federated learning: collaborative machine learning without centralized training data (2022)
15. New crawdad data set. srfg/lte-4g-highway-drive-tests-salzburg. https://crawdad.org/srfg/lte-4g-highway-drive-tests-salzburg/2022-01-18

16. Mnih, K.K.S.D. V.: Human-level control through deep reinforcement learning. Nature **518**, 529–533 (2015). https://doi.org/10.1038/
17. Yi, C., Cai, J., Su, Z.: A multi-user mobile computation offloading and transmission scheduling mechanism for delay-sensitive applications. IEEE Trans. Mobile Comput. **1**(19) (2020)

Crowdsourcing Task Recommendation Method Based on Heterogeneous Graph Feature Anomaly Detection

Kai Wei[1], Qingxian Pan[1(✉)], Song Yu[2], Zequn Fan[1], and Jinru Li[1]

[1] School of Computer and Control Engineering, Yantai University, Yantai 264005,
China
pqx@ytu.edu.cn

[2] School of Computer and Information Science, Southwest University,
Chongqing 400715, China

Abstract. The crowdsourcing task recommendation method addresses worker selection overload by intelligently matching workers with tasks. However, existing research often overlooks the inherent characteristics of workers and tasks, the long-term behavioral preferences of workers, and abnormal information about workers and tasks, which impacts the accuracy of recommendations. To address these issues, we propose a novel crowdsourcing task recommendation method based on anomaly detection using multi-attribute heterogeneous graph features. This method first establishes the connection relationships between crowdsourcing workers and tasks to construct a worker-task heterogeneous graph. DeepWalk generates initial node features, and the message-passing mechanism in the graph neural network is employed to explore the feature information of workers and task nodes. During message transmission, the graph convolutional autoencoder drives the detection of worker and task feature information. Finally, Bi-GRU captures the long-term behavioral preferences of workers, and link prediction constructs links based on node similarity to complete the recommendation of sensing tasks. We evaluate nine real datasets, and the experimental results demonstrate that the proposed method outperforms the baseline method.

Keywords: Mobile crowdsourcing · task recommendation · graph neural network · anomaly detection

1 Introduction

Mobile crowdsourcing (MCS) is an innovative model for solving complex problems using decentralized intelligence [1,2]. In most existing crowdsourcing task recommendation studies, researchers often consider only the characteristics of individual workers, neglecting the potential correlation between crowdsourcing tasks and workers [3]. Additionally, there may be fraudulent workers and malicious task requests within the task recommendation process [4]. For example,

L. Sun and Y. Chen (Eds.): CWSN 2024, CCIS 2341, pp. 40–51, 2025.
https://doi.org/10.1007/978-981-96-2186-6_4

when a worker performs an invalid task request, it can decrease worker remuneration and reduce the accuracy of platform task recommendations. Therefore, accurately identifying abnormal feature information between crowdsourcing workers and tasks and recommending tasks to the appropriate workers becomes a critical issue. Existing research on crowdsourcing task recommendations ignores the complex potential relationships and anomalous feature information between workers and tasks, reducing the accuracy of task recommendations. This paper analyses the features associated with crowdsourced workers and tasks and constructs a heterogeneous worker-task graph. As there may be abnormal information in the features of workers and tasks, this paper proposes a novel task recommendation method based on heterogeneous graph feature abnormality detection (HGFA) for detecting the feature information of workers and tasks and accomplishing task recommendation and the specific flowchart is shown in Fig. 1. The main contributions of this paper are as follows:

- Considering the potential relationship between crowdsourced workers and tasks, we construct a multi-attribute heterogeneous graph that effectively fuses the feature information of workers and tasks.
- A task recommendation method based on heterogeneous graph feature detection (HGFA) is proposed to detect the feature information of workers and task nodes and predict whether there is a link between a work node and a task by mining the potential relationship between task nodes and work nodes. Finally, Bi-GRU is introduced to capture workers' long-term preferences.
- The experimental results show that the method HGFA of this paper is superior to the advanced baseline method.

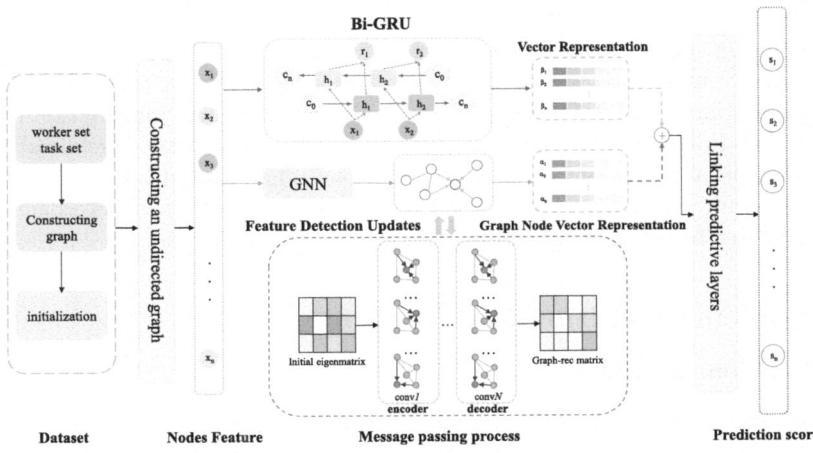

Fig. 1. Model Flowchart

2   Related Work

Mobile crowdsourcing performs large-scale sensing tasks through many users and mobile devices, and the scale of tasks and data is much larger than traditional crowdsourcing. Therefore, mobile crowdsourcing requires more advanced task allocation strategies. In mobile crowdsourcing (MCS), task allocation becomes a critical research problem. Liu et al. [5] highlighted the importance of task allocation and task dependency, proposing a multi-stage complex task allocation method that optimizes task distribution in spatial crowdsourcing using greedy and gaming algorithms to maximize profits. Effective crowdsourcing task allocation should maximize the number of tasks completed and consider the quality of task completion and user satisfaction [6]. Xie et al. [7] addressed the issue of user satisfaction by proposing a quality-aware task assignment method, designing greedy and game algorithms aimed at maximizing overall user satisfaction.

Workers may have different preferences in various scenarios, and considering these preferences can improve execution efficiency. Huang et al. [8] proposed a preference-based online stable task allocation method that effectively addresses the task allocation problem in crowdsourcing by constructing a weighted partition graph and a linear programming model. The increase in the number of users of crowdsourcing platforms has placed demands on collaboration among crowdsourcing workers [9]. Liang et al. [10] proposed a many-to-many task allocation manifold, specifically cluster multi-role collaborative allocation, to formalize the team allocation problem in crowdsourcing by introducing higher-order cardinality and role-conflicting agent constraints. They experimentally validated the high efficiency of this approach. In recent years, heterogeneous features between crowdsourcing workers and tasks have become a research hotspot. Yang et al. [11] proposed a deep neural framework based on heterogeneous features and multiple interactions that can flexibly combine different task features to solve the crowdsourcing cold-start problem.

The above methods propose many effective schemes for crowdsourcing task recommendations. Still, they do not fully consider the strange information in the potential relationship between crowdsourcing workers and tasks, which leads to a decrease in the accuracy of task recommendations. Therefore, this paper proposes a task recommendation method based on anomaly detection of heterogeneous graph features to solve the above problems.

3   Problem Definition and Method

3.1   Problem Definition

The approach proposed in this paper consists of five main parts: building a heterogeneous graph, node representation, graph structure message passing, feature-driven anomaly detection, and perceptual task recommendation.

Theorem 1. *Heterogeneous Graph: Construct a worker-task graph by analyzing the correlation between crowdsourced workers and tasks. Since the relationship* *between workers and tasks is mutual, the worker-task graph is undirected $G = (V, E)$, where V denotes the set of all nodes and E denotes the edges between all nodes.*

Theorem 2. *Node Representation: For known nodes, we use the majority voting method to obtain the initial representation of the node. For nodes without initial information, we employ a random walk (DeepWalk) to generate the feature representation of the new node.*

Theorem 3. *Graph Structure Messaging: To further explore the deep relationship between crowdsourcing worker w_i and task t_j, two different messaging mechanisms for worker and task are designed for aggregating the reductive neighbor nodes and updating their representations.*

Theorem 4. *Feature-driven anomaly detection: During the node feature update process defined in (3), we perform feature-driven detection. Suppose the current node is i and its feature representation is X. The encoder in the feature detection component can learn the embedding representation $Z = f_{enc}(X, A)$ of the node, and A is the adjacency matrix. The decoder reconstructs the original features to obtain $\tilde{X} = f_{dec}(Z)$.*

Theorem 5. *Perceived Task Recommendation: By calculating the similarity between heterogeneous nodes, we establish worker-task links using link prediction and select appropriate workers to accomplish the perceived task.*

3.2 Method

In this paper, crowdsourcing workers and tasks are modeled as heterogeneous graphs, and they utilize the Deep Walk algorithm and a majority voting method to generate the initial features of the graph nodes. Then, we use the message-passing mechanism in graph neural networks to mine the intrinsic association between worker and task nodes, and we use a two-way GRU model to capture workers' long-term behavioral preferences. During the message-passing process, the graph convolutional self-encoder detects anomalies in the worker and task feature information matrices and reconstructs the feature information. Finally, the link prediction layer accomplishes perceptual task recommendations based on node similarity. The following section describes each component of the HGFA approach in detail. Figure 1 illustrates the overall process.

Constructing Isomorphic Maps: The heterogeneous graph constructed in this paper consists of worker nodes w_i and task nodes t_j, with only cross-category connections between nodes. A unique ID identifies each worker and task node to reflect the specific attributes of the crowdsourcing platform. In the undirected graph, we set up n workers and m crowdsourced tasks, where a graph task node can be categorized into k categories. Each worker node has three attributes: label (the label given to the task when the worker completes it), gold label (the gold label of the task as determined by majority voting), and time (the time taken to complete the task).

Obtaining Node Representations: Having mined the potential associations between workers and tasks and modeled them as heterogeneous graphs in Sect. 4.1, this section describes the methods for initializing the node representations: the majority voting method and the DeepWalk algorithm. For any worker node, w_i and task node t_j $(w_i, t_j) \in V$, their characteristics can be calculated using the majority voting method, as shown in Eq. (1):

$$r_1(w_i) = \frac{|\{j \in J(w_i) \,|\, l_{ij} = g_j\}|}{|J(w_i)|} \qquad r_1(t_j) = 1 - \frac{|\{i \in P(t_j) \,|\, l_{ij} = g_j\}|}{|P(t_j)|} \qquad (1)$$

Here, $J(w_i)$ denotes the set of tasks performed by worker w_i, and $P(t_j)$ denotes the set of workers performing task t_j. l_{ij} represents the label assigned to task t_j at the end of the worker's execution, while g_j is the gold label determined by most votes or experts. It is generally believed that when the label given to a task by a worker matches the gold label more frequently, it indicates that the worker is more capable of performing the task. Conversely, the more categories of labels a worker assigns to a task, the more complex the task is considered to be.

The above methods provide an initial assessment of worker ability and task difficulty, but considering only the end-of-task phase is insufficient. Therefore, we extend the feature dimensions of workers and tasks to include time information. First, the efficiency feature $r_2(wi)$ for worker w_i is defined as shown in Eq. (2):

$$r_2(w_i) = 1 - \frac{\sum\limits_{j \in J(w_i)} T_{ij}}{\sum\limits_{j \in J(w_i)} a_j} \qquad r_2(t_j) = \frac{a_j}{|V_T| \times \sum\limits_{j \in V_T} a_j} \qquad (2)$$

$J(w_i)$ denotes the set of tasks completed by worker w_i, T_{ij} denotes the total time spent by worker w_i to complete task t_j, and a_j denotes the average time to complete task t_j. For the feature modeling of task difficulty as $r_2(t_j)$, V_T denotes the set of all task nodes, and $|V_T|$ reflects the size of the set of task nodes. As shown in Eq. (2). Finally, the resulting features are normalized.

It is generally believed that workers with shorter average task execution times are more efficient, while tasks with longer execution times are more complex. DeepWalk is used to obtain the initial representation for nodes without initial information. DeepWalk, used mainly for graph structure data mining, integrates the random walk strategy and the word2vec model to uncover the implicit feature vectors of network nodes.

Graph Structure Message Passing: This section introduces the graph message-passing mechanism between workers and task nodes in HGFA. Suppose that at time step T, the message passing process depends on the message function M_j^i and the node update function U_T, and the hidden state r^T of each node is updated according to the message function $m^{(T+1)}(w_i)$. Eqs describe the specific process. (3) and (4):

$$m^{(T+1)}(w_i) = \sum_{j \in J(w_i)} \lambda_{ij} M_j^i \left(r^T(w_i), r^T(t_j), r^T(e_{ij}) \right) \tag{3}$$

$$r^{(T+1)}(w_i) = U_T \left(c_w r^T(w_i), (1 - c_w) m^{(T+1)}(w_i) \right) \tag{4}$$

Where λ_{ij} denotes the attention weight, $r^T(w_i)$ denotes the feature embedding of the worker node w_i, in the time step T, $r^T(t_j)$ denotes the task node embedding, $r^T(e_{ij})$ denotes the feature of the edge, and the weight $c_w \in [0,1]$. The calculation method of λ_{ij} is as follows Eq. (5):

$$\lambda_{ij} = \frac{\exp \left(W_1 \left(M_j^i \left(r^T(w_i), r^T(t_j), r^T(e_{ij}) \right) \oplus r^T(w_i) + b_1 \right) \right)}{\sum_{m \in J(w_i)} \exp \left(W_1 \left(M_m^i \left(r^T(w_i), r^T(t_m), r^T(e_{im}) \right) \oplus r^T(w_i) + b_1 \right) \right)} \tag{5}$$

Where m is a single task in the task set performed by the worker, exp is an exponential function, W_1 is the weight matrix, and b is the bias term. This paper's potential association between workers and tasks includes node feature information, crowdsourcing labels, and time dimension information. Therefore, this paper's message function M_j^i considers the worker-task node characteristics. For any worker node, the message function is calculated as shown in Eq. (6):

$$\underset{j \in J(w_i)}{\forall} M_j^i \left(r^T(w_i), r^T(t_j), r^T(e_{ij}) \right) = \Phi \left(W^x \left(r^T(t_j) \oplus \left(W_e^x r^T(e_{ij}) \right) \right) \right) \tag{6}$$

Here, Φ is a nonlinear activation function, W^x and W_e^x are parameter matrices. The model then transmits the information generated by the work node to the task node. For the message passing phase of the task node, the task node will get the message from the connecting edge and the worker node as Eq. (7):

$$r^{(T+1)}(t_j) = \Phi(c_t r^T(t_j) + (1 - c_t) \sum_{i \in P(t_j)} \theta_{ji} M_i^j (r^T(t_j), r^T(w_i), r^T(e_{ij}))) \tag{7}$$

Similar to the above, θ is the attention weight, weight $c_t \in [0,1]$, M_i^j is the message function, and $P(t_j)$ represents the set of workers performing the task t_j. Similarly, the attention weight θ and the task node message function are shown in Eqs. (8) and (9), respectively:

$$\theta_{ji} = \frac{\exp \left(W_2 \left(M_i^j \left(r^T(t_j), r^T(w_i), r^T(e_{ij}) \right) \oplus r^T(t_j) + b_2 \right) \right)}{\sum_{p \in P(t_j)} \exp \left(W_2 \left(M_p^j \left(r^T(t_j), r^T(w_p), r^T(e_{jp}) \right) \oplus r^T(t_j) + b_2 \right) \right)} \tag{8}$$

$$\underset{p \in P(t_j)}{\forall} M_p^j \left(r^T(t_j), r^T(w_p), r^T(e_{pj}) \right) = \Phi \left(W^y \left(r^T(w_p) \oplus \left(W_e^y r^T(e_{pj}) \right) \right) \right) \tag{9}$$

The node representation of the worker-task graph is obtained through a multi-layer Graph Neural Network. At the same time, Bi-GRU is used to capture workers' long-term behavioral preferences. Bi-GRU, composed of two reverse GRU units, processes sequence data in both directions. The working data is converted into an embedding vector, inputted into the Bi-GRU, and updated through multi-layer stacking. Finally, the Bi-GRU output is connected with the GNN layer output to form a comprehensive vector representation.

Feature-Driven Anomaly Detection: Section 4.3 introduces the message-passing mechanism between worker and task nodes. Typically, during message transmission, the current node will receive the message from a neighboring abnormal node. In order to solve the problem of abnormal characteristic information of workers and task nodes present in the message-passing process, this paper designs a graph convolutional autoencoder. This autoencoder extracts the feature representation of graph nodes and learns the low-dimensional representation of graph structure data. Assume that at time step T, the detection process is expressed as follows Eqs. (10), (11):

$$\underset{i,j \in V}{\forall} Genc\left(\left(r^T\right)^\upsilon (w_i, t_j)\right) = ReLU\left(r^T (w_i, t_j)^\omega \cdot W^{conv}\right) \odot Dropout\,(p)\ (\upsilon \leq \omega) \tag{10}$$

$$Gdec\left(\left(r^T\right)^\omega (w_i, t_j)\right) = ReLU\left(\left(r^T\right)^\upsilon (w_i, t_j) \cdot W^{deconv}\right) \tag{11}$$

Here, ω, υ represent the feature dimension, W_{conv} represents the graph convolution layer, G_{enc}, and G_{dec} are graph encoders and decoders. The above formula combines the anomaly detection expressions of workers and task nodes.

Recommendations for Perception Tasks: After completing the above steps, we obtain the final feature vector embeddings of workers and tasks after feature-driven detection and the long-term preferences of workers captured by Bi-GRU. We can predict the connectivity between workers and tasks using these final vector embeddings and link prediction. The connectivity is obtained as follows Eq. (12):

$$H_{w,t} = \Phi\left(r_w^L, r_t^L\right) \tag{12}$$

where r_w^L, and r_t^L denote the final embedded worker w_i and task t_j.

4   Experiment

This section conducts extensive experiments on nine publicly available datasets to validate the effectiveness of the methods in this paper. The experimental platform of this paper is Window11, 12th generation Intel(R) Core(TM) i5-12490F 3.00 GHz, GTX 1660 SUPER, and the model is implemented based on Pytorch1.13 and DGL1.1.2 cu117.

4.1   Dataset

This section briefly describes the nine publicly available real data sets used for the experiments:

- Music Genre: MG is an audio-type dataset from Tzanetakis and Cook.
- WS-AMT: WS-AMT is a weather sentiment dataset provided by AMT.
- Top Personality: Top Personality Dataset contains information such as worker ID, movie ID, and movie ratings.
- Amazon Reviews: This dataset contains over 6,643,669 consumer reviews of different Amazon products.
- Workers Browser Activity: This dataset contains the assignment results of 3 different crowdsourcing tasks launched on CrowdFlower, along with the associated worker behavior.
- Wine Tasting: A wine-tasting dataset containing 130 k wine reviews posted to WineEnthusiast.
- Tomatoes movies: Rotten Tomatoes Movies and Critics Review Dataset.
- Book-Crossing: A book rating dataset containing 278858 users who have provided 1149780 ratings on about 271379 books.
- Toloka Aggregation Relevance 5: This dataset contains about 1 million anonymous crowdsourcing tags collected in the Relevance 5 Gradations project in 2016.

4.2   Comparison Experiment

- GAT [12]: GAT is a graph neural network based on an attention mechanism.
- GraphSAGE [13]: GraphSAGE is a GNN based on sampled neighbour aggregation.
- KGA [14]: KGA is a knowledge graph enhancement method that includes text in the embedding model without modifying its loss function.
- LowFER [15]: LowFER is a factorization bilinear pooling model that allows better integration of entities and relations, resulting in efficient and unconstrained models.
- DeepFM [16]: DeepFM is a model that combines Factorization Machines and Deep Neural Networks to solve the recommendation problem for large-scale sparse feature data.

4.3   Experimental Results

This paper compares the proposed method with six different methods using Area Under the Curve (AUC) as a comparison metric. Table 1 shows that the HGFA method proposed in this paper significantly outperforms other advanced baseline methods on the AR, BOOK, and TOLOKA datasets. It also performs better than the baseline methods on the TP, WBA, WINE, and TOMATO datasets. However, on the MG and WS datasets, the performance of the HGFA method is slightly worse than that of some baseline methods. The problem may be because there are fewer entities and more relationships in these datasets, which affects the recommendation performance of our method for multi-relational data with fewer entities. Overall, the HGFA method surpasses existing baseline methods, demonstrating its effectiveness and advancement.

Table 1. AUC comparison Table

Dataset	GAT	GraphSAGE	KGA	LowFER	DeepFM	HGFA
MG	0.752	0.868	**0.878**	0.854	0.822	<u>0.874</u>
WS-AMT	0.711	0.724	0.710	**0.944**	0.812	<u>0.923</u>
TP	0.676	<u>0.934</u>	0.560	0.447	0.833	**0.945**
AR	0.770	<u>0.869</u>	0.520	0.479	0.810	**0.988**
WBA	0.775	<u>0.923</u>	0.403	0.700	0.805	**0.929**
WINE	0.864	<u>0.955</u>	0.501	0.753	0.817	**0.962**
TOMATO	0.743	<u>0.946</u>	0.530	0.459	0.840	**0.956**
BOOK	0.735	0.930	0.579	0.774	<u>0.931</u>	**0.985**
TOLO	0.762	0.912	0.611	0.831	<u>0.913</u>	**0.981**

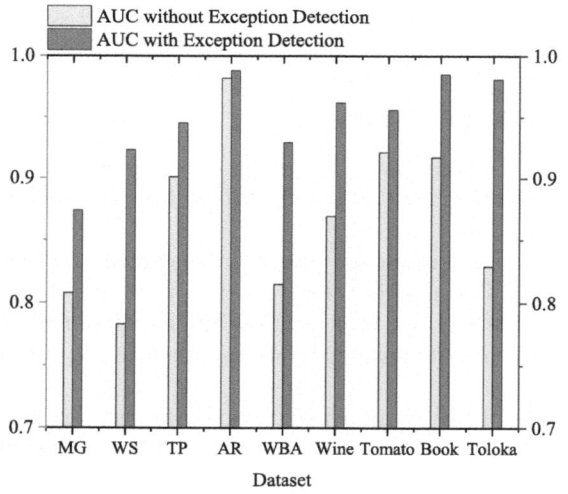

Fig. 2. Ablation experiment

Comparative Experiment of Ablation and Feature Dimension: The ablation experiment is shown in Fig. 2, introducing the detection method based on worker-task characteristics significantly improves the AUC index of the model across eight datasets, with a slight improvement on the Amazon Reviews dataset. This experiment demonstrates the effectiveness of the proposed method in recognizing worker and task anomaly feature information in task recommendations.

Table 2. Comparative experiments on feature dimensions

Dataset	32	64	128	256
MG	0.812	0.832	0.874	0.87
WS-AMT	0.792	0.865	0.923	0.922
TP	0.913	0.925	0.945	0.946
AR	0.934	0.965	0.988	0.989
WBA	0.874	0.902	0.929	0.92
WINE	0.912	0.93	0.962	0.964
TOMATO	0.872	0.915	0.956	0.959
BOOK	0.898	0.937	0.985	0.982
TOLOKA	0.873	0.904	0.981	0.949

Secondly, the experiment explores the influence of node feature dimensions on model performance, and the results show that dimension has a significant effect on performance, as shown in Table 2. The model performance is poor when the dimension is 32 or 64 due to insufficient features. Increasing the dimension to 128 significantly improves performance. However, further increasing the dimension to 256 yields limited performance improvement and reduces training efficiency. Therefore, 128 dimensions are determined to be the optimal input.

Negative Sampling Comparison Experiment: This paper investigates the effect of negative sampling number (m value 1∽5) on the model performance by adjusting it and presenting the results on TOMATO, TOLOKA, MG, and BOOK datasets. As shown in Fig. 3, the model performance fluctuates with the m-value, but there is no significant difference. The model is most stable when m is set to 4.

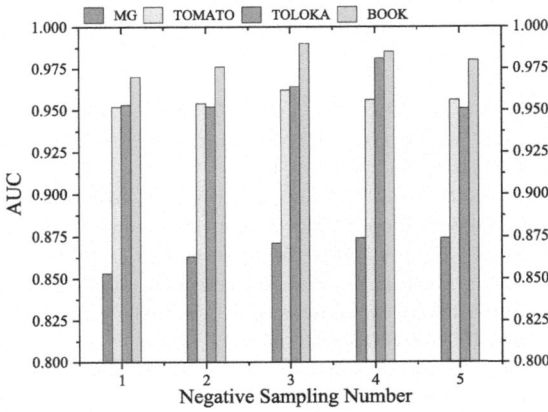

Fig. 3. Negative sampling number comparison.

5   Conclusion

This paper proposes a novel task recommendation method based on heterogeneous graph feature anomaly detection, which mines the potential associations between workers and task nodes, addresses abnormal feature issues, and captures workers' long-term behavioral preferences. This method effectively improves the accuracy of task recommendations, and extensive experiments demonstrate its effectiveness. The next step will optimize the model to achieve even more accurate recommendations.

References

1. Tong, Y., Zhou, Z., Zeng, Y., Chen, L., Shahabi, C.: Spatial crowdsourcing: a survey. VLDB J. **29**(1), 217–250 (2019). https://doi.org/10.1007/s00778-019-00568-7
2. Abhinav, K., Bhatia, G.K., Dubey, A., Jain, S., Bhardwaj, N.: Tasrec: a framework for task recommendation in crowdsourcing. In: Proceedings of ACM/IEEE International Conference on Global Software Engineering, ICGSE, pp. 86–95 (2020). https://doi.org/10.1145/3372787.3390435
3. Hettiachchi, D., Kostakos, V., Goncalves, J.: A survey on task assignment in crowdsourcing. ACM Comput. Surv. **55**(3), 1–35 (2022). https://doi.org/10.1145/3494522
4. Zhao, Y., Chen, X., Deng, L., Kieu, T., Guo, C., Yang, B., Zheng, K., Jensen, C.S.: Outlier detection for streaming task assignment in crowdsourcing. In: Proceedings of ACM Web Conference on 2022, pp. 1933–1943 (2022). https://doi.org/10.1145/3485447.3512067
5. Liu, Z., Li, K., Zhou, X., Zhu, N., Gao, Y., Li, K.: Multi-stage complex task assignment in spatial crowdsourcing. Inf. Sci. **586**, 119–139 (2022). https://doi.org/10.1016/j.ins.2021.11.084
6. Rahman, M.M., Abdullah, N.A.: A trustworthiness-aware spatial task allocation using a fuzzy-based trust and reputation system approach. Expert Syst. Appl. **211**, 118592 (2023). https://doi.org/10.1016/j.eswa.2022.118592
7. Xie, Y., Wang, Y., Li, K., Zhou, X., Liu, Z., Li, K.: Satisfaction-aware task assignment in spatial crowdsourcing. Inf. Sci. **622**, 512–535 (2023). https://doi.org/10.1016/j.ins.2022.11.081
8. Huang, W., Li, P., Li, B., Nie, L., Bao, H.: Towards stable task assignment with preference lists and ties in spatial crowdsourcing. Inf. Sci. **620**, 16–30 (2023). https://doi.org/10.1016/j.ins.2022.11.048
9. Zhao, P., Li, X., Gao, S., Wei, X.: Cooperative task assignment in spatial crowdsourcing via multi-agent deep reinforcement learning. J. Syst. Architect. **128**, 102551 (2022). https://doi.org/10.1016/j.sysarc.2022.102551
10. Liang, L., Fu, J., Zhu, H., Liu, D.: Solving the team allocation problem in crowdsourcing via group multirole assignment. IEEE Trans. Comput. Social Syst. (2022). https://doi.org/10.1109/TCSS.2022.3155868
11. Yang, B., Wang, X., Zhang, S., Gao, M., Tian, J., Tan, G., Yang, L., Su, J.: Joint modelling of task requirements and worker preferences based on heterogeneous features and multiple interactions for knowledge-intensive crowdsourcing recommendation. INT. J. BIO-INSPIR. COM. **22**(2), 105–116 (2023). https://doi.org/10.1504/IJBIC.2023.134974

12. Veličković, P., Cucurull, G., Casanova, A., Romero, A., Lio, P., Bengio, Y.: Graph attention networks. arXiv preprint arXiv:1710.10903 (2017). https://doi.org/10.48550/arXiv.1710.10903

13. Hamilton, W., Ying, Z., Leskovec, J.: Inductive representation learning on large graphs. Adv. Neural Inf. Process. Syst. **30** (2017). https://doi.org/10.48550/arXiv.1706.02216

14. Wang, J., Ilievski, F., Szekely, P., Yao, K.T.: Augmenting knowledge graphs for better link prediction. arXiv preprint arXiv:2203.13965 (2022). 10.48550/arXiv.2203.13965

15. Amin, S., Varanasi, S., Dunfield, K.A., Neumann, G.: Lowfer: low-rank bilinear pooling for link prediction. In: International Conference on Machine Learning, ICML. pp. 257–268. PMLR (2020). https://doi.org/10.48550/arXiv.2008.10858

16. Guo, H., Tang, R., Ye, Y., Li, Z., He, X.: Deepfm: a factorization-machine based neural network for ctr prediction. arXiv preprint arXiv:1703.04247 (2017). https://doi.org/10.24963/ijcai.2017/239

Topology Inference of IoT Edge Network Based on Network Flow Behavior Analysis

Xiaofeng Zhang[1,2], Jinfa Wang[1,2(✉)], Chunyang Zheng[1,2], Haiqiang Fei[1,2], Wenhao Li[3], and HongSong Zhu[1,2]

[1] Institute of Information Engineering, Chinese Academy of Sciences, Beijing 100190, China

{zhangxiaofeng,wangjinfa,zhengchunyang,feihaiqiang,zhuhongsong}@iie.ac.cn

[2] School of Cyber Security, University of Chinese Academy of Sciences, Beijing 10587, China

[3] School of Software, Henan University, Kaifeng 475000, China

liwenhao@henu.edu.cn

Abstract. Internet of Things (IoT) networks have become increasingly characterized by diverse device types, complex partitioned management, and cumbersome security policy configurations. These factors pose significant challenges for fault localization, asset inventory, and security protection within IoT environments. Understanding the network topology of the IoT edge is crucial to addressing these challenges. However, in IoT edge structures, technologies like Network Address Translation (NAT) typically hinder traditional active probing methods from effectively penetrating private networks. In response to this limitation, this paper introduces a novel approach that infers device scale, calculates node correlation coefficients, and determines node relationships, all based on network flow behavior analysis. This approach accurately infers the topology of deep-layer private networks following NAT deployment. The primary objective is to precisely map the topology of deep-layer IoT edge networks. Experimental results demonstrate the exceptional performance of this approach in topology inference, achieving a host device scale metric of 0.8, with link completeness, accuracy, and recall rates of 0.87, 0.84, and 0.73. These results validate the feasibility and effectiveness of the proposed approach, underscoring its capability to accurately infer the topology of deep-layer private network.

Keywords: Topology Inference · IoT Edge Network · Network Flow Behavior · Flow Correlation Coefficient · Private Network Topology

1 Introduction

The Internet of Things (IoT) enhances traditional cyber-physical systems by connecting sensor-based edge devices to network-accessible services and resources. The advent of emerging technologies such as intelligent transportation, urban

L. Sun and Y. Chen (Eds.): CWSN 2024, CCIS 2341, pp. 52–63, 2025.
https://doi.org/10.1007/978-981-96-2186-6_5

computing, building automation, and particularly industrial IoT, has spurred an unprecedented demand for large-scale IoT deployments [8]. These deployments, notably in industrial control settings as shown in Fig. 1, involve a massive number of edge devices that form complex networks, with especially deep network architectures emerging on the edge side of IoT systems [15].

Detecting the network structures as depicted in Fig. 1 in industrial IoT edge environments has become crucial for fault localization [3], asset inventory, and security protection. Traditional detection methods, however, struggle to accurately infer the complexity of these network structures [14]. This challenge is further compounded by the widespread use of Network Address Translation (NAT) services in many internal networks [6]. NAT, a common network technology that enables the use of private IP addresses within a local area network (LAN) while employing public IP addresses on the Internet, enhances network security and simplifies management. Nonetheless, it interferes with traffic-based topology inference by altering packet data [10].

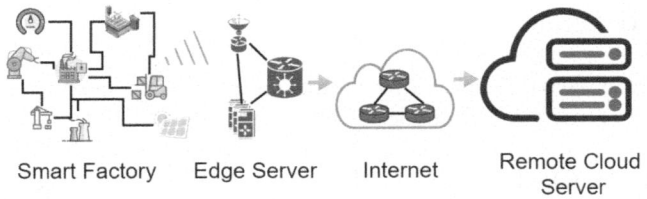

Smart Factory   Edge Server   Internet   Remote Cloud
                                                    Server

Fig. 1. Application Scenario of Industrial Internet

Owing to the presence of NAT, numerous difficulties arise in network topology inference, such as accurately determining the number of internal devices and their relationships. Traditional methods that rely on external traffic capture face significant challenges [13]. Although recent approaches have utilized variations in TCP/IP protocol fields or traffic clustering for topology inference [1], these methods often focus solely on detecting NAT devices and determining host scales, resulting in significant inaccuracies in network topology inference.

To overcome these limitations, this paper proposes a novel approach based on network flow behavior modeling to infer deep internal network topologies in industrial IoT environments, ultimately characterizing the structure of IoT edge networks. The significance of this research lies in its potential to enhance the reliability and security of IoT systems by providing a more accurate depiction of their network architecture. By addressing the limitations of existing methods, this approach offers a solution for understanding and managing the intricate structures of IoT deployments.

Experimental results demonstrate that this method performs well in topology inference, achieving a terminal device scale metric of 0.8, and link completeness, accuracy, and recall rates of 0.87, 0.84, and 0.73. These metrics underscore the method's effectiveness and accuracy in mapping the deep-layer private networks of IoT settings.

The main contributions of this paper can be summarized as follows:

- We introduce a network flow behavior analyzing approach to accurately infer internal network topologies, effectively determining device scale and interrelationships within IoT edge environments.
- We develop a device scale inference algorithm that classifies all NTP traffic by host, utilizing characteristics such as destination IP addresses and timing intervals of NTP request packets during synchronization to estimate the scale of host devices.
- We present a device traffic clustering algorithm that uses the time difference between the second and third TCP handshake packets to calculate one-way delays between NAT and internal network devices, facilitating the clustering of TCP handshake flows by host.

2   Related Work

Recent studies have focused on various methodologies for detecting and identifying devices behind NAT (Network Address Translation) setups. Dai Xianlong et al. [2] propose a tethering behavior detection architecture based on RTT measurement of TCP flows, which effectively identifies tethering activities but does not infer network topology between devices or address the detailed structure of NATed networks. Arman Pashamokhtari et al. [12] propose a method for inferring IoT devices from IPFIX records in residential ISP networks by leveraging flow-level telemetry to identify device types post-NAT. However, their method primarily relies on flow-level features and does not effectively infer the network topology between devices. Christelle Nader et al. [9] propose learning methodologies and clustering algorithms to classify NATed IoT devices, but their approaches are less effective in accurately fingerprinting internal network structures and primarily focus on detecting malicious activities. Khatouni et al. [4] propose a method that achieves high performance in accurately detecting NAT devices and identifying hosts within the network, including multi-layer NAT setups, and adapts well to changes in network topology. However, it requires extensive datasets and computational resources, has limited scalability due to the need for retraining with new data, and may not be applicable to certain types of NAT devices. Hanbyeol Park et al. [11] propose a method for identifying hosts behind a NAT device using multiple fields of IP and TCP packets, but it relies on passive traffic observation, leading to potential limitations in certain scenarios, has high algorithmic complexity, and may fail if NAT devices modify traffic fields. Jianjin Zhao et al. [16] propose IOTPROFILE, which uses simple packet-level features and convolutional transformations for IoT device identification, but it may face challenges with real-time data imbalance and cannot effectively handle edge devices behind NAT.

In summary, while these studies provide valuable insights into detecting devices behind NAT setups, they often fall short in inferring the detailed network topology and handling edge devices effectively. This paper aims to address these gaps by proposing a novel approach that leverages network flow behavior analysis to provide a more comprehensive understanding of device interactions within NATed environments and ultimately enhancing our ability to infer the internal topology of IoT edge.

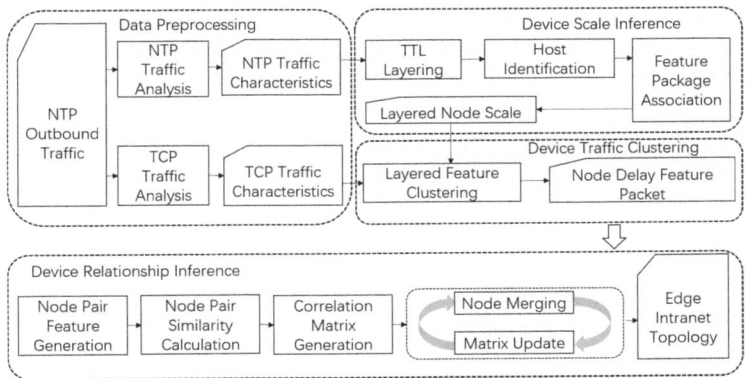

Fig. 2. Diagram of Deep-layer Edge Network Topology Inference Method

3   Architecture

To address the challenge of probing deep-layer private network structures that active probing techniques cannot reach, this chapter proposes a traffic-based method for inferring deep-layer private network topology. This method aims to accurately infer the topology of complex private networks through four main steps: data preprocessing, device scale inference, device traffic clustering, and device relationship inference, as illustrated in Fig. 2. This comprehensive approach ensures a detailed mapping and understanding of the intricate connections within deep-layer private network.

3.1   Data Preprocessing

In data preprocessing step, traffic at the exit of the NAT router is monitored and analyzed. This traffic is then parsed according to protocol types-specifically NTP and TCP—to extract structured data for further analysis. Given the vast volume of traffic, only packets containing key characteristic values essential for topology inference are analyzed. These characteristic values are critical for describing the state of network devices, facilitating subsequent phases of device scale inference and traffic clustering.

NTP Traffic Analysis. Building on the foundation laid by our data preprocessing, we delve into a detailed analysis of NTP traffic. This method utilizes the
destination IP address and periodic characteristics of NTP request packets to
infer the number of devices within a deep-layer private network. The following
features from NTP traffic packets are selected to form a four-tuple structure:
(*capture_time, mode, ttl, dest_ip*).

1. *capture_time*: This represents the time when the NAT router captures the
   data packet. Although the exact time when the target device sends the request
   cannot be obtained, the delay from the target device to the NAT router is
   stable in a steady network. Therefore, the interval between capture times can
   approximate the interval between requests sent by the target device.
2. *mode*: This field indicates the mode of the NTP request packet. When `mode=3`,
   it represents client mode. This analysis focuses on the intervals at which the
   target device sends requests to the NTP server, so only NTP packets with
   `mode=3` are analyzed.
3. *ttl*: This is the value of the time-to-live field. The default initial TTL values
   for Linux and Windows devices are typically constant. Linux devices usually
   have a TTL of 64, while Windows devices typically have a TTL of either 64
   or 128, depending on the operating system.
4. *dest_ip*: This records the IP address of the NTP server. For Windows devices,
   the NTP server address is generally constant.

Since the values of *capture_time, mode, ttl*, and *dest_ip* remain unchanged
after NAT translation, they can serve as distinguishing features for devices.
Consequently, these features help in inferring the number of devices.

By analyzing the *capture_time, mode, ttl*, and *dest_ip*, it is possible to
derive the number of devices behind a NAT device. This method assumes that
the periodic nature of NTP requests and the stability of the network can be
used to estimate the frequency and number of requests, thereby estimating the
number of devices.

Focusing on *mode* = 3 packets ensures that only client-initiated requests are
considered, simplifying the analysis and increasing accuracy. The use of TTL
values helps distinguish between different types of operating systems, further
refining the device count estimate. The destination IP helps maintain consistency, particularly for Windows devices that use a constant NTP server.

This structured approach to NTP traffic analysis provides a reliable method
for inferring device counts and understanding the topology of deep-layer private
network.

TCP Traffic Analysis. Continuing our exploration of traffic analysis, we shift
our focus to the examination of TCP traffic packets, which are crucial for understanding the relationships between network nodes. This method employs an analysis of TCP traffic packets to infer relationships between network nodes. During
the analysis, key fields are extracted from each TCP handshake packet, including
the capture time (*capture_time*), sequence number (*seq_num*), acknowledgment

number (ack_num), synchronization flag (SYN), acknowledgment flag (ACK), and time-to-live (TTL). These fields facilitate the identification and grouping of packets that belong to the same handshake sequence, enabling a detailed examination of network interactions.

For each grouped sequence, a tuple is constructed, comprising the capture time (the timestamp of the third handshake packet), the delay time (representing the one-way delay from the target device to the NAT router), and the TTL (indicating the network layer of the device). The capture time aids in assembling arrays of associated delays for devices that communicate at closely timed intervals. The delay time provides a measure of the one-way delay from the NAT router to the target device, and the TTL serves to identify the device's network layer. These characteristics, which remain consistent following NAT translation, ensure that the tuples derived from TCP traffic packets serve as a reliable basis for inferring inter-node relationships in the network.

3.2   Device Scale Inference

The core components of a deep-layer private network are the device nodes. The inference process targets these devices, determining their scale by classifying NTP traffic by device, and identifying the connections between them. For Linux devices, modern distributions such as Ubuntu, Debian, Arch Linux, and OpenSUSE typically employ systemd-timesyncd as their time synchronization tool. This tool generally schedules NTP requests at intervals ranging from 32 to 2048 s, adhering to powers of two. If the interval between two requests follows this, they are likely from the same device. NTP packets are first processed by layer based on their Time to Live (TTL) values. The analysis focuses on the time relationships between NTP request packets sent by Linux devices within the same layer, producing two key outputs: an array of indices representing the associated packets for each packet, and a time interval matrix that records values only when the intervals between two packets meet specific criteria, otherwise it is recorded as zero. Following this, associated packets that show real correlations are categorized into the same group. Further analysis is conducted to determine if these grouped packets belong to the same device, based on whether the number of associated packets exceeds two or the time intervals approximate 2048 s. These steps collectively complete the grouping and classification of the packets until all are accurately grouped. This structured approach enables precise analysis and categorization of NTP packets, enhancing the understanding of device behaviors and interactions within the network.

3.3   Traffic Clustering

Due to significant variations in link delay across different connections, and considering that the link delay from the same device typically remains within a certain range when unaffected by network status changes, clustering methods are utilized to categorize TCP handshake traffic packets originating from the same device. Analysis of TCP three-way handshake packets reveals that half of the time difference between the captures of the last two handshakes can approximate the one-way delay from the host device to the NAT router under ideal conditions.

Initially, all TCP traffic is stratified by Time To Live (TTL) values. Subsequently, within each layer, traffic is clustered based on the one-way delay of host devices. The k-means clustering algorithm is employed, using *delay_ time* as the feature for clustering. The number of clusters is determined based on the inferred scale of devices from the previous step. Upon completion of the clustering, inferred results regarding the ownership of each TCP handshake packet are recorded in a label field (`label`).

Furthermore, the feature data is organized into tuples (`capture_time`, `delay_time`, `ttl`, `label`), where the `label` field identifies individual devices for subsequent analysis. This process enables the aggregation of arrays containing TCP handshake packets for various devices, which are then used to generate arrays of delay times sorted by device. These sorted arrays will be instrumental in the next phase for inferring the relationships between devices.

3.4 Device Relationship Inference

To depict the relationships between devices based on their inter-device correlations, the merging process of device nodes is structured as follows:

(1) Initialization: Source and destination node sets are created for NAT routers and target nodes respectively, starting with an empty set of connections.
(2) Correlation Matrix Construction: Feature arrays are created for each device pair, focusing on similar timestamp delays. These arrays are used to calculate correlation coefficients and cosine similarities, which are then used to form a correlation matrix.
(3) Selection of Most Similar Devices: Devices with cosine similarities above a set threshold and the highest correlation coefficients are merged.
(3) Correlation Matrix Update: The matrix is updated to reflect the new relationships post-merger.
(4) Termination: The process ends if only one node remains, connecting it to the source node. Otherwise, it repeats from the selection stage.

This methodological approach ensures a systematic analysis of network structures, allowing for an accurate modeling of device interconnectivity within the network.

4 Experiment

4.1 Environment Setup

To validate the effectiveness of the proposed method for inferring the topology of deep-layer private network based on network traffic, an experimental topology was designed using EVE-NG [7], as illustrated in Fig. 3. This topology includes ten terminal devices, labeled 1 through 10, and six routers, labeled $R1$ through $R6$, with router $R1$ configured to provide NAT services. The setup features eleven paths from the NAT router to all the host devices and a total of fifteen paths between devices, denoted as $l1$ through $l5$. Each link's delay settings, as shown in Table 1, simulate the inherent delays typically present in network environments. This experimental configuration provides a controlled environment to assess the method's accuracy and reliability in replicating real-world network dynamics.

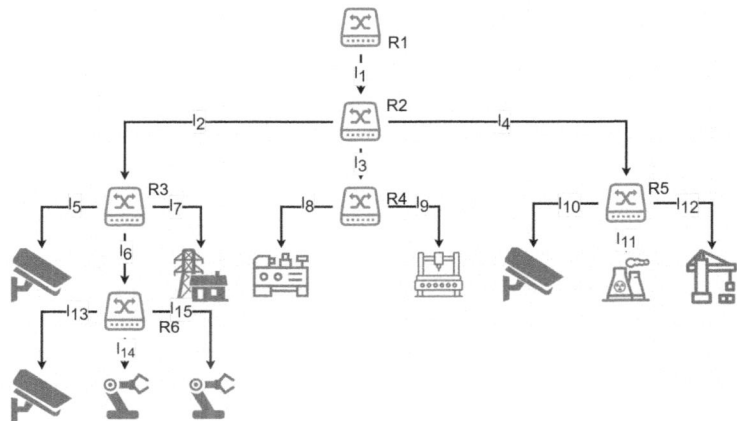

Fig. 3. Original Network Topology.

An NTP server was installed to stabilize Linux device synchronization due to the reliance on frequent NTP requests for device scale inference.To simulate a realistic and complex private network environment, the experimental setup included multiple IoT device terminals.

Table 1. The inherent delay of each link in the simulated topology

Link	1	2	3	4	5	6	7	8	9	10	11	12	13	14	15
Delay/ms	40	50	10	30	20	20	30	10	20	20	10	30	30	10	20

Under the NAT router, three routers were set up to simulate network core layer routers. The first router connects to two devices and another router, which itself connects to three devices; the second router connects to two devices; and the third router connects to three devices. These routers each feature different device connection configurations, simulating a complex, real-world network environment.

4.2 Traffic Data Generation

In this research, the experimental environment's traffic was stimulated through scripts leveraging the curl utility to fetch a range of services, effectively emulating real-world interactions and producing handshake traffic data packets. By amalgamating this synthetic traffic with the existing organic network traffic and deliberate visits to prevalent web services, a foundational traffic mix was established for the experiments, sufficiently aligning with the study's demands.

4.3 Results and Discussion

Traffic capture was conducted using Wireshark [5], both at the entry and exit points of the NAT router. Traffic at the exit point served as the primary data source for inferring the topology of the deep-layer private network, while traffic at the entry point provided insights into the network's IP addresses, aiding in the evaluation of the clustering effects and topology inference. This approach allowed for the association of NAT-transformed traffic with specific device labels, facilitating assessments of clustering performance and device relationships. The simulation environment was configured to capture two hours of traffic per session, with each packet capture involving over 100,000 packets. To minimize variability and experimental error, this process was repeated at different time intervals for a total of ten sessions, with the mean of these ten outcomes serving as the final result.

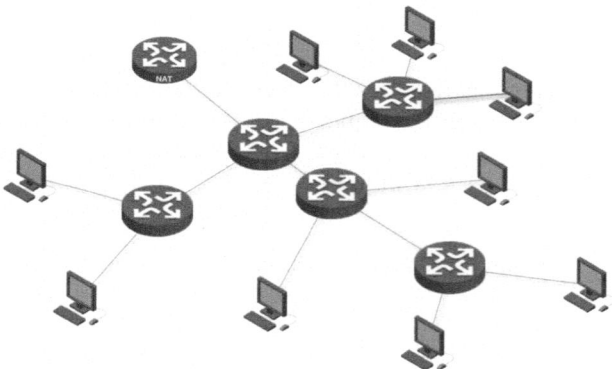

Fig. 4. Infered Network Topology.

To minimize errors caused by network and other objective factors, the inference process was repeated ten times at different time intervals, with the average of the ten results recorded as the final outcome for each metric, as shown in Table 3. The inference was conducted by capturing the outbound traffic at the NAT router. A single experiment yielded the deep-layer private network topology illustrated in Fig. 3. Subsequently, the effectiveness of the topology inference from the ten experiments was analyzed in detail based on both basic and extended metrics, the inferred topology results are shown in the Fig. 4.

The results of clustering the TCP traffic from the experimental topology using different clustering algorithms are shown in Table 2. From Table 2, it is evident that the spectral clustering algorithm performs poorly, which is mainly due to its suitability for handling high-dimensional data. The hierarchical clustering algorithm and the k-means clustering algorithm perform better because the dataset consists of categorical data, which is well-suited for processing with hierarchical and k-means clustering algorithms. Since k-means is a distance-based iterative clustering algorithm that assigns data points to the nearest cluster center and adjusts the cluster centers through multiple iterations to achieve the final clustering results, k-means outperforms the other algorithms in all metrics.

Table 2. Comparison results of clustering methods.

Clustering Method	Homogeneity	Completeness	V-Measure	F-Score
Hierarchical Clustering	0.846	0.919	0.881	0.858
Spectral Clustering	0.762	0.832	0.796	0.761
DBSCAN	0.567	0.671	0.614	0.587
k-means	0.908	0.974	0.940	0.913

Table 3 presents the results of the topology inference experiment. The inferred host device scale achieved a ratio of 0.8 compared to the actual scale, indicating that 8 out of 10 devices were correctly inferred. The network hierarchy inference was entirely accurate, maintaining a perfect ratio of 1.0. The system type inference for Linux devices also achieved a perfect ratio of 1.0, correctly identifying all 6 Linux devices. However, the inference for Windows devices was less accurate, with a ratio of 0.5, identifying only 2 out of 4 devices correctly. The link completeness ratio was 0.87, suggesting that 13 out of 15 links were correctly identified. Link accuracy and recall ratios were 0.84 and 0.73, respectively, indicating that while the majority of links were correctly identified, there is room for improvement in ensuring all relevant links are captured. These results validate the feasibility and effectiveness of the proposed method for inferring the topology of deep-layer private networks post-NAT deployment, particularly in terms of host device scale and network hierarchy.

Table 3. General overview of topological extrapolation

Metric	Actual Result	Average Inference Result	Ratio
Host Device Scale	10	8	0.8
Network Hierarchy	4	4	1.0
Link Completeness	15	13	0.87
Link Accuracy	1.0	0.84	0.84
Link Recall	1.0	0.73	0.73

5   Conclusion

The method presented in this paper, based on NTP and TCP traffic analysis, has demonstrated its high accuracy in inferring the topology of IoT networks within simulated environments. Accurate inference of IoT edge network topology holds significant value for the security and management of IoT systems, as it provides visibility into the network structure, which is essential for assessing security risks and optimizing network performance. However, with the rapid evolution of IoT technology and the ever-changing network landscape, this method will need to be further enhanced in terms of adaptability and precision to meet new challenges and demands. Therefore, ongoing research and development are necessary to maintain the effectiveness and relevance of this approach.

Acknowledgments. This work was partially supported by the National Key Research and Development Program of China (2022YFB3103904), the National Natural Science Youth Foundation (62002342), the National Natural Science Foundation of China (61931019) and the Youth Innovation Promotion Association CAS (id. E3YY021104).

References

1. Changazi, S.A., et al.: Optimization of network topology robustness in IoTs: a systematic review. Comput. Netw. 110568 (2024)
2. Dai, X., Cheng, G., Lu, G., Jin, B.: Tethering behavior detection architecture based on RTT measurement of TCP flows. J. Beihang Univ. (Aeronaut. Astronaut.) **49**(6), 1414–1423 (2021)
3. Khalil, T.Y., et al.: Deep learning in the industrial internet of things: potentials, challenges, and emerging applications. IEEE Internet Things J. **8**(14), 11016–11040 (2021)
4. Khatouni, I., Zincir-Heywood, N.: Exploring NAT detection and host identification using machine learning. In: 2019 15th International Conference on Network and Service Management (CNSM), pp. 1–8. IEEE (2019)
5. Lamping, U., Warnicke, E.: Wireshark user's guide. Interface **4**(6), 1 (2004)
6. Leivadeas, A., Falkner, M.: A survey on intent-based networking. IEEE Commun. Surv. Tutor. **25**(1), 625–655 (2022)

7. Mazin, A.M., Ab Rahman, R., Kassim, M., et al.: Performance analysis on network automation interaction with network devices using python. In: 2021 IEEE 11th IEEE Symposium on Computer Applications & Industrial Electronics (ISCAIE), pp. 360–366. IEEE (2021)
8. McKee, D.W., et al.: Massive-scale automation in cyber-physical systems: vision & challenges. In: 2017 IEEE 13th International Symposium on Autonomous Decentralized System (ISADS), pp. 5–11. IEEE (2017)
9. Nader, C.: Identifying IoT devices behind a NAT by using empirical data and learning methods. Master's thesis, The University of Texas at San Antonio (2022)
10. Olson, E., et al.: Doomed to repeat with IPv6? Characterization of NAT-centric security in SOHO routers. ACM Comput. Surv. **55**(14s), 1–37 (2023)
11. Park, C., et al.: Identification of hosts behind a NAT device utilizing multiple fields of IP and TCP. In: 2016 International Conference on Information and Communication Technology Convergence (ICTC), pp. 484–486. IEEE (2016)
12. Pashamokhtari, Y., Nakahara, M., Gharakheili, H.H.: Inferring connected IoT devices from IPFIX records in residential ISP networks. In: 2021 IEEE 46th Conference on Local Computer Networks (LCN), pp. 57–64. IEEE (2021)
13. Peixoto, T.P.: Descriptive vs. Inferential Community Detection in Networks: Pitfalls, Myths and Half-Truths. Cambridge University Press (2023)
14. Qiu, T., Chi, J., Zhou, X., Ning, Z., Atiquzzaman, M., Wu, D.O.: Edge computing in industrial internet of things: architecture, advances and challenges. IEEE Commun. Surv. Tutor. **22**(4), 2462–2488 (2020)
15. Yu, W., et al.: A survey on the edge computing for the internet of things. IEEE Access **6**, 6900–6919 (2017)
16. Zhao, J., et al.: Efficient IoT device identification via network behavior analysis based on time series dictionary. IEEE Internet Things J. (2023)

SmartTask: Efficient Dispatching for Low-Latency Tasks on Dynamic Edge Networks

Zhi Ding, Boyu Kong, Jiamei Lv, Yi Gao$^{(\boxtimes)}$, and Wei Dong

College of Computer Science and Technology, Zhejiang University, Hangzhou 310027, Zhejiang, China
{dingzhi,kongby,lvjm,gaoyi,dongw}@zju.edu.cn

Abstract. With the increasing adoption of edge computing, the necessity to offload tasks to edge servers is growing. Task dispatching becomes crucial in multi-server environments. Nevertheless, this process encounters difficulties due to the real-time acquisition complexities of communication and computation latency. Prior efforts have explored these latencies, but they presume easy acquisition of latency metrics, which is unrealistic in dynamic edge networks. To overcome these challenges, we introduce SmartTask, an innovative edge task dispatching system employing responsive network tomography to assess communication latency and deep neural networks to predict computation latency. To optimize the balance between dispatching speed and solution accuracy, SmartTask utilizes reinforcement learning for task scheduling. Additionally, SmartTask integrates curriculum learning to improve the performance and generalization of reinforcement learning. Evaluations indicate that SmartTask decreases end-to-end latency by an average of 26–86% compared to the baseline.

Keywords: Edge computing · task dispatching · reinforcement learning

1 Introduction

Edge computing (EC) addresses computational limitations, energy consumption of end devices, and high cloud latency. Task dispatching in EC has been extensively studied [1–5]. Efficient task dispatching to suitable edge servers in dynamic EC networks is essential. Most existing studies [1–4] assume readily available communication latency between the user and the server when dispatching tasks. While this is feasible in a nearly static network, it becomes difficult to accurately obtain communication latency in a highly heterogeneous edge server network. Fluctuating network latency adversely affects latency-sensitive edge computing tasks such as live streaming and edge cloud gaming. Current task scheduling schemes and tools [1,2,4,5] neglect varying server communication latency, and

L. Sun and Y. Chen (Eds.): CWSN 2024, CCIS 2341, pp. 64–75, 2025.
https://doi.org/10.1007/978-981-96-2186-6_6

network monitoring [6] is not efficiently integrated with task offloading algorithms. The complexity and variability of real-world edge networks result in highly variable network topology and communication latency, making existing work unsuitable for dynamic edge network task scheduling.

We proposed edge task dispatching strategy, termed SmartTask, assuming edge servers deployed on base stations (BS) for efficient task offloading via wireless hop. SmartTask, a modular server-side extension, comprises a task scheduling module, a network probing module, and a computational latency prediction module. Upon receiving a client task request, SmartTask probes network for communication latency and predicts computation latency, then dispatches task to minimize end-to-end latency. To efficiently dispatch tasks in a dynamic edge network with fluctuating latency and topology, SmartTask requires accurate network probing and rapid decision-making.

SmartTask faces two challenges. **Challenge 1: Probing the dynamic edge network accurately.** Task dispatching relies on end-to-end latency, where network fluctuations significantly impact communication latency. Traditional strategies [7] probe latency on each link, impractical in large-scale scenarios. Leveraging network tomography [8], SmartTask introduces responsive network tomography, enhancing precision in communication latency estimation. By judiciously selecting monitors and adaptively choosing servers, SmartTask optimizes network probing efficiency while ensuring accurate latency assessment, especially in varying network topologies. **Challenge 2: Expediting task dispatching decisions.** Even when armed with essential data, task dispatching remains NP-Hard, amalgamating influencing factors like task requests, server capacity and network conditions. SmartTask, akin to prior studies, employs reinforcement learning (RL) for task dispatching. Though RL training demands time, edge task dispatching becomes efficiently solvable post-training. Given the challenge of RL's generalization in complex and volatile environments [9], curriculum learning (CL) [9] is utilized to formulate curricula for enhancing RL training. However, conventional CL methods reliant on predetermined rules are ill-suited for fluctuating network contexts. We gauge and devise curricula based on performance gaps between trained RL and baseline. Once trained within a dynamic network, SmartTask attains superior performance and enhances dispatching decisions.

SmartTask adapts task dispatching policies to varied workloads, task requests, and network conditions. Unfortunately, there are no public datasets containing relevant data on network fluctuations in our target setting. Therefore, we created a dataset to evaluate SmartTask in a simulation. Our evaluation indicates that SmartTask reduces mean latency by 26–86% with lower overhead compared to the baseline. In summary, we make the following contributions: (1) We probe the client-server network latency using *responsive network tomography*. (2) We model the task dispatching policies and apply *reinforcement learning* for the policies. (3) We incorporate *curriculum learning* into the reinforcement learning training for task dispatching in dynamic edge networks.

2   Related Work

Dispatching policies are increasingly significant in evolving edge cloud scenarios. Xu et al. [10] propose an online task dispatching algorithm for edge servers with uniform computational capabilities. OnDisc [5] performs online task dispatch in edge clouds, while Dedas [4] greedily schedules tasks and considers replacing existing ones to meet new deadlines, but they all overlook network fluctuations, which affect communication latency. The SDGP [11] enhances NAS by generalizing performance predictors across search spaces but presupposes substantial domain similarities, limiting its applicability in heterogeneous environments. Qiang et al. [12] propose the FACT algorithm to optimize latency and accuracy in MAR via server assignment and frame resolution selection; however, their method is domain-specific. Conversely, SmartTask dynamically adjusts task dispatching based on real-time network latency, offering greater adaptability across diverse network conditions and task types.

Network tomography [8] aims to estimate the network performance from link measurements. Performance and capacity weighted routing methods to avoid congestion and enhance user experience are discussed in [13]. The traffic controller uses real-time measurements for routing and traffic balancing decisions. Existing research primarily focuses on determining network latency via edge-to-edge measurements. SmartTask extends this by using tomography to optimize task dispatching strategies.

3   Motivation and Overview

We evaluate various task-dispatching strategies in mobile contexts and present the SmartTask system for near-optimal task dispatching. We compare four strategies: (1) **Lowest Communication Latency First**, dispatching the task to the server with minimum communication latency; (2) **Lowest Computation Latency First**, dispatching the task to the server with minimum computation latency; (3) **Periodic Network Probing**, periodically probing network latency to dispatch tasks to the server with the minimum end-to-end latency; and (4) **Optimal**, theoretically using perfect latency knowledge for minimal end-to-end latency, although practically unattainable due to unpredictable delays and NP-hard computation complexity (Table 1).

The evaluation uses three network topologies from the Internet Topology Zoo dataset. Results (Fig. 1) indicate that Periodic Network Probing outperforms others with latency that is 1.11-3.71× worse than the Optimal The Lowest Communication Latency First performs the worst (2.12-11.95× worse). Periodic Network Probing excels by simultaneously gathering crucial information, but the Optimal policy is superior in larger networks due to accurate round-trip delay data essential for task dispatching. The study reveals that leveraging communication and computation latency data for task dispatching significantly enhances performance (i.e., end-to-end task latency). However, the Optimal policy's practical application is hindered by its reliance on future communication and com-

Table 1. Three different network topologies in our evaluation.

Network Topology	Scale	Number of Nodes	Number of Links
Abilene	Small	11	14
Bell Canada	Middle	48	65
Kdl	Large	754	899

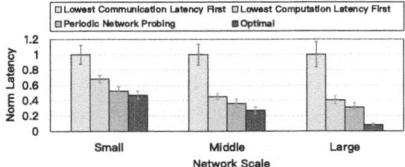

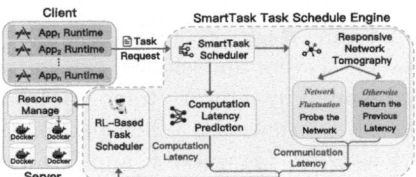

Fig. 1. Average latency of four policies.   **Fig. 2.** Overview of SmartTask.

Table 2. Notations used in SmartTask

Symbol	Description
$\mathcal{G}_t = (V, L_t)$	The t-th topology with node set V and link set L_t
$\mathcal{G}_{prune}^{(t)}$	The pruned graph of $\mathcal{G}_t(t = 1, ..., T)$
$\mathcal{I}^{(t)}$	The set of link to be probed (denoted as **interesting link**)
$\mathcal{H}^{(t)}$	The helper vertex set of $G_{prune}^{(t)}$
$V(\mathcal{D}), L(\mathcal{D})$	The set of nodes/links in graph $\mathcal{D}$
F	Monitor assignment constraints

putation latencies, rendering its upper bound unrealistic. Based on the comparison of the strategies, we propose SmartTask, which utilizes communication and computation latency data for task dispatching. Specifically, it employs efficient server workload network analysis and reinforcement learning strategies for real-time task scheduling, achieving near-optimal performance benefits in practice. Addressing this objective entails tackling two primary challenges: **efficiently gathering time-varying communication and computation latency data across edge devices and networks**, and **effectively dispatching tasks amidst computational complexity to align with dynamic network conditions.**

Figure 2 shows the workflow of SmartTask. When requesting the task, the edge server network is a black box to the client. SmartTask probes the network to obtain the communication latency (Sect. 4.1) and predict the computation latency with DNN (Sect. 4.2). SmartTask utilizes these latencies to dispatch tasks by employing reinforcement learning and curriculum learning methods (Sect. 5.2).

4   Efficient End-to-End Latency Estimation

The task's end-to-end latency contains *communication latency* probed by *responsive network tomography* (Sect. 4.1) and *computation latency* predicted by DNN (Sect. 4.2).

4.1   SmartTask's Responsive Network Tomography

Dispatching tasks requires an understanding of the communication latency between servers and clients. SmartTask develops *responsive network tomography* inspired by network tomography. Network topology varies frequently due to network fluctuations. When probing the network, SmartTask denotes the network as $G_t(V, L_t)$ where V and L_t are the node and link sets of the t-th topology, respectively. Table 2 shows the notations in SmartTask, some of which will be explained later. A subset of servers in V is assigned as monitors to probe the network for the communication latency of the interesting links. To probe the network efficiently, we use the two-stage graph pruning algorithm in Scalpel [14] to prune the network. Scalpel [14] outputs the pruned graph G_{prune} and the set H of *helper vertex* sets. Then, detecting the probing paths can obtain the communication latency information for all the interesting paths in G.

When the client requests tasks for the first time, SmartTask probes the network to analyze communication latency to the servers. If the client has requested services before, SmartTask checks for significant changes in latency due to network fluctuations. The network is probed only if there is evidence that latency has varied enough to affect task dispatching. When the client requests the task again, it gathers latency information from the K nearest servers, where K is fixed for the specific network topology. If the relative order of latency values among these servers changes significantly or if any latency value exceeds a threshold, re-probing is deemed necessary.[1] At this time, the *interesting links* include all links that end with the K closest servers to the client.

Due to network fluctuations, the edge network topology varies over time. There may be some overlap in network topologies across time slots, which leads to certain monitors potentially suitable for measuring the performance of interesting links in multiple time slots. To deploy monitors in dynamic topologies, SmartTask employs the Algorithm 1[2] to responsively probe the network when necessary. The basic idea is to express the deployment constraints of monitors in each time slot's topology G_t in the form of $\{(S_i, k_i)|i = 1, 2, ...\}$, where S_i is a

---

[1] We discuss the impact of different K values and thresholds in Sect. 6.

[2] *Connected* graph has at least one path from any vertex to any other vertex. A graph is *biconnected* if it stays *connected* after removing any one vertex, and *triconnected* if it stays *connected* after removing any two vertices. A *2-vertex cut* is a vertices set $\{v_1, v_2\}$ that removing v_1 or v_2 alone does not disconnect *connected* graph G, but removing both disconnects G. The *Cut-l* is a link connects the two vertices in a *2-vertex cut*. The *SPQR* component is a *Triconnected* components without *interesting links* connected to only one *2-vertex cut*, and cycles with no *interesting links* except for *cut-l*.

set of candidate monitors and k_i is the minimum number of monitors that need to be selected from S_i. Then, by solving an optimization problem with these constraints, a monitor deployment to probe the *interesting link* in different time slots' topologies is obtained.

Algorithm 1: SmartTask's Monitor Nodes Assignment

Input: $\mathcal{G}_t, \mathcal{H}^{(t)}, \mathcal{I}^{(t)}$
Output: Monitor assignment policy M^S
1   $F \leftarrow$ Empty set of monitor assignment constraints;
2   $\mathcal{G}_{prune}^{(t)} \leftarrow$ Pruned the graph $\mathcal{G}_t$ with Scalpel;
3   **foreach** *pruned graph* $\mathcal{G}_{prune}^{(t)}$ **do**
4   **foreach** *connected component* $\mathcal{C}$ *of* $\mathcal{G}_{prune}^{(t)}$ **do**
5   divide $\mathcal{C}$ into *biconnected components* $\mathcal{B}_1, \mathcal{B}_2,...$;
6   **foreach** $\mathcal{B}_i$ *with at least three nodes* **do**
7   divide $\mathcal{B}_i$ into *SPQR* components $\mathcal{R}_1, \mathcal{R}_2,...$;
8   **foreach** *SPQR component* $\mathcal{R}_j$ **do**
9   ExtractedConstrainct($\mathcal{R}_j, \mathcal{H}^{(t)}, \mathcal{I}^{(t)}, F$);
10   **end**
11   **end**
12   ExtractedConstrainct($\mathcal{C}, \mathcal{H}^{(t)}, \mathcal{I}^{(t)}, F$);
13   **end**
14 **end**
15 Express the constraint F as an optimization problem and obtain M^S by solving the optimization problem;

SmartTask obtains the monitor deployment by solving the following problem, where $|M|$ is the number of monitor servers, V is the set of nodes in the network, $Resoure_m$ is the current computation resource occupation on the server m, C_m is the total calculation resource on server m and $TH_{resource}$ is the threshold of computation resource occupation (empirically set to 80%).

$$\text{minimize: } |M| \tag{1}$$

$$\text{subject to: } |M \cap S_i| \geq k_i \qquad \forall (S_i, k_i) \in F, M \subseteq V \tag{2}$$

$$Resource_m < C_m \cdot TH_{resource} \qquad \forall m \in M \tag{3}$$

Equation (2) constrains the monitor should obey the constraints generated by Algorithm 1, and Eq. (3) constrains that the server does not act as a monitor when the resource consumption is higher than the threshold. Choosing the subset $M \subseteq V$ to obey Eq. (2) is NP-hard. So we design heuristics to solve the above equations.

4.2   SmartTask's DNN-Based Computation Latency Prediction

We construct a prediction model for the computation latency of the current task on the server based on our dataset. Our dataset contains the amount of computational resources required for tasks (e.g., CPU/GPU/memory requirements, etc.), the features of tasks (e.g., complexity of tasks, etc.), the current resource usage on the server (e.g., CPU/GPU/memory usage, etc.), and the number of tasks currently running on the target server. We trained a DNN (Deep-Learning Neural Network) to predict the computation latency of a specific task on a specific server by using our dataset. During training, the inputs to the network are task type, resource requirements, complexity and the server's resource usage, and the output is the predicted computation latency of the task. When a client requests a task, its task request contains its computation resource requirements. SmartTask predicts the computation latency based on the task's resource requirements and the server's current computational resource load and uses this to guide the dispatching of the task. Details on how to utilize these predicted network latencies will be elaborated in Sect. 5.1.

5   Efficient Task Dispatching Decisions

The solution to SmartTask's optimal task dispatching is NP-hard and the network fluctuation introduces additional complexity. We formulate the task dispatching problem (Sect. 5.1) and present an RL-based solution strategy (Sect. 5.2).

5.1   Task Dispatching Problem Formulation

Given M servers (each of which can serve certain kinds of tasks among all K kinds), SmartTask dispatches different tasks from N clients to different servers and assumes that each task is only dispatched to one server. We denote $T_{n,k}$ and $H_{n,k}$ as the end-to-end latency when the client n request for the task k and the threshold of the latency, respectively. $x_{n,k}^m$ is the boolean variable to describe whether the task k from client n is dispatched to the server m. y_k^m is the boolean variable to describe whether the server m can serve for the task k. The communication latency from client n to server m is denoted as t_n^m and the calculation latency for the client n's task k on server m is denoted as $s_{n,k}^m$. The calculation resource for client n's task k is denoted as $c_{n,k}$. When the current computation resource occupation on the server is high, tasks assigned to the server will wait until the resource load on that server is reduced below the threshold $TH_{resource}$. The optimization goal is to minimize the end-to-end latency of the clients, i.e.,

$$\text{minimize:} \sum_{n=1}^{N} \sum_{m=1}^{M} \sum_{k=1}^{K} x_{n,k}^m \cdot (t_n^m + s_{n,k}^m) \tag{4}$$

where t_n^m is probed by *responsive network tomography* (Sect. 4.1) and $s_{n,k}^m$ is predicted by the computation latency prediction (Sect. 4.2). When there are many tasks on the server, the task waiting latency on the server is also included in $s_{n,k}^m$. The minimization problem is subject to:

$$T_{n,k} = \sum_{m=1}^{M} x_{n,k}^m \cdot (t_n^m + s_{n,k}^m) \tag{5}$$

$$T_{n,k} \leq H_{n,k} \qquad \forall n \in [N], k \in [K] \tag{6}$$

$$\sum_{n=1}^{N} \sum_{k=1}^{K} x_{n,k}^m \cdot c_{n,k} \leq C_m \cdot TH_{resource} \quad \forall m \in [M] \tag{7}$$

$$x_{n,k}^m = 1 \rightarrow y_k^m = 1 \quad \forall n \in [N], m \in [M], k \in [K] \tag{8}$$

$$\sum_{m=1}^{M} x_{n,k}^m = 1 \quad \forall n \in [N], k \in [K] \tag{9}$$

$$x_{n,k}^m \in \{0,1\} \qquad \forall n \in [N], m \in [M], k \in [K] \tag{10}$$

$$y_k^m \in \{0,1\} \qquad \forall m \in [M], k \in [K] \tag{11}$$

Equation (5) defines the end-to-end latency of task k from client n. Equation (6) constrains the end-to-end latency not to exceed the task's latency threshold. Equation (7) constrains that the server resources consumed by all tasks cannot exceed the threshold, otherwise the tasks will wait to be served. Equation (8) constrains tasks that can only be dispatched to the server that can service that kind of task. Equation (9) constrains each task to be offloaded to only one server. Equation (10) and Eq. (11) constrain that the decision variable and y_k^m variable should be boolean. Since the problem is NP-Hard, traditional solvers will cause a large latency, SmartTask develops the RL-based solution for task dispatching.

5.2 Learning Method for Task Dispatching

SmartTask uses *reinforcement learning* to solve task scheduling problems and uses *curriculum learning* to guide reinforcement learning training.

SmartTask's Reinforcement Learning Model. SmartTask uses reinforcement learning (RL)[3] to dispatch the tasks. The agent's goal is to maximize the expected cumulative discounted reward $E\left[\sum_{t=0}^{\infty} \gamma^t r_t\right]$[4]. The **state** is the current task dispatching. The **action** is to change the task-dispatching policy to maximize the reward. SmartTask uses **critic-only reinforcement learning (CORL)** [15] which trains only a critic network. In CORL, the network tomography module and DNN-based communication prediction module are part of the critic network. Besides, the critic network and the constraint execution module act as task dispatchers. The end-to-end latency is treated as the **reward**.

---

[3] SmartTask chose RL over Deep Reinforcement Learning (DRL) because RL already achieves good performance and its models are lighter and easier to train.

[4] The discount factor $\gamma \in [0, 1]$ relates the rewards to the time domain and cares for the rewards agent achieved in the past, present, and future.

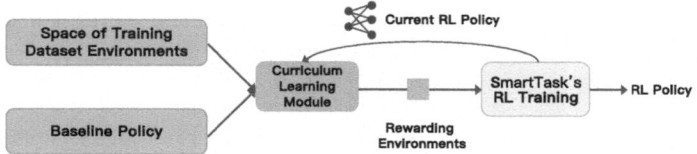

Fig. 3. Curriculum Learning creates curricula for SmartTask's RL training.

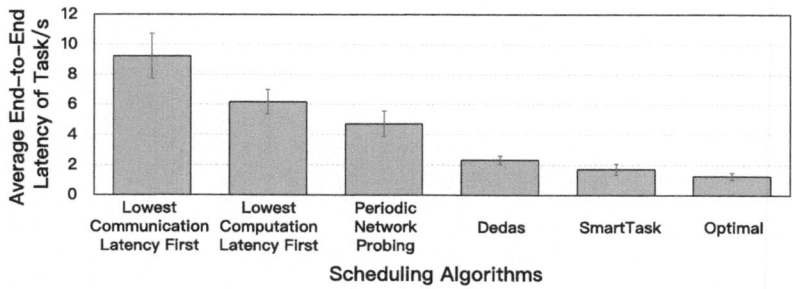

Fig. 4. Overall performance of SmartTask versus different baselines.

SmartTask's Curriculum Learning Method. When dispatching the task, RL may perform poorly if the training distribution spans a wide range of environments and curriculum learning (CL) [9][5] can improve RL training. In the early stages of CL, easier environments are selected to comprise a smooth loss function. When harder environments are introduced into training, the result model is a good starting point, reducing the smoothness of the loss function and making it harder to optimize. Optimizing the model with progressively less smooth loss functions gradually moves the parameters closer to the global optimum. However, it's challenging to define the difficulty of the environment for RL training. We measure environment difficulty by the performance gap between the trained agent and the Dedas baseline [4]. A large gap indicates a *rewarding* environment, which allows the RL model to significantly improve by learning from the baseline. A small gap suggests either the environment is difficult, the RL already performs well, or the baseline performs poorly but the RL has room for improvement. As shown in Fig. 3, each iteration in SmartTask's CL involves three steps: updating the RL model with the current environment distribution, selecting *rewarding* environments where the RL model has a large gap from the baseline, and promoting these environments in the next training distribution.

6   Evaluation

We evaluate SmartTask through simulation, showing a 26–86% improvement in average end-to-end request latency over other baselines. We use the tasks from

---

[5] CL gradually increases training environment difficulty, allowing the model to optimize less smooth loss functions and avoid local minima.

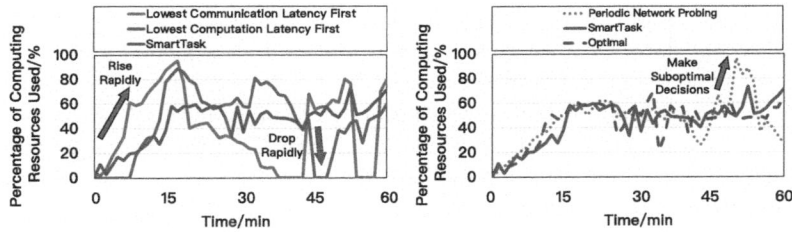

Fig. 5. The percentage of computation resource usage when using different policy.

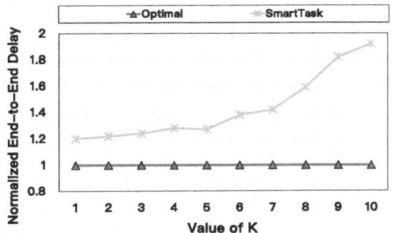

Fig. 6. Impact of K.   **Fig. 7.** Impact of Threshold.

Google Cluster, server network topologies from the Internet Topology Zoo [16], communication latency from the PlanetLabData [17] and CloudLab [18], and clients' movement trajectories from the Geolife [19] to simulate realistic edge task scenarios. We compare SmartTask with baselines described in Sect. 3 and Dedas [4].

End-to-End Latency Speedups. We evaluate the Kdl network topology with 50 clients by injecting 200 tasks. Figure 4 shows SmartTask reduces average end-to-end latency by 26–86% compared to baselines. This is because Smart-Task responsively probes the network for accurate communication latency and sequentially plans task execution on the server side to minimize the end-to-end latency of the task and to benefit existing and future tasks.

Load Balancing Between Servers. We evaluate load balancing in the Kdl topology with 10 clients, each sending identical tasks simultaneously. Figure 5 shows that SmartTask achieves better load balancing, with smaller server load fluctuations. SmartTask improves system reliability, scalability, performance, and security by leveraging near-real-time communication and computation latency data, unlike other policies that lead to greater load fluctuations and sub-optimal decisions.

Varying Tomography Parameters Settings. The performance of SmartTask is affected by the value of K and threshold (both defined in Sect. 4.1). We evaluate the performance of SmartTask when these properties vary.

a. Impact of K. Figure 6 shows the impact of K on SmartTask's performance, with end-to-end latency normalized to the Optimal approach. In the Kdl network, end-to-end delay increases slowly with $K \leq 5$ but significantly with $K > 5$. Thus, $K = 5$ is optimal for Kdl network and can balance network scans and performance, probably because the relative latency of the five servers neighboring the client portrays the fluctuation of the edge server network better. Smaller K values slightly improve performance but increase overhead, while larger K values reduce accuracy and degrade performance. Although the performance of Smart-Task varies with the value of K, grid-based search can determine the appropriate K for different network topologies.

b. Impact of Threshold. Figure 7 shows the impact of the threshold on Smart-Task's performance, with normalized end-to-end latency of Optimal approach. In the Kdl network, end-to-end delay increases slowly with a threshold up to 12%, but increases rapidly beyond that. Thus, a 12% threshold is optimal. Smaller thresholds slightly improve performance but increase network scans, while larger thresholds reduce accuracy and degrade performance. Although the performance of SmartTask varies with the value of threshold, grid-based search can determine the optimal threshold for different network topologies.

SmartTask's Overhead. We evaluate SmartTask's overhead. Memory overhead of each client's task request log depends on the number of task requests and servers, with each requiring 8 bytes for storage. This results in less than 2 MB per client even for large systems, making the memory overhead negligible. CPU and network overheads range from 1.50%–2.58% and 1.17%–3.13%, respectively. These overheads are acceptable given SmartTask's significant reduction in end-to-end latency.

7   Conclusion

We present SmartTask, an edge task dispatching policy for dynamic edge computing network scenarios. Unlike previous task dispatching policies, SmartTask dynamically adjusts its dispatching policies based on responsively probing the communication latency and predicting the server's load. Besides, SmartTask adaptively improves its dispatching policy based on reinforcement learning and generates the curricula for RL training by curriculum learning. Its dynamic task dispatching based on real-time network conditions makes it valuable for scenarios requiring low latency and efficient resource allocation such as smart cities, healthcare and industrial IoT. Evaluation results show that SmartTask reduces the end-to-end request latency of edge tasks by 26–86% compared to existing layout policies.

Acknowledgement. This work is supported by the "Pioneer" and "Leading Goose" R&D Program of Zhejiang under grant No.2023C01033 and the National Natural Science Foundation of China under grant no. 62272407.

References

1. Ren, T., Hu, Z., He, H., Niu, J., Liu, X.: Feat: towards fast environment-adaptive task offloading and power allocation in MEC. In: IEEE INFOCOM, pp. 1–10 (2023)
2. Li, Y., Zeng, T., Zhang, X., Duan, J., Wu, C.: Tapfinger: task placement and finegrained resource allocation for edge machine learning. In: IEEE INFOCOM, pp. 1–10 (2023)
3. Liu, Y., Mao, Y., Liu, Z., Ye, F., Yang, Y.: Joint task offloading and resource allocation in heterogeneous edge environments. In: IEEE INFOCOM, pp. 1–10 (2023)
4. Meng, J., Tan, H., Li, X.-Y., Han, Z., Li, B.: Online deadline-aware task dispatching and scheduling in edge computing. IEEE TPDS **31**(6), 1270–1286 (2020)
5. Han, Z., Tan, H., Li, X.-Y., Jiang, S.H.-C., Li, Y., Lau, F.C.M.: Ondisc: online latency-sensitive job dispatching and scheduling in heterogeneous edge-clouds. IEEE ToN **27**(6), 2472–2485 (2019)
6. Chen, Y., et al.: Norma: towards practical network load testing. In: NSDI, pp. 1733–1749 (2023)
7. Noor, J., Srivastava, M., Netravali, R.: Portkey: adaptive key-value placement over dynamic edge networks. In: Proceedings of SOCC, pp. 197–213 (2021)
8. Vardi, Y.: Network tomography: estimating source-destination traffic intensities from link data. JASA **91**, 365–377 (1996)
9. Narvekar, S., Peng, B., Leonetti, M., Sinapov, J., Taylor, M.E., Stone, P.: Curriculum learning for reinforcement learning domains: a framework and survey. JMLR **21**(1), 7382–7431 (2020)
10. Xu, Z., Liang, W., Xu, W., Jia, M., Guo, S.: Efficient algorithms for capacitated cloudlet placements. IEEE TPDS **27**(10), 2866–2880 (2016)
11. Ma, L., Kang, H., Yu, G., Li, Q., He, Q.: Single-domain generalized predictor for neural architecture search system. IEEE Trans. Comput. **73**(05), 1400–1413 (2024)
12. Liu, Q., Huang, S., Opadere, J., Han, T.: An edge network orchestrator for mobile augmented reality. In: IEEE INFOCOM 2018 - IEEE Conference on Computer Communications, pp. 756–764 (2018)
13. Schlinker, B., et al.: Engineering egress with edge fabric: steering oceans of content to the world. In: Proceedings of SIGCOMM, pp. 418–431 (2017)
14. Gao, Y., Dong, W., Wu, W., Chen, C., Li, X.Y., Bu, J.: Scalpel: scalable preferential link tomography based on graph trimming. IEEE ToN **24**(3), 1392–1403 (2016)
15. Alibekov, E., Kubalik, J., Babuska, R.: Policy derivation methods for critic-only reinforcement learning in continuous spaces. EAAI **69**, 178–187 (2018)
16. Knight, S., Nguyen, H.X., Falkner, N., Bowden, R., Roughan, M.: The internet topology zoo. IEEE JSAC **29**(9), 1765–1775 (2011)
17. Zhu, R., Liu, B., Niu, D., Li, Z., Zhao, H.V.: Network latency estimation for personal devices: a matrix completion approach. IEEE/ACM ToN **25**(2), 724–737 (2017)
18. Maricq, A., Duplyakin, D., Jimenez, I., Maltzahn, C., Stutsman, R., Ricci, R.: Taming performance variability. In: OSDI, pp. 409–425 (2018)
19. Zheng, Y., Fu, H., Xie, X., Ma, W.-Y., Li, Q.: Geolife GPS Trajectory Dataset - User Guide (2011). https://www.microsoft.com/en-us/research/publication/geolife-gps-trajectory-dataset-user-guide/

BM²SS: Blockchain-Aided Multi-authority and Multi-keyword Searchable Scheme for IoT

Yao Huang[1,2], Zhongyuan Yu[3], Guijuan Wang[1,2(✉)], Baobao Chai[4], Hongliang Zhang[1,2], and Jiguo Yu[5]

[1] Key Laboratory of Computing Power Network and Information Security, Ministry of Education, Shandong Computer Science Center, Qilu University of Technology (Shandong Academy of Sciences), Jinan 250353, China
guijuan_wang@126.com
[2] Shandong Provincial Key Laboratory of Industrial Network and Information System Security, Qilu University of Technology (Shandong Academy of Sciences), Jinan 250353, China
[3] School of Information Science and Engineering, Lanzhou University, Lanzhou 730000, China
[4] School of Computer Science and Engineering, Shandong University of Science and Technology, Qingdao 266590, China
bbchai_915@sdust.edu.cn
[5] School of Computer Science and Engineering, University of Electronic Science and Technology of China, Chengdu 611731, China

Abstract. Owing to security and privacy concerns of outsourced data, numerous studies have been dedicated to attaining fine-grained access control and keyword-based search. Nevertheless, achieving decentralized attribute management and efficient multi-keyword search remains an untoward issue. In this paper, we propose a blockchain-aided multi-authority and multi-keyword searchable scheme, named BM²SS. Our scheme employs a set of attribute authorities to manage attributes and generate attribute decryption keys for authorized users. Subsequently, resource-limited users can efficiently outsource the decryption to the cloud with attribute decryption keys. Also, the hash value of plaintext data stored in the blockchain allows for effortless verification of cloud computation results. Additionally, we utilize smart contract to match search trapdoor and index without worrying about the correctness of search results. Simulation results demonstrate the efficiency and applicability of our scheme in IoT scenarios.

Keywords: Internet of Things · Multi-authority · Multi-keyword search · Blockchain · Privacy protection

1 Introduction

The rapid advancement and widespread adoption of Internet of Things (IoT) have led to the deployment of thousands of IoT devices across various scenarios

L. Sun and Y. Chen (Eds.): CWSN 2024, CCIS 2341, pp. 76–91, 2025.
https://doi.org/10.1007/978-981-96-2186-6_7

[1]. The data generated by various IoT applications usually contains privacy-sensitive information such as user identities and home addresses [2]. As a result of the semi-trusted nature of cloud servers, IoT data is frequently encrypted and stored on third-party cloud servers. Although this approach can prevent cloud servers from compromising privacy and abusing IoT data for commercial purposes, the functions such as fine-grained access control and ciphertext search are sacrificed [3].

Attribute-based encryption (ABE), a promising cryptographic technique, enables fine-grained access control and confidentiality protection for IoT data stored in the cloud. Some variants of ABE including ciphertext-policy ABE (CP-ABE) and key-policy ABE (KP-ABE) have been applied in various fields [4]. In a CP-ABE enabled IoT data sharing system, the data owners do not need to perform any encryption calculations upon adding a new data user. However, the centralized attribute authority easily exposes the system to single point of failure [5]. Therefore, multi-authority CP-ABE is introduced in the design of IoT data sharing system, where a set of authorities is responsible for managing separate attribute sets. Nevertheless, there are still some issues that affect the application of current decentralized schemes. Specifically, there is a deficiency and trust issue in key generation and data integrity, which leads to computational complexity and risk of data forgery in the key generation request and data integrity verification processes.

In practical scenarios, a cloud server provides computing and storage services to multiple users [6]. Consequently, searchable encryption is essential for efficiently retrieving the required data from a vast amount of encrypted data. To alleviate the bottleneck of low accuracy caused by single-keyword search, multi-keyword SE schemes are designed to match the multi-keyword index and search trapdoor [7]. Yet, search efficiency and reliability of search results are still the problems faced by the current research. In a multi-keyword search scheme, the search computation will increase because of the requirements of matching multiple keywords in one search. Also, since the search operation is usually conducted by a third-party cloud, the search results are subject to some malicious manipulation for profit purposes.

Blockchain can enable traceability and verification within the data sharing process, offering potential solutions to the security and privacy issues associated with cloud computing [8]. Data integrity and computation results can be verified on the blockchain with smart contract, thus ensuring unambiguous system execution and fostering trust among users.

Motivation. Given the challenges faced by current solutions, we propose a blockchain-based approach in this paper. The motivations are as follows: First, to enhance efficiency and trust in decentralized attribute management. The computation of attribute keys is often resource-intensive, and it is crucial to address the challenge of preventing malicious requests during key generation and computation. Second, to improve search efficiency and result reliability. It is essential to minimize computational overhead in search operations while optimizing the benefits of multi-keyword searches. Additionally, the approach should ensure high accuracy of search results and provide mechanisms to prevent malicious manipulation.

In this paper, we propose a blockchain aided multi-authority and multi-keyword searchable scheme (BM^{2}SS). The contributions of the paper are outlined as follows:

- Decentralized attribute management and fine-grained access control. BM^{2}SS utilizes a set of attribute authorities for the generation of attribute decryption keys, which not only eliminates the potential performance bottleneck brought by a centralized attribute authority but also guarantees fine-grained data access control based on attributes.
- Multi-keyword search. BM^{2}SS facilitates multi-keyword search, enhancing the precision of search results compared to single-keyword search. Furthermore, the matching process between the search trapdoor and index is executed on the blockchain through smart contract.
- BM^{2}SS is proved to be statically secure and indistinguishable under chosen keyword attacks (IND-CKA). Additionally, the simulation results indicate a superior performance of BM^{2}SS compared to other schemes.

The subsequent sections of this paper are organized as follows: Sect. 2 provides a concise overview of the relevant literature. The system framework of BM^{2}SS is presented in Sect. 3. We detail the concrete construction BM^{2}SS in Sect. 4. In Sect. 5, the theoretical analysis of BM^{2}SS is demonstrated. Section 6 involves the performance analysis and evaluation of the proposed scheme. Lastly, Sect. 7 offers the conclusion.

2   Related Work

This section presents a comprehensive overview of relevant studies.

In [9], Song et al. initially introduced the concept of searchable encryption (SE), allowing keyword-based search over ciphertext without compromising privacy. Next, in [10], Boneh et al. devised a keyword-based searchable public key encryption scheme. The data user can generate a search trapdoor in the scheme with the associated secret key. In [11], Zhang et al. designed a lightweight SE scheme to alleviate the computational burdens of IoT devices. Their scheme implemented multi-keyword search and dynamic user identity management. Nevertheless, the computational overheads related to search and encryption are still too heavy. In [12], Meng et al. developed an Attribute-Based Searchable Encryption (ABSE) scheme that offloads the majority of computational burdens to fog nodes. However, the scheme incurs significant overheads in trapdoor generation.

Some studies concentrate on employing the aforementioned cryptographic techniques to tackle security and privacy concerns in IoT. In [13], a multi-value independent ABSE scheme resistant to key recovery attacks was developed. Nevertheless, their scheme uses an AND-gate access policy and does not consider how to perform multi-keyword search on the ciphertext. In [14], Wang et al. devised an ABSE scheme utilizing an access tree structure. This approach involves the centralized generation of attribute keys by an attribute authority, raising concerns about performance and the risk of SPoF. In [15], Huang et al. proposed an ABSE scheme that constructed a Bloom filter tree structure for a collection of documents stored on the cloud, avoiding the need to match keywords by traversing the entire collection. Two single keyword-based SE schemes were provided in [16] and [17]. However, the indices are collaboratively generated by users and a trusted authority, which is prone to causing performance bottlenecks with massive IoT data.

In [18], Su et al. developed an Ethereum-based ABSE, which utilizes smart contract to perform search and verification. Nevertheless, the unconditional openness of Ethereum introduces security concerns for file indexes, and complex search operations incur high gas consumption. In [19], Liu et al. investigated three different levels of secure verification and proposed a certificate-based verifiable search scheme in conjunction with blockchain. In [20], Liu et al. devised a blockchain aided ABSE scheme tailored for cloud-based IoT. They utilize blockchain to conduct decentralized key management and maintain a user revocation list. In [21], for obtaining full decentralization, Yu et al. introduced a decentralized ABSE scheme with user revocation at the cost of sacrificing efficiency in system initialization. In [22], Zhang et al. proposed an anonymous ABSE scheme using blockchain and achieved confidentiality of attributes and verifiability of results. In [23], Gao et al. dedicated to addressing potential interest conflicts between data user and data owner. Their scheme ensures data integrity and transaction fairness through blockchain and smart contract. However, their single-keyword search approach makes the scheme less practical than a multi-keyword search scheme.

ABSE schemes ensure the privacy of outsourced data while providing flexible access control and keyword-based search functionality. However, the semi-trusted nature of cloud computing poses challenges in detecting malicious tampering and ensuring the correctness of cloud-generated results. Although blockchain offers practical solutions to these issues, further research is needed to enhance the efficiency of multi-keyword searches and to strengthen resistance against malicious manipulation of search results.

3   System Framework

3.1   System Model

BM²SS comprises six entities, namely the Trusted Authority, Attribute Authorities, Data Owners, Data Users, Cloud Service Provider, and Blockchain, as shown in Fig. 1.

- *Trusted Authority* (TA). The TA functions as a fully trusted entity. It is responsible for initializing the entire system, generating the public parameters PP, assigning users a set of attributes based on their identities by launching a blockchain record Tx_{reg}, and maintaining the system.

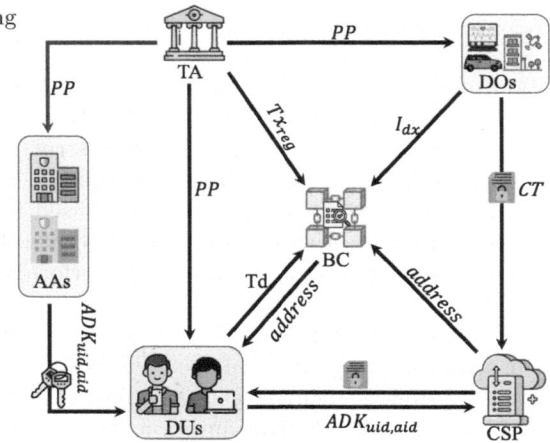

Fig. 1. Framework of BM^{2}SS scheme.

- *Attribute Authorities* (AAs). BM^{2}SS includes a group of AAs within the system. These AAs individually manage disjoint attribute sets and generate corresponding attribute decryption keys for authorized users. Specifically, AAs are in charge of computing attribute decryption keys $ADK_{uid,aid}$ for DUs.

- *Data Owners* (DOs). The DOs usually possess vast amounts of data, including privacy-sensitive information. To ensure efficient data sharing while preserving user privacy, DOs are accountable for computing the data ciphertext CT and data index I_{dx}. Specifically, DOs commonly utilize predefined access policies to encrypt IoT data. Additionally, DOs may extract keywords from IoT data for multi-keyword search.

- *Data Users* (DUs). The DUs possess attributes along with corresponding attribute decryption keys. Additionally, DUs can generate search trapdoors Td based on their preferred keywords. These search trapdoors are submitted to BC, and the searching process is performed through a smart contract.

- *Cloud Service Provider* (CSP). The CSP possesses sufficient storage capacity and computational resources, offering reliable storage services as well as ciphertext transformation services. After the ciphertext is uploaded to CSP by DOs, the storage *address* of the encrypted data is logged on BC.

- *Blockchain* (BC). The BC is responsible for ensuring information consistency and validating the results of outsourced decryption. Multi-keyword search operations are executed on the BC via smart contracts. Upon completion of the search, the corresponding data storage address is returned to the Data Users. Hyperledger Fabric[1] is used as the blockchain emulation platform. We assume that at least 51% of the participating entities (e.g., nodes or miners) are honest and trustworthy. This assumption is consistent with the standard security model of blockchain, where the majority of the network's computational power is controlled by honest participants, ensuring the integrity and immutability of the blockchain.

---

[1] https://github.com/hyperledger/fabric.

3.2   Algorithm Definition

- **Initialization**(1^{θ}) → PP. Taking a security parameter θ as the input, the algorithm, performed by the TA, outputs the public parameters PP.
- **AASetup**(PP) → (PK_{aid}, SK_{aid}). Taking the public parameters PP as the input, the algorithm, performed by an AA aid, outputs a public key PK_{aid} and a private key SK_{aid}, where $aid \in AID$.
- **UKeyGen**(PP) → ($PK_{uid/oid}, SK_{uid/oid}$). Taking the public parameters PP as the input, the algorithm, performed by a DU uid or a DO oid, outputs a public key PK_{uid}/PK_{oid} and a private key SK_{uid}/SK_{oid}, where $uid/oid \in UID$.
- **ADKGen**($PP, SK_{aid}, PK_{uid}, S_{uid,aid}$) → $ADK_{uid,aid}$. Taking the public parameters PP, a private key SK_{aid}, a public key PK_{uid} and an attribute set $S_{uid,aid}$ of DU as the input, where the attribute set $S_{uid,aid}$ is managed by an AA, the algorithm, performed by the AA aid, outputs the attribute decryption key $ADK_{uid,aid}$ over the attribute set $S_{uid,aid}$.
- **DataEnc**($PP, \{PK_{aid}\}, (\mathbb{A}, \delta), F$) → CT. Taking the public parameters PP, a public key set $\{PK_{aid}\}$, an access policy $(\mathbb{A}, \delta)$, and the IoT data file F as the input, the algorithm, performed by a DO, outputs the ciphertext CT associated with $(\mathbb{A}, \delta)$.
- **KwEnc**(PP, PK_{oid}, KW) → I_{dx}. Taking the public parameters PP, public key PK_{oid} of a DO oid and a keyword set KW extracted from IoT data file F as the input, the algorithm, performed by a DO, outputs the data index I_{dx} of IoT data file F.
- **TdGen**(PP, SK_{uid}, KW') → Td. Taking the public parameters PP, private key SK_{uid} of a DU uid and a keyword set KW' as the input, the algorithm, performed by the DU, outputs the search trapdoor Td.
- **Match**(I_{dx}, Td) → 0/1. Taking the data index I_{dx} and search trapdoor Td as the input, the algorithm, performed by blockchain consensus nodes, if the keywords specified by a DU match the keywords extracted from IoT data file F, blockchain returns the storage *address* of ciphertext CT.
- **SemiDec**($PP, PK_{uid}, \{ADK_{uid,aid}\}, CT$) → SCT. Taking the public parameters PP, a public key PK_{uid}, an attribute decryption key set $\{ADK_{uid,aid}\}_{aid \in AID}$ of a DU, and ciphertext CT as the input, the algorithm, performed by CSP, outputs the semi-decrypted ciphertext SCT.
- **FiDec**(SCT, SK_{uid}) → F. Taking the semi-decrypted ciphertext SCT and private key SK_{uid} of a DU uid as the input, the algorithm, performed by a DU, outputs the IoT data file F without complex decryption computations.

3.3   Security Model

BM²SS is statically and IND-CKA secure against any probabilistic polynomial time (PPT) adversary. The security models are introduced between adversary $\mathcal{A}$ and challenger $\mathcal{C}$.

The static security model is described as follows.

Setup: $\mathcal{C}$ generates PP and sends it to $\mathcal{A}$.

Adversary queries: $\mathcal{A}$ specifies a set of corrupted AAs $C_{AAs} \subseteq AID$. Then, $\mathcal{A}$ can make the following queries.

- $\mathcal{A}$ queries a set of public keys of uncorrupted AAs N_{AAs}, where $C_{AAs} \cap N_{AAs} = \emptyset$.
- $\mathcal{A}$ sends attribute decryption key queries to $\mathcal{C}$ by submitting $\{uid, S_{uid}\}$, with the restriction that the queried attributes are not associated with corrupted AAs.
- $\mathcal{A}$ submits two messages of equal length $m_0, m_1 \in \mathbb{G}_T$, and an access structure$(\mathbb{A}^*, \delta^*)$ to obtain a ciphertext CT^* on m_0 or m_1 from $\mathcal{C}$. The $(\mathbb{A}^*, \delta^*)$ has a maximum size of $q \times q$.

Challenger replies: $\mathcal{C}$ randomly selects a message m_b, where $b \in \{0,1\}$, and responses $\mathcal{A}$ as follows.

- $\mathcal{C}$ returns public keys of uncorrupted AAs N_{AAs} by executing **AASetup** algorithm.
- $\mathcal{C}$ returns the attribute decryption keys by executing **ADKGen** algorithm.
- $\mathcal{C}$ returns challenge ciphertext on m_b by executing the **DataEnc** algorithm.

Guess: $\mathcal{A}$ outputs its guess bit $b' \in \{0,1\}$.

Definition 1. *Let $\mathcal{A}$'s advantage in winning the above static security game be $Adv_{\mathcal{A}}^{static}(1^\theta) = |2Pr[b' = b] - 1|$. The BM^2SS scheme is secure against static attacks if any PPT adversary has a negligible advantage in statically breaking our scheme under the static security model.*

The IND-CKA security model is described as follows.

Setup: $\mathcal{C}$ generates PP and sends it to $\mathcal{A}$.

Phase 1: $\mathcal{A}$ sends trapdoor queries to $\mathcal{C}$ by submitting a set of keywords. $\mathcal{C}$ responds with the outputs of running the **TdGen** algorithm.

Challenge: $\mathcal{A}$ randomly selects two keywords kw_0, kw_1 of equal length and submits kw_0, kw_1 to $\mathcal{C}$. The keywords queried in *Phase 1* are not allowed to be submitted. $\mathcal{C}$ runs the **KwEnc** algorithm to randomly encrypt a keyword kw_b, where $b \in \{0,1\}$, and returns the challenge index to $\mathcal{A}$.

Phase 2: $\mathcal{A}$ issues query as in *Phase 1*. The keywords queried in *Challenge* cannot be submitted.

Guess: $\mathcal{A}$ outputs its guess bit $b' \in \{0,1\}$.

Definition 2. *Let $\mathcal{A}$'s advantage in winning the above IND-CKA security game be $Adv_{\mathcal{A}}^{IND-CKA}(1^\theta) = |2Pr[b' = b] - 1|$. The BM^2SS scheme is secure against chosen-keyword attacks if any PPT adversary has a negligible advantage in breaking our scheme under IND-CKA security model.*

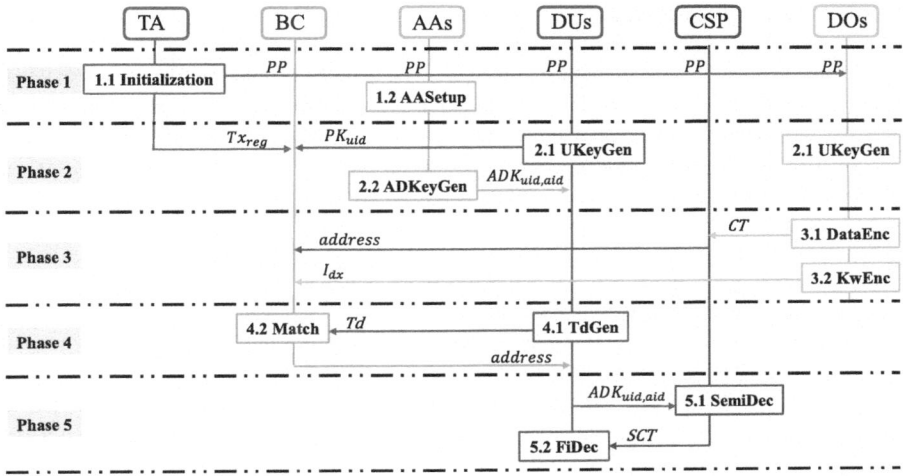

Fig. 2. Workflow of BM²SS scheme.

4 Construction of BM²SS

The BM²SS is divided into 5 phases: *System Initialization, Key Generation, Encryption, Search,* and *Decryption.* The workflow of the proposed scheme is illustrated in Fig. 2.

Phase 1. System Initialization

1.1 The TA performs the **Initialization** algorithm to choose two multiplicative cyclic groups $\mathbb{G}$, $\mathbb{G}_T$ with the prime order p. Let $g \in \mathbb{G}$ be a generator of group $\mathbb{G}$. In addition, the algorithm defines a bilinear map $\hat{e} : \mathbb{G} \times \mathbb{G} \to \mathbb{G}_T$ and picks three hash functions H, H_0, and H_1, where H maps strings to elements in $\mathbb{Z}_p$, H_0 maps unique identities in UID to elements in $\mathbb{G}$ and H_1 maps attributes to elements in $\mathbb{G}$. Finally, the algorithm random chooses $\gamma \in \mathbb{Z}_p$ and outputs the public parameters:

$$PP = \{\mathbb{G}, \mathbb{G}_T, p, g, \hat{e}, g^\gamma, H, H_0, H_1\}.$$

1.2 The AAs perform the **AASetup** algorithm to complete initialization. Each AA with a unique identity *aid* respectively manages a disjoint set of attributes. The algorithm randomly chooses $\alpha_{aid}, \beta_{aid} \in \mathbb{Z}_p$, then calculates the public key and private key as the following:

$$PK_{aid} = \{g^{\alpha_{aid}}, g^{\beta_{aid}}\}, SK_{aid} = \{\alpha_{aid}, \beta_{aid}\}.$$

Phase 2. Key Generation

2.1 Each DU/DO with a unique identifier performs the **UKeyGen** algorithm to generate a key pair $(PK_{oid}/PK_{uid}, SK_{oid}/SK_{uid})$ with PP as the input. The algorithm randomly chooses $z_{oid}/z_{uid} \in \mathbb{Z}_p$ as the private key and computes public key $PK_{oid} = g^{z_{oid}}/PK_{uid} = g^{z_{uid}}$. Then, the algorithm outputs a key pair of DO or DU:

$$(PK_{oid} = g^{z_{oid}}/PK_{uid} = g^{z_{uid}}), (SK_{oid} = z_{oid}/SK_{uid} = z_{uid}).$$

By sending PK_{uid} and identifier uid to the blockchain, an attribute set S_{uid} is assigned to a data user. Finally, TA launches a blockchain record $Tx_{reg} = \{uid, S_{uid}, Timestamp\}$.

2.2 Each AA aid runs the **ADKGen** algorithm to generate attribute decryption keys for its attributes. For an attribute $att_i \in S_{uid,aid}$, AA randomly chooses $t \in \mathbb{Z}_p$ and computes:

$$K_{uid,att_i} = g^{z_{uid}\alpha_{aid}} H_0(uid)^{\beta_{aid}} H_1(att_i)^t, L_{uid,att_i} = g^t.$$

Then, the algorithm outputs attribute decryption key $ADK_{uid,aid}$ related to $S_{uid,aid}$: $ADK_{uid,aid} = (\{K_{uid,att_i}, L_{uid,att_i}\}_{att_i \in S_{uid,aid}})$.

Phase 3. Encryption

3.1 DO runs the **DataEnc** algorithm and formulates an access policy $(\mathbb{A}, \delta)$, where $\mathbb{A} \in \mathbb{Z}_p^{l \times n}$ is a matrix of l rows and n columns. DO randomly chooses $s, v_2, ..., v_n, y_2, ..., y_n \in \mathbb{Z}_p$, then creates two vectors $\boldsymbol{v} = (s, v_2, ..., v_n), \boldsymbol{w} = (0, y_2, ..., y_n)$. For each row $\mathbb{A}_i$ of $\mathbb{A}$, the algorithm computes $\lambda_i = \mathbb{A}_i \cdot \boldsymbol{v}$ and $w_i = \mathbb{A}_i \cdot \boldsymbol{w}$, where λ_i represents the share of s and w_i represents the share of 0 in row $\mathbb{A}_i$. In addition, we define two functions δ and ρ mapping rows of $\mathbb{A}$ to attributes and AAs, respectively. DO randomly chooses $t_i \in \mathbb{Z}_p$ and computes the ciphertext components as the following:

$$C_0 = F \cdot \hat{e}(g,g)^s, C_{1,i} = g^{\lambda_i} g^{\alpha_{\rho(i)} t_i}, C_{2,i} = g^{\beta_{\rho(i)} t_i} g^{w_i}, C_{3,i} = g^{-t_i}, C_{4,i} = H_1(\delta(i))^{t_i}.$$

Then, DO outputs the ciphertext: $CT = (C_0, \{C_{1,i}, C_{2,i}, C_{3,i}, C_{4,i}\}_{i \in [l]})$.

3.2 DO runs the **KwEnc** algorithm and extracts a set of keywords $KW = \{kw_1, ..., kw_d\}$ from IoT data and encrypts the keywords for privacy concerns. The algorithm randomly selects $\tau, \tau_1 \in \mathbb{Z}_p$ and computes the index as follows:

$$W_1 = g^{z_{oid}\tau}, W_2 = g^{\gamma\tau_1}, W_3 = g^{\tau_1}, W_i = g^{\gamma H(kw_i)\tau}.$$

Then, the algorithm outputs multi-keyword index: $I_{dx} = (W_1, W_2, W_3, \{W_i\}_{i \in [d]})$.

After finishing data encryption and index construction, DO sends $\{Hash(CT), CT\}$ and $\{I_{dx}, Hash(CT)\}$ to CSP and BC, respectively, where

Hash is a collision-resistant hash function. Any malicious modifications to *CT* can be easily detected depending on the tamper-resistance of blockchain. The CSP records the storage address *address* of ciphertext CT on BC with $\{Hash(CT), I_{dx}, address\}$.

Phase 4. Search

4.1 DO runs the **TdGen** algorithm to generate a search trapdoor in correspondence with interested keywords $KW' = \{kw'_1, ..., kw'_{d'}\}$. The algorithm randomly chooses $\eta \in \mathbb{Z}_p$ and computes:

$$T_1 = g^{\eta z_{uid}}, T_2 = g^{\gamma \eta z_{uid}}, T_3 = \prod_{i=1}^{d'} g^{\gamma H(kw'_i)}.$$

The algorithm then outputs the search trapdoor Td and sends it to BC for ciphertext retrial: $Td = (T_1, T_2, T_3)$.

4.2 The **Match** algorithm is implemented with smart contract and takes index I_{dx} and search trapdoor Td as inputs. Upon receiving the search trapdoor from DU, the consensus nodes proceed to verify the following equation through the execution of a smart contract:

$$\hat{e}(T_1, W_2)\hat{e}(PK_{oid}, \prod_{i=1}^{d'} W_i) = \hat{e}(T_2, W_3)\hat{e}(T_3, W_1). \tag{1}$$

If the equation holds, the algorithm outputs 1 and returns the ciphertext storage *address* to DU. Otherwise it outputs 0 indicating search failed.

Phase 5. Decryption

5.1 CSP performs the **SemiDec** algorithm to complete complex decryption computations instead of DU. The algorithm aborts if DU's attributes do not satisfy the access policy. Otherwise, let $I = \{i : \delta(i) \in S_{uid}\}_{i \in [l]}$. CSP computes tct_i for $i \in I$:

$$tct_i = V_{1,i} \cdot V_{2,i} \cdot V_{3,i} \cdot V_{4,i} = \hat{e}(g,g)^{z_{uid}\lambda_i}\hat{e}(H_0(uid),g)^{w_i}. \tag{2}$$

The intermediate values $V_{1,i}, V_{2,i}, V_{3,i}, V_{4,i}$ are: $V_{1,i} = \hat{e}(PK_{uid}, C_{1,i})$, $V_{2,i} = \hat{e}(K_{uid,att_i}, C_{3,i})$, $V_{3,i} = \hat{e}(H_0(uid), C_{2,i})$, $V_{4,i} = \hat{e}(L_{uid,att_i}, C_{4,i})$. There exists a set of constants $c_i \in \mathbb{Z}_p$ such that $\sum_{i \in I} c_i\lambda_i = s$ and $\sum_{i \in I} c_iw_i = 0$, where $\sum_{i \in I} c_i\mathbb{A}_i = (1, 0, ..., 0)$. CSP computes tct with $\{c_i\}_{i \in I}$:

$$tct = \prod_{i \in I}(tct_i)^{c_i} = \prod_{i \in I}(\hat{e}(g,g)^{z_{uid}\lambda_i}\hat{e}(H_0(uid),g)^{w_i})^{c_i} = \hat{e}(g,g)^{z_{uid}s}.$$

Finally, CSP returns $SCT = \{C_0 = F \cdot \hat{e}(g,g)^s, tct\}$ to DU.

5.2 DU performs the **FiDec** algorithm to recover the plaintext data by computing:

$$\frac{C_0}{tct^{\frac{1}{SK_{uid}}}} = \frac{F \cdot \hat{e}(g,g)^s}{(\hat{e}(g,g)^{z_{uid}s})^{\frac{1}{z_{uid}}}} = F.$$

Since the hash value of plaintext data has been recorded on the blockchain in the data encryption phase, any modifications to the outsourced data can be noticed by comparing the hash value of the data encryption phase and the data decryption phase.

5   Security Analysis

Before starting the concrete security proof, we first introduce the Decisional Bilinear Diffie-Hellman (DBDH) assumption.

Decisional Bilinear Diffie-Hellman (DBDH) Problem: The challenger randomly chooses $a, b, c \in \mathbb{Z}_p$ and gives $\{\mathbb{G}, \mathbb{G}_T, p, \hat{e}\}$, g^a, g^b, g^c to the adversary. The advantage of a PPT adversary who intends to distinguish the term g^{abc} and $z \in \mathbb{G}$ is always negligible.

Theorem 1. *If the q-DPBDHE2 problem [24] is hard, then no probabilistic polynomial time (PPT) adversary can break the BM^{2}SS scheme by statically corrupting a set of attribute authorities.*

Proof of Theorem 1

Suppose a PPT adversary $\mathcal{A}$ can break the proposed scheme in the static security model with an advantage ε. Then, a simulator $\mathcal{B}$ can be constructed based on $\mathcal{A}$ to solve the q-DPBDHE2 problem. In our scheme, the private key of DU is embedded in the attribute description key through exponentiation calculation. The concrete proof process is similar to that in [24]. Due to space limitations, we omit the complete proof.

Theorem 2. *If the DBDH problem is hard, then no PPT adversary can break the BM^{2}SS scheme by chosen-keyword attacks.*

Proof of Theorem 2

Suppose a PPT adversary $\mathcal{A}$ can break the proposed scheme in IND-CKA security model with an advantage ε. Then, a simulator $\mathcal{B}$ can be constructed based on $\mathcal{A}$ to solve the DBDH problem. Following is the detailed proof process:

Setup: $\mathcal{B}$ generates PP with the **Initialization** algorithm and sends PP to $\mathcal{A}$.

Phase 1: $\mathcal{A}$ issues trapdoor queries by submitting keyword set $KW' = \{kw_1', ..., kw_d'\}$ to $\mathcal{B}$. Then $\mathcal{B}$ randomly selects $\eta \in \mathbb{Z}_p$ and performs **TdGen** algorithm to generate a trapdoor associated to queried KW', $Td = (T_1 = g^{\eta z_{uid}}, T_2 = g^{\gamma \eta z_{uid}}, T_3 = \prod_{i=1}^{d'} g^{\gamma H(kw_i')}$.

Challenge: $\mathcal{A}$ sends two random keyword sets KW_0', KW_1' that are not queried in *Phase 1* to $\mathcal{B}$. Then $\mathcal{B}$ randomly encrypts a keyword set KW_b' with **KwEnc** algorithm to generates challenge index I_{dx}^*, where $b \in \{0, 1\}$.

Phase 2: Queries in *Phase 1* can be resubmitted by $\mathcal{A}$ in this, but queries on the ciphertext of KW_0' or KW_1' are not allowed.

Guess: $\mathcal{A}$ gives a bit b' as its guess result. If $b' = b$, $\mathcal{A}$ wins the simulation.

If $\mathcal{A}$ can break the IND-CKA security game with an advantage ϵ, then $\mathcal{A}$ has an advantage of $\epsilon/2$ in distinguishing g^{φ} and $g^{\gamma H(kw_0)\tau}$, where $\varphi \in \mathbb{Z}_p$. The advantage of $\mathcal{A}$ in distinguishing $g^{\gamma H(kw_0)\tau}$ and $g^{\gamma H(kw_1)\tau}$ is the same as in distinguishing g^{φ} and $g^{\gamma\tau}$. As the DBDH problem is hard, then ϵ is negligible and the scheme is INK-CKA secure.

Table 1. Comparison Of Storage Overheads

Scheme	[11]	[12]	[17]	BM²SS
$ADK_{uid,aid}$	$3N_u\|\mathbb{G}\|$	$(2N_u + 4)\|\mathbb{G}\|$	$(N_u + 3)\|\mathbb{G}\|$	$2N_u\|\mathbb{G}\|$
Index	$(d + 4)\|\mathbb{G}\|$ $+(2d + 1)\|\mathbb{G}_T\|$ $+d\|\mathbb{Z}_p\|$	$2d\|\mathbb{G}\| + \|\mathbb{G}_T\|$	$(2N_u + 2)\|\mathbb{G}\|$	$(d + 3)\|\mathbb{G}\|$
Trapdoor	$N_u\|\mathbb{G}\| + \|\mathbb{G}_T\|$ $+d'\|\mathbb{Z}_p\|$	$(2d' + 1)\|\mathbb{G}\|$	$(N_u + 2)\|\mathbb{G}\|$	$3\|\mathbb{G}\|$
SCT	$2\|\mathbb{G}_T\|$	$2\|\mathbb{G}_T\|$	–	$2\|\mathbb{G}_T\|$
CT	$(k + 4)\|\mathbb{G}\|$ $+(2k + 1)\|\mathbb{G}_T\|$ $+(d + 1)\|\mathbb{Z}_p\|$	$(2k + 2)\|\mathbb{G}\|$ $+2d\|\mathbb{G}\|$ $+2\|\mathbb{G}_T\|$	$4k\|\mathbb{G}\| + 2\|\mathbb{G}_T\|$	$4k\|\mathbb{G}\| + \|\mathbb{G}_T\|$

Table 2. Comparison Of Computation Overheads

Scheme	[11]	[12]	[17]	BM²SS
KwEnc	$(2N_u + 7)E + 2N_uP$	$2dE$	$(3N_u + 2)E$	$(d + 3)E$
TdGen	$(N_u + 1)E + P$	$(2N_u + d')E$	$(N_u + 2)E$	$3E$
Match	$(2N_u + 4)E + 3P$	$2E + (N_ud' + 1)P$	$(2k + 1)P$	$4P$
DataEnc	–	$(2k + 4)E + 2P$	$(6k + 4)E$	$(4k + 1)E$
FiDec	$2E$	P	$(2k + 1)P$	E

6 Performance Analysis and Evaluation

We first analyze the storage and computation costs of BM²SS and compare it with other schemes [11,12,17]. The scheme in [17] supports single-keyword search, whereas [11] and [12] all support multi-keyword search. Additionally, [11] involves a set of attribute authorities, while [12] and [17] utilize centralized attribute authority responsible for the generation of attribute decryption keys. Subsequently, we implement BM²SS with Charm framework and evaluate the efficiency of the main algorithms under three security levels. Within the Charm framework, three elliptic curves, i.e., SS512 (80-bit security), MNT159 (70-bit security), and MNT201 (90-bit security), are employed for pairing to attain various security levels.

6.1 Theoretical Comparison

Some notations used in this section are described as follows. N_u is the number of user's attributes. d is the number of keywords extracted from plaintext. d' is the number of keywords queried in trapdoor. k is the number of attributes in access policy. E is exponentiation in group. P is pairing operation in $\hat{e}$. $|\mathbb{G}|$, $|\mathbb{G}_T|$, and $|\mathbb{Z}_p|$ are respectively the element size in $\mathbb{G}$, $\mathbb{G}_T$, and $\mathbb{Z}_p$.

According to the analysis of storage overheads in Table 1, the size of the attribute decryption key of BM²SS is $(2N_u)|\mathbb{G}|$, which is similar to the size of a single attribute authority scheme (e.g., [12]). The storage overheads of the index in schemes [11,12], and BM²SS are all linearly related to the number of keywords defined by the data owners. BM²SS has the lowest index storage overheads, surpassing other methods and achieving the optimum. The integration of access control into search algorithm causes the index storage overheads of [17] to grow with the number of attributes. Moreover, each search process of [17] can only match a single keyword. Only BM²SS attains a constant storage overheads in terms of the trapdoor size. The trapdoor sizes in schemes [11,12], and [17] are linearly correlated with the number of query keywords or user attributes, resulting in a significant storage overhead, particularly as the number of query keywords grows. All comparison schemes entail equal storage overheads of semi-decrypted ciphertext. With the exception of [11], the sizes of ciphertexts in all schemes tend to increase with the growth of the attribute number in the access policy.

As seen in Table 2, both [11] and BM²SS have the same exponential costs in the generation of attribute decryption keys. Since [11] and BM²SS both involve a set of attribute authorities to manage the system's attributes separately, there will be slightly higher computational overhead compared to schemes with a single attribute authority. Nevertheless, the utilization of multiple authorities better aligns with practical requirements. BM²SS incurs the lowest exponential computation overheads in index generation. During the matching process of trapdoors and indexes, the Match algorithm of BM²SS requires constant-level bilinear pairing computation costs, i.e., 4P. The DataEnc algorithm of our scheme requires a cost of $(4k + 1)$E for generating ciphertext. All comparison schemes can outsource the complex decryption to cloud. BM²SS offloads the pairing computation of $(4k)$P to the cloud, thereby reducing the computational burden on the user side to a single exponentiation calculation.

6.2   Simulation Results

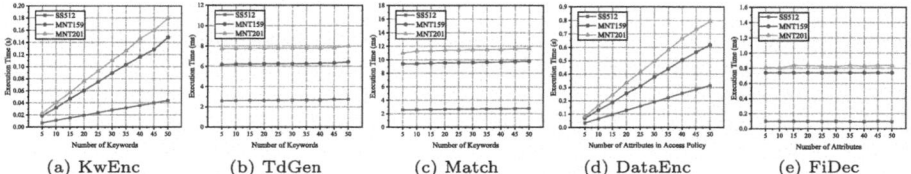

(a) KwEnc   (b) TdGen   (c) Match   (d) DataEnc   (e) FiDec

Fig. 3. Simulation results

The execution time of the KwEnc algorithm is depicted in Fig. 3a, which is roughly linear to the number of keywords extracted by data owner. There is an apparent increase in the execution time as the number of keywords increases. The index can be constructed in less than 0.2 ms for 50 keywords under three security levels, demonstrating high efficiency for resource-constrained applications.

From Fig. 3b and Fig. 3c, the execution time of TdGen and Match algorithms remains nearly constant as the number of keywords increases. The main computational costs of TdGen and Match algorithms are 3E and 4P, respectively. Nevertheless, it is crucial to emphasize that the performance of these two algorithms is still impacted by the number of keywords. Specifically, TdGen and Match algorithms involve hash and multiplication computations, which minimally impact the execution time.

The execution time of DataEnc algorithms rises as the number of attributes increases, according to Fig. 3d. For the DataEnc algorithm, when the number of attributes is 50, it takes 0.3 ms, 0.6 ms, and 0.8 ms respectively to generate ciphertext for SS512, MNT159, and MNT201. Such time consumption is all less than 1 s and is suitable for IoT application scenarios.

As shown in Fig. 3e, the FiDec algorithm carried out on the user side incurs negligible computational overheads, regardless of the number of attributes, which aligns with the theoretical analysis. For different security levels, the FiDec algorithm demonstrates an average execution time of less than 1 ms.

7   Conclusion

We propose a blockchain aided multi-authority and multi-keyword searchable scheme (BM²SS). First, we achieve decentralized attribute management by employing multiple attribute authorities instead of a single one. Second, multi-keyword search is implemented in the scheme, which enables higher search accuracy. Also, the search trapdoor and index are matched on the blockchain through a match smart contract. Third, the outsourced decryption computations can be completed without the necessity of computing an outsourced key. For the future, as IoT networks grow, ensuring the scalability of the BM^{2}SS will be critical. Possible research may include strategies for optimizing performance and resource management to handle large-scale deployments.

Acknowledgements. This work was supported by the Major Program of Shandong Provincial Natural Science Foundation for the Fundamental Research under Grant ZR2022ZD03, the National Science Foundation of China under Grants 62272256, 62202250, the National Science Foundation of Shandong Province under Grant ZR2021QF079, the Talent Cultivation Promotion Program of Computer Science and Technology in Qilu University of Technology (Shandong Academy of Sciences) under Grant 2023PY059, and the Colleges and Universities 20 Terms Foundation of Jinan City under Grant 202228093.

References

1. Wu, Y.: Cloud-edge orchestration for the internet of things: Architecture and aipowered data processing. IEEE Internet Things J. **8**(16), 12792–12805 (2021)
2. Yu, J., Yan, B., Qi, H., Wang, S., Cheng, W.: An efficient and secure data sharing scheme for edge-enabled IoT. IEEE Trans. Comput. **73**(1), 178–191 (2024)
3. Shi, J., Yu, Y., Yu, Q., Li, H., Wang, L.: Toward data security in 6G networks: a public-key searchable encryption approach. IEEE Network **36**(4), 166–173 (2022)
4. Rasori, M., Manna, M.L., Perazzo, P., Dini, G.: A survey on attribute-based encryption schemes suitable for the internet of things. IEEE Internet Things J. **9**(11), 8269–8290 (2022)
5. Liu, S., Yu, J., Chen, L., Chai, B.: Blockchain-assisted comprehensive key management in CP-ABE for cloud-stored data. IEEE Trans. Netw. Serv. Manage. **20**(2), 1745–1758 (2023)
6. Miao, Y., et al.: Privacy-preserving attribute-based keyword search in shared multi-owner setting. IEEE Trans. Dependable Secure Comput. **18**(3), 1080–1094 (2021)
7. Xu, P., Tang, S., Xu, P., Wu, Q., Hu, H., Susilo, W.: Practical multi-keyword and boolean search over encrypted e-mail in cloud server. IEEE Trans. Serv. Comput. **14**(6), 1877–1889 (2021)
8. Xu, M., Liu, S., Yu, D., Cheng, X., Guo, S., Yu, J.: Cloudchain: a cloud blockchain using shared memory consensus and RDMA. IEEE Trans. Comput. **71**(12), 3242–3253 (2022)
9. Song, D.X., Wagner, D., Perrig, A.: Practical techniques for searches on encrypted data. In: Proceeding 2000 IEEE Symposium on Security and Privacy. S&P 2000, pp. 44–55 (2000)
10. Boneh, D., Di Crescenzo, G., Ostrovsky, R., Persiano, G.: Public key encryption with keyword search. In: Cachin, C., Camenisch, J.L. (eds.) EUROCRYPT 2004. LNCS, vol. 3027, pp. 506–522. Springer, Heidelberg (2004). https://doi.org/10.1007/978-3-540-24676-3_30
11. Zhang, K., Long, J., Wang, X., Dai, H.-N., Liang, K., Imran, M.: Lightweight searchable encryption protocol for industrial internet of things. IEEE Trans. Industr. Inf. **17**(6), 4248–4259 (2021)
12. Meng, F., Cheng, L.,Wang, M.: ABDKS: attribute-based encryption with dynamic keyword search in fog computing. Front. Comput. Sci. **15**(5) (2021)

13. Wang, H., Dong, X., Cao, Z.: Multi-value-independent ciphertext-policy attribute based encryption with fast keyword search. IEEE Trans. Serv. Comput. **13**(6), 1142–1151 (2020)
14. Wang, M., Miao, Y., Guo, Y., Wang, C., Huang, H., Jia, X.: Attribute-based encrypted search for multi-owner and multi-user model. In: ICC 2021 - IEEE International Conference on Communications, pp. 1–7 (2021)
15. Huang, Q., Wei, Q., Yan, G., Zou, L., Yang, Y.: Fast and privacy-preserving attribute-based keyword search in cloud document services. IEEE Trans. Serv. Comput. **16**(5), 3348–3360 (2023)
16. Chaudhari, P., Das, M.L.: Privacy preserving searchable encryption with fine-grained access control. IEEE Trans. Cloud Comput. **9**(2), 753–762 (2021)
17. Yin, H., Li, Y., Li, F., Deng, H., Zhang, W., Li, K.: An efficient and access policy-hiding keyword search and data sharing scheme in cloud-assisted IoT. J. Syst. Architect. **128**, 102533 (2022)
18. Su, J., Zhang, L., Mu, Y.: BA-RMKABSE: blockchain-aided ranked multi-keyword attribute-based searchable encryption with hiding policy for smart health system. Futur. Gener. Comput. Syst. **132**, 299–309 (2022)
19. Liu, H., Ming, Y., Wang, C., Zhao, Y., Zhang, S., Lu, R.: Blockchain-assisted verifiable certificate-based searchable encryption against untrusted cloud server for industrial internet of things. Futur. Gener. Comput. Syst. **153**, 97–112 (2024)
20. Liu, S., Yu, J., Xiao, Y., Wan, Z., Wang, S., Yan, B.: BC-SABE: blockchain-aided searchable attribute-based encryption for cloud-IoT. IEEE Internet Things J. **7**(9), 7851–7867 (2020)
21. Yu, J., Liu, S., Xu, M., Guo, H., Zhong, F., Cheng, W.: An efficient revocable and searchable MA-ABE scheme with blockchain assistance for C-IoT. IEEE Internet Things J. **10**(3), 2754–2766 (2023)
22. Zhang, K., Zhang, Y., Li, Y., Liu, X., Lu, L.: A blockchain-based anonymous attribute-based searchable encryption scheme for data sharing. IEEE Internet Things J. **11**(1), 1685–1697 (2024)
23. Gao, H., Huang, H., Xue, L., Xiao, F., Li, Q.: Blockchain-enabled fine-grained searchable encryption with cloud-edge computing for electronic health records sharing. IEEE Internet Things J. **10**(20), 18414–18425 (2023)
24. Rouselakis, Y., Waters, B.: Efficient statically-secure large-universe multiauthority attribute-based encryption, pp. 315–332. Springer, Heidelberg (2015)

Fog-Enabled Network Intrusion Detection Based on Variational Autoencoder for Internet of Vehicles

Shizhao Tian[1,2(✉)], Haiqiang Fei[1,2(✉)], Yongji Liu[1,2], Hongsong Zhu[1,2], and Limin Sun[1,2]

[1] Institute of Information Engineering, Chinese Academy of Sciences, Beijing, China
{tianshizhao,feihaiqiang,liuyongji,zhuhongsong,sunlimin}@iie.ac.cn
[2] School of Cyber Security, University of Chinese Academy of Sciences, Beijing, China

Abstract. The Internet of Vehicles (IoV), a burgeoning application of the Internet of Things (IoT), confronts a growing array of cyber-attacks, necessitating a robust network intrusion detection system (NIDS) to safeguard its security. Current NIDS solutions have limitations in key performance metrics such as accuracy, recall, and false positive rate, and they exhibit inadequate generalization in identifying novel attack patterns. To address these challenges, we design an anomaly-based network intrusion detection system within a fog computing architecture. Our model employs a Variational Autoencoder (VAE) to extract deep features from network traffic and establish a baseline of normal behavior patterns. Any traffic that deviates significantly from this baseline is identified as an anomaly, potentially indicating an attack. By utilizing the Receiver Operating Characteristic (ROC) curve, we carefully select the optimal decision threshold to enhance the model's detection performance. We conduct a comprehensive evaluation on the BoT-IoT dataset, and the results indicate that our method's accuracy and recall is 4% to 11% and 3% to 15% higher than other methods, respectively. These results highlight the potential of our approach in providing advanced network security protection in the IoV environment.

Keywords: Intrusion detection · IoV · Fog computing · Variational autoencoder

1 Introduction

The burgeoning Internet of Things (IoT) landscape has ushered in a plethora of innovative applications, with the Internet of Vehicles (IoV) emerging as a prominent example. By seamlessly integrating vehicles with an array of external devices, IoV enables dynamic communication and data exchange through vehicle-to-vehicle (V2V), vehicle-to-infrastructure (V2I), and vehicle-to-network (V2N) [1]. This technological leap promises not only a significant boost to traffic safety by mitigating the risk of accidents but also a marked enhancement

L. Sun and Y. Chen (Eds.): CWSN 2024, CCIS 2341, pp. 92–103, 2025.
https://doi.org/10.1007/978-981-96-2186-6_8

in traffic management and overall driving experience. Nonetheless, the intricate communication ecosystem and the open architecture of IoV networks render vehicles susceptible to a spectrum of cyber threats, which pose a dire risk to the system's security and integrity.

To counter these threats, network intrusion detection system (NIDS) has become a crucial line of defense for the security of IoV. Traditional signature-based network intrusion detection system (SNIDS) [2] excels at detecting known attacks but are powerless against the rapidly evolving new types of attacks. In contrast, anomaly-based network intrusion detection systems (ANIDS) analyze and learn the behavior patterns of the system during normal operation to construct a baseline model that reflects normal behavior. Any network traffic that significantly deviates from this baseline is judged to be an attack, which gives ANIDS a significant advantage in detecting unknown attacks. However, ANIDS may make incorrect judgments when distinguishing between normal and abnormal data. Therefore, for ANIDS, in addition to detection accuracy, the false positive rate is also an important evaluation index. To improve the detection capabilities of ANIDS, many current studies have begun to apply deep learning technology. With its excellent feature extraction and modeling capabilities, deep learning provides strong support for improving the detection performance of ANIDS in complex network environments.

In light of this, we introduce an ANIDS that utilizes deep learning to enhance the detection capabilities against emerging attack patterns. We have chosen to implement this model within a fog computing architecture [3] to reduce communication overhead with the cloud and to improve the efficiency of data processing. At the fog layer, we perform collection, preprocessing, and feature selection of the traffic data, which not only significantly alleviates the communication burden with the cloud but also provides a refined dataset for model training in the cloud. Subsequently, the feature-selected data is transmitted to the cloud for training the intrusion detection model. We employ Variational Autoencoder (VAE) technology to model and reconstruct normal behavior patterns comprehensively, capturing the intrinsic structural characteristics of normal data. Through ROC curve analysis, we determine the optimal decision threshold for distinguishing between normal and abnormal behaviors, aiming to achieve high-accuracy detection while minimizing the potential for false positives. Ultimately, the trained model is deployed on vehicles to enable real-time detection of network intrusions. The main contributions are as follows:

- Introducing an anomaly-based intrusion detection approach for Internet of Vehicles.
- Designing the intrusion detection system in the fog computing architecture effectively reduces the amount of data transmission to the cloud, thereby significantly reducing communication costs.
- Utilizing VAE technology for precise modeling of normal behavior patterns significantly improves detection performance and generalization capabilities.

This paper is organized as follows: Sect. 2 reviews the previous work on intrusion detection for IoV. Section 3 details the proposed method. Section 4 focuses on evaluation and results. Finally, the conclusion is presented in Sect. 5.

2   Related Work

With the progression of IoV technology, the sphere of intrusion detection research is witnessing an ongoing deepening of expertise. In this section, we review signature-based network intrusion detection methods and anomaly-based network intrusion detection methods, and sort out the current research progress.

Signature-based methods rely on predefined attack characteristics or patterns to identify intrusions. In recent research progress, the authors of [4] propose a signature-based intrusion detection system that combines centralized and distributed modules. This system achieves rapid and precise detection and response to malicious behaviors by comparing network activities against a database of known attack signatures. Another research [5] addresses the specific needs of IoV by proposing a lightweight signature-based intrusion detection system. It analyzes attack patterns like packet loss, replay, and tampering, and carefully selects five key signatures to detect abnormal traffic and content. Simulation experiments demonstrate the method's efficiency in detecting packet loss and replay attacks. Although signature-based methods perform well in recognizing known attacks, their detection capabilities against unknown attacks still need improvement.

Anomaly-based methods do not rely on known attack signatures and possess a stronger capability to detect new types of attacks. The authors of [6] introduce a lightweight anomaly-based intrusion detection method specifically designed for Internet of Vehicles (IoV). They generate a dataset simulating IoV scenarios, including both normal traffic and UDP flood attack traffic and then deploy Support Vector Machine (SVM) and J48 decision tree classifiers to accurately classify the traffic data, effectively identifying and responding to potential network attack threats. The authors of [7] propose an anomaly-based intrusion detection method utilizing SVM and Random Forest machine learning algorithms to analyze network data. To improve detection efficiency, they also explores feature selection for handling large amounts of missing data. Experimental results show that Random Forest slightly outperforms SVM in detection accuracy, and both algorithms effectively identify and classify attack behaviors.

With the advancement of deep learning, an increasing number of deep learning models are being applied to anomaly-based intrusion detection. These models enable automatic extraction of complex features from network traffic and facilitate the learning of patterns in normal behavior. In the paper [8], researchers adopt an innovative deep learning architecture, namely an LSTM-based autoencoder model, to learn the data characteristics of normal network traffic. This model can identify intrusion behaviors by comparing the reconstruction error of the traffic with a set threshold, effectively detecting potential attacks in the IoV.

3   Proposed Method

In this section, we provide a detailed description of our anomaly-based intrusion detection method designed within fog computing architecture, illustrated in Fig. 1. Our framework encompasses three essential layers: the IoV device layer, fog layer, and cloud layer. At the IoV devices layer, extensive communication occurs between vehicles, between vehicles and infrastructure (V2I), between vehicles and networks(V2N), resulting in substantial and dynamically changing network traffic. At the fog layer, we utilize traffic collection tools to capture network data, followed by data preprocessing and feature selection to minimize the data volume transmitted to the cloud, thereby reducing communication overhead. At the cloud layer, we employ the feature-selected normal network data to train the VAE, establishing a baseline for normal behavior patterns in the IoV. Subsequently, we determine the optimal decision threshold for the VAE for intrusion detection. Once trained, the model is deployed to vehicles to facilitate real-time detection of IoV traffic. Upon detection of abnormal traffic or potential attack behavior, immediate response measures are implemented to ensure the security and stability of IoV.

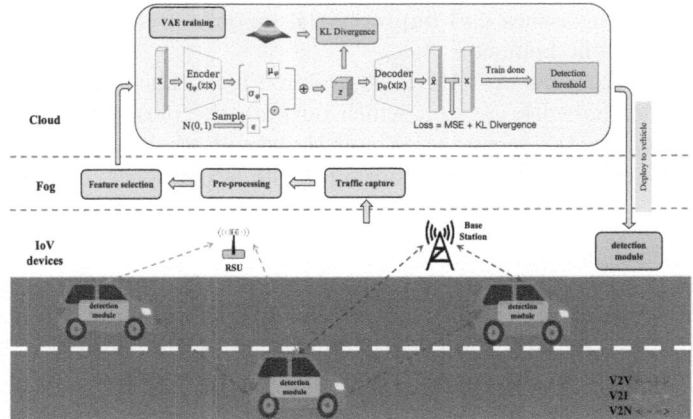

Fig. 1. Workflow of the proposed framework.

3.1   Feature Selection

Network traffic contains a large number of features, but not all features are helpful for intrusion detection. In order to reduce the complexity of the model and improve the training speed, we need to perform feature selection. In this paper, we employ the Mutual Information (MI) [9] method due to its effectiveness in measuring the information correlation between features and target variables, particularly its sensitivity to nonlinear relationships. During the feature selection process, we calculate the mutual information value between each feature X_i and the target variable Y:

$$MI(X_i, Y) = \sum_{x_i \in X_i} \sum_{y \in Y} p(x_i, y) log \frac{p(x_i, y)}{p(x_i)p(y)} \tag{1}$$

where $p(x_i, y)$ is the joint probability distribution of X_i and Y, $p(x_i)$ and $p(y)$ are the marginal probability distributions of X_i and Y, respectively. Based on calculated MI values, features are ranked by their contribution to the target variable, prioritizing those with higher MI values.

3.2 Variational Autoencoder

To accurately and comprehensively model normal network traffic behavior, we utilize a VAE. As a deep generative model, VAE employs an encoder to learn underlying data distributions deeply. Using these learned latent features, the decoder reconstructs data and generates new instances resembling the original input. VAE introduces randomness in the latent space to prevent the model from memorizing training data mechanically, enhancing its flexibility in modeling the diversity and dynamics of normal traffic. This approach effectively mitigates overfitting issues and improves the model's ability to generalize and detect network traffic behavior.

The model structure of VAE is shown in Fig. 1. The input data x is fed into the encoder network $q_\phi(z|x)$, which outputs the parameters of the latent variables z, namely the mean $\mu_\phi(x)$ and the standard deviation $\sigma_\phi(x)$. These parameters define a Gaussian distribution in the latent space, expressed as:

$$q_\phi(z|x) = \mathcal{N}(z|\mu_\phi(x), \sigma_\phi^2(x)) \tag{2}$$

To ensure that gradients can be propagated through the stochastic process, VAE employs the reparameterization trick which involves sampling a random noise term ϵ from the standard normal distribution and then generating the latent variable z according to the parameters output by the encoder:

$$z = \mu_\phi(x) + \sigma_\phi(x) \odot \epsilon \tag{3}$$

Subsequently, the decoder network receives the latent variable z and attempts to reconstruct the input data x. The decoder outputs the parameters of the probability distribution of the reconstruct data $\hat{x}$, which are typically also the mean $\mu_\theta(z)$ and standard deviation $\sigma_\theta(z)$ of a Guassian distribution:

$$p_\theta(x|z) = \mathcal{N}(x|\mu_\theta(z), \sigma_\theta^2(z)) \tag{4}$$

The training objective of VAE is to minimize the negative Evidence Lower Bound(ELBO), which is the loss function. The loss function consists of two parts: the reconstruction loss and the Kullback-Leibler (KL) divergence, expressed as:

$$\mathcal{L}(\theta, \phi; x) = -\mathbb{E}_{q_\phi(z|x)}[\log p_\theta(x|z)] + KL(q_\phi(z|x)||p(z)) \tag{5}$$

here, the first term $-\mathbb{E}_{q_\phi(z|x)}[\log p_\theta(x|z)]$ is the reconstruction loss, which measures the model's ability to reconstruct the input x based on the latent variables z. The expectation is computed with respect to the variational distribution $q_\phi(z|x)$, which is used to approximate $p_\theta(x|z)$. The second term $KL(q_\phi(z|x)||p(z))$ measures the difference between the variational distribution $q_\phi(z|x)$ and the prior distribution $p(z)$. By including this term in the loss function, we encourage the model's latent representation z to not only aid in reconstructing the input data but also to follow the prior distribution $p(z)$ that we have chosen, which is typically a standard normal distribution.

Through the above process, VAE can learn the latent representation of the input data and reconstruct new instances similar to the original data, while introducing randomness in the modeling process to effectively prevent overfitting.

3.3 Detection Threshold Selection

By training VAE with normal data, it learns the statistical distribution of normal data and can evaluate its reconstruction probability when new data points enter the system. This probability reflects the consistency between the data points and the learned normal distribution. When new normal data passes through VAE, it will have a higher reconstruction probability due to sharing similar distribution characteristics with the training data. On the contrary, abnormal data that deviates from the distribution of normal data will result in a lower probability of reconstruction. Based on this principle, we can set a threshold τ: if the reconstruction probability P_R of a data point is lower than this threshold, it will be marked as attack:

$$DetectionResult = \begin{cases} normal & \text{if } P_R > \tau, \\ attack & \text{otherwise .} \end{cases} \tag{6}$$

The estimation of P_R is achieved using Monte Carlo method, which involves multiple sampling of latent variables. Each sampling generates data reconstruction through the decoder and calculates its probability. The average of these probabilities is the P_R:

$$P_R = \frac{1}{L} \sum_{l=1}^{L} p_\theta(x|z^{(l)}) \tag{7}$$

where $p_\theta(x|z^{(l)})$ is the probability of reconstructing the original data x under the latent variable z, L is the number of samples taken.

In the selection of the optimal threshold τ^*, we adopt Receiver Operating Characteristic Curve (ROC) analysis to determine the optimal P_R threshold for distinguishing between normal and abnormal network traffic. Our goal is to select a threshold that minimizes the False Positive Rate (FPR) while maximizing the True Positive Rate (TPR) of the model which is expressed as the following optimization goal:

$$\tau^* = \arg\max_\tau(\sqrt{(FPR_\tau)^2 + (1 - TPR_\tau)^2} \tag{8}$$

4   Evaluation and Results

4.1   Dataset

We employ the BoT-IoT dataset [10] to evaluate our method. Although the BoT-IoT dataset is designed for IoT environments, the network traffic patterns and attack types it contains can be valuable resource for studying intrusion detection in IoV. BoT-IoT involves a substantial volume of normal traffic and four category of attack traffic: Denial of Service(DoS), Distributed Denial of Service(DDoS), Reconnaissance and Data Theft, the statistics of which is shown in Table 1. We preprocess the dataset and obtain the top 40 features using the MI method. After feature selection, the amount of data can be reduced by 62%, greatly reducing the amount of transmission to the cloud and reducing communication overhead.

Table 1. Statistics of BoT-IoT.

Category	Records
DDoS	2194787
DoS	2287339
Reconnaissance	1828872
Data Theft	262497
Normal	4601121
Total	11174616

4.2   Evaluation Indicators

We evaluate our method using several metrics, involving accuracy rate, detection rate, precision rate, false alarm rate, f1-Score and receiver operating curve (ROC), which are calculated through the confusion matrix, shown in Table 2.

Table 2. Confusion Matrix.

	Predicted Attack	Predicted Normal
Actual Attack	TP	FN
Actual Normal	FP	TN

1) **Accuracy:** Accuracy is the ratio of the number of correct predictions to the total number of predictions, which provides a simple measure of the overall performance of the model.

$$Accuracy = \frac{TP + TN}{TP + TN + FP + FN} \qquad (9)$$

2) Detection Rate (DR): also known as recall, is the ratio of the number of correctly identified positive instances to the total number of actual positive instances, which measures the model's ability to capture all positive instances.

$$DR = \frac{TP}{TP + FN} \tag{10}$$

3) Precision: Precision is the ratio of the number of correctly predicted positive instances to the total number of instances the model predicted as positive. It measures the proportion of positive predictions that are actually correct.

$$Precision = \frac{TP}{TP + FP} \tag{11}$$

4) False Alarm Rate (FAR): also known as the false positive rate, is the ratio of the number of false positive predictions to the total number of actual negative instances.

$$FAR = \frac{FP}{FP + TN} \tag{12}$$

5) F1-Score: F1-Score is the harmonic mean of precision and detection rate, balancing the two metrics and providing a single performance measure that considers both.

$$F1\text{-}Score = 2 \times \frac{Precision \times DR}{Precision + DR} \tag{13}$$

6) Receiver Operating Characteristic Curve (ROC): The ROC curve is an essential tool for binary classification, depicting the True Positive Rate (TPR) versus the False Positive Rate (FPR) at various threshold levels. It aids in selecting the optimal threshold, identified as the point on the curve closest to the top-left corner, maximizing TPR while minimizing FPR.

4.3   Experiment Setups

1) Simulation environment: This experiment is conducted on a server equipped with Intel(R) Xeon(R) Gold 5218 CPU @ 2.30GHz and 256GB of memory, along with 4 GeForce RTX 3090 graphics cards to meet the computation needs.

2) Implementation details: We select 60% of the normal traffic data to train the VAE model. To determine the optimal decision threshold, we construct a validation set composed of the remaining 20% of normal data and 50% of each type of attack data. Using this validation set, we will plot the ROC curve to select the best threshold. Finally, the remaining data is allocated as the test set to assess the model's performance and generalization ability.

Our VAE adopts a symmetrical encoder and decoder structure, with the encoder reducing the dimensionality from 40 neurons to a 10-dimensional latent space, and the decoder symmetrically expanding back to 40 neurons, which ensures efficient data learning and reconstruction. We employ the Adam optimizer for weight updates, setting the initial learning rate to 0.001. In addition, in order to prevent overfitting and improve the generalization ability of the model, we introduce a dropout layer in the network, and the dropout rate is set to 0.1. With a batch size of 40, we balance computational efficiency with performance, training the model for 100 epochs to thoroughly capture the data's distribution. The ReLU activation function is utilized across the network, facilitating gradient flow and mitigating the vanishing gradient issue.

4.4   Detection Performance

Throughout the training process, the loss of VAE gradually stabilize with successive iterations, as illustrated in Fig. 2. To determine the optimal decision threshold, we apply the method proposed in Sect. 3.3 to calculate the reconstruction probabilities of various traffic types in the validation dataset. By setting a series of different reconstruction probability values as the threshold τ, we compute the corresponding FPR and TPR, and plot these data to form ROC curve, as shown in Fig. 3. According to our strategy (8), we find the best threshold τ^* to be 0.64.

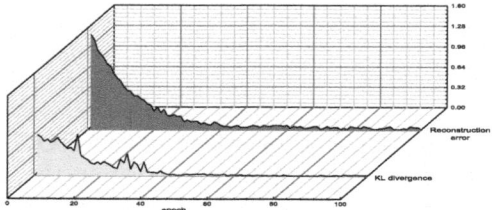

Fig. 2. Training loss: KL divergence and reconstruction error.

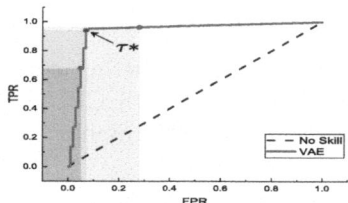

Fig. 3. Finding optimal threshold τ^*.

Furthermore, we conduct detection on normal traffic and various types of attack traffic on the test set. Traffic records are fed into the trained VAE for reconstruction, and reconstruction probabilities are computed, as shown in

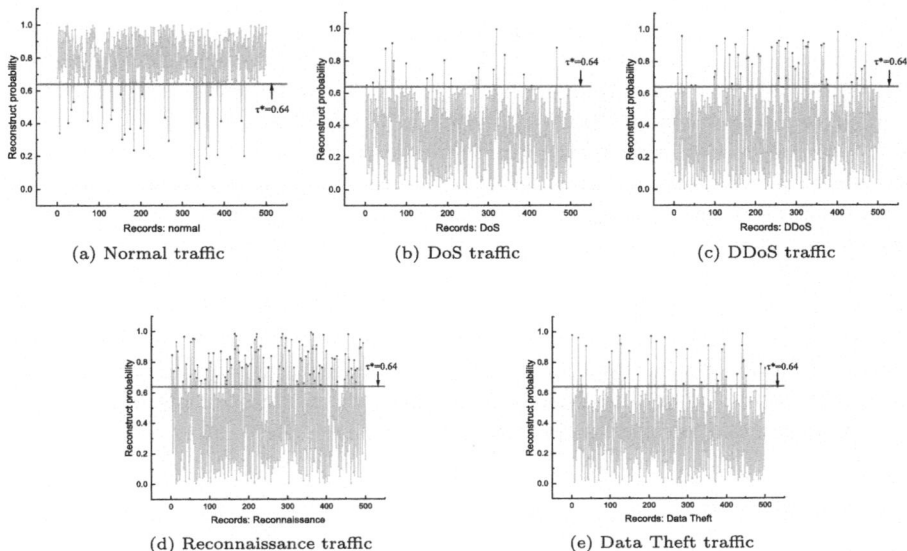

(a) Normal traffic   (b) DoS traffic   (c) DDoS traffic

(d) Reconnaissance traffic   (e) Data Theft traffic

Fig. 4. Intrusion detection.

Fig. 4. Due to space constraints, we show only 500 records for each traffic category. Figure 4a shows the reconstruction probability of normal traffic. It can be seen that the reconstruction probability of most traffic exceeds the optimal threshold, which shows that VAE has the ability to accurately reconstruct normal traffic and has good generalization ability. Figures 4b to 4c show the reconstruction probabilities of four types of attacks, indicating that the reconstruction probabilities of attack traffic are generally lower than the optimal threshold. However, it is worth noting that the reconstruction probabilities of a considerable part of reconnaissance attacks exceed the optimal threshold, indicating that some reconnaissance traffic may go undetected. Through analysis, we find that reconnaissance attacks typically occur relatively infrequently and are able to lurk in the network without raising suspicion, thus resembling normal traffic patterns and not easily detected.

Table 3. Overall performance.

Method	Accuracy(%)	DR(%)	Precision(%)	FAR(%)	F1-Score(%)
BN	83.97	75.42	92.55	9.74	83.11
PCA	87.49	79.27	95.89	4.14	86.79
AE	90.13	87.26	93.67	4.36	90.35
Ours	94.26	90.35	96.78	3.29	93.45

To further prove the performance of our method, we compare our method with other anomaly-based intrusion detection methods such as Bayesian Networks (BN), Principal Component Analysis (PCA), and Autoencoders (AE), as detailed in Table 3. On the BoT-IoT test set, traditional methods like BN and PCA perform poorly in reconstructing normal records, failing to effectively capture nonlinear relationships, thus resulting in lower accuracy and detection rates. In contrast, the deep learning method Autoencoder (AE) demonstrates superior performance due to its stronger modeling capability of normal traffic. Our proposed model shows significant advantages in accuracy, detection rate, precision, far and f1-score, highlighting its precise modeling of normal traffic and robust generalization ability. Furthermore, our approach using threshold selection based on reconstruction probability proves effective in distinguishing between normal and attack traffic. Therefore, based on comparative results, our method exhibits clear superiority in the field of intrusion detection.

5   Conclusion

Our analysis of existing intrusion detection methods reveals that most models have poor detection performance and weak generalization capabilities. To address these issues, we introduce an anomaly-based method using a VAE to model the network's normal state. By selecting the optimal decision threshold through the ROC curve, we significantly enhance the model's detection performance. Experimental results demonstrate that our method exhibits superior performance. In the future work, we plan to test our model on additional datasets and further improve its performance.

Acknowledgment. We are grateful to the anonymous reviewers for their work and insightful feedback. This work was supported by the National Natural Science Foundation of China (No. 61931019).

References

1. Abboud, K., Omar, H.A., Zhuang, W.: Interworking of DSRC and cellular network technologies for V2X communications: a survey. IEEE Trans. Veh. Technol. **65**(12), 9457–9470 (2016)
2. Tu, S., Waqas, M., Badshah, A., Yin, M., Abbas, G.: Network intrusion detection system (NIDS) based on pseudo-siamese stacked autoencoders in fog computing. IEEE Trans. Serv. Comput. (2023)
3. Yi, S., Li, C., Li, Q.: A survey of fog computing: concepts, applications and issues. In: Proceedings of the 2015 Workshop on Mobile Big Data, pp. 37–42 (2015)
4. Ioulianou, P., Vasilakis, V., Moscholios, I., Logothetis, M.: A signature-based intrusion detection system for the internet of things. Information and Communication Technology Form (2018)
5. Jin, S., Chung, J.-G., Xu, Y.: Signature-based intrusion detection system (IDS) for in-vehicle can bus network. In: 2021 IEEE International Symposium on Circuits and Systems (ISCAS), pp. 1–5. IEEE (2021)

6. Sai, K.M., Gupta, B.B., Colace, F., Chui, K.T., et al.: A lightweight anomaly based DDoS flood attack detection for internet of vehicles. In: SysCom, pp. 139–146 (2021)
7. Yihunie, F., Abdelfattah, E., Regmi, A.: Applying machine learning to anomaly-based intrusion detection systems. In: 2019 IEEE Long Island Systems, Applications and Technology Conference (LISAT), pp. 1–5. IEEE (2019)
8. Ashraf, J., Bakhshi, A.D., Moustafa, N., Khurshid, H., Javed, A., Beheshti, A.: Novel deep learning-enabled LSTM autoencoder architecture for discovering anomalous events from intelligent transportation systems. IEEE Trans. Intell. Transp. Syst. **22**(7), 4507–4518 (2020)
9. Pluim, J.P., Maintz, J.A., Viergever, M.A.: Mutual-information-based registration of medical images: a survey. IEEE Trans. Med. Imaging **22**(8), 986–1004 (2003)
10. Koroniotis, N., Moustafa, N., Sitnikova, E., Turnbull, B.: Towards the development of realistic botnet dataset in the internet of things for network forensic analytics: Bot-IoT dataset. Futur. Gener. Comput. Syst. **100**, 779–796 (2019)

Enabling Sub-second QoS-Aware Scheduling for Dynamic Serverless Workloads

Haodong Tian, Tianyu Huang, Mengyang Liu, Fang Dong$^{(\boxtimes)}$,
and Ruiting Zhou

School of Computer Science and Engineering, Southeast University, Nanjing 210096,
China
{hdtian,213211490,myliu,fdong,ruitingzhou}@seu.edu.cn

Abstract. Serverless computing platforms face significant challenges in
fulfilling the Quality-of-Service (QoS) demands of serverless functions.
Existing resource management strategies rely on time-consuming online
fine-tuning processes and are limited by the static nature of container
resource configurations. Moreover, the cold start problem leads to unpredictable performance degradation under dynamic workloads. To address
these challenges, we propose a novel system that integrates *Process-Level
Checkpoint/Restore* (PLCR) techniques with a *Real-time Workload-and-
QoS-Aware Scheduling* algorithm. PLCR enables rapid switching of
serverless functions within the lifespan of a container instance, effectively
mobilizing idle containers to assist functions at risk of QoS degradation
while significantly alleviating cold start delays. The scheduling algorithm
dynamically adapts to workload fluctuations and workflow changes to
maintain sub-second responsiveness and proactively ensure QoS compliance. Experimental results demonstrate significant improvements in the
system's ability to handle dynamic workload variations, with our PLCR
mechanism achieving 2.2×–28.1× faster function switching compared to
cold starts, reducing QoS violation rates by up to 13.5% across different functions, and outperforming the state-of-the-art Aquatope system
by over 15% in QoS compliance during the critical initial deployment
phase.

Keywords: Serverless Computing · Quality of Service (QoS) ·
Process-Level Checkpoint/Restore (PLCR) · Real-time Scheduling

1 Introduction

Serverless computing has emerged as a transformative cloud computing
paradigm, enabling developers to focus solely on writing and deploying functions without the burden of managing the underlying infrastructure. Major
cloud providers, such as Amazon Web Services (AWS) and Microsoft Azure,
have widely adopted serverless computing, offering platforms like AWS Lambda

© The Author(s), under exclusive license to Springer Nature Singapore Pte Ltd. 2025
L. Sun and Y. Chen (Eds.): CWSN 2024, CCIS 2341, pp. 104–117, 2025.
https://doi.org/10.1007/978-981-96-2186-6_9

[1] and Azure Functions [9]. However, despite its growing popularity, serverless computing faces significant challenges in meeting the Quality-of-Service (QoS) requirements of latency-sensitive applications, such as machine learning workflows [18] and real-time data processing [6].

Existing approaches to enhancing QoS in serverless computing primarily focus on adaptive resource allocation strategies [20]. These strategies aim to intelligently allocate resources to function instances based on their QoS requirements while minimizing overall resource consumption. However, these approaches are limited by the static nature of container resource configurations, making the process of fine-tuning these configurations time-consuming and potentially detrimental to QoS. Furthermore, the prevalent cold start problem, which occurs when a new function instance is launched, leads to unpredictable performance degradation under dynamic workloads.

To address these challenges, we propose a novel system that integrates PLCR techniques with a *Real-time Workload-and-QoS-Aware Scheduling* algorithm. PLCR enables rapid switching of serverless functions within the lifespan of a container instance, effectively leveraging idle containers to support functions at risk of QoS violations. By capturing and restoring the state of individual processes, PLCR significantly reduces cold start delays compared to traditional approaches that require the creation of new containers. The scheduling algorithm, designed to operate in sub-second time frames, dynamically adapts to workload fluctuations and workflow changes, ensuring proactive QoS compliance.

We implement our system on a Kubernetes cluster and evaluate its performance under various workload scenarios. The experimental results demonstrate a significant improvement in the system's ability to handle dynamic workload variations, with notable reductions in tail latencies and enhanced QoS compliance compared to state-of-the-art approaches. Our system achieves a 50% reduction in QoS violations within the first 10 min of operation, showcasing its rapid adaptability.

The main contributions of this paper are as follows:

- A novel approach for rapid serverless function switching using PLCR techniques, significantly reducing cold start latency compared to container-level checkpointing and traditional cold start mitigation strategies.
- A *Real-time Workload-and-QoS-Aware Scheduling* algorithm that adapts to workload dynamics in sub-second time frames and proactively ensures QoS compliance, outperforming state-of-the-art resource management approaches.
- A comprehensive evaluation of the proposed system, demonstrating its effectiveness in handling diverse workload scenarios, reducing tail latencies, and improving overall performance and resource utilization.

The rest of the paper is organized as follows: Sect. 2 provides background information on serverless computing and discusses related work. Section 3 presents the challenges and motivations behind our proposed system. Section 4 describes the system design and architecture in detail. Section 5 presents the experimental evaluation and results. Finally, Sect. 6 summarizes our work and concludes the paper.

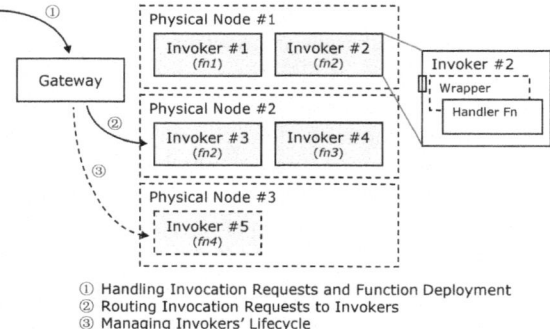

① Handling Invocation Requests and Function Deployment
② Routing Invocation Requests to Invokers
③ Managing Invokers' Lifecycle

Fig. 1. Architecture of serverless platforms.

2   Background and Related Works

2.1   Architecture of Serverless Platforms

Serverless platforms simplify application deployment by providing *Function-as-a-Service*. Developers write event-triggered functions, and the platform manages resource allocation, scaling, and execution within secure *sandbox* environments like containers [11] or lightweight VMs [3]. The platform typically consists of a *Gateway* for request routing and an *Invoker* for function execution (Fig. 1).

2.2   Eliminating Cold Starts

The phenomenon of cold starts, a common issue in serverless platforms, poses a major challenge in serverless platforms, as they considerably extend the time it takes for a function to complete. Serverless functions are often ephemeral, with 75% running for less than 10 s, making the cold start duration a dominant factor in their execution timeline [13,14]. An accumulation of cold starts on a single node may also engender severe collocation interference, compromising the performance of co-located containers. Strategies to mitigate cold starts include container caching [13,14], where frequently invoked function containers are retained to enable warm starts. Other approaches involve caching function dependencies and libraries [8,10] to speed up the initialization process. Recently, snapshot-based optimizations have gained attention, such as capturing function state for rapid restoration [2,17], in-memory snapshotting [16], and optimizing post-restore performance [15].

2.3   Quality-of-Service in Serverless Computing

Serverless applications often specify QoS requirements, typically in terms of latency percentiles (e.g., P95 latency) [7]. Platforms aim to satisfy these requirements while minimizing resource consumption. Adaptive resource management techniques have been proposed, utilizing performance prediction models to estimate function execution latencies under different configurations [4,5]. These models are built through online profiling [12,18,20] and guide resource allocation decisions. State-of-the-art approaches dynamically adjust resources during runtime to meet QoS objectives, with techniques like Bayesian optimization showing promising results in handling the uncertainty and variability of serverless environments [20].

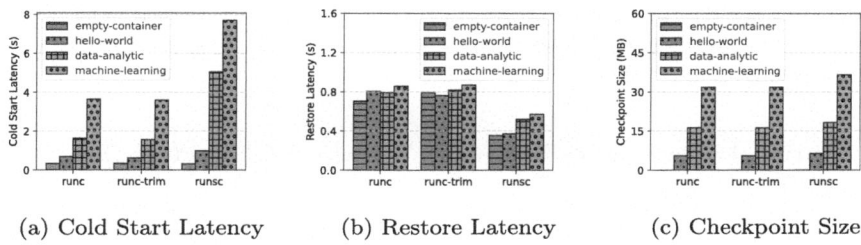

(a) Cold Start Latency   (b) Restore Latency   (c) Checkpoint Size

Fig. 2. Performance of Container-Level Checkpoint/Restore

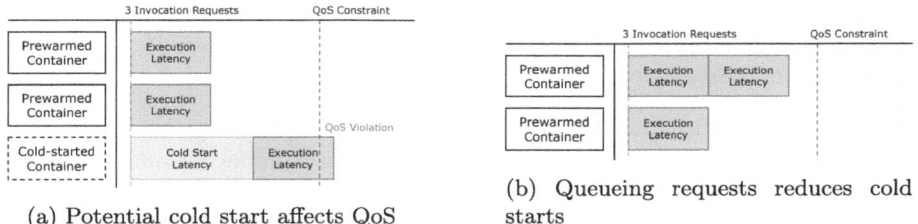

(a) Potential cold start affects QoS

(b) Queueing requests reduces cold starts

Fig. 3. Potential to judiciously queue requests in the same container while preserving QoS constraints.

3 Challenges and Motivations

Challenge 1: Prolonged Fine-Tuning Process

Existing resource management strategies rely on performance prediction models that require extensive online profiling, as offline profiling is infeasible due to data privacy and consistency concerns [7]. This online fine-tuning is time-consuming, risks QoS degradation, and incurs overheads from container restarts. State-of-the-art approaches take nearly 20 min to converge to a near-optimal configuration, which is problematic for time-sensitive applications and when new functions are introduced.

Challenge 2: Harmful Cold Start Impacts

Cold start latency is a significant portion of the overall function invocation delay and can unexpectedly violate QoS constraints. It is especially problematic in serverless platforms with high container colocation and network traffic [19]. Pre-warm container pools [14] are not always effective, as they can be insufficient during bursty workloads, leading to cold starts and increased tail latency [2].

As shown in Fig. 2, even with container-level checkpoint/restore techniques, the restore latency is significant compared to the function execution time, indicating that the container initialization phase is a major bottleneck. This insight motivates the need for a more efficient approach to rapidly switch between serverless functions.

Motivation 1: Leveraging Real-time Workload Characteristics

Current resource management techniques focus on individual function execution latency without considering the potential to consolidate requests in the same container while meeting QoS constraints (Fig. 3). By leveraging workload characteristics in real-time, we can reduce the number of active containers, avoid unnecessary cold starts, and improve resource efficiency without violating QoS.

Motivation 2: Rapid Function Switching via Process-Level Checkpoint/Restore

PLCR enables rapid switching of serverless functions within a container's lifespan by recovering only the necessary process state. This approach is more efficient than container-level restoration, as it avoids the overhead of recreating *cgroups* and *namespaces*. By leveraging PLCR, we can quickly mobilize idle containers to support functions at risk of QoS violations, minimizing the impact of cold starts.

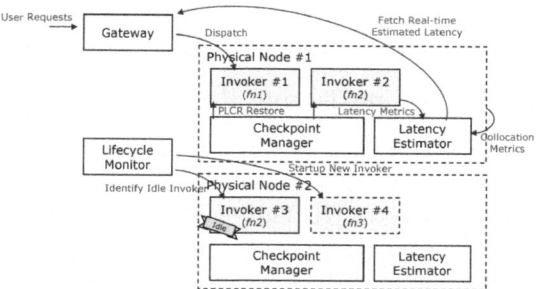

Fig. 4. System architecture of our proposed system.

4   System Design

4.1   Architecture

Our proposed system architecture (Fig. 4) integrates PLCR techniques for rapid serverless function deployment and a *Real-time Workload-and-QoS-Aware Scheduling* algorithm to adapt to dynamic workloads while ensuring sub-second QoS compliance. The system consists of the following key components:

- **Gateway**: The entry point for incoming requests, responsible for routing them to the appropriate function instances based on the scheduling algorithm's decisions. It interacts with the *Latency Estimator* to obtain function instance latency predictions.
- **Invoker**: Manages the execution of serverless functions within secure sandbox environments (e.g., containers). It handles the lifecycle of function instances, including pausing and restoring *handler* processes via the *Checkpoint Manager*, and dispatches tasks to the *handler* processes.
- **Checkpoint Manager**: Takes the responsibility of capturing and restoring the state of *handler* processes using PLCR techniques. It stores the checkpointed states and facilitates rapid function switching within the lifespan of a container instance.
- **Latency Estimator**: Predicts the execution latency of function instances based on their resource configurations and collocation metrics. It employs a Mondrian Forest model for efficient online learning and provides the scheduling algorithm with accurate latency estimates.
- **Lifecycle Monitor**: Oversees the lifecycle of *Invoker* instances, adjusting their number based on the incoming workload. It identifies idle *Invokers* that can be quickly repurposed to support functions at risk of QoS violations.

The system operates as follows. Incoming requests are received by the *Gateway*, which consults the scheduling algorithm to determine the optimal function instance placement. The scheduling algorithm leverages the *Latency Estimator*'s predictions and the current system state to make sub-second placement decisions that minimize QoS violations. The *Gateway* forwards the request to the selected *Invoker*, which manages the execution of the corresponding function instance. If the scheduling algorithm determines that a function requires additional support to meet QoS constraints, it instructs the *Lifecycle Monitor* to repurpose an idle *Invoker* using PLCR techniques. The *Checkpoint Manager* captures and restores the state of *handler* processes as needed, enabling rapid function switching within the lifespan of a container instance. The *Invoker* continuously reports runtime metrics to the *Latency Estimator*, allowing it to refine its predictions and adapt to changing workload conditions.

4.2   Process-Level Checkpoint/Restore (PLCR) Mechanism

The swift transition between serverless functions during a container's lifespan is facilitated by the PLCR mechanism. For instance, this approach involves the *wrapper* process terminating the previous *handler* and retrieving the subsequent *handler* from the *Checkpoint Manager* – the dedicated storage system present on each node that retains the states of *handler* processes.

We pivoted to a user-space strategy of *Checkpoint/Restore in Userspace* (CRIU), which is both flexible and adaptable to our requirements. CRIU is a mature and widely-adopted tool that engages less intrusive methods and takes advantage of established kernel mechanisms.

One of the primary obstacles in integrating CRIU within a container framework is the elimination of redundant, time-intensive tasks associated with capturing and restoring the full process state. A substantial portion of the restoration delay stems from reinstating *cgroup* and *namespace* primitives. However, our use case, which involves restoration inside an existing container, renders the reestablishment of these components unnecessary. By devising methodologies that avoid certain restoration steps, we have significantly minimized the time to revive a process.

Another hurdle facing us is `pid` conflicts, a consequence of CRIU's restriction that mandates restoration with the identical `pid` as the original process. Such a stipulation poses a genuine concern in serverless infrastructures, where simultaneous processing of numerous requests can naturally lead to `pid` clashes. Our approach circumvents this by embracing the *pid namespace* isolation provided by the container runtime. This utilization of *namespace* safeguards the uniqueness of the `pid` upon restoration within the confines of the container, thereby averting potential conflicts.

Table 1. Description of mathematical notations.

Notation	Description
$\mathcal{F}$	Set of all deployed serverless functions
QoS_j	QoS threshold for function j
$\mathcal{K}$	Set of all available *Invokers*
$\mathcal{K}^j$	Set of *Invokers* that serving function j
$\mathcal{K}^{idle}$	Set of *Invokers* identified as idle
EA_k	Estimated Available time on *Invoker* k
$\mathcal{N}$	Set of all nodes in the serverless platform
$Node(k)$	Node on which *Invoker* k is running
$EL_{n,j,0}$	Execution latency of function j on node n
$EL_{n,j,1}$	Restore latency of function j on node n
$\mathcal{R}$	Set of all incoming invocation requests
$\mathcal{R}^j$	Set of invocation requests for function j
$\mathcal{A}$	Set of invocation assignments
$\mathcal{S}$	Set of restoration assignments

4.3   Real-Time Workload-and-QoS-Aware Scheduling Algorithm

The *Real-Time Workload-and-QoS-Aware Scheduling* Algorithm is the core component of our system, ensuring QoS compliance by intelligently leveraging workload characteristics and the rapid function switching capabilities provided by PLCR. The algorithm is designed to be resilient and adaptable to the dynamic nature of serverless computing environments, making real-time decisions based on current workload conditions and latency predictions, ensuring QoS requirements are met and resource utilization is optimized.

Scheduling Objective. The scheduling algorithm operates at scheduled intervals to determine the best possible dispatch of influx invocation requests $\mathcal{R}$. It consistently seeks to uphold low tail latencies and limit the occurrences of QoS violations for each serverless function. In this process, the algorithm relies on the estimated availability window EA_k for every *Invoker* k and is informed by the execution $EL_{n,j,0}$ and restoration $EL_{n,j,1}$ latencies provided by the *Latency Estimator*. The mathematical notations used in the algorithm are summarized in Table 1.

Latency Estimation. The *Latency Estimator* is a crucial component that predicts the execution latency of function instances, considering both the specific characteristics of each function and the impact of co-located functions on the same node. Our adoption of the Mondrian Forest model demonstrates fast convergence during initial training and adapts well to the dynamic nature of serverless workloads. Specifically, compared to traditional incremental learning models, the Mondrian Forest methodology enhances accuracy by a notable 20% after the preliminary 10 batches of training. The estimator is trained using runtime metrics collected by the *Invokers*, such as function execution time, resource utilization, and performance counters. By accurately predicting the execution latency, the scheduling algorithm can make informed decisions to meet QoS requirements and optimize resource allocation.

First-Fit and Best-Fit Allocation. The scheduling algorithm employs a combination of First-Fit and Best-Fit allocation strategies to assign invocation requests to *Invokers*. The First-Fit strategy (Algorithm 1, lines 3–14) aims to allocate requests to the first available *Invoker* that can execute them within the QoS constraints. It iterates through the *Invokers* associated with each function, assigning requests until the estimated completion time exceeds the QoS threshold. The Best-Fit strategy (Algorithm 1, lines 15–19) is employed for requests that cannot be accommodated by the First-Fit strategy. It selects the *Invoker* that minimizes the estimated completion time for each remaining request, reducing the overall tail latency.

Algorithm 1. First-Fit and Best-Fit Assignment

Input: Estimated Available EA, Invocation Requests $\mathcal{R}$
Output: Assignment $\mathcal{A} = \{(r,k)|r \in \mathcal{R}, k \in \mathcal{K}\}$
1: $\mathcal{A} \leftarrow \emptyset$
2: **for** $j \in \mathcal{F}$ **do**
3:    **for** $k \in \mathcal{K}^j$ **do**
4:       **while** $\mathcal{R}^j \neq \emptyset$ **do**
5:          $n \leftarrow Node(k)$
6:          **if** $EA_k + EL_{n,j,0} \leq QoS_j$ **then**
7:             $r \leftarrow \mathcal{R}^j.pop()$
8:             $\mathcal{A} \leftarrow \mathcal{A} \cup \{(r,k)\}$
9:             $EA_k \leftarrow EA_k + EL_{n,j,0}$
10:          **else**
11:             break
12:          **end if**
13:       **end while**
14:    **end for**
15:    **for** $r \in \mathcal{R}^j$ **do**
16:       $k \leftarrow \arg\min_{k \in \mathcal{K}^j}(EA_k + EL_{Node(k),j,0})$
17:       $\mathcal{A} \leftarrow \mathcal{A} \cup \{(r,k)\}$
18:       $EA_k \leftarrow EA_k + EL_{Node(k),j,0}$
19:    **end for**
20: **end for**
21: **return** $\mathcal{A}$

Algorithm 2. Iterative Restore

Input: Estimated Available EA, Invocation Requests $\mathcal{R}$
Output: Assignment $\mathcal{A} = \{(r,k)|r \in \mathcal{R}, k \in \mathcal{K}\}$, Restoration $\mathcal{S} = \{(k,j)|k \in \mathcal{K}, j \in \mathcal{F}\}$
1: $\mathcal{A} \leftarrow$ **First-Fit-and-Best-Fit**$(EA, \mathcal{R})$
2: $\mathcal{S} \leftarrow \emptyset$
3: **while** $\mathcal{K}^{idle} \neq \emptyset$ **and** $\mathcal{A}$ causes QoS breaches **do**
4:    $k \leftarrow \mathcal{K}^{idle}.pop()$
5:    $j \leftarrow$ **Select-Fn-To-Help**$(\mathcal{A}, k)$
6:    $\mathcal{S} \leftarrow \mathcal{S} \cup \{(k,j)\}$
7:    $EA_k \leftarrow EA_k + EL_{Node(k),j,1}$
8:    $\mathcal{K}^j \leftarrow \mathcal{K}^j \cup \{k\}$
9:    $\mathcal{A} \leftarrow$ **First-Fit-and-Best-Fit**$(EA, \mathcal{R})$
10: **end while**
11: **return** $\mathcal{A}, \mathcal{S}$

Iterative Restore. To further improve QoS compliance and resource utilization, the scheduling algorithm incorporates an Iterative Restore technique (Algorithm 2) that leverages idle *Invokers* to support functions at risk of QoS violations. When the First-Fit and Best-Fit allocation strategies result in potential QoS breaches, the algorithm identifies the function that requires the most assistance and restores an idle *Invoker* to support it using PLCR. The restored

Invoker assumes the role of the overloaded function, allowing the original *Invokers* to be relieved. The allocation process is then repeated until QoS constraints are satisfied or no more idle *Invokers* are available.

The Iterative Restore technique introduces an additional restore latency $EL_{n,j,1}$ for the selected idle *Invoker*, which is accounted for when updating its estimated available time EA_k. By dynamically adapting to workload fluctuations and proactively provisioning resources, the scheduling algorithm ensures sub-second QoS compliance and efficient resource utilization.

5 Evaluation

5.1 Experimental Setup

We conduct experiments on a Kubernetes v1.28.4 cluster with 22 nodes. Half of the nodes have 4 Intel Xeon Gold 6252 CPUs, 200 GB DDR4 memory, and two 400 GB ATA disks, while the other half have 4 Intel Xeon Gold 6330 CPUs, 256 GB DDR4 memory, and one 960 GB SCSI disk. The nodes run CentOS Stream 9 with Linux kernel 5.14.0 and are connected by a 10 Gbps Ethernet network (Table 2).

Table 2. Function Descriptions

Function Name	Description
HW: **H**ello-**W**orld	Simplest function
ML: **M**achine-**L**earning	Do typical calculations in machine-learning
VP: **V**ideo-**P**rocessing	Process some frames for high-intensity areas
DA: **D**ata-**A**nalytic	Sort and filter a CSV dataset

Our workload consists of four Python functions adapted from the Aliyun serverless benchmark suite. We use Locust to generate realistic traffic patterns based on the Azure Function Dataset [9]. A 30-min segment is chosen to represent a wide range of load variations.

5.2 Performance of PLCR Function Switching

We evaluate the performance of our PLCR mechanism for function switching and compare it with alternative approaches. Figure 5 shows the average function switching delay for different methods. PLCR significantly outperforms all other approaches, being 2.2×–28.1× faster than cold starts and Zygote Repack [8], and 0.6×–1.5× faster than container-level restoration.

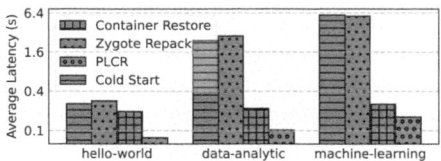

Fig. 5. Function switching delay comparison.

Our experiments also demonstrate the superior scalability of PLCR under high concurrency compared to container-level restoration. PLCR maintains low latency and high throughput even when multiple function switches occur simultaneously. Specifically, PLCR achieves a 2.3× lower latency and a 1.9× higher throughput compared to container-level restoration when handling 100 concurrent function switches. These results showcase PLCR's ability to efficiently handle bursty serverless workloads without compromising performance.

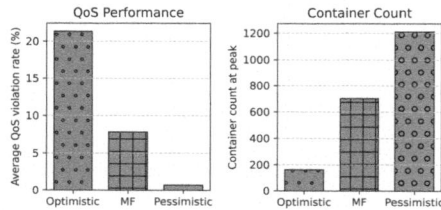

Fig. 6. Average QoS violation rate and container provision counts between different estimators.

5.3   Accuracy and Efficiency of Latency Estimation

The accuracy and efficiency of the *Latency Estimator* are crucial for the performance of our scheduling algorithm. Our Mondrian Forest-based estimator demonstrates fast convergence and high accuracy, enabling precise latency predictions with minimal training data. It effectively balances the trade-off between QoS violations and resource utilization, outperforming both optimistic and pessimistic estimators.

Figure 6 shows the impact of the *Latency Estimator* on the end-to-end QoS violation rate and container provisioning. The Mondrian Forest model achieves a low QoS violation rate of 7.8%, compared to 21.3% for an optimistic estimator. At the same time, it provisions 701 containers, which is 27% fewer than the 964 containers provisioned by a pessimistic estimator. These results highlight the effectiveness of our *Latency Estimator* in minimizing QoS violations while efficiently utilizing resources.

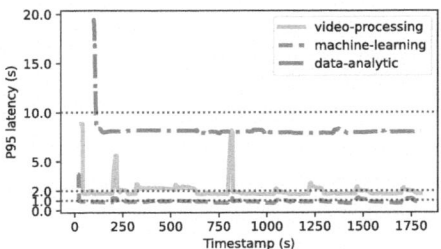

Fig. 7. 95th percentile latency of recent 1000 requests of different function invocations.

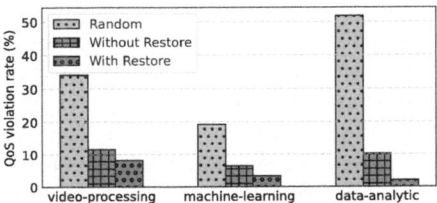

Fig. 8. QoS violation rate of different scheduling strategies across different applications.

5.4 Effectiveness of QoS-Aware Scheduling

We evaluate the effectiveness of our scheduling algorithm in maintaining QoS compliance under dynamic workloads. Figure 7 presents the 95th percentile latency for different functions over time. Our algorithm consistently keeps the latency below the QoS thresholds, even during sudden workload spikes. Figure 8 compares the QoS violation rates of different scheduling strategies. Our algorithm, with the Iterative Restore technique, achieves the lowest violation rates across all functions. Removing Iterative Restore leads to a 3.2%–8.3% performance degradation, highlighting its importance in handling workload fluctuations.

5.5 Overall Performance

We compare the overall performance of our proposed system against Aquatope [20], a state-of-the-art QoS-aware serverless resource management system. During the initial 10-min deployment phase, our system demonstrates a significant advantage, reducing the QoS violation rate by over 15% compared to Aquatope. This improvement can be attributed to the fast convergence of our Mondrian Forest-based *Latency Estimator*, which enables accurate and timely scheduling decisions.

The rapid adaptation of our system to changing workload conditions is further highlighted by its ability to maintain low QoS violation rates throughout the entire experimental period. By leveraging the PLCR mechanism for fast function switching and the real-time scheduling algorithm, our system consistently outperforms Aquatope in terms of QoS compliance and resource utilization.

These results demonstrate the effectiveness of our proposed system in handling dynamic serverless workloads while ensuring sub-second QoS-aware scheduling. The combination of PLCR, accurate latency estimation, and real-time scheduling enables our system to achieve superior performance compared to state-of-the-art approaches.

6 Conclusion

This research tackles critical challenges in serverless computing, not only solving the cold start problem but also enabling sub-second, QoS-aware scheduling for fluctuating workloads. A PLCR strategy was developed to minimize cold starts, while a Mondrian Forest-based latency estimator ensures precise performance prediction. Dynamic resource management is achieved through a newly developed Real-Time Workload-and-QoS-Aware Scheduling algorithm. Extensive experiments using real-world serverless workloads proved the system's effectiveness in swiftly adapting to workload changes. The proposed approach substantially reduces QoS violations in various scenarios, surpassing existing solutions in managing dynamic workloads. This advancement in serverless computing enhances performance and resource utilization for fluctuating workloads, laying the groundwork for more efficient and responsive serverless platforms.

References

1. Amazon Web Services: AWS Lambda (2024). https://aws.amazon.com/lambda/
2. Du, D., et al.: Catalyzer: sub-millisecond startup for serverless computing with initialization-less booting. In: Proceedings of the Twenty-Fifth International Conference on Architectural Support for Programming Languages and Operating Systems, ASPLOS 2020, pp. 467–481. Association for Computing Machinery, New York (2020). https://doi.org/10.1145/3373376.3378512
3. Firecracker Community: Firecracker (2024). https://firecracker-microvm.github.io/
4. HoseinyFarahabady, M.R., Zomaya, A.Y., Tari, Z.: A model predictive controller for managing QoS enforcements and microarchitecture-level interferences in a lambda platform. IEEE Trans. Parallel Distrib. Syst. **29**(7), 1442–1455 (2018). https://doi.org/10.1109/TPDS.2017.2779502
5. HoseinyFarahabady, M., Lee, Y.C., Zomaya, A.Y., Tari, Z.: A QoS-aware resource allocation controller for function as a service (FAAS) platform. In: Maximilien, M., Vallecillo, A., Wang, J., Oriol, M. (eds.) Service-Oriented Computing, pp. 241–255. Springer, Cham (2017)
6. Jarachanthan, J., Chen, L., Xu, F., Li, B.: Astrea: auto-serverless analytics towards cost-efficiency and QoS-awareness. IEEE Trans. Parallel Distrib. Syst. **33**(12), 3833–3849 (2022). https://doi.org/10.1109/TPDS.2022.3172069
7. Li, S., Wang, W., Yang, J., Chen, G., Lu, D.: Golgi: performance-aware, resource-efficient function scheduling for serverless computing. In: Proceedings of the 2023 ACM Symposium on Cloud Computing, SoCC 2023, pp. 32–47. Association for Computing Machinery, New York (2023). https://doi.org/10.1145/3620678.3624645

8. Li, Y., Zeng, D., Gu, L., Ou, M., Chen, Q.: On efficient zygote container planning toward fast function startup in serverless edge cloud. In: IEEE INFOCOM 2023 - IEEE Conference on Computer Communications, pp. 1–9 (2023). https://doi.org/10.1109/INFOCOM53939.2023.10228916
9. Microsoft Azure: Azure Functions (2024). https://azure.microsoft.com/en-us/services/functions/
10. Oakes, E., et al.: SOCK: rapid task provisioning with serverless-optimized containers. In: 2018 USENIX Annual Technical Conference (USENIX ATC 2018), pp. 57–70. USENIX Association, Boston, MA (2018). https://www.usenix.org/conference/atc18/presentation/oakes
11. Open Container Initiative: runc (2024). https://github.com/opencontainers/runc
12. Patel, T., Tiwari, D.: CLITE: efficient and QoS-aware co-location of multiple latency-critical jobs for warehouse scale computers. In: 2020 IEEE International Symposium on High Performance Computer Architecture (HPCA), pp. 193–206 (2020). https://doi.org/10.1109/HPCA47549.2020.00025
13. Shahrad, M., et al.: Serverless in the wild: characterizing and optimizing the serverless workload at a large cloud provider. In: 2020 USENIX Annual Technical Conference (USENIX ATC 2020), pp. 205–218. USENIX Association, Online (2020). https://www.usenix.org/conference/atc20/presentation/shahrad
14. Suo, K., Son, J., Cheng, D., Chen, W., Baidya, S.: Tackling cold start of serverless applications by efficient and adaptive container runtime reusing. In: 2021 IEEE International Conference on Cluster Computing (CLUSTER), pp. 433–443 (2021). https://doi.org/10.1109/Cluster48925.2021.00018
15. Ustiugov, D., Petrov, P., Kogias, M., Bugnion, E., Grot, B.: Benchmarking, analysis, and optimization of serverless function snapshots. In: Proceedings of the 26th ACM International Conference on Architectural Support for Programming Languages and Operating Systems, ASPLOS 2021, pp. 559–572. Association for Computing Machinery, New York (2021). https://doi.org/10.1145/3445814.3446714
16. Venkatesh, R.S., Smejkal, T., Milojicic, D.S., Gavrilovska, A.: Fast in-memory criu for docker containers. In: Proceedings of the International Symposium on Memory Systems, MEMSYS 2019, pp. 53–65. Association for Computing Machinery, New York (2019). https://doi.org/10.1145/3357526.3357542
17. Wang, K.T.A., Ho, R., Wu, P.: Replayable execution optimized for page sharing for a managed runtime environment. In: Proceedings of the Fourteenth EuroSys Conference 2019. EuroSys 2019. Association for Computing Machinery, New York (2019). https://doi.org/10.1145/3302424.3303978
18. Wu, H., Deng, J., Fan, H., Ibrahim, S., Wu, S., Jin, H.: QoS-aware and cost-efficient dynamic resource allocation for serverless ml workflows. In: 2023 IEEE International Parallel and Distributed Processing Symposium (IPDPS), pp. 886–896 (2023). https://doi.org/10.1109/IPDPS54959.2023.00093
19. Zhang, Y., et al.: Workload consolidation in Alibaba clusters: the good, the bad, and the ugly. In: Proceedings of the 13th Symposium on Cloud Computing, SoCC 2022, pp. 210–225. Association for Computing Machinery, New York (2022). https://doi.org/10.1145/3542929.3563465
20. Zhou, Z., Zhang, Y., Delimitrou, C.: Aquatope: QoS-and-uncertainty-aware resource management for multi-stage serverless workflows. In: Proceedings of the 28th ACM International Conference on Architectural Support for Programming Languages and Operating Systems, ASPLOS 2023, vol. 1, pp. 1–14. Association for Computing Machinery, New York (2022). https://doi.org/10.1145/3567955.3567960

EdgeMeter: Towards Efficient and Accurate Latency Prediction of Neural Network Model Inference on Edge Devices

Songtao Lu[1], Weilong Wang[1], Borui Li[1], Shuai Wang[1], Xiaolei Zhou[2], and Zhao-Dong Xu[3](✉)

[1] School of Computer Science and Engineering, Southeast University,
Nanjing 210000, Jiangsu, China
{seu_lst,wang_wl,libr,shuaiwang_iot}@seu.edu.cn
[2] The Sixty-Third Research Institute, National University of Defense Technology,
Nanjing 210000, Jiangsu, China
zhouxiaolei@nudt.edu.cn
[3] School of Civil Engineering, Southeast University, Nanjing 210000, Jiangsu, China
xuzhdgyq@seu.edu.cn

Abstract. With the continuous development of Internet of Things (IoT) and Artificial Intelligence (AI) technologies, edge computing is emerging as a near-data source computing model. Due to the limited computing resources of edge devices, it is essential to measure and analyze the performance of neural network models to ensure efficient use of these resources during inference on edge devices. However, most existing prediction techniques are based on the model or kernel operator level. They require access to the specific code of the neural network model, making them unsuitable for black-box models. Additionally, most current prediction technologies necessitate large-scale data sample collection, which incurs substantial time overhead on edge devices. In response to these challenges, this paper proposes a prediction algorithm based on machine learning that does not require internal details of the neural network model. The algorithm leverages Bayesian Optimization to optimize the hyperparameters of the training model and employs a Gaussian process regression model to guide targeted data sampling, thereby reducing overall training costs. Furthermore, experimental results verify the algorithm's stability and excellence in model performance prediction, as well as its feasibility in constructing an accurate performance model with a small amount of sample data.

Keywords: Edge devices · Neural network model · Inference cost prediction · Gaussian process regression

1 Introduction

With the continuous development of Internet of Things (IoT) and Artificial Intelligent (AI), edge computing as a near data source computing mode is gradually emerging [1]. At the same time, the popularity of technologies such as the Internet of Things and intelligent terminals has also made it possible to deploy intelligent applications on mobile devices. For example, in the fields of intelligent monitoring and intelligent transportation, edge computing has already made a huge impact [2].

However, the limited computing resources of edge devices, such as processing power and storage capacity, conflict with the high computing resource requirements of the neural network model itself [3]. In many latency-sensitive applications, predicting the inference cost of the neural network model deployed on the edge device is important for better resource scheduling. With the increasing research on implementing deep learning on edge devices, inference latency has become a key metric for running deep neural network (DNN) models on various mobile and edge devices [4–6].

Existing works on inference cost prediction of neural network models can be divided into the following categories: feature selection based [7–9], graph based [10,11] and neural network structure based [4,9,12,13,15].

The selection of features is diverse, encompassing aspects such as the optimizer within the neural network model, batch size, processor configuration of the hardware, memory bandwidth, etc. [7,8]. Additionally, numerous studies employ FLOPs (Floating Point Operations) to predict the inference time of neural network models [4,16].

Methods based on neural network architecture can be further divided into three categories: neural network level [9,12], hierarchy level [7,13,17], and operator kernel level [14,15,18]. Hierarchical and operator level or kernel level neural network model inference time prediction algorithms tend to have higher accuracy. However, they require complex and precise modeling of the model kernel and even the device kernel. In order to build prediction models, it takes a lot of time to collect data samples. In the case of nn-Meter, it takes 2.5 days to build a kernel on the CPU and 4.4 days on the VPU [15].

Among existing prediction methods, most algorithms require extensive data sampling. This results in significant time overhead when performed on edge devices. Additionally, hierarchical and operator/kernel-level prediction techniques often need open-source model code. This is necessary to decompose the model or segment the kernel. For some black-box models, this algorithm does not work.

From this, we propose EdgeMeter, a Bayesian Optimization (BO) based inference cost prediction framework. Unlike other methods, EdgeMeter does not perform hierarchical or operator-level analysis of the model's internal structure. It uses random forest regression to directly capture the relationship between the batch size of different neural network models and the model inference time. We use the idea of Bayesian Optimization to optimize the hyperparameter combination of the training model to obtain better training results. Moreover, we design a sampling-guided algorithm based on Gaussian process regression to reduce the sampling cost.

EdgeMeter has two challenges. First, the selection of hyperparameters for the training model impacts its performance. In machine learning, the combination of hyperparameters significantly affects the model's training results. Second, sampling time on edge devices is costly. Edge devices have limited computing resources, making the inference time for neural network models much higher than on processors with abundant resources. Thus, large-scale and intensive sampling methods are not suitable for predicting the inference time of models on edge device CPUs.

We summerize our key contribution as follows:

- We propose and design the EdgeMeter, which uses Bayesian Optimization to adjust the hyperparameters of the training model, and intersperses the sampling update during the iteration process to improve the prediction performance.
- We design a sampling guided algorithm based on Gaussian process regression to reduce sampling costs.
- We test 10 neural network models on real edge devices to validate the feasibility of EdgeMeter. The results show that EdgeMeter is more than 85% accurate in predicting the inference cost of most NN models with ±10% accuracy.
- We conduct a series of experiments to demonstrate the effectiveness of hyperparameter optimization and sampling guidance.

2   Background and Motivation

2.1   Inference Time of Neural Network Models

The influence of machine learning on numerical prediction is powerful, and a wide variety of machine learning models can be used for numerical prediction [19–21]. Most machine learning models have limitations, and they are unlikely to be good predictors for all types of data.

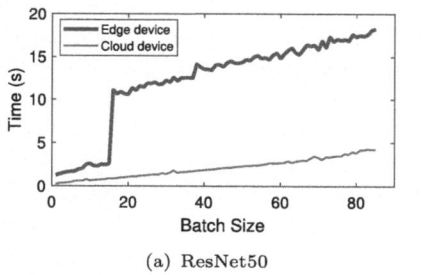
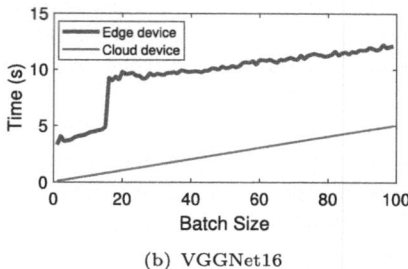

| | |
| (a) ResNet50 | (b) VGGNet16 |

Fig. 1. Inference time on edge and cloud devices varies with batch size

Due to the limited computing power of edge devices, the inference performance of neural network model will decrease as the computing load of edge devices increases. Given the nonlinear characteristics of the data in Fig. 1, we choose to use random forest regression [22] as the basis of the prediction algorithm with good processing ability for complex nonlinear data. Many studies have adopted random forest regression algorithm to model data sets with complex nonlinear relationships, and have obtained good prediction results [23].

2.2 Hyperparameter Optimization

In machine learning, the combination of hyperparameters often significantly impacts the results of model training. Common hyperparameters include weight, learning rate, and regularization parameters. Changes in these values affect the model's performance and generalization ability [24].

The hyperparameters of the selected random forest model are as follows:

(1) n_estimators: Increasing the number of trees can improve the stability and generalization ability of the model, but also increase the computational cost.
(2) max_depth: Controlling the depth of the tree can limit the complexity of the model and avoid over fitting.
(3) min_samples_split: Controlling the number of min_samples_split can control the growth of the tree and prevent overfitting (Table 1).

Table 1. Hyperparameter combination values and ±15% accuracy

Combination	n_estimators	max_depth	min_samples_split	±15% Accuracy
Params1	381	4	0.2573823443	51.76%
Params2	880	7	0.6198324796	38.82%
Params3	754	2	0.6574620844	8.33%

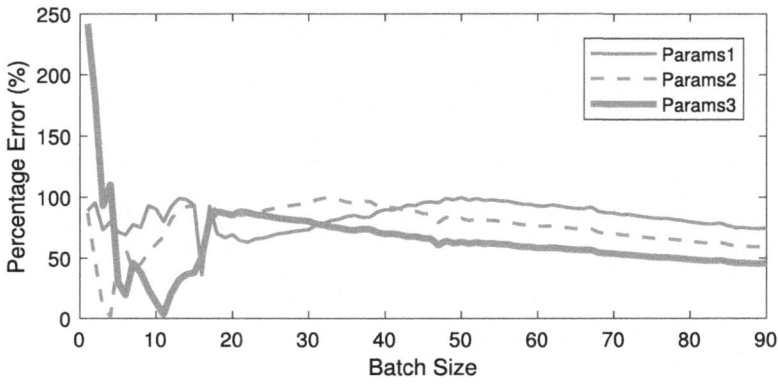

Fig. 2. Percentage Error of the same data under three hyperparameter combinations

As shown in Fig. 2, selecting the most appropriate combination of hyperparameters for the machine learning model and the data to be trained can significantly improve the training efficiency and quality of the model.

2.3   Excessive Sampling Overhead

Machine learning needs ample training data for better performance, which can cause substantial time overhead. Due to limited computing resources on edge devices, neural network inference times there are much higher-often tens or even hundreds of times longer than on powerful processors. In the case of nn-Meter, it takes 2.5 days to build a kernel on a CPU and 4.4 days on a VPU [15].

We design a sampling guide function to guide the model to sample the parts with poor prediction accuracy twice during the training process, so as to reduce the sampling cost on the premise of ensuring the prediction performance of the model.

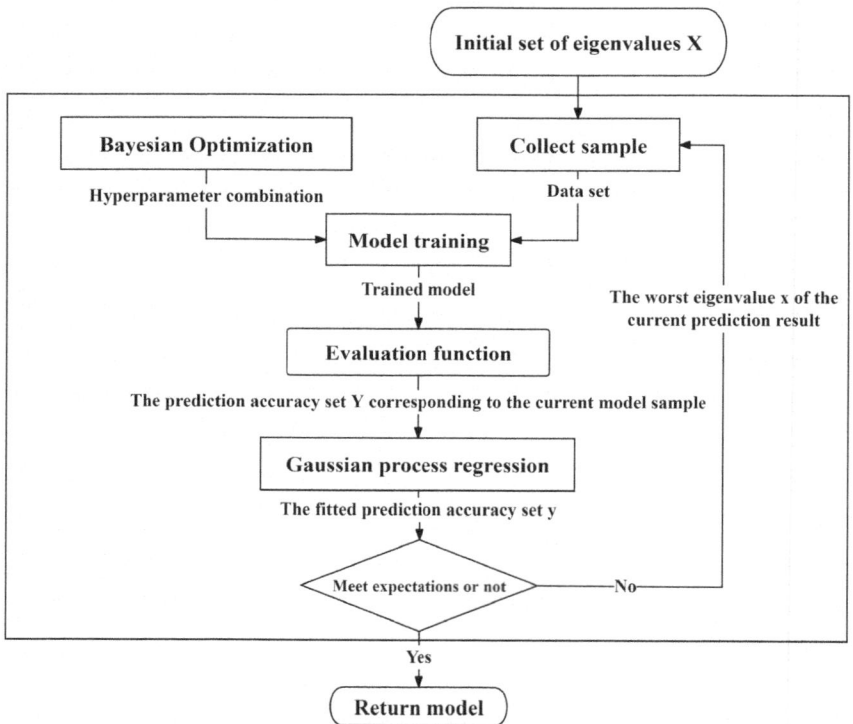

Fig. 3. EdgeMeter flow chart

3   EdgeMeter Design

EdgeMeter does not need to delve deeply into the neural network model to segment it. Instead, EdgeMeter models parameters such as the batch size and corresponding inference time. As shown in Fig. 3, during the modeling process, EdgeMeter also uses Bayesian methods to optimize the hyperparameter combination of the random forest model. This approach aims to further improve training efficiency and final performance. Meanwhile, EdgeMeter fully considers the problem of excessive sampling cost on edge devices. We employ a Gaussian process regression model to guide the sampling process during model training, thereby reducing sampling costs.

3.1 Performance Optimization Based Bayesian Optimization

The hyperparameter combination of machine learning models often significantly impacts the results of model training. To address this, EdgeMeter aims to use Bayesian Optimization to enhance the model's prediction performance. To minimize the waste of computational and time resources on extreme or meaningless hyperparameter values during Bayesian Optimization, we restrict the value range of the hyperparameters to be optimized, as shown in Table 2.

Table 2. The value range of the hyperparameter

hyperparameter	Value range
n_estimators	[10,1000]
max_depth	[1,20]
min_samples_split	[0.01,1.0]

The objective function assesses model performance for a given hyperparameter set. Bayesian Optimization [25] improves search efficiency by evaluating this function, quantifying model performance for each configuration, and guiding the selection of the next set of hyperparameters.

In order to better evaluate the performance indicators of the model, we adopt the idea of cross-validation to formulate the objective function [26]. There are two main types of Cross Validation: Simple Cross Validation and K-fold cross validation.

Considering that K-fold cross-validation maximizes the use of all data samples and is more suitable for models with small sample sizes, we choose to employ K-fold cross-validation to formulate the objective function. We use Mean Squared Error (MSE) as the performance index of the final model.

$$MSE = (\frac{1}{n}) \sum_{i=1}^{n} (y_i - \tilde{y}_i)^2 \tag{1}$$

where n indicates the number of data samples. $\tilde{y}_i$ is the predicted value of the model for the first sample (here refers to the predicted value of the inference time). y_i is the true inference time for sample i.

Mean Squared Error (MSE) serves as a metric for evaluating the performance of regression models. A smaller MSE implies predictions that are closer to the actual values and higher accuracy. This is in line with EdgeMeter's objective of enhancing prediction accuracy.

3.2 Sampling Guidance Based Gaussian Process Regression

In EdgeMeter, we use a Gaussian process regression model [27] to guide sampling during model training. As a non-parametric regression method, it does not require assumptions about the data distribution or the function form. Instead, it models by learning the relationship between data, making it ideal for establishing the link between eigenvalues and prediction accuracy.

Algorithm 1. Sampling guidance

Require: Set of eigenvalues X
Ensure: The current model predicts the worst-performing eigenvalue point min_X
1: $Y = Eval(X, T)$
2: $gpModel = GaussianProcessRegressor()$
3: $gpModel.fit(X, Y)$
4: $y\_pred = gpModel.predict(X)$
5: $min\_X\_index = np.argmin(y\_pred)$
6: $min\_X = X[min\_X\_index]$ // Get the eigenvalues of the worst prediction performance of the current model
7: **return** min_X

To identify the eigenvalue points with the poorest prediction performance, it is essential to model the eigenvalue set and the corresponding prediction accuracy. As shown in Fig. 3, the algorithm uses the evaluation function to determine the prediction accuracy for each eigenvalue of the current model. The specific formula is as follows:

$$y_i = (1 - |\tilde{t}_i - t_i|/t_i)^2 \qquad (2)$$

where y_i is the prediction accuracy corresponding to each sample eigenvalue x_i. $\tilde{t}_i$ is the inference time predicted by the current model for x_i. t_i is the inference time obtained by sampling corresponding to the eigenvalue x_i of the sample.

After modeling with Gaussian process regression, we obtain predictions for the training model's accuracy at each eigenvalue interval. Using this information, we identify the worst prediction performance. Next, we collect data samples near this point on the edge device and incorporate them into the original dataset for further training.

4 Evaluation

Experiments on ten different size neural network models (such as AlexNet, DenseNet121, InceptionNetv3, MNASNet1, MobileNetv2, ResNet50,

ResNext50_32x4d, ShuffleNetv2, SqueezeNet1, VGGNet16, etc. [28]) are performed at Jetson Xavier NX which is a representative edge device for inference time prediction. For baselines, we choose two baselines, one based on FLOPs [4,16], which we call FLOPs, and the other based on random forest regression, which we call RF. For the first, we use FLOPs to build a linear regression model to estimate the inference time of neural network models. For the second, we only use random forest regression for modeling to verify the feasibility of EdgeMeter in reducing sampling overhead.

Figure 4 compares the performance of Edgemeter and FLOPs within a ±10% accuracy range. In terms of prediction performance, Edgemeter consistently demonstrates higher accuracy, typically exceeding 85%. Compared to FLOPs-based prediction technology, Edgemeter exhibits significant predictive effectiveness.

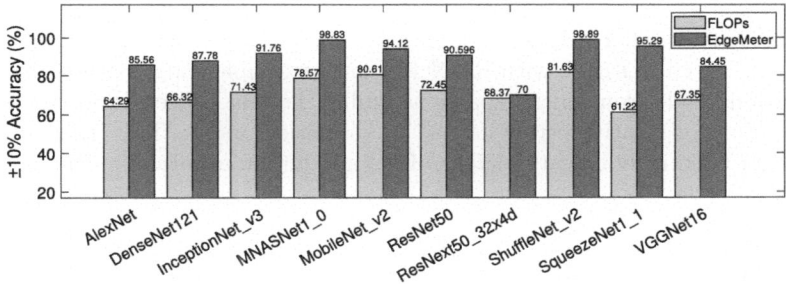

Fig. 4. Comparison of ±10% accuracy between EdgeMeter and FLOPs

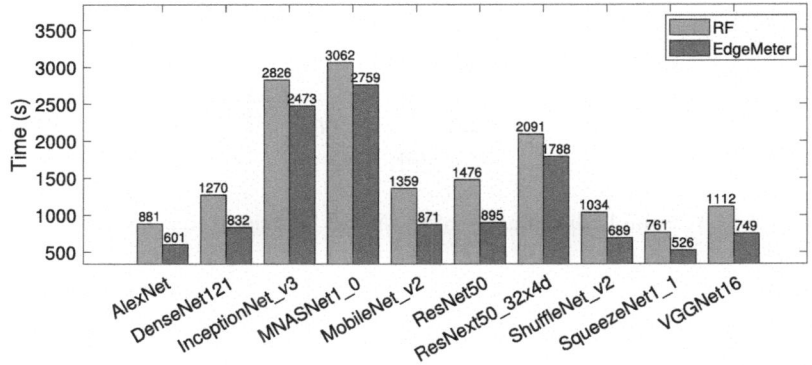

Fig. 5. The overall sampling time of EdgeMeter and RF

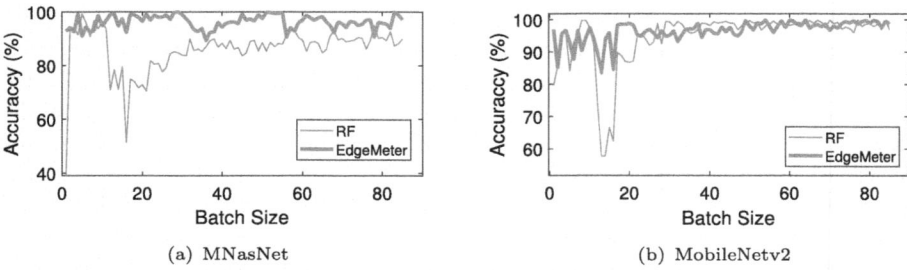

(a) MNasNet   (b) MobileNetv2

Fig. 6. Prediction accuracy of EdgeMeter and RF under the same sample size

Figure 6 shows that when the sample size is approximate, EdgeMeter's ability
to predict the inference time of neural network models is significantly better than
RF.

Figure 5 shows that EdgeMeter generally has a smaller overall sampling time
than RF. As seen in Fig. 7, with ResNet50 as an example, EdgeMeter's sampling
distribution, aside from initial sparse sampling, largely concentrates in areas of
mutated data or relative errors caused by numerical issues. This indicates that
EdgeMeter effectively targets regions of low prediction accuracy in the sampling
process.

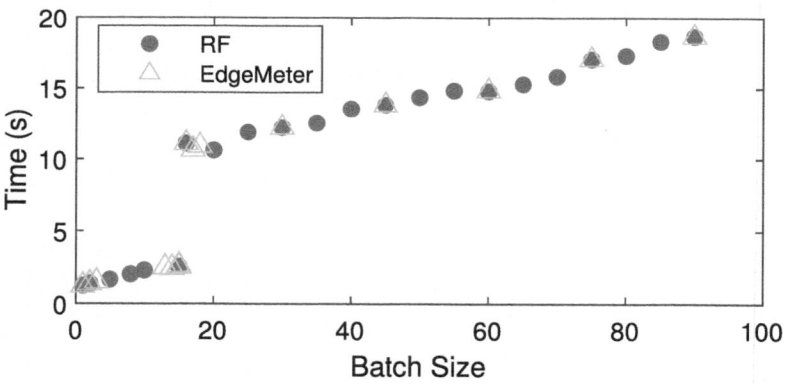

Fig. 7. Sample distribution of ResNet50 by EdgeMeter and RF

5   Discussion

EdgeMeter aims to reduce sampling time and computational overhead on edge
devices, verifying its feasibility through experiments. However, predicting inference delays by DNNs on diverse devices necessitates separate modeling for each

device. Future research will focus on establishing an inter-device performance model based on device specifications, enabling transferability of existing device prediction models to new devices.

6 Related Work

The inference time of neural network models on edge devices is mainly affected by the model itself and the hardware configuration. Many prediction algorithms only consider the model's influence, ignoring the heterogeneity of edge devices, leading to low prediction accuracy. For example, Liu et al. used FLOPs to predict the inference cost of DNNs in Darf [16]. Gujarati A et al. predicted inference time by representing DNN model inference as a definite sequence of mathematical operations [9].

The algorithm based on neural network model operator kernel level has the highest prediction accuracy. For example, Kaufman S et al. [14] constructed a cost model to predict the execution time of each TPU kernel. Zhang et al. [15] proposed and developed a novel and efficient system nn-Meter, which achieved high accuracy. However, most of the prediction algorithms based on operator kernel need to obtain the internal code of the model, which is not applicable to the black box model.

In addition, all the above algorithms carry out large-scale sampling in the process of modeling, which will cause a lot of time cost on edge devices.

7 Conclusion

We propose EdgeMeter to optimize model training with targeted sampling, reducing significant time and computing overhead on edge devices. It effectively constructs prediction models for neural network inference costs. Testing on Jetson NX with ten neural network models, we compare their performance against classical algorithms to validate EdgeMeter's effectiveness.

Acknowledgements. This work is supported by the Major Project of Fundamental Research on Frontier Leading Technology of Jiangsu Province (BK20222006), National Natural Science Foundation of China (62302096), and Zhishan Young Scholar Program of Southeast University (3209002402A2).

References

1. Xue, F., Fang, W.W.: EdgeMI: deep learning multi-device collaborative reasoning under resource-constrained conditions. In: Modern Computer, pp. 27–32+43 (2020). issn: 1007-1423
2. Szegedy, C., et al.: Rethinking the inception architecture for computer vision. In: Proceedings of the IEEE Conference on Computer Vision and Pattern Recognition, pp. 2818–2826 (2016)

3. Kong, X., et al.: Real-time mask identification for COVID-19: an edge-computing-based deep learning framework. IEEE Internet Things J. **8**(21), 15929–15938 (2021)
4. He, Y., et al.: Amc: Automl for model compression and acceleration on mobile devices. In: Proceedings of the European Conference on Computer Vision (ECCV), pp. 784–800 (2018)
5. Ma, L., et al.: Pareto-wise ranking classifier for multi-objective evolutionary neural architecture search. IEEE Trans. Evol. Comput. (2023)
6. Vasu, P.K.A., et al.: Mobileone: an improved one millisecond mobile backbone. In: Proceedings of the IEEE/CVF Conference on Computer Vision and Pattern Recognition, pp. 7907–7917 (2023)
7. Justus, D., et al.: Predicting the computational cost of deep learning models. In: IEEE international conference on big data (Big Data) 2018, PP. 3873–3882. IEEE (2018)
8. Qi, H., Sparks, E.R., Talwalkar, A.: Paleo: a performance model for deep neural networks. In: International Conference on Learning Representations (2022)
9. Gujarati, A., et al.: Serving DNNs like clockwork: performance predictability from the bottom up. In: 14th USENIX Symposium on Operating Systems Design and Implementation (OSDI 20), pp. 443–462 (2020)
10. Baghsorkhi, S.S., et al.: An adaptive performance modeling tool for GPU architectures. In: Proceedings of the 15th ACM SIGPLAN Symposium on Principles and Practice of Parallel Programming, pp. 105–114 (2010)
11. Gao, Y., et al.: Runtime performance prediction for deep learning models with graph neural network. In: 2023 IEEE/ACM 45th International Conference on Software Engineering: Software Engineering in Practice (ICSE-SEIP), pp. 368–380. IEEE (2023)
12. Adolf, R., et al.: Fathom: reference workloads for modern deep learning methods. In: IEEE International Symposium on Workload Characterization (IISWC) 2016, pp. 1–10. IEEE (2016)
13. Stamoulis, D., et al.: Single-path NAS: designing hardware-efficient convnets in less than 4 hours. In: Brefeld, U., Fromont, E., Hotho, A., Knobbe, A., Maathuis, M., Robardet, C. (eds.) ECML PKDD 2019. LNCS (LNAI), vol. 11907, pp. 481–497. Springer, Cham (2020). https://doi.org/10.1007/978-3-030-46147-8_29
14. Kaufman, S., Phothilimthana, P.M., Burrows, M.: Learned TPU cost model for XLA tensor programs. In: Proceedings of Workshop ML Systems, NeurIPS, pp. 1–6 (2019)
15. Zhang, L.L., et al.: Nn-meter: towards accurate latency prediction of deep learning model inference on diverse edge devices. In: Proceedings of the 19th Annual International Conference on Mobile Systems, Applications, and Services, pp. 81–93 (2021)
16. Liu, H., Simonyan, K., Yang, Y.: Darts: differentiable architecture search. arXiv preprint arXiv:1806.09055 (2018)
17. Lee, J., Ham, B.: AZ-NAS: assembling zero-cost proxies for network architecture search. In: Proceedings of the IEEE/CVF Conference on Computer Vision and Pattern Recognition, pp. 5893–5903 (2024)
18. Wu, B., et al.: Fbnet: hardware-aware efficient convnet design via differentiable neural architecture search. In: Proceedings of the IEEE/CVF Conference on Computer Vision and Pattern Recognition, pp. 10734–10742 (2019)
19. Seber, G.A.F., Lee, A.J.: Linear Regression Analysis. John Wiley & Sons, Hoboken (2012)
20. Quinlan, J.R.: Induction of decision trees. Mach. Learn. **1**, 81–106 (1986)

21. Cortes, C., Vapnik, V.: Support-vector networks. Mach. Learn. **20**, 273–297 (1995)
22. Breiman, L.: Random forests. Mach. Learn. **45**, 5–32 (2001)
23. Vijh, M., et al.: Stock closing price prediction using machine learning techniques. Procedia Comput. Sci. **167**, 599–606 (2020)
24. Murphy, K.P.: Machine Learning: A Probabilistic Perspective. MIT press, Cambridge (2012)
25. Santos, M.: Bayesian optimization for hyperparameter tuning. J. Bioinf. Artif. Intell. **2**(2), 1–13 (2022)
26. Stone, M.: Cross-validatory choice and assessment of statistical predictions. J. Roy. Stat. Soc. Ser. B (Methodological) **36**(2), 111–133 (1974)
27. Frazier, P.I.: A tutorial on Bayesian optimization. arXiv preprint arXiv:1807.02811 (2018)
28. Paszke, A., et al.: Pytorch: an imperative style, high-performance deep learning library. In: Advances in Neural Information Processing Systems, vol. 32 (2019)

Enhancing IoT Compliance Checking with Distributed Process Mining: A Scalable Framework for Log Data Streams

Chao Song[✉], Zheng Ren, Ruilin Hu, and Li Lu

School of Computer Science and Engineering,
University of Electronic Science and Technology of China, Chengdu, China
{chaosong,luli2009}@uestc.edu.cn, {renzheng,huruilin}@std.uestc.edu.cn

Abstract. The integration of the Internet of Things (IoT) into various industries has led to an exponential increase in the volume of data generated, posing significant challenges for compliance monitoring. Traditional compliance checking methods are often inadequate due to their inability to handle the high velocity and volume of real-time data streams emanating from IoT devices. In this paper, we introduce a novel distributed computing framework specifically designed to address these challenges by leveraging process mining techniques on IoT log data streams. The proposed framework is built to scale horizontally, allowing for the parallel processing of massive data sets while maintaining real-time performance. It is capable of identifying compliance patterns, detecting deviations, and providing actionable insights to ensure that IoT systems operate within the confines of established regulations and standards. To evaluate the performance and effectiveness of the proposed framework, we conducted extensive experiments using a publicly available industrial IoT log dataset. The results demonstrate the framework's ability to process large volumes of data in real-time, offering a significant improvement over existing centralized approaches.

Keywords: compliance checking · distributed framework · internet of things · log data stream · process mining

1 Introduction

The proliferation of the Internet of Things (IoT) [1] has led to an exponential growth in the generation of data from a multitude of connected devices. These devices, ranging from simple sensors to complex smart systems, produce streams of data that capture the nuances of various processes across different domains such as manufacturing, healthcare, logistics, and smart cities [2]. The sheer volume, velocity, and variety of IoT data present both significant challenges and opportunities for businesses and researchers alike. Process mining (PM) is an emerging field that offers a set of techniques to analyze event logs from processes, providing insights into their behavior and performance. When applied to IoT, process mining can help in making sense of the complex interactions between IoT devices and the processes they support [3,4]. It enables the discovery of process models from event data, conformance checking to ensure that actual process executions adhere to predefined process models, and the detection of bottlenecks, inefficiencies, and areas for improvement [5–7].

In Internet of Things (IoT), the scale of data generated by interconnected devices is staggering, posing significant challenges for process mining endeavors [8]. The volume of data is massive, with billions of devices potentially contributing to a continuous influx of information. This vast amount of data is accompanied by the velocity challenge, where data streams are generated in real-time, requiring process mining solutions that can keep pace with the speed of incoming data to provide timely insights [9]. The sheer size of data can overwhelm traditional process mining techniques, which may not be designed to handle the scale of data production in IoT environments. IoT data is often time-sensitive, necessitating process mining methods that can analyze and provide feedback on processes as they occur, without significant delays. IoT devices vary widely in their data output, leading to diverse data formats and structures that must be standardized for effective process mining. As the IoT ecosystem expands, the process mining framework must scale accordingly to accommodate an increasing number of devices and data points. IoT environments are highly dynamic, with devices frequently joining or leaving the network, which can affect the continuity and reliability of process mining analyses.

In this paper, we propose a Distributed Process Mining Framework (DPMF) for IoT environments to address these challenges. DPMF is a real-time scalable compliance checking method, based on a distributed fusion stream data processing structure. DPMF utilizes a distributed fusion stream data processing framework, which can process in real-time as the data stream enters the system, and can be checked in real-time according to specific compliance requirements. Building upon traditional centralized computing, DPMF offers the three data processing methods of distributed computing, offline analysis, and stream data processing. It has the advantages of real-time processing, flexibility, scalability, high availability, and reliability. To validate the performance and effectiveness of our proposed framework, we conducted experiments using a publicly available industrial IoT log dataset. The results of these experiments demonstrate the framework's ability to process and analyze IoT log data streams efficiently, providing a robust solution for compliance monitoring in IoT environments.

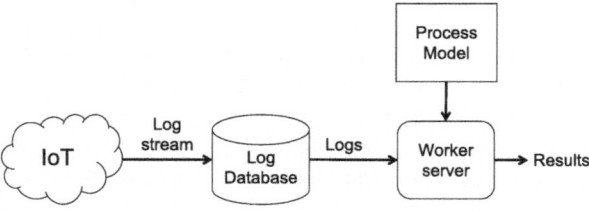

Fig. 1. Centralized compliance checking for offline log data from IoT

2   Related Work

In the realm of Internet of Things (IoT) process mining, a multitude of studies have paved the way for understanding and analyzing the complex data generated by IoT devices within business processes. This section reviews the related work that has been conducted in this field, highlighting the methodologies, applications, and contributions of each study. Stertz et al. in [3] present an approach where they focus on detecting and analyzing the root causes of concept drifts in business processes using sensor event streams. Their work leverages Dynamic Time Warping (DTW) to compare time sequences and identify deviations that may lead to concept drifts, providing a novel online algorithm for real-time analysis and process optimization. Mohammad et al. in [4] propose a multilayered framework for process mining in industrial IoT security that integrates process mining techniques within the context of industrial IoT. The framework aims to enhance security in industrial IoT environments by utilizing existing device or sensor logs to detect anomalies, respond to incidents, monitor compliance, and assess risks. Zisgen et al. introduce a tool in [10] that generates synthetic IoT sensor event logs. This tool allows users to model processes and configure them with parameters such as duration, frequency, and noise level. Gruger et al. propose an XES extension named "SensorStream" in [11]. This extension enables the integration of IoT sensor data with process events, providing a comprehensive context for data analysis. Malburg et al. in [12] introduce an IoT-enriched XES event log generated by a physical smart factory. The study aims to address the scarcity of real-world IoT-based event logs for research, offering a more realistic dataset for process mining in smart factory settings.

3   Problem Statement

Compliance checking ensures that the IoT system's operations comply with industry standards and legal requirements, and validates that the IoT processes are executed as intended without unauthorized deviations. It identifies and addresses potential risks or non-compliant behaviors that could lead to system failures or security breaches. Thus, compliance checking ensures that IoT systems operate efficiently and as intended, and demonstrates adherence to industry regulations and legal requirements. It proactively identifies and mitigates risks associated with non-compliant behavior, and also enhances the reliability and trustworthiness of IoT systems.

Figure 1 shows a typical centralized structure of compliance checking for offline log data from IoT. In the compliance checking for log data from IoT, the raw data generated by IoT devices, capturing the state changes, activities, and events over time. The predefined sequences of activities or rules that represent the correct or expected behavior of the IoT system. The specific criteria or conditions that the IoT system must meet to be considered compliant. The tools or algorithms used to analyze the event logs in real-time or near-real-time to detect compliance deviations.

The compliance checking for log data from IoT exists many challenges. IoT devices produce data at a high rate, making it challenging to process and analyze all events for compliance in real-time. IoT systems consist of various devices with different data formats and protocols, complicating the integration and analysis of event logs. IoT systems are subject to change due to device updates, environmental factors, or operational adjustments, which can affect compliance. Over time, the behavior of IoT systems may deviate from the initial process models, requiring updates to the compliance rules. Inaccurate or noisy data from sensors can lead to false compliance alerts or missed violations.

4 Solution

4.1 Process Model

Process discovery algorithms are pivotal in identifying an appropriate process model that encapsulates the sequence of events or activities within a process execution. Three typical algorithms are: (1) The Alpha Miner constructs a Petri net model characterized by visible and distinct transitions that correspond to categorized events, such as specific activities; (2) The Inductive Miner operates on the principle of identifying a 'cut' within the event log, which could be sequential, parallel, concurrent, or a loop; (3) The Heuristic Miner is an algorithm that functions on the Directly-Follows Graph, offering a method to manage noise and identify common structural elements, such as dependencies between activities or AND-joins.

4.2 Distributed Process Mining Framework

To enhance IoT compliance checking with log data streams, we propose a Distributed Process Mining Framework (DPMF) as shown in Fig. 2. In DPMF, a data storage module uses a database to store log data, benchmark process models, evaluation results, and other data. Databases such as MySQL can be selected for this purpose. A log collection module is responsible for acquiring anonymized operational log data from data sources as system input. Tools like Flume can be chosen for log collection. A log distribution module as master distributes log data to various working nodes of the data processing module throughout the system and saves new anonymized operational log data to the database. Tools like

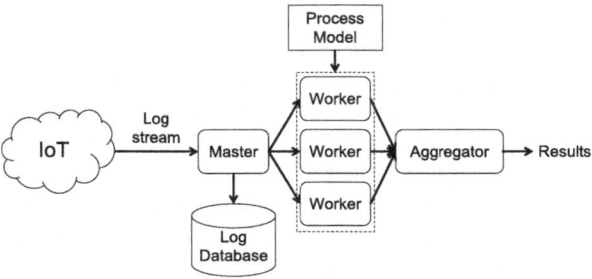

Fig. 2. Distributed process mining framework with IoT log data stream.

Kafka can be selected for log distribution. The data processing module at each worker operates the compliance evaluation algorithms and outputs the results. Frameworks such as Spark or Storm can be chosen for data processing.

The data processing module at each worker utilizes a distributed stream data processing framework (such as Spark Streaming, Storm) to handle data. It reads the new IoT log data from the master into memory and processes the data in memory at certain intervals, that is, to perform compliance checking. The compliance checking algorithms, including Token-based Replay [13], Alignments [14], Footprints [15], use a graph-based benchmark process model (such as Petri nets, knowledge graphs) to compare the IoT log data with the benchmark process model, achieving quantification and diagnosis of deviations. The input to the compliance checking algorithm is an event log, the basic unit of which is an event, representing a basic event unit. Multiple events form a trace, representing a single operation record. The basic idea of the compliance checking algorithm is to replay each trace from the log data on the Petri net graph of the benchmark process model to determine whether the operation record is compliant.

DPMF integrates three processing methods: (1) Offline Analysis Method: All input IoT log data are treated as a single collection and input into the compliance checking algorithm for evaluation against the benchmark process model. (2) Stream Data Processing Method: Events in the IoT log data arrive in the form of streaming data and are processed in real-time to assess compliance. (3) Distributed Computing Method: To improve processing efficiency, the IoT log data are distributed to multiple working nodes for computation and the results are aggregated.

Specially, the distributed computing method is as follows: During distributed processing, log data are partitioned according to partitioning rules based on key-value pairs. Whether it is offline analysis or stream data processing, it is essential to ensure that events within the same trace are partitioned into the same partition. If events of the same trace exist in different partitions, the trace will be considered different in each partition, which can affect the compliance checking results. Therefore, it is necessary to convert events in the log into key-value pairs according to their trace, and then perform partitioning operations. Compliance checking is conducted within each partition, yielding results for each partition, which are then aggregated. The compliance checking include: (1) the proportion of log records with non-compliant operational events (event) in the log data, represented by the fitness indicator; (2) identifying which log record operational events (event) are non-compliant.

Therefore, DPMF has the following four different computational modes for compliance checking of IoT log data: (1) Centralized Offline Computing Mode: The compliance checking system proposed adopts a single working node to process all IoT log data in a centralized manner, where the node caches all log data before performing compliance checks. (2) Centralized Stream Computing Mode: The system uses a single working node to process all IoT log data in a centralized manner, with incoming log data being directly processed in real-time as streaming data without the need for caching on the working node. (3) Distributed Offline Computing Mode: The system utilizes multiple working nodes to process IoT log data in a distributed manner, where each node caches the allocated log data before conducting compliance checks. (4) Distributed Stream Computing Mode: The system employs multiple working nodes to process IoT log data in a distributed manner, with incoming log data being directly processed in real-time as streaming data without the need for caching on the working nodes.

5   Experiment Results

5.1   Experiment Setup

5.1.1   Experiment Environment

The deployment environment for our experiment consists of the following software and hardware configurations: (1) Flume 1.7.0, used for efficient log collection and aggregation. (2) Kafka 2.11-0.10.1.0, serving as a distributed streaming platform for handling high volumes of data. (3) Spark (with Spark Streaming) 2.4.5, employed for processing large-scale data streams. (4) MySQL 8.0.32, utilized as the relational database management system. (5) Python 3.7.1, the programming language used for scripting and additional data processing tasks. (6) The operating system is Ubuntu 20.04, providing a stable and secure platform for the software stack.

The server is Dell PowerEdge R740, which contains 24 CPUs with Intel(R) Xeon(R) Silver 4214R CPU @ 2.40 GHz, and has 127.62 GB of RAM, providing ample memory for data-intensive tasks. The storage space is 7.15 TB, ensuring sufficient capacity for data storage and logging.

5.1.2   Dataset

The experimental dataset we used is a log generated by executing processes as described in [12], controlled in a process-based manner through Workflow Management Systems (WfMSs) on the production line. The event log is in XES format, containing a total of 16 workflows, where a single execution of a workflow corresponds to a trace in the log, which includes multiple events.

There are two versions of the log dataset, one is the original Data Quality Issues Event Log, and the other is Cleaned Event Log after preprocessing the original log dataset. In addition to basic preprocessing, errors in the data have

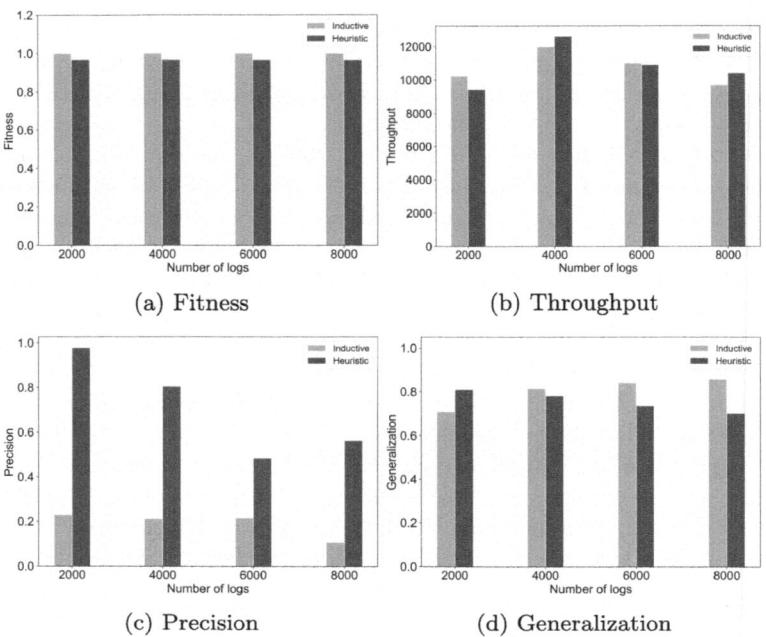

Fig. 3. Comparison with process discovery algorithms

also been corrected, including recovering missing events, deleting duplicate data, generating missing data, and correcting errors caused by time shifts, etc. When building the process model, use the corrected dataset, and when performing compliance checking, use the original dataset. The Cleaned Event Log has 301 traces, and 9,471 events. The Data Quality Issues Event Log contains 271 traces, and 8,607 events.

5.2   Process Discovery Algorithms

The compliance checking algorithm uses the Token-based replay algorithm, with the model construction dataset being Cleaned Event Log and the evaluation dataset being Data Quality Issues Event Log. We took the first n events from the dataset, recording the fitness values corresponding to the inductive and heuristic algorithms, with n taking four different values. We compared the compliance checking fitness of models generated by different process model generation algorithms, and the experimental results are shown in the Fig. 3a. Due to the limitations of the alpha algorithm, the fitness of the model constructed for compliance checking is 0, hence the alpha algorithm was not included in the results. The results show that the fitness of the models generated by both the inductive and heuristic algorithms is relatively high, with the inductive algorithm performing slightly better than the heuristic algorithm on this dataset. We compared the throughput, precision, and generalization during compliance checking of models generated by different process model generation algorithms, as shown in Figs. 3b,

3c, and 3d, respectively. From the results, it can be observed that on this dataset, as the number of events increases, the generalization of the model produced by the inductive algorithm gradually increases, while the generalization of the model produced by the heuristic algorithm gradually decreases.

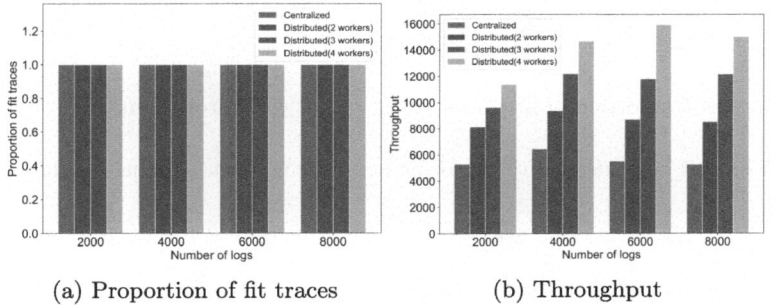

(a) Proportion of fit traces   (b) Throughput

Fig. 4. Comparison with conformance checking for offline log data

5.3   Offline and Streaming Log Data

The model generation algorithm uses the Inductive algorithm, and the compliance checking algorithm uses the Token-based replay algorithm. The dataset for model construction is Cleaned Event Log, and the evaluation dataset is Data Quality Issues Event Log. We took the first n events from the dataset, recording the proportion of compliant traces in offline scenarios for centralized, distributed (2 workers), distributed (3 workers), and distributed (4 workers) compliance checks, with n taking four different values. We compared the proportion of compliant traces when executing the compliance checking algorithm under centralized offline and distributed offline processing methods, as shown in the Fig. 4a. It can be observed that under the offline processing scenario, the compliance checking results obtained using different numbers of nodes in the distributed processing method are completely consistent with those of the centralized processing method, verifying the correctness of the distributed processing approach proposed in the paper. We compared the throughput when executing the compliance checking algorithm under centralized offline and distributed offline processing methods, as shown in the Fig. 4b. It can be observed that under the offline processing scenario, with the same number of log events, as the distributed algorithm is adopted and the number of distributed computing nodes increases, the system's throughput gradually rises.

The model generation algorithm uses the Inductive algorithm, and the compliance checking algorithm uses the Token-based replay algorithm. The dataset for model construction is Cleaned Event Log, and the evaluation dataset is Data Quality Issues Event Log. We took the first n events from the dataset, recording the proportion of compliant traces in the streaming data processing scenario for centralized, distributed (2 workers), distributed (3 workers), and distributed (4

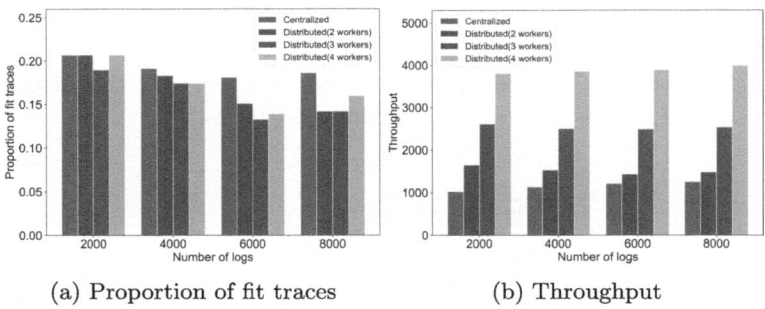

(a) Proportion of fit traces   (b) Throughput

Fig. 5. Comparison with conformance checking for streaming log data

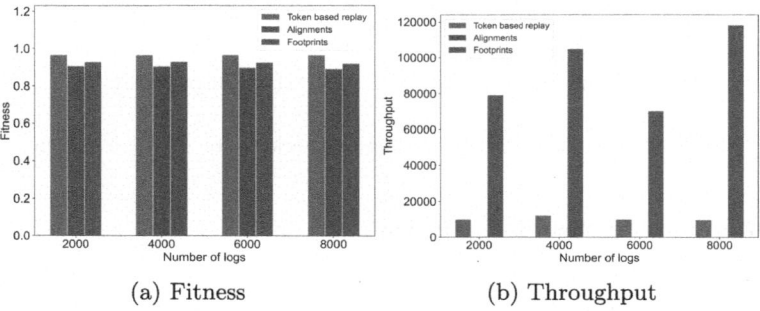

(a) Fitness   (b) Throughput

Fig. 6. Comparison with conformance checking algorithms

workers) compliance checks, with n taking four different values. We compared the proportion of compliant traces when executing the compliance checking algorithm under centralized streaming and distributed streaming processing methods, as shown in the Fig. 5a. From the results, it can be observed that in the streaming processing scenario, the proportion of compliant traces obtained by the model is relatively lower compared to the offline scenario, and not completely consistent, whether it is centralized or distributed processing. This may be due to the streaming data processing algorithm of PM4PY. We compared the throughput when executing the compliance checking algorithm under centralized streaming and distributed streaming processing methods, as shown in the Fig. 5b. From the results, it can be observed that in the streaming processing scenario, with the same number of log events, as the distributed algorithm is adopted and the number of distributed computing nodes increases, the system's throughput gradually rises.

5.4   Conformance Checking Algorithms

The model generation algorithm uses the Heuristic algorithm, with the model construction dataset being Cleaned Event Log and the evaluation dataset being Data Quality Issues Event Log. We take the first n events from the dataset, recording the fitness values corresponding to the token-based Replay algorithm, alignments algorithm, and footprints algorithm, with n taking four different values. We compared the fitness of compliance checks using different compliance checking algorithms, as shown in the Fig. 6a. From the results, it can be seen that on this dataset, with the same model generation algorithm, the compliance checking results obtained by the three different compliance checking algorithms are all relatively high, with the token-based Replay algorithm performing slightly better than the other two. We compared the throughput of compliance checks using different compliance checking algorithms, as shown in the Fig. 6b. The results indicate that among the three compliance checking algorithms, the footprints algorithm has the highest throughput during execution, while the alignments algorithm, due to its most complex execution process, has a significantly lower throughput compared to the other two algorithms (it's only a little over 100 and is not visible in the figure).

6 Conclusion

This paper has conducted a comprehensive evaluation of compliance checking within IoT environments by employing various process model generation and compliance checking algorithms. We introduce a novel distributed computing framework specifically designed to address these challenges by leveraging process mining techniques on IoT log data streams. The experiments were designed to assess not only the fitness and throughput of different algorithms but also their precision in a streaming context. The results indicate that while the token-based replay algorithm demonstrated a slightly superior performance in terms of fitness, the footprints algorithm outperformed others in throughput.

Acknowledgments. This work is supported by the National Key R&D Program of China under Grant 2021YFB3101303; the Sichuan Science and Technology Program No.2024NSFSC0492; the National Natural Science Foundation of China under Grant No. 82241060, 62020106013.

References

1. Kong, L., et al.: Edge-computing-driven internet of things: a survey. ACM Comput. Surv. **55**(8), 174–117441 (2023)
2. Seiger, R., Malburg, L., Weber, B., Bergmann, R.: Integrating process management and event processing in smart factories: a systems architecture and use cases. J. Manuf. Syst. **63**, 575–592 (2022). https://doi.org/10.1016/j.jmsy.2022.05.012
3. Stertz, F., Rinderle-Ma, S., Mangler, J.: Analyzing process concept drifts based on sensor event streams during runtime. In: Proceedings of 18th International Conference on Business Process Management (BPM) (2020)
4. Mohammad, N., Shaikh, E., Tariq, Z., McClean, S.: A multilayered framework for process mining in industrial iot security. In: IEEE Smart World Congress (SWC), pp. 764–769 (2023)

5. Montali, M., Plebani, P.: Iot-based compliance checking of multi-party business processes modeled with commitments. In: Proceedings of European Conference on Service-Oriented and Cloud Computing (2017). https://doi.org/10.1007/978-3-319-67262-5_14

6. Singh, P., et al.: Using log analytics and process mining to enable self-healing in the internet of things. Environ. Syst. Decis. **42**, 234–250 (2022). https://doi.org/10.1007/s10669-022-09859-x

7. Franceschetti, M., et al.: Proambition: online process conformance checking with ambiguities driven by the internet of things. In: Proceedings of the 35th International Conference on Advanced Information Systems Engineering (CAiSE 2023), vol. 3413, pp. 52-59 (2023). https://ceur-ws.org/Vol-3413/paper8.pdf

8. Meroni, G., Baresi, L., Montali, M., Plebani, P.: Multi-party business process compliance monitoring through iot-enabled artifacts. Inf. Syst. **73**, 61–78 (2018). https://doi.org/10.1016/j.is.2017.12.009

9. Seiger, R., Zerbato, F., Burattin, A., García-Bañuelos, L.,Weber, B.: Towards iot driven process event log generation for conformance checking in smart factories. In: 24th IEEE International Enterprise Distributed Object Computing Workshop, pp. 20–26 (2020)

10. Zisgen, Y., Janssen, D., Koschmider, A.: Generating synthetic sensor event logs for process mining. In: Proceedings of Intelligent Information Systems, vol. 452, pp. 130–137 (2022)

11. Grüger, J., et al.: Sensorstream: an XES extension for enriching event logs with iot-sensor data. CoRR arxiv:2206.11392 (2022)

12. Malburg, L., Grüger, J., Bergmann, R.: An iot-enriched event log for process mining in smart factories. CoRR arxiv:2209.02702 (2022). https://doi.org/10.48550/ARXIV.2209.02702

13. Rozinat, A., Aalst, W.M.P.: Conformance checking of processes based on monitoring real behavior. Inf. Syst. **33**(1), 64–95 (2008). https://doi.org/10.1016/j.is.2007.07.001

14. Adriansyah, A., Munoz-Gama, J., Carmona, J., Dongen, B.F., Aalst, W.M.P.: Alignment based precision checking. In: Business Process Management Workshops (BPM), vol. 132, pp. 137–149 (2012)

15. Aalst, W.M.P.: Process Mining - Discovery, Conformance and Enhancement of Business Processes (2011). https://doi.org/10.1007/978-3-642-19345-3

Internet of Things Security and Privacy Protection

EMLogger: Inferring Computer Activities via EM Side-Channel of Disks

Wenfan Song[1], Jianwei Liu[1,2], and Jinsong Han[1(✉)]

[1] Zhejiang University, Hangzhou, China
{wenfansong,jianweiliu,hanjinsong}@zju.edu.cn
[2] Hangzhou City University, Hangzhou, China

Abstract. In computer systems, the built-in disk is essential for data storage as computers typically need to read and write data from the disk during operations. Some existing works have utilized the read/write characteristics of disks to infer sensitive information, such as browsing websites. However, previous research primarily focuses on hard disk drives (HDDs). With solid state drives (SSDs) gradually becoming the mainstream option for computer disks, these approaches have shown limitations. In this paper, we reveal a novel side-channel vulnerability targeting both HDDs and SSDs, named EMLogger. Specifically, we find that attackers can exploit the electromagnetic (EM) radiation leaked by the disk to detect ongoing activities on the computer. To enhance the strength of EM signals, we propose a sub-signal fusion method. Besides, we employ machine learning techniques for feature extraction and activity classification from the enhanced EM signals. Finally, we conduct real-world experiments on computers equipped with HDDs or SSDs. Our experimental results demonstrate that EMLogger achieves an accuracy of over 98% in inferring computer activities. Furthermore, the experiments validate the robustness of EMLogger at varying attack distances.

Keywords: Electromagnetic Emanation · Side-channel Attack · Disk

1 Introduction

The built-in disks, including hard disk drives (HDDs) and solid state drives (SSDs), are essential in computer systems for storing operating systems, applications, and user data. However, recent studies [1,2] have demonstrated that disks can be exploited as an attack vector to steal sensitive information from the host, such as the websites being accessed. This is due to the dependency of computer activities, like browsing websites and watching videos, on the data read and write operations performed by the disk. Specifically, these studies have focused on leveraging the physical movements of the read/write head in HDDs to infer ongoing activities on the host [1,2]. The read/write head's position and movements over the disk's platters can reveal the computer activities. However, these approaches [1,2] have a limitation: they are only applicable to HDDs,

L. Sun and Y. Chen (Eds.): CWSN 2024, CCIS 2341, pp. 143–154, 2025.
https://doi.org/10.1007/978-981-96-2186-6_12

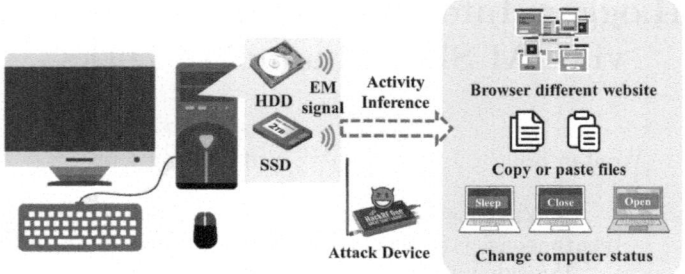

Fig. 1. EMLogger can capture EM signals leaked from the computer's disk through an attack device to infer computer activities, thereby endangering the user privacy.

whereas a majority of computers now use SSDs [3]. This is because SSDs are based on flash storage technology, and do not rely on the mechanical movement of magnetic heads and rotating platters like HDDs.

In this paper, we introduce a novel physical side-channel vulnerability, namely EMLogger, targeting both HDDs and SSDs to infer computer activities. Specifically, we find that the EM signals leaked by the common components in both HDDs and SSDs, i.e., the clock modules and DRAM modules, can reveal fine-grained information about the computer's ongoing activities. As shown in Fig 1, an attacker can hide the attack device under a table, When the victim operates the computer on this table, the attack device can capture the EM signals emitted by the disk inside the computer. The attacker can then infer the host activities based on these EM signals. This poses a serious threat to the victim's privacy. For instance, an attacker could determine which websites the victim is browsing. The leakage of website information provides attackers with at least two key insights. First, attackers can target precise advertisements based on the victim's preferences. Second, attackers can infer sensitive information about the victim, such as their interests and health status.

To implement EMlogger, we address two challenges. **(1) How to capture high-quality EM signals in a noisy environment?** On one hand, electromagnetic compatibility (EMC) standards impose strict limits on the intensity of the EM emanation emitted by the disk [4]. On the other hand, other electronic devices in the ambient environment also emit EM signals, which may interfere with the EM signal of the disk. These factors result in a low signal-to-noise ratio (SNR) for the captured EM signals from the disk. To tackle this challenge, we adopt a sub-signal fusion technique. Particularly, the EM radiation from the disk consists of a series of sub-clock signals. The amplitude of these sub-clocks varies consistently over time, and the frequency intervals between these sub-clocks are uniform. Based on these consistencies, we aggregate the sub-clock signals in the frequency domain to enhance the leaked EM signals from the disk. **(2) How to extract representative features from the EM signals emitted by the disk to infer computer activities?** We first theoretically analyze and model the EM signals leaked by the disk to explore characteristics related to computer activities. Then, we use machine learning to further learn and classify these features to accurately infer computer activities. To validate the threat posed by EMLogger, we also conduct real-world attack experiments on computers equipped with HDDs and SSDs. The experimental results indicate that the accuracy of inferring computer activities can reach over 98%. Additionally, we confirm the robustness of EMLogger at different attack distances: within a range of 15 cm, the accuracy remains above 83%. In summary, our contributions are as follows:

- We explore a new electromagnetic side-channel attack targeting both HDDs and SSDs, namely EMLogger. Our theoretical model demonstrates that activities on a computer can be covertly monitored through the EM side channel.
- We propose a sub-signal fusion method to enhance the SNR of the EM signals leaked by the disk. Besides, we also adopt machine learning techniques to extract activity-related features.
- We conduct real-world experiments on computers equipped with HDDs and SSDs. The experimental results show that EMLogger can achieve an accuracy of over 98% in inferring computer activities, which demonstrates the potential privacy threats posed by EMLogger.

2 Related Work

EM emanations leaked by computing devices have been widely leveraged for various side-channel attacks, such as theft of encryption keys [5,6] and interference with private information [1,7–9]. These emanations are primarily generated by the high-speed switching circuits [9] and clock modules [5–7] within the devices, which makes them valuable for constructing covert channels for data leakage. The essence of using EM signals for side-channel attacks is that different activities inside the device emit EM signals with distinct characteristics. For example, Alam et al. [5] and Genkin et al. [6] successfully recover the full RSA key and ECDSA secret signing keys via EM emanations, respectively. The work in [7] infers website fingerprinting and keystroke timing vulnerabilities in GPUs using EM side-channel analysis. Moreover, Enev et al. [9] use in-display fingerprint sensors to extract fingerprint information for deceiving and unlocking smartphones. The work in [8] utilizes EM emanations from in-display fingerprint sensors to extract fingerprint information for deceiving and unlocking smartphones. Biedermann et al. [1] exploit the EM emanations from HDD heads for attacks. Similar to this work, we use EM signals leaked from the disk to infer the computer activities. Despite the similarities, our approach diverges fundamentally and demonstrates superior efficacy. Firstly, our attack has a broader scope, encompassing both HDDs and SSDs, whereas work [1] is limited to HDDs. This difference arises from our utilization of EM signals emitted by common components of HDDs and SSDs (i.e., clock module and DRAM module) to achieve attacks, while the work [1] relies on the unique EM signals emitted by HDD

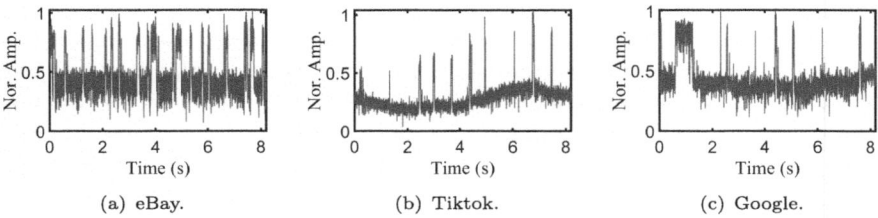

(a) eBay.   (b) Tiktok.   (c) Google.

Fig. 2. EM signals leaked from the disk when browsing different websites. Nor. Amp means normalized amplitude.

magnetic heads. Secondly, the attack distance of our method is longer (15 cm) compared to that of [1] (3 cm). This is because we have investigated techniques to amplify the EM signals of interest, enabling effective EM signals capture at larger distances. Finally, the accuracy of our approach far exceeds that of [1] (i.e., 98% >> 75%), attributed to our use of deep neural networks (DNN) to effectively extract fine-grained features from EM signals, which leads to efficient classification.

3   Threat Model

The goal of EMLogger is to eavesdrop on the EM signals emitted by the disk inside the victim computer and then extract sensitive information, such as the websites the victim is browsing. In real-world scenarios, we assume the victim places his/her computer (e.g., a laptop) on a table in a public place (e.g., a cafe or meeting room). The attacker pre-hides the attack device (i.e., a software-defined radio (SDR) like a HackRF) near the victim computer (such as under the table). In this case, the attacker can remotely monitor the EM leakage from the disk inside the victim computer. Since the activities of the computer rely on the disk, the EM emanations from the disk can be utilized to infer the computer's activities. Subsequently, the attacker can obtain the user's sensitive information, such as hobbies, and behavioral habits. Furthermore, we assume that attackers can determine the computer model by observing its appearance, and then further search online for the model of the disk inside the computer. Subsequently, the attacker can acquire an identical model of the computer from the market for further study. It is worth noting that the victim computer is not assumed to have any malicious software or physical tampering.

4   Privacy Leakage Exploration

To investigate the feasibility of EMLogger attack, we first develop a theoretical model for the EM emanations of hard drives and the associated privacy leakage process. Subsequently, we conduct a series of experiments to demonstrate the viability of such EM side-channel attacks.

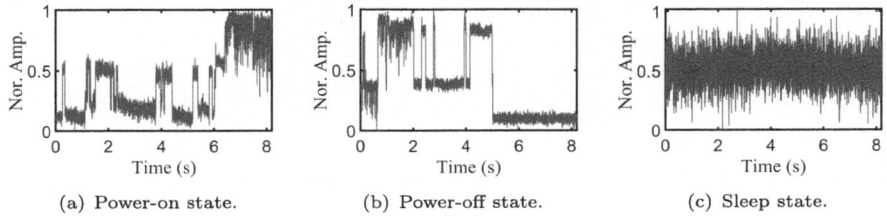

(a) Power-on state.   (b) Power-off state.   (c) Sleep state.

Fig. 3. EM signals leaked from the disk when the computer is in different power states. Nor. Amp means normalized amplitude.

4.1   Side-Channel Modeling

Different activities performed on a computer exert various loads on its inside disk, which depends on the frequency and volume of disk reads and writes. The fluctuation in disk load induces changes in the EM signals emitted by the disk. Consequently, by eavesdropping on these EM signals, we can infer the computer's activities.

The EM emanations of the disk mainly originate from two modules: the clock module and the DRAM module. The clock module is responsible for coordinating the timing sequence of read and write operations and controlling the data transfer rate. Meanwhile, the DRAM module is used for temporary storage and quick access to data and instructions being processed. For the clock module, we can observe that its EM signals $m_{clk}(t)$ consist of a series of sub-clocks, usually distributed on the side-band below the clock frequency f_0, which can be expressed as:

$$m_{clk}(t) = \{m_{clk}[1,t], m_{clk}[2,t], ..., m_{clk}[N,t]\}. \tag{1}$$

Specifically, the n-th sub-clock can be expressed as:

$$m_{clk}[n,t] = A_{clk}(n)\sin(2\pi f_{clk,n}t), n \in [1,N] \tag{2}$$

where $A_{clk}(n)$ and $f_{clk,n} = f_0 - nf_m, 1 \leq n \leq N$ are the amplitude and frequency of the n-th sub-clock, respectively. f_m represents the frequency interval between adjacent sub-clocks, and N represents the total number of sub-clocks. When the computer conducts activities (e.g., browsing websites), it performs a series of reading and writing operations on the DRAM module of the disk. This leads to the emission of EM signals by the disk (denoted as $m_{dram}(t)$), which are then amplitude-modulated onto the clock's electromagnetic signal ($m_{clk}(t)$). It is worth noting that although $m_{dram}(t)$ alters the amplitude of $m_{clk}(t)$, it does not affect the spectral pattern of the clock. Considering the effect of host activity on the load of the DRAM (denoted as $\alpha(t)$), the EM signal of the DRAM module can be further expressed as $m_{dram}\{\alpha(t)\}$. In this case, the EM emanation leaked by the disk (denoted as $m_{disk}(t)$) can be expressed as:

$$m_{disk}(t) = m_{dram}\{\alpha(t)\} * \{m_{clk}[1,t], m_{clk}[2,t], ..., m_{clk}[N,t]\}. \tag{3}$$

In this formula, we can observe that the intensity of the sub-clock's electromagnetic radiation varies in proportion to the load of the (i.e., $\alpha(t)$). Due to the strong correlation between $\alpha(t)$ and host activities, different activities introduce different DRAM loads. Therefore, by analyzing the EM signals leaked by the disk, an attacker can infer the host activities, such as browsing different websites.

4.2 Preliminary Experiment Validation

In this work, we focus on three kinds of activities that could leak user privacy, namely (1) browsing different websites, (2) the power state of the computer, and (3) writing to/reading from files to the disk. To explore the potential for identifying these activities via EM signals, we conduct a series of preliminary experiments. Specifically, we use a software-defined radio (HackRF SDR), a Foresight low-noise amplifier, and a 3dBi antenna to collect the EM signals emitted by the internal disk of a Lenovo Xiaoxin Pro 14 laptop while performing different activities. Since the amplitude variation of sub-clocks over time is similar (determined by the DRAM load $\alpha(t)$), we only capture one sub-clock signal to explore inferring computer activities using EM signals.

■ **Websites.** In this experiment, we browse eBay, Tiktok, and Google respectively, and record the corresponding EM emanations. Figure 2 shows the normalized EM signals while the computer performs various activities. We can observe that there are noticeable differences in the EM signals corresponding to these three websites. This is because each website caches different content to the disk, leading to variations in the disk load. Therefore, the EM signals corresponding to different websites exhibit distinct characteristics. Consequently, attackers can exploit these EM signals to infer the websites that users are browsing.

■ **Power state.** Similar to the website inference experiment, we set the computer to power-on, power-off, and sleep states separately and record the corresponding EM signals leaked from the disk. Figure 3 shows significant differences in the EM signals corresponding to these three computer power states. This is because the load of the disk varies depending on the power state. In sleep mode, the disk is in a low-power state. When powered on, the disk transitions from a powered-off state to an active state, and vice versa when powered off. Therefore, attackers can utilize EM signals to detect the computer's power state.

■ **Write/read files to/from the computer.** In this experiment, we write/read files to/from the computer and record the corresponding EM signals. As shown in Fig 4, we can observe significant differences in the EM signals corresponding to these two types of computer activities. The reason is that these two types of activities involve various hardware operations and data transfer processes, resulting in differences in the load of the disk. Therefore, attackers can exploit EM signals to detect the read/write activities of the computer.

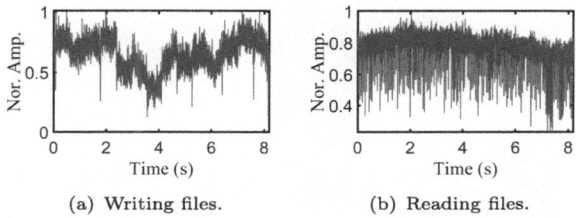

(a) Writing files.   (b) Reading files.

Fig. 4. EM signals leaked from the disk when writing/reading files to/from the disk.

5   Methodology

With the captured EM signals, an attacker can infer the activities being performed by a computer. To achieve this goal, we first employ sub-clock fusion to enhance the signal-to-noise ratio (SNR) of the EM signals. After that, we induce a DNN-based approach to accurately infer computer activities.

5.1   Sub-clock Fusion

As mentioned in Sect. 4.1, the amplitudes of the sub-clock signals can reflect the variation in disk load (i.e., $\alpha(t)$), which depends on the activities being executed by the computer. Nevertheless, unlike the clock signals which are distributed at a single frequency, the EM emanations from the disk clock module are spread across a range of frequencies. This dispersion significantly reduces the signal-to-noise ratio (SNR) of the clock EM signal [10]. Additionally, electromagnetic noise from surrounding devices further decreases the SNR of the disk EM signals. To address the challenge of low SNR, we adopt the sub-clock fusion technique [7] to amplify the EM signal of the disk.

The core idea of sub-clock fusion is that (1) the amplitude variations of different sub-clocks are consistent over time, and (2) the frequency intervals between adjacent sub-clocks are uniform. This consistency allows us to effectively enhance the SNR of the clock module's EM signals by summing these sub-clock signals. Specifically, assume that the EM signal of the clock module (i.e., m_{clk}) comprises N sub-clocks, where $m_{clk}[i, t](i \in [1, N])$ represents the i-th sub-clock signal. We can obtain the spectrum of these N sub-clock signals through the short-time Fourier transform. Subsequently, we sum these N sub-clocks and obtain the fused clock signal (denoted as $m_{fused}(t)$) ,which can be expressed as:

$$m_{fused}(t) = \sum_{n=1}^{N} A_{clk}(n) \sin(2\pi f_{clk,n} t). \tag{4}$$

We can observe that the amplitude of the fused clock signal (i.e., $|m_{fused}(t)|$) is significantly enhanced compared to that of the i-th sub-clock ($|A_{clk}(i) \sin(2\pi f_{clk,i} t)|$). In this case, the amplified EM signal of the disk can

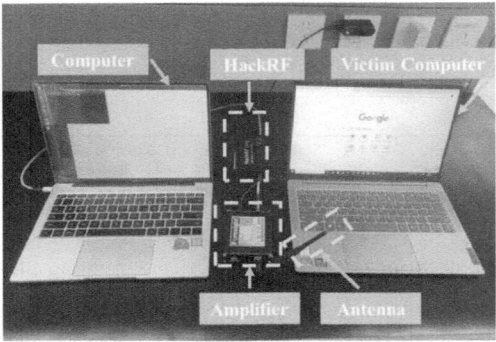

Fig. 5. EMLogger setup.

be expressed as $m'_{disk} = m_{fused}(t) * m_{dram}\{\alpha(t)\}$. In the following, we will utilize a DNN-based approach to extract features of the disk load (*i.e.*, $\alpha(t)$) from the amplitude trace of m'_{disk}, thereby accurately inferring the activities of the computer.

5.2   Activity Inference

Given the excellent feature extraction capabilities of DNN [11], we attempt to design a DNN-based learning model to mine the 'deep-hidden' features of the disk load from the amplitude trace of m'_{disk}.

As the amplitude traces are time-series data and one-dimensional convolution kernels are efficient in feature extraction, we opt for one-dimensional convolutional layers as the primary components of the DNN. To extract deep-level disk load features for inferring computer activities, we employ three convolutional layers. Each convolutional kernel involves tuning three parameters: channel number, kernel size, and stride. The channel number critically influences the model's representational capacity: too few channels risk information loss, whereas an excessive number may escalate computational demands. Similarly, the kernel size dictates the granularity in feature extraction; too diminutive a kernel might overlook crucial features, while a large one could yield overly generalized features. The stride parameter governs the size of output feature maps, with an excessively small stride risking information loss and a too-large one imposing higher computational costs and memory usage. Based on our experiments, we set the kernel size to $16 * 1$ and the stride to $8 * 1$. The channel numbers of the three convolutional layers are set to 16, 32, and 64, respectively. Additionally, each convolutional layer is followed by a batch normalization (BN) function [12] and a rectified linear unit (ReLU) [13], which help enhance the network's generalization ability and improve its expressive power. Subsequently, we add two fully connected layers after the third convolutional layer to map the features into a probability space. To enhance the DNN's nonlinearity, we also add a sigmoid function after the fully connected layers. Then, we employ the cross-entropy loss function to measure the difference between the probability distribution output by the model and the actual labels, which continuously optimizes the trained DNN model. The cross-entropy loss function can be expressed as:

$$Loss = \frac{1}{N} \sum_{i=1}^{N} q_i log(p_i),$$ (5)

where N represents the number of the activity categories. q_i represents the probability distribution of the true activity category labels. p_i represents the probability distribution of the activity categories predicted by the model. Based on computational loss, we utilize the Adam optimizer to iteratively update the parameters in the DNN until the loss converges or reaches a predefined stopping condition.

6 Evaluation

In this section, we first introduce the real-world experiment setup and then detail the performance of EMLogger attacks.

■ **Experiment Setup.** We build the prototype of EMLogger based on a software-defined radio (HackRF SDR), a Foresight low-noise amplifier, and a 3dBi omnidirectional antenna. As shown in Fig 5, we place the antenna above the internal disk of the compromised disk to capture its leaked EM signals. These received signals are then amplified by the amplifier before being transmitted to the HackRF. Following this, we employ a Huawei KLV-W19L PC equipped with an Intel(R) Core(TM) i5-8265U CPU to further process the EM signals received from the HackRF.

■ **Data Collection.** To evaluate the robustness of EMLogger across various environments,we conduct experiments in three environments: a cafe, an office, and a meeting room. In each environment, we test the performance of EMLogger using two types of internal disks within the host: the HDD (model WD10EZEX) within the computer (model Dell OptiPlex 7060) and the SSD (model UMIS AM6A1) within the computer (model Lenovo Xiaoxin 14pro). For each disk, we capture its EM signals when the computer is executing 10 common activities. These ten activities are divided into three major categories: (1) web browsing, including eBay, Tiktok, BiliBili, Spotify, and Google; (2) computer power status: including power-on, power-off, and sleep states; (3) file transfer: copying or moving files to the disk. EM signals are sampled at a rate of 20 MHz with a bandwidth of 10 MHz. We collect over 4000 EM signals, with each EM signal corresponding to one activity the computer performed. Each EM signal comprises 5000 samples within a 4.1-second duration.

■ **Metric.** We define accuracy for computer activity class determination. The accuracy is the probability that an activity class of an EM signal sample is correctly identified.

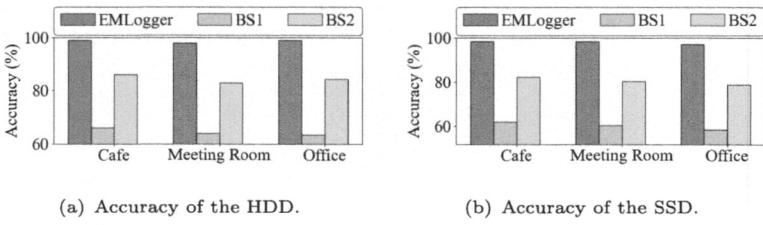

(a) Accuracy of the HDD.   (b) Accuracy of the SSD.

Fig. 6. Activity classification accuracy of HDD and SSD under different environments.

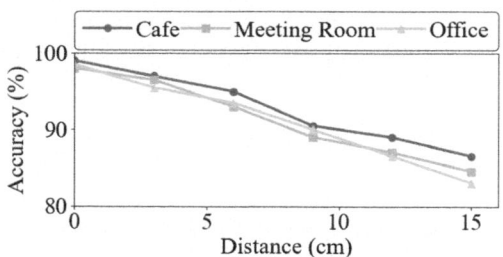

Fig. 7. The impact of attack distance on EMLogger.

6.1 Overall Effectiveness

We first evaluate the overall performance of EMLogger in three different environments. Particularly, we use 50% signal samples for DNN model training and the rest 50% for testing. To show the superiority of our sub-clock fusion method and the DNN method, we compare EMLogger with two baselines. Baseline (BS1): we directly use DNN to classify the raw EM signals without signal enhancement. Baseline (BS2): we use the support vector classifier (SVM) to classify the enhanced EM signal. Figure 6 shows the results of accuracy of inferring activities from EM signals leaked by the HDD and SSD under three different environments. We can observe that the average accuracy of EMLogger exceeds 98%, while the averages of these two baselines are 62.4% and 82.6%, respectively. The high accuracy of EMLogger demonstrates the outstanding classification performance in different environments. These comparisons with two baselines indicate that sub-clock fusion and DNN classification can effectively enhance the EM signals and extract features.

6.2 Impact of Attack Distance

We use the disk inside the computer Lenovo Xiaoxin 14pro to evaluate the impact of distance between the attack device and the disk in three different environments. Particularly, the attack device is placed under the computer. We set the attack distance range from 0 cm to 15 cm in a step of 3 cm. The training set is collected at 0 cm, and we calculate the classification accuracy of activities at other attack distances. As shown in Fig 7, EMLogger achieves the highest accuracy when both the test set and training set are collected at the same position (i.e., 0 cm). As the attack distance increases, the accuracy decreases slightly. However, within the attack distance range of 15 cm, EMLogger can still guarantee a high accuracy (within 83%). These results demonstrate that the features extracted by EMLogger from EM signals are robust to distance variations.

7 Conclusion

In this paper, we propose a new EM side-channel attack targeting the disks inside the computers, namely EMLogger. We first build a theoretical model to show that the computer activities can be inferred by the EM signals leaked from the disks. To improve the SNR of EM signals, we propose the sub-clock fusion method. Then ,we design a DNN model to extract features from the EM signals and then achieve activity classification. Our real-world experiments show that EMLogger can effectively infer the computer activities from the EM signals and is robust to varying attack distances.

Acknowledgements. This paper is supported by the National Natural Science Foundation of China under grant U21A20462 and 62372400, "Pioneer" and "Leading Goose" R&D Program of Zhejiang under grant No. 2023C01033, and the Postdoctoral Fellowship Program of CPSF under Grant Number GZC20241488.

References

1. Biedermann, S., Katzenbeisser, S., Szefer, J.: Hard drive side-channel attacks using smartphone magnetic field sensors. In: Böhme, R., Okamoto, T. (eds.) FC 2015. LNCS, vol. 8975, pp. 489–496. Springer, Heidelberg (2015). https://doi.org/10.1007/978-3-662-47854-7_30
2. Gold, B.D., Linde, R.R., Cudney, P.F.: Kvm/370 in retrospect. In: 1984 IEEE Symposium on Security and Privacy, pp. 13–13 (1984). https://doi.org/10.1109/SP.1984.10002
3. Quicke, S.: SSD becoming the norm in laptops (2020). https://www.computerweekly.com/microscope/news/252478552/SSD-becomingthe-norm-in-laptops
4. Morgan, D.: A Handbook for EMC Testing and Measurement, vol. 8. Iet (1994)
5. Alam, M., et al.: One&Done: a single-decryption em-based attack on OpenSSL's constant-time blinded RSA. In: 27th USENIX Security Symposium (USENIX Security 18), pp. 585–602 (2018)
6. Genkin, D., Pachmanov, L., Pipman, I., Tromer, E., Yarom, Y.: Ecdsa key extraction from mobile devices via nonintrusive physical side channels. In: Proceedings of the 2016 ACM SIGSAC Conference on Computer and Communications Security, pp. 1626–1638 (2016)
7. Zhan, Z., Zhang, Z., Liang, S., Yao, F., Koutsoukos, X.: Graphics peeping unit: exploiting em side-channel information of gpus to eavesdrop on your neighbors. In: 2022 IEEE Symposium on Security and Privacy (SP), pp. 1440–1457. IEEE (2022)

8. Ni, T., Zhang, X., Zhao, Q.: Recovering fingerprints from in-display fingerprint sensors via electromagnetic side channel. In: Proceedings of the 2023 ACM SIGSAC Conference on Computer and Communications Security, pp. 253–267 (2023)
9. Enev, M., Gupta, S., Kohno, T., Patel, S.N.: Televisions, video privacy, and powerline electromagnetic interference. In: Proceedings of the 18th ACM Conference on Computer and Communications Security, pp. 537–550 (2011)
10. Chen, H.-W., Wu, J.-C.: A spread spectrum clock generator for emi reduction. IEICE Trans. Electron. 84(12), 1959–1966 (2001)
11. Krizhevsky, A., Sutskever, I., Hinton, G.E.: Imagenet classification with deep convolutional neural networks. Commun. ACM **60**(6), 84–90 (2017)
12. Bjorck, N., Gomes, C.P., Selman, B., Weinberger, K.Q.: Understanding batch normalization. Adv. Neural Inf. Process. Syst. **31** (2018)
13. Hara, K., Saito, D., Shouno, H.: Analysis of function of rectified linear unit used in deep learning. In: 2015 International Joint Conference on Neural Networks (IJCNN), pp. 1–8 (2015). IEEE

A Lightweight Authentication Protocol for LAFED

Yuzhao Liu[✉]

Department of Computer Science, University of Liverpool, Liverpool, UK
sgyliu96@liverpool.ac.uk

Abstract. Federated learning is an innovative distributed machine learning method that allows for the construction of effective and secure shared models through cooperative learning of data between devices while ensuring data privacy protection. However, current federated learning methods often require uploading some key parameters to a centralized server for model merging, a process that may lead to the risk of privacy leakage. Recently, blockchain technology provides new solutions for the security of federated learning. This paper introduces a lightweight authentication scheme in a blockchain-based federated learning system. Through extensive experimental verification, our method can increase the system performance when the computing capabilities of central nodes and local nodes are unbalanced.

Keywords: Federated learning · Blockchain · Lightweight authentication

1 Introduction

Previously, AI was largely confined to executing straightforward, pre-programmed tasks, with more intricate operations still necessitating direct human intervention. Nonetheless, strides made in deep learning technology have propelled AI into assuming responsibilities that were once exclusively within human purview, augmenting and, in some cases, supplanting human roles across various sectors [1,2].

At the core of Artificial Intelligence, machine learning has garnered significant interest for its efficacy, while simultaneously sparking privacy debates. Conventionally, the process entailed amassing substantial user data in centralized systems, thereby posing privacy risks, as this data frequently encompasses delicate personal information such as health records or political affiliations [3].

In addressing privacy concerns, McMahan and colleagues introduced federated learning, a novel technique that facilitates the training of a universal model through local computations without the need to exchange individual data, as outlined in their work [4]. This strategy proves especially advantageous for smart city applications, significantly reinforcing privacy safeguards in sectors such as healthcare and mobile communications networks [5,6].

L. Sun and Y. Chen (Eds.): CWSN 2024, CCIS 2341, pp. 155–167, 2025.
https://doi.org/10.1007/978-981-96-2186-6_13

However, federated learning encounters security challenges encompassing confidentiality, accessibility, and integrity breaches, which stem from weaknesses in public channel data exchanges [7–9]. To tackle these issues, node authentication protocols play a vital role in protecting data privacy by verifying identities securely throughout communication [10].

Thus, this paper propose a lightweight authentication mechanism for the blockchain-integrated federated learning systems LAFED presented in [6]. The key contributions of this paper can be encapsulated as follows: (1) A novel lightweight authentication protocol is designed for blockchain-facilitated federated learning. (2) The security of UECDH is formally analyzed. The analysis outcomes demonstrate that UECDH accomplishes the security objectives.

The rest of this paper is introduced as follows. The related work is shown in Sect. 2. Section 3 is preliminary. Section 4 discusses the proposed protocol. Section 5 is the security analysis. Section 6 reports the performance evaluation results. Section 7 is the conclusion of this paper.

2   Related Work

2.1   Federated Learning Based on Blockchain

Recently, scholars have integrated blockchain technology with federated learning to enhance security and privacy. Traditional federated learning, which centralizes model updates, faces challenges when the central server fails or is compromised. To address this, FLChain [11] employs blockchain to create an immutable record of local model parameter updates. Specifically, it introduces a blockchain peer-to-peer network-based federated learning architecture where the global model is stored in the blockchain using a Merkle Patricia Tree (MPT) structure. FL Block [12] is another blockchain-based federated learning approach that employs a distributed hash table to ensure efficient block generation. It utilizes the Proof of Work (PoW) consensus mechanism to maintain consistency across the global model. Kim et al. [13] introduced blockchain into federated learning to address the single-point failure issue and analyzed the optimal block generation rate, although their work did not fully consider the privacy protection of intermediate parameters.

Awan et al. [14] proposed a blockchain-based privacy protection framework that eliminates the semi-honest assumption of participants, leveraging encryption techniques to safeguard data privacy. However, the risk of a single-point failure in the parameter server remains. BAFFLE [15] mitigates this by utilizing decentralized smart contracts to manage model aggregation and parameter updates in federated learning. It also enhances computational performance through scoring and bidding strategies by dividing the global parameter space into multiple blocks. Zhao et al. [16] proposed a reputation-based federated learning system for mobile edge computing, incorporating differential privacy to protect sensitive information. This system aims to enhance the security and privacy of federated learning by rewarding high-quality contributions and penalizing poor or malicious ones.

The integration of blockchain with federated learning presents a promising direction for addressing the challenges of centralization, single-point failure risks, and privacy concerns inherent in traditional federated learning setups.

2.2   Diffie-Hellman Protocol

In the realm of federated learning, the Diffie-Hellman protocol is particularly noteworthy for its role in enhancing communication security. It is a building block of Secure Sockets Layer (SSL), which is widely used in this area. Various studies, such as those by Ma et al. [17,18], and [19], have demonstrated the enhancement of data transmission security among participants through the incorporation of the Diffie-Hellman protocol. The application of the Diffie-Hellman protocol is especially significant in the context of federated learning within the Internet of Things (IoT) environment. It substantially improves the security of data transmission between IoT devices and effectively mitigates security threats, such as man-in-the-middle attacks. This protocol offers a secure platform for data exchange [?] when IoT devices engage in local model training and contribute to global model updates.

3   Priliminary

In this section, we present the system model and security model.

3.1   The Framework of LAFED

In this section, we elaborate on the framework for LAFED, as detailed in [6] and illustrated in Fig. 1.

The process commences with each participant acquiring a unique user ID and training their model locally. Subsequently, the trained models are uploaded to the system, and consensus information is retrieved. The selection of consensus committee members is predicated on their contributions and the outcomes of the consensus process. Ultimately, the members of the consensus committee verify the identities of participants who have uploaded models, utilizing zero-knowledge proofs to maintain anonymity. The schematic representation of the framework is provided in Fig. 1.

To elaborate, prior to engaging in the federated learning task, all participants are required to register and obtain a user ID. Concurrently, their registration details are recorded in the blockchain for user authentication purposes. Thereafter, the management node, typically a trusted server, initiates the global model and disseminates it among all participants. Participants then proceed to train the model using their respective local datasets.

This approach ensures a robust and secure framework for federated learning, where the integrity of the process is maintained through the use of blockchain technology and zero-knowledge proofs, thereby fostering trust and privacy among participants.

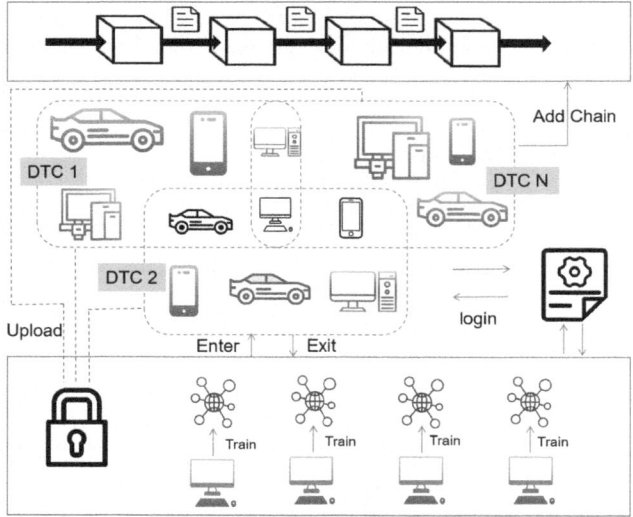

Fig. 1. The architecture of LAFED.

3.2 Security Model

For our authentication protocol, we consider *key indistinguishability with partial forward security* IND-pFS with passive attacker. We define the security from a security game (or mental experiment) between a challenger and a adversary. We formalize security against the polynomial probabilistic-time (PPT) adversaries. Informally, the challenger maintains the environment and sets the system parameters of AKE. The behavior of attacking from the adversary is modelled by the query to oracles hold by the challenger. The boolean value outputted by the game indicates the adversary breaks IND-pFS-security or not. The game is given in Fig. 2 by code-based playing [?].

Suppose there are at most μ parties and each party may involve in at most n_s sessions in our setting. π_i^s is the formalized oracle indicating that party i in session s. The security of key indistinguishability is captured by the TEST query, which will return a random or real key to the adversary $\mathcal{A}$, if the adversary's guess is correct we say it wins the security game. I.e., the adversary is able to distinguish the real key from the random one. Note line 3 in TEST query, the initiator cannot be corrupted but that is not the case for the responder, since we are modeling partial forward security. Therefore, we have

$$\mathsf{Adv}^{\mathsf{ind\text{-}pfs}}_{\mathcal{A},\mathsf{KE}}(n) \leq \Pr[b = b'].$$

Adversary may eavesdrop the communication, corrupt a party to get its secret key, or reveal the session key directly. The eavesdropping is formalized as EXECUTE query, which returns the messages generated by KE. We note that the internal randomness is implicit since we do not take the ephemeral secret leakage, and we use randomly sampled messages and key to represent the procedure.

GAME IND-pFS

---

1 : $b \leftarrow_\$ \{0, 1\}$

2 : **for** $i \in [\mu]$:

3 : $(\mathsf{pk}_i, \mathsf{sk}_i) \leftarrow_\$ \mathsf{KGen}(1^n); \mathsf{Sid} := 0$

4 : $\mathsf{RevList} := \mathsf{CorrList} := \emptyset$

5 : $\mathsf{SKeyList}[\cdot] := \perp$

6 : $b' \leftarrow_\$ \mathcal{A}^O(1^n, \{pk_i\}_{i \in [\mu]})$

7 : **return** $b = b'$

EXECUTE(i, j)

---

1 : **if** $i \notin [\mu] \vee j \notin [\mu]$: **return** $\perp$

2 : $\mathsf{Sid} + +; s := \mathsf{Sid}$

3 : $(msg, msg', k) \leftarrow_\$ \mathsf{KE}(pk_i, pk_j, sk_i, sk_j)$

4 : $\mathsf{SkeyList}[s] := \{i, j, k\}$

5 : **return** (msg, msg')

REVEAL(s)

---

1 : **if** $\mathsf{SkeyList}[s] = \perp$: **return** $\perp$

2 : $\mathsf{RevList} := \mathsf{RevList} \cup \{s\}$

3 : **parse** $\{i, j, k\} \leftarrow \mathsf{SkeyList}[s]$

4 : **return** k

CORRUPT(i)

---

1 : $\mathsf{CorrList} := \mathsf{CorrList} \cup \{i\}$

2 : **return** sk_i

TEST(s)

---

1 : **if** $s \in \mathsf{RevList} \vee \mathsf{SkeyList}[s] = \perp$: **return** $\perp$

2 : **parse** $\{i, j, k\} \leftarrow \mathsf{SkeyList}[s]$

3 : **if** $i \in \mathsf{CorrList}$: **return** $\perp$

4 : $k_0 := k; k_1 \leftarrow_\$ \mathcal{K}$

5 : **return** k_b

Fig. 2. Security game IND-pFS

We need every session key is independent to each other, in other words, the leak-age of some other session keys will not afflict the security of the testing one. This kind of property is modeled by REVEAL query. The corruption is captured by CORRUPT query, which is used to analysis our partial forward security.

4   The Proposed Protocol

In this section, the newly designed protocol is described.

4.1   Registration

To ensure the authenticity of nodes, zero-knowledge proofs and the UECDH key exchange authentication are utilized. All nodes must register and obtain public parameters before joining the blockchain. The registration process is as follows:

1. Generate common parameters shared by P and DTC_k: comm $= (\mathbb{Z}_q^*, E, G)$.
2. Generate private and public keys for P: (SK_P, PK_P), where $SK_P \in \mathbb{Z}_q^*$ and $PK_P = SK_P \times G$. SK_P is secretly held by P. PK_P is public and accessible to DTC_k.
3. Generate private and public keys for DTC_k: (SK_D, PK_D) where $SK_D \in \mathbb{Z}_q^*$ and $PK_D = SK_D \times G$. SK_D is secretly held by DTC_k. PK_D is public and accessible to P.
4. Generate local parameters, including a random number r, a random symbol sequence s (with s taking a value of either –1 or 1), and a sequence $(s_1, s_2, ..., s_k)$.
5. Select a large integer m and calculate $v_i = s_i^2 \mod q$ for each i, which will be used to form the public parameter information for the zero-knowledge proof.
6. The registration information is compiled as $reg = (id, (v_1, v_2, ..., v_k), PK_P)$ and broadcasted to the blockchain network, where id represents the node's identification information.

4.2   Authentication Stage

The authentication process (see Fig. 3) of the protocol is as follows:

Step 1: User P requests the consensus committee DTC to query and obtain the public parameters registered by DTC members. These parameters are generated from DTC node k's ID, zero-knowledge proof public parameters $(s_1, s_2, ..., s_k)$, and PK_P. Compute $U_P = R_P + SK_P$, where R_P is a random number and SK_P is the node's private key. P then sends its user ID id_u, timestamp t_1, U_P, PK_P, and a random number N_1 to DTC_k.

Step 2: Upon receiving P's message, DTC_k calculates $U_D = R_D + SK_D$ and $T_D = U_D \times G$, where R_D is a random number and SK_D is DTC_k's private key. DTC_k also randomly generates a binary string $(a_1, a_2, ..., a_k)$ with values of 0 or 1, and sends it to P along with the node ID id_k, timestamp t_2, T_D, PK_D, and N_2 (where $N_2 = N_1 + 1$).

Step 3: DTC_k requests P's registration information.

Step 4: Upon receiving the binary string from DTC_k, P calculates the zero-knowledge proof parameters based on the random number r and $(s_1, s_2, ..., s_k)$. It then sends these to DTC_k with a timestamp t_3 and N_3 (where $N_3 = N_2 + 1$).

Step 5: P calculates $K_P = R_P \times (T_D - PK_P)$. It then encrypts the information with K and sends it to DTC_k.

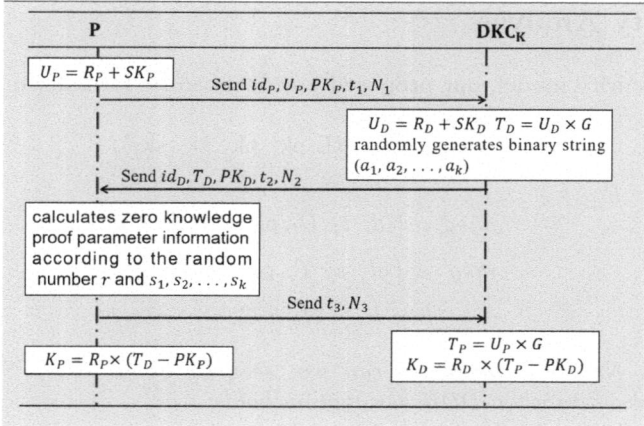

Fig. 3. Authentication stage.

Step 6: Upon receiving P's message, DTC_k verifies P's identity using the zero-knowledge proof protocol. If verification is successful, P's identity is confirmed as authentic. DTC_k computes $T_P = U_P \times G$ and $K_D = R_D \times (T_P - PK_P)$ using P's registration data from the blockchain. It then decrypts P's message and encrypts the response with K before sending it back to P. The session key K is subsequently used for secure data exchange between P and DTC_k.

4.3   Correctness

From the equations presented, it is evident that K_P and K_D are equal upon successful completion of the protocol.

$$
\begin{aligned}
K_P &= R_P \times (T_D - PK_D) \\
&= R_P \times ((R_D + SK_D) \times G - PK_D) \\
&= R_P \times (R_D \times G) \\
&= R_P \times R_D \times G.
\end{aligned}
$$

$$
\begin{aligned}
K_D &= R_D \times (T_P - PK_P) \\
&= R_D \times ((R_P + SK_P) \times G - PK_P) \\
&= R_D \times (R_P \times G) \\
&= R_P \times R_D \times G.
\end{aligned}
$$

5   Security Analysis

Under our security model, our proposed protocol can be formalized as

$$(msg, msg', k) \leftarrow \mathsf{KE}(\mathsf{pk}_i, \mathsf{pk}_j, \mathsf{sk}_i, \mathsf{sk}_j),$$

where

$$msg = \{id_i, t_1, U_i, \mathsf{pk}_i, N_1\},$$
$$msg' = \{id_j, t_2, T_j, \mathsf{pk}_j, N_2\},$$
$$k = R_i \times R_j \times G.$$

Theorem 1. *No PPT adversary can win security game* IND-pFS *with non-negligible probability when DDH assumption holds.*

Proof: We sketch the proof here. Given a DDH instance (X, Y, Z), we construct a PPT algorithm $\mathcal{C}$ to solve the DDH problem with the help of adversary $\mathcal{A}$. In other words, if there exists such an adversary, we can then solve the problem with non-negligible probability (greater than $1/p(n)$ for some polynomial p), which contradicts to the DDH hardness assumption, our protocol is therefore secure.

Let $\mathcal{C}$ simulates the security game sequence for $\mathcal{A}$. We modify each games a little bit with introducing a failure/invalid probability, which in each game we will show that is negligible. In other words, $\mathcal{A}$ cannot distinguish the real security game from the modified one. In the final game we conclude with a solution to DDH problem and the introduced probability is still polynomial bounded.

GAME 0. This game is identical to game IND-pFS. It is trivial to show each response of queries.

GAME 1. We aborts $\mathcal{C}$ if there are any key collision happens. This brings a negligible probability if we pick big enough group to sample our keys, say a finite elliptic curve cyclic group of size $q = 2^{256}$. This step exclude possible parameter collision, which may affect the analysis of the following game. We can treat the key outputted by $\mathsf{KGen}(1^\lambda)$ as unique.

GAME 2. We first pick a party i^* randomly and set its public key as $\mathsf{pk}_i = X$. We abort $\mathcal{C}$ if $\mathcal{A}$ corrupts i. Secondly, we pick a session s^* randomly. We aborts $\mathcal{C}$ if $\mathcal{A}$ does not pick s^* to test or s^* is not a session of i^*. This step brings the main security loss since we have to pick one reducible session from $\mu \cdot n_s$. Also, we modify the EXECUTE query in Fig. 4. Suppose $u = r' + x$ for some unknown r'. We denote $x = Dlog(X)$ with $x \times G = X$ and $y = Dlog(y)$ with $y \times G = Y$. Note that if $DH(X, Y) = Z$, in condition $i = i^* \wedge s = s^*$, we have $k := u \times Y - Z = r' \times y \times G$, which is a valid session key for s^* in the view of $\mathcal{A}$. And the similar reason for case $s \neq s^*$, the session keys of i are computable and we can deal with the corresponding REVEAL queries. Therefore, $\mathcal{C}$ can simulate the EXECUTE and REVEAL queries perfectly.

Finally, $\mathcal{C}$ outputs what $\mathcal{A}$ outputs.   ∎

EXECUTE$'(i, j)$

1 : **if** $i \notin [\mu] \lor j \notin [\mu]$: **return** $\perp$

2 : $\mathsf{Sid} + +; s := \mathsf{Sid}$

3 : **if** $i = i^*$:

4 : $(u, U) \leftarrow\$ \mathsf{KGen}(1^n)$;

5 : $msg := \{id_i, t_1, u, \mathsf{pk}_i, N_1\}$;

6 :   **if** $s = s^*$:

7 : $msg' := \{id_j, t_2, Y + \mathsf{pk}_j, \mathsf{pk}_j, N_2\}$

8 : $k := u \times Y - Z$

9 :   **elseif** $s \neq s^*$:

10 : $(r, R) \leftarrow\$ \mathsf{KGen}(1^n)$;

11 : $msg' := \{id_j, t_2, R + \mathsf{pk}_j, \mathsf{pk}_j, N_2\}$

12 : $k := r \times (U \times G - \mathsf{pk}_i)$

13 : $\mathsf{SkeyList}[s] := \{i, j, k\}$

14 :   **return** (msg, msg')

15 : $(msg, msg', k) \leftarrow\$ \mathsf{KE}(pk_i, pk_j, sk_i, sk_j)$

16 : $\mathsf{SkeyList}[s] := \{i, j, k\}$

17 : **return** (msg, msg')

Fig. 4. Modified EXECUTE query

6 Performance Analysis

6.1 Protocol Performance Analysis

In this subsection, we analyze the benefits of the UECDH protocol. We conducted experiments to measure computation time and the overall execution time. The experimental setup is detailed in Table 1. Here, T_A^D denotes the time taken to execute algrithm A on device D (Fig. 5).

Experiment I. We used two identically configured laptops to represent the two communication parties of the proposed protocol. From Fig. 6, we can see that the average total computing time $T_{UECDH}^P < T_{ECDH}^P$.

Experiment II. We utilized two Raspberry Pis for our experiment: one with a frequency of 0.6 GHz to represent the participant end (P end), and the other with a frequency of 1.2 GHz to represent the device end (D end). As illustrated in Fig. 6, $T_{UECDH}^P < T_{ECDH}^P$ and $T_{UECDH} < T_{ECDH}$.

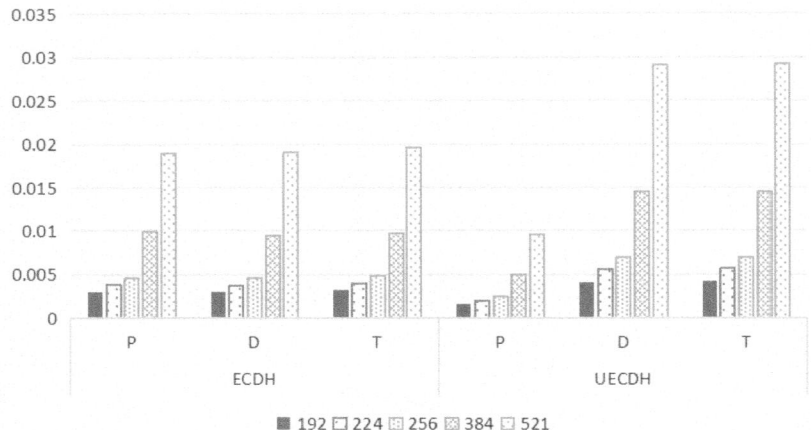

Fig. 5. I average computing time

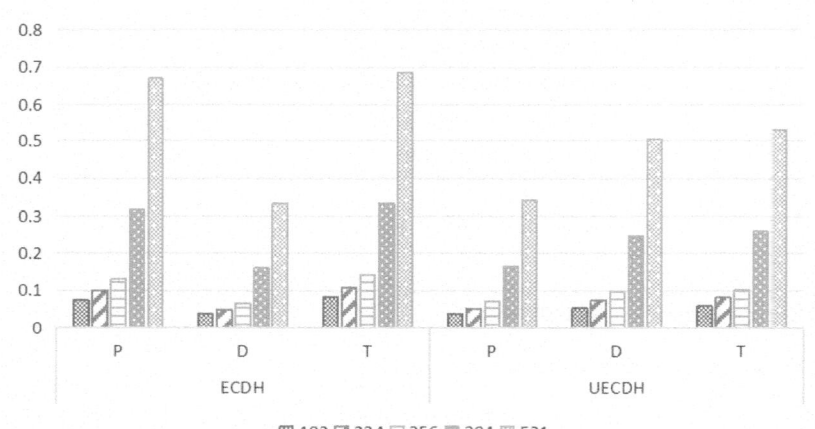

Fig. 6. II average computing time

Table 1. Experiment Setting

	Device	CPU	Core	RAM	Programming language	Elliptic curves
Experiment1	Laptop	i7-8750H 2.20 GHz	6	16 GB	Python	P-192-P-521
	Laptop	i7-8750H 2.20 GHz	6	16 GB	Python	P-192-P-521
Experiment2	Raspberry Pi	0.6 GHz	6	2 GB	Python	P-192-P-521
	Raspberry Pi	1.2 GHz	6	2 GB	Python	P-192-P-521

6.2   Federal Learning Performance Analysis

Federated Learning is based on the Anaconda environment, trained using Python version 3.8 and Pytorch framework version 1.3, Syftpy version 0.3.4 and relies on GPU-based Rocm. Hardware standards for the system include an Intel i5-10600kf CPU, AMD Radeon RX 6700 GPU and 64 GB of RAM.

MINST Dataset. The MNIST Dataset is made up of 0 to 9 handwritten digit images and digit labels, consisting of 60,000 training samples and 10,000 test samples, each of which is a 28 * 28 pixel greyscale image of a handwritten digit.

Federal Learning Experimental Model. There are three nodes involved in the experiment, including a central node (Server) as well as two slave nodes (Alice, Bob). Alice and Bob each hold half of the dataset, while Server holds the model parameters. In each training epoch, Server first distributes the model to Alice and Bob, then receives and merges the trained models from both ends.

We use a conventional convolutional neural network (CNN) for training, consisting of two convolutional layers, a pooling layer, a Dropout layer, and a fully connected layer. The convolutional layers use 32 and 64 small convolutional kernels, respectively, to extract image features, and each layer applies a ReLU activation function. The pooling layer uses maximum pooling to reduce the data dimensions and retain the most important features. The Dropout layer is used to prevent overfitting. Finally, a fully connected layer containing 128 neurons and an output layer (using the softmax function) form the tail end of the network, which completes the recognition of handwritten digits in 10 categories.

Training and Evaluations. We started the training script on the 2 participating nodes and used local data for training. We set the training generation to 100, the learning rate to 0.01, the number of batches trained per cycle to 64, and the momentum parameter to 0.5 to ensure that the model converges on each node.

After each epoch of training, we record metrics such as training loss, test loss, and test accuracy. We show our training results in Fig. 7. From the figure, we can see that the test loss always stays within a small range, and the accuracy of the test gradually improves as the training epoch increases. In addition, the training using federated learning requires more rounds than convential CNN.

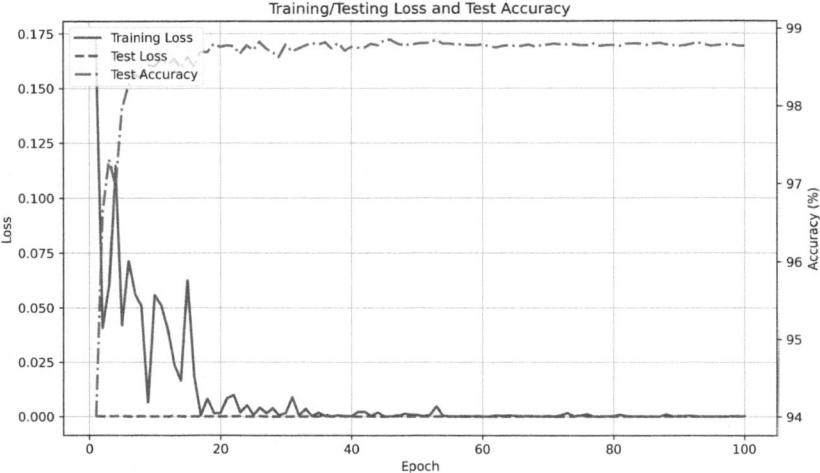

Fig. 7. Training and Testing loss and accuracy

7   Conclusion

Federated learning represents a groundbreaking advancement in distributed machine learning, enabling the collaborative development of robust models across devices while preserving data privacy. Despite its merits, conventional federated learning systems entail the central server aggregating critical model components, thereby posing potential privacy risks. The integration of blockchain technology has lately emerged as a promising avenue to bolster security within this framework. This study presents an optimized authentication protocol designed for a federated learning ecosystem underpinned by blockchain. Extensive experimental evaluations demonstrate the efficacy of our approach in enhancing system efficiency, particularly in scenarios where there exists a disparity in computational power between the central and participant nodes.

Acknowledgment. Thank my team members for their outstanding contributions at every stage, including data collection, experimental design, and result analysis.

References

1. Polaski, D.R., Brienza, M.J.: Managing ai: risks and opportunities (2023)
2. Bhadoria, R.S., Bhoj, N., Srivastav, M.K., Kumar, R., Raman, B.: A machine learning framework for security and privacy issues in building trust for social networking. Cluster Computing **26**(6), 3907–3930 (2023)
3. Mohassel, P., Zhang, Y.: Secureml: a system for scalable privacy-preserving machine learning. In: 2017 IEEE symposium on security and privacy (SP), pp. 19–38. IEEE (2017)

4. McMahan, B., Moore, E., Ramage, D., Hampson, S., y Arcas, B.A.: Communication-efficient learning of deep networks from decentralized data. In: Artificial Intelligence and Statistics, pp. 1273–1282. PMLR (2017)

5. Zhu, J., Cao, J., Saxena, D., Jiang, S., Ferradi, H.: Blockchain-empowered federated learning: challenges, solutions, and future directions. ACM Comput. Surv. **55**(11), 1–31 (2023)

6. Ji, S., Zhang, J., Zhang, Y., Han, Z., Ma, C.: Lafed: a lightweight authentication mechanism for blockchain-enabled federated learning system. Futur. Gener. Comput. Syst. **145**, 56–67 (2023)

7. Fang, M., Cao, X., Jia, J., Gong, N.: Local model poisoning attacks to {Byzantine-Robust} federated learning. In: 29th USENIX security symposium (USENIX Security 20), pp. 1605–1622 (2020)

8. Huang, Y., Gupta, S., Song, Z., Li, K., Arora, S.: Evaluating gradient inversion attacks and defenses in federated learning. Adv. Neural. Inf. Process. Syst. **34**, 7232–7241 (2021)

9. Ma, C., et al.: On safeguarding privacy and security in the framework of federated learning. IEEE Netw. **34**(4), 242–248 (2020)

10. Kumar, P., Chouhan, L.: A privacy and session key based authentication scheme for medical iot networks. Comput. Commun. **166**, 154–164 (2021)

11. Bao, X., Su, C., Xiong, Y., Huang, W., Hu, Y.: Flchain: a blockchain for auditable federated learning with trust and incentive. In: 2019 5th International Conference on Big Data Computing and Communications (BIGCOM), pp. 151–159. IEEE (2019)

12. Qu, Y., et al.: Decentralized privacy using blockchain-enabled federated learning in fog computing. IEEE Internet Things J. **7**(6), 5171–5183 (2020)

13. Kim, H., Park, J., Bennis, M., Kim, S.-L.: Blockchained on-device federated learning. IEEE Commun. Lett. **24**(6), 1279–1283 (2019)

14. Awan, S., Li, F., Luo, B., Liu, M.: Poster: a reliable and accountable privacy-preserving federated learning framework using the blockchain. In: Proceedings of the 2019 ACM SIGSAC Conference on Computer and Communications Security, pp. 2561–2563 (2019)

15. Ramanan, P., Nakayama, K.: Baffle: Blockchain based aggregator free federated learning. In: 2020 IEEE International Conference on Blockchain (Blockchain), pp. 72–81. IEEE (2020)

16. Zhao, Y., Zhao, J., Jiang, L., Tan, R., Niyato, D., Li, Z., Lyu, L., Liu, Y.: Privacy-preserving blockchain-based federated learning for iot devices. IEEE Internet Things J. **8**(3), 1817–1829 (2020)

17. Ma, J., Naas, S.-A., Sigg, S., Lyu, X.: Privacy-preserving federated learning based on multi-key homomorphic encryption. Int. J. Intell. Syst. **37**(9), 5880–5901 (2022)

18. Aljrees, T., Kumar, A., Singh, K.U., Singh, T.: Enhancing IoT security through a green and sustainable federated learning platform: leveraging efficient encryption and the quondam signature algorithm. Sensors **23**(19), 8090 (2023)

19. Fang, H., Qian, Q.: Privacy preserving machine learning with homomorphic encryption and federated learning. Future Internet **13**(4), 94 (2021)

Generalizable and Robust Log Anomaly Detection Based on Transformer

Zhaoyang Lou, Xiaolin Chai, Ce Shang, and Yan Sun$^{(\boxtimes)}$

Beijing University of Posts and Telecommunications, Beijing, China
{zzzzy0302,xiaolin_chai,shangce,sunyan}@bupt.edu.cn

Abstract. Log anomaly detection plays a crucial role in maintaining the security and reliability of Internet of Things devices. Unsupervised deep learning methods have made significant progress in anomaly detection by modeling normal log sequences. However, the approach of only considering the normal patterns of sequences leads to limited generalization ability of the model. To address this problem, we propose GRLog to enhance the performance and generalization ability of anomaly detection models based on log sequences. First, we introduce auxiliary datasets to enhance the model's ability to represent log sequences when learning the local and global information of log sequences based on Transformer. Second, we propose a similar log detection method to handle previously unseen logs. GRLog achieves higher F1 scores on three public datasets and their evolution datasets, which shows that our proposed model can better detect anomalies in log sequences and effectively address log evolution.

Keywords: Anomaly Detection · Transformer Encoder · Generalization Ability · Log Evolution

1 Introduction

With the widespread deployment of Internet of Things devices, the logs generated by systems have become increasingly complex and voluminous. Log anomaly detection has become a crucial tool for ensuring the security and stability of systems in the IoT domain. Many studies have proposed machine learning methods [14,16,24] for log anomaly detection. However, these methods often struggle to fully capture the complex patterns and temporal dependencies within log data, leading to suboptimal detection performance.

In recent years, deep learning-based anomaly detection methods have gradually become a research hotspot, mainly divided into supervised and unsupervised methods. Supervised methods [3,7,9,15,26] primarily perform binary classification based on log labels. Although these methods can achieve good performance, most of them require balanced normal and abnormal data for training. In practical scenarios, log labels are often difficult to obtain and abnormal events rarely occur, which makes supervised methods difficult to apply. Unsupervised models detect anomalies by learning the sequence patterns of normal log data, mostly based on RNN [2,5,6,17] and Transformer Encoder [1,8,11–13,20,23]. RNNs effectively capture long-term dependencies and temporal patterns in sequence data, while Transformer Encoders leverage self-attention [22] mechanisms to better capture global information. These methods achieve good results by learning the normal performance patterns of the system as much as possible, but they still face two issues. First, models that only learn normal log data patterns may overfit, leading to poor performance. Second, some methods that do not consider log semantics are unable to handle log evolution in practice. For example, a log statement like "User login attempt" might later be replaced with "User login attempt: username= , ipAddress= " to provide more information. When the model, which has learned the sequence patterns during the training phase, encounters updated log entries that do not match the expected patterns, it might incorrectly identify these entries as anomalies, thus reducing the effectiveness of the detection methods.

In this paper, we solve the above problems through GRLog. This method uses a Transformer Encoder to learn the patterns of log sequences through two training tasks. The first task is a mask prediction task, inspired by BERT's MLM [4], where parts of normal log sequences are masked, and the true log content is predicted using the contextual information of the logs. The second task is a sequence representation learning task, where normal log data and log data from other systems are used as auxiliary data for training. This ensures that normal sequences are close to each other in the vector space while being distant from the auxiliary data, thereby learning the representation of log sequences. Finally, we use a pre-trained language model to extract semantic vectors of logs. By employing a log replacement strategy, we effectively mitigate the impact of changes in log format and content, addressing log evolution.

Overall, the contributions of this paper are as follows: (1) Based on the Transformer Encoder, we use an auxiliary dataset to better learn log sequence patterns through global and local tasks. (2) Using a pre-trained language model to handle log evolution enhances the model's generalization ability.

2 Related Work

Traditional machine learning approaches such as IsolationForest [16] have shown limited effectiveness in practical applications of log anomaly detection due to challenges in capturing complex patterns and temporal dependencies within log data.

With advancements in deep learning techniques, there has been extensive research and application of deep learning-based methods in log anomaly detection. Supervised approaches like logRobust [26] and LogFormer [9] leverage semantic information of log events for binary classification tasks, demonstrating strong performance in handling log instability. However, these methods often struggle with the imbalance between normal and abnormal data in log systems, posing challenges in real-world applications.

Unsupervised methods such as DeepLog [5], LogAnomaly [17], and LogBERT [8] focus on capturing dependencies within normal log sequences to identify abnormal patterns. These methods are capable of adapting to different time scales and effectively handling complex data patterns and variations. Nonetheless, their reliance on modeling normal data to learn sequence patterns often lacks domain adaptability for abnormal distributions and effective handling of new log events.

In this paper, we propose a novel unsupervised learning approach that addresses these challenges. By utilizing easily accessible log data as auxiliary datasets, we introduce domain biases to mitigate issues related to abnormal distributions. We design global and local tasks to enhance learning of log sequence patterns and improve anomaly detection performance. Additionally, we employ pre-trained language models to develop an online detection system capable of addressing challenges posed by log evolution.

3   Methodology

In this section, we describe the overall framework of GRLog. In Fig. 1, GRLog consists of three main components: preprocessing, offline training, and online detection. We will proceed to provide detailed explanations in the following sections.

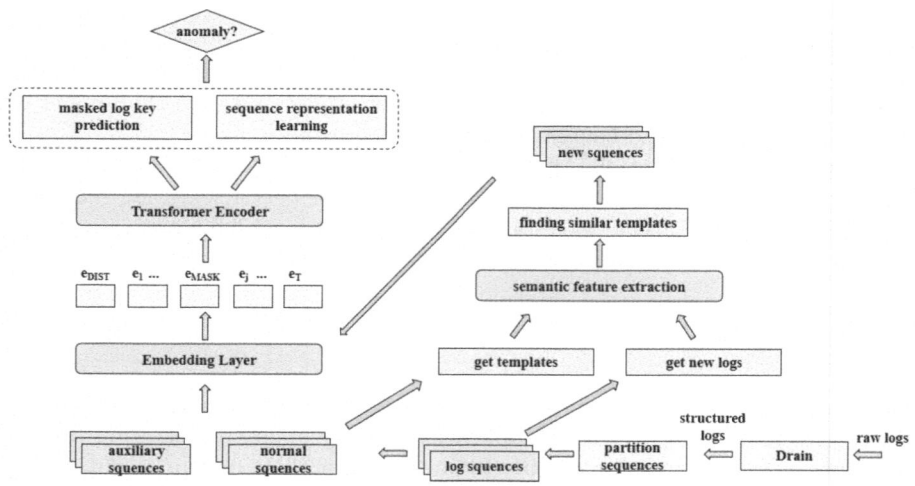

Fig. 1. The overview of GRLog

3.1   Preprocess

We preprocess logs using the Drain [10] parsing algorithm. Drain is an efficient online log parsing method that employs a fixed-depth tree structure to effectively group logs and generate normalized log keys (log templates). Its strengths lie in its real-time processing capabilities, low computational overhead, and suitability for handling large-scale log data processing scenarios. After parsing the logs, we segment the structured log key data into time windows, resulting in a continuous sequence of log keys $S = \{k_1, \ldots, k_t, \ldots, k_T\}$, where $k_t \subseteq K$ denotes the log keys at position t, and K represents a set of log keys extracted from log messages. These processed log key sequences serve as input data for model training and anomaly detection, aiming to enhance system efficiency and accuracy.

3.2 Offline Training

Given normal and auxiliary log sequences, we prepend a special token "DIST" at the beginning of each sequence as the first log key, representing the entire log sequence. The embedding of "DIST" is used to constrain the distribution of normal and auxiliary sequences. Each log key in the sequence is passed through an Embedding Layer and represented as an embedding vector, which is obtained by adding the token embedding and position embedding. We use Transformer Encoder to learn dependencies between log keys in log sequences through the following two tasks.

Masked Log Key Prediction (MLKP). It is adapted from BERT's Masked Language Model (MLM) task to capture patterns in normal log sequences. In this task, a subset of log keys in the input log key sequence is randomly masked, and the model predicts these masked log keys based on context. The model generates embeddings for the masked log key sequence and outputs probabilities for each position predicting the log key. For the masked positions, the cross-entropy loss between the predicted log key and the actual log key is computed as follows:

$$\mathcal{L}_{\text{MLKP}} = - \sum_{i \in \text{masked positions}} \log P(x_i | \text{context}) \tag{1}$$

Here, i represents the masked position, x_i denotes the actual log key, context refers to the contextual information from the log key sequence, and $P(x_i|\text{context})$ represents the probability of predicting log key x_i given the log key sequence.

Normal log sequences exhibit specific patterns and structures. Through this approach, the model learns how to predict masked log keys based on contextual cues within the log sequence, thereby capturing the patterns of normal log sequences. Since anomalous sequences deviate significantly from normal sequences in terms of patterns, the model's accuracy in predicting masked log keys decreases substantially for anomalous sequences. Hence, anomalies can be identified based on this decreased prediction accuracy during masked prediction.

Sequence Representation Learning Task (SRL). To ensure learning the differences between normal and abnormal log samples, we designed a spherical objective function to adjust the distribution of normal and abnormal log sequences. The motivation behind SRL is to concentrate normal log sequences closely together in the embedding space, while pushing anomalous log sequences farther away. We use context embeddings of the DIST-marked log sequences encoded by a Transformer Encoder as representations of the log sequences in the embedding space. At the beginning of each training round, we compute the mean of the embedding vectors of normal data sequences as the center of the hypersphere $c = \frac{1}{m} \sum_{i=1}^{m} h_{\text{DIST}i}$, where $h_{\text{DIST}i}$ is the representation of the i-th normal log sequence. The loss function for this task is as follows:

$$\mathcal{L}_{\text{SRL}} = \frac{1}{n} \sum_{i=1}^{n} \left[y_i (h_i - c)^2 + (1 - y_i) \log \left(1 + \exp[-(h_i - c)^2] \right) \right] \tag{2}$$

where $y_i \in \{0, 1\}$, $y_i = 0$ represents anomalous samples (auxiliary data), and $y_i = 1$ represents normal samples (target system). The left term of the loss function ensures compactness of normal data, minimizing their distance to the hypersphere center c. The right term increases the distance of anomalous data from the hypersphere center c. The center c encodes common patterns in normal log sequences. By bringing normal sequences closer to c and pushing anomalous sequences farther away, this method helps the model explicitly learn to distinguish between normal and anomalous data during training.

This approach enhances the model's understanding of normal data characteristics, enabling better utilization of correlations among normal data during masked log key prediction, and improving accuracy in predicting masked log keys in normal log sequences.

Finally, the training objective function $\mathcal{L}$ is defined as:

$$\mathcal{L} = \mathcal{L}_{\text{MLKP}} + \alpha \mathcal{L}_{\text{SRL}} \tag{3}$$

where α is a hyperparameter used to balance the two training tasks.

3.3 Online Detection

First, the raw log data to be detected is transformed into structured log key data using the Drain algorithm. For newly appearing log keys, we use a pre-trained sentence-transformers [21] model to extract their semantic vectors. Next, the semantic vectors of these new log keys are compared with the normal log keys used during the training phase to calculate the distance between them and determine their similarity s. Specifically, if the calculated distance is less than a predefined threshold t, we replace the new log key with the most similar log key; otherwise, we retain the new log key without replacement. Finally, the processed log keys are passed to the trained model for detection. This approach allows us to map newly appearing log keys to the log keys used during training as the log data evolves, thereby maintaining the model's stability and detection performance.

For anomaly detection, we randomly add a certain proportion of masks to the log key sequences to be detected, and then use the model to predict the actual log keys at these masked positions. The number of failed predictions in a sequence is used to determine whether the sequence is anomalous. Since the model has learned the patterns of normal log key sequences, which are significantly different from anomalous sequences, it is likely to correctly predict the actual log keys at masked positions if the sequence is normal, and unlikely to do so if the sequence is anomalous. For each mask, the model generates a probability list l indicating the likelihood of different log keys appearing at that position. Following the LogBERT method, we define a candidate set containing the top k log keys from the probability list l. If the actual log key is within the candidate set, the prediction is considered successful and the log key at the masked position is deemed normal; otherwise, the prediction fails and the log key is considered anomalous. We set a sequence log key anomaly threshold r, and if the number of anomalous log keys in a sequence is below the threshold r, the sequence is considered normal; otherwise, it is considered anomalous. Here, k and r are hyperparameters that need to be adjusted.

4   Experiments

To evaluate the performance of our model, we compared our method with existing methods on multiple benchmark datasets. Since only normal labels from the target system were used, GRLog was evaluated as an unsupervised method.

4.1   Experimental Setup

Datasets: We evaluated the improved model on three log datasets from Loghub[1]: HDFS, BGL, and Thunderbird. The HDFS [18] dataset is generated and collected from the Amazon EC2 platform through running Hadoop-based map-reduce jobs. We divided sequences by the block ID in each log entry. The BGL and Thunderbird datasets [19,25] contain logs collected from a two-supercomputer system at Sandia National Labs (SNL) in Albuquerque. For these datasets, we defined a time sliding window to divide the sequences, with window sizes of 5 min and 1 min, respectively.

Table 1 shows the statistical information of the datasets. For each dataset, we used 40% of the normal data sequences and 5% auxiliary data from other systems for training. In reality, log data often evolves over time. To simulate the instability of log data, We modified 2%, 5%, and 10% of the log data respectively. Specifically, after log preprocessing, we constructed log evolution processes by using synonym replacements, truncations, and random replacements on part of the parsed log templates. The modified templates were then mapped back to the structured log data.

Baselines. We compare our model with the following four publicly available benchmark methods:

---

[1] https://github.com/logpai/loghub.

Table 1. Statistics of evolution datasets

Dataset	Log Messages	Anomalies	LogKeys	Log Sequences in Test Dataset	
				Normal	Anomalous
HDFS	11,172,157	284,818	46(15)	553,366	10,647
BGL	4,747,963	348,460	1000(192)	10,045	2,630
Thunderbird-mini	20,000,000	758,562	1206(1059)	71,155	45,385

IsolationForest isolates data points by constructing a random forest, thereby identifying those log entries that are significantly different from the majority as anomalies.

DeepLog uses LSTM to learn normal patterns in log sequences and identifies anomalies based on the probabilities of log key predictions.

LogAnomaly utilizes a Bi-LSTM network and self-attention mechanism to model log sequences, learning normal patterns to detect both sequential and quantitative log anomalies.

LogBERT is a BERT-based log anomaly detection method that learns log sequence patterns through the masked language model (MLM) task and volume minimization hypersphere learning.

4.2 Experimental Results

We compared the performance of our model with these baseline methods on the same datasets. Table 2 presents our results on the BGL, HDFS, and Thunder-Bird datasets. It is evident that Isolation Forest performs poorly across all three datasets, achieving high recall but failing to balance precision and recall effectively, resulting in very low F1 scores. In contrast, the three deep learning-based baselines show reasonable F1 scores, highlighting the advantage of using deep learning models to capture sequence patterns. Furthermore, our model consistently achieves the highest F1 scores compared to all baseline methods, albeit occasionally with slightly lower precision or recall than these three deep learning methods. Notably, these deep learning methods exhibit significant discrepancies between precision and recall, whereas our model demonstrates superior balancing capabilities. This indicates that combining auxiliary datasets with global and local tasks can effectively enhance the learning of log sequence patterns.

Figure 2 illustrates the performance of these methods on the BGL dataset at different log change rates (2%, 5%, 10%). Table 3 presents the test results of various methods on three datasets (HDFS, BGL, Thunderbird) with a 10% log change. The experimental design aims to explore the performance of each method under different dataset conditions and log change rates comprehensively. The results clearly show that the precision and F1 scores of the three baseline deep learning methods significantly decrease, while the recall may increase due to deteriorating model performance, regardless of whether it is under varying log change rates within the same dataset or uniform log change rates across different datasets. In contrast, our method demonstrates stability in precision, recall, and F1 scores. This is primarily because these deep learning methods output a probability list for the log keys at masked positions, representing the likelihood of encountering these log keys during training, which cannot handle new logs effectively. In contrast, our approach replaces new logs with the most semantically similar log based on vector embeddings, mitigating the impact of log changes. Hence, our method exhibits greater potential for practical applications in scenarios involving continuous log evolution.

Table 2. Performance comparison on different datasets

Method	HDFS			BGL			Thunderbird		
	Precision	Recall	F-1 score	Precision	Recall	F-1 score	Precision	Recall	F-1 score
iForest	5.24	**100**	9.96	10.61	**100**	19.18	39.17	**100**	56.29
DeepLog	92.66	45.58	61.10	93.00	77.91	84.79	90.70	99.62	94.95
LogAnomaly	**93.33**	43.10	58.97	91.94	79.44	85.23	91.47	99.61	95.37
LogBERT	80.14	63.79	71.04	91.15	92.57	91.86	**99.65**	93.79	96.63
GRLog	79.72	72.94	**76.18**	**93.85**	92.42	**93.13**	95.13	99.16	**97.13**

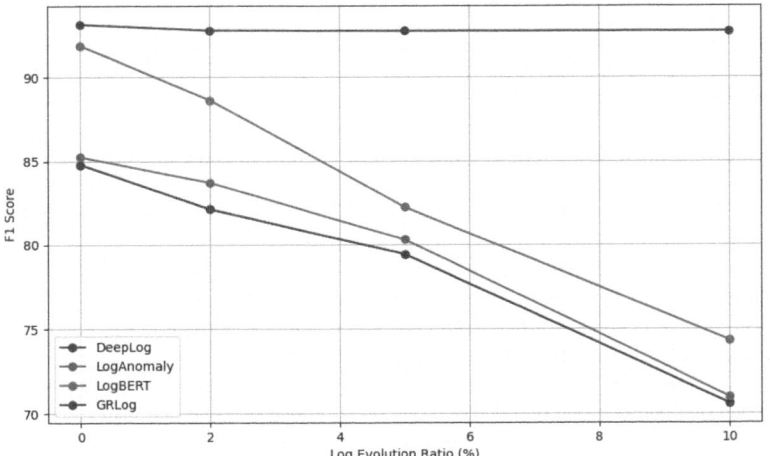

Fig. 2. F1 scores of different methods at various evolution ratios on BGL dataset.

Table 3. Performance comparison on different datasets (10% evolution)

Method	HDFS			BGL			Thunderbird		
	Precision	Recall	F-1 score	Precision	Recall	F-1 score	Precision	Recall	F-1 score
DeepLog	71.84	11.87	20.38	60.10	85.57	70.61	68.76	**99.76**	81.41
LogAnomaly	73.99	17.40	28.17	61.02	84.84	70.99	68.75	**99.76**	81.40
LogBERT	1.89	**99.85**	3.71	61.83	**93.15**	74.32	71.05	97.93	82.35
GRLog	**79.62**	72.82	**76.07**	**92.69**	92.73	**92.71**	**92.98**	99.16	**95.97**

5 Conclusion

In this paper, we propose GRLog. The model is based on Transformer Encoder and utilizes auxiliary datasets to learn log sequence patterns through global and local tasks. Additionally, we designed an online processing workflow to handle previously unseen logs. Experimental results show that our method achieves the highest scores across three datasets. Furthermore, it demonstrates excellent generalization ability on evolving log samples.

Future work includes but is not limited to integrating large language models into the log anomaly detection system to improve anomaly detection accuracy.

Acknowledgments. This work is supported by the National Natural Science Foundation of China under Grant 61877005 and 62172051.

References

1. Chen, S., Liao, H.: Bert-log: anomaly detection for system logs based on pre-trained language model. Appl. Artif. Intell. **36**(1), 2145642 (2022)
2. Chen, Y., Luktarhan, N., Lv, D.: Logls: research on system log anomaly detection method based on dual LSTM. Symmetry **14**(3), 454 (2022)
3. Chen, Z., Gao, Q., Moss, L.S.: Neurallog: natural language inference with joint neural and logical reasoning. arXiv preprint arXiv:2105.14167 (2021)
4. Devlin, J.: Bert: pre-training of deep bidirectional transformers for language understanding. arXiv preprint arXiv:1810.04805 (2018)
5. Du, M., Li, F., Zheng, G., Srikumar, V.: Deeplog: anomaly detection and diagnosis from system logs through deep learning. In: Proceedings of the 2017 ACM SIGSAC Conference on Computer and Communications Security, pp. 1285–1298 (2017)
6. Elbasani, E., Kim, J.D.: Llad: life-log anomaly detection based on recurrent neural network LSTM. J. Healthc. Eng. **2021**(1), 8829403 (2021)
7. Fu, Y., Liang, K., Xu, J.: Mlog: mogrifier LSTM-based log anomaly detection approach using semantic representation. IEEE Trans. Serv. Comput. **16**(5), 3537–3549 (2023)
8. Guo, H., Yuan, S., Wu, X.: Logbert: log anomaly detection via bert. In: 2021 International Joint Conference on Neural Networks (IJCNN), pp. 1–8. IEEE (2021)
9. Guo, H., et al.: Logformer: a pre-train and tuning pipeline for log anomaly detection. In: Proceedings of the AAAI Conference on Artificial Intelligence, vol. 38, pp. 135–143 (2024)

10. He, P., Zhu, J., Zheng, Z., Lyu, M.R.: Drain: an online log parsing approach with fixed depth tree. In: 2017 IEEE International Conference on Web Services (ICWS), pp. 33–40. IEEE (2017)
11. Huang, S., et al.: Hitanomaly: hierarchical transformers for anomaly detection in system log. IEEE Trans. Netw. Serv. Manag. **17**(4), 2064–2076 (2020)
12. Huang, S., Liu, Y., Fung, C., Wang, H., Yang, H., Luan, Z.: Improving log-based anomaly detection by pre-training hierarchical transformers. IEEE Trans. Comput. **72**(9), 2656–2667 (2023)
13. Lee, Y., Kim, J., Kang, P.: Lanobert: system log anomaly detection based on bert masked language model. Appl. Soft Comput. **146**, 110689 (2023)
14. Li, K.L., Huang, H.K., Tian, S.F., Xu, W.: Improving one-class svm for anomaly detection. In: Proceedings of the 2003 International Conference on Machine Learning and Cybernetics (IEEE Cat. No. 03EX693), vol. 5, pp. 3077–3081. IEEE (2003)
15. Li, X., Chen, P., Jing, L., He, Z., Yu, G.: Swisslog: robust and unified deep learning based log anomaly detection for diverse faults. In: 2020 IEEE 31st International Symposium on Software Reliability Engineering (ISSRE), pp. 92–103. IEEE (2020)
16. Liu, F.T., Ting, K.M., Zhou, Z.H.: Isolation forest. In: 2008 Eighth IEEE International Conference on Data Mining, pp. 413–422. IEEE (2008)
17. Meng, W., et al.: Loganomaly: unsupervised detection of sequential and quantitative anomalies in unstructured logs. In: IJCAI, vol. 19, pp. 4739–4745 (2019)
18. Nedelkoski, S., Bogatinovski, J., Acker, A., Cardoso, J., Kao, O.: Self-supervised log parsing. In: Dong, Y., Mladenić, D., Saunders, C. (eds.) ECML PKDD 2020. LNCS (LNAI), vol. 12460, pp. 122–138. Springer, Cham (2021). https://doi.org/10.1007/978-3-030-67667-4_8
19. Oliner, A., Stearley, J.: What supercomputers say: a study of five system logs. In: 37th annual IEEE/IFIP International Conference on Dependable Systems and Networks (DSN 2007), pp. 575–584. IEEE (2007)
20. Qi, J., et al.: Logencoder: log-based contrastive representation learning for anomaly detection. IEEE Trans. Netw. Serv. Manag. **20**(2), 1378–1391 (2023)
21. Reimers, N., Gurevych, I.: Sentence-bert: sentence embeddings using siamese bert-networks. arXiv preprint arXiv:1908.10084 (2019)
22. Vaswani, A.: Attention is all you need. arXiv preprint arXiv:1706.03762 (2017)
23. Wang, W., Lu, S., Luo, J., Wu, C.: Deepuserlog: deep anomaly detection on user log using semantic analysis and key-value data. In: 2023 IEEE 34th International Symposium on Software Reliability Engineering (ISSRE), pp. 172–182. IEEE (2023)
24. Xu, W., Huang, L., Fox, A., Patterson, D., Jordan, M.I.: Detecting large-scale system problems by mining console logs. In: Proceedings of the ACM SIGOPS 22nd Symposium on Operating Systems Principles, pp. 117–132 (2009)
25. Yao, K., Li, H., Shang, W., Hassan, A.E.: A study of the performance of general compressors on log files. Empir. Softw. Eng. **25**(5), 3043–3085 (2020). https://doi.org/10.1007/s10664-020-09822-x
26. Zhang, X., et al.: Robust log-based anomaly detection on unstable log data. In: Proceedings of the 2019 27th ACM Joint Meeting on European Software Engineering Conference and Symposium on the Foundations of Software Engineering, pp. 807–817 (2019)

Internet of Things Service
and Application Technology

Research on the Method of Face Recognition Based on Attention Mechanism

Wenbin Liu$^{(\boxtimes)}$, Guoqing Xu, and En Wang

Jilin University, Changchun, Jilin, China
{liuwenbin,wangen}@jlu.edu.cn

Abstract. In recent years, as large model technology gradually becomes integrated into people's daily lives, the potential risks it poses have also raised societal alarms. Consequently, traditional computer vision problems such as face recognition have regained public attention. Research on face recognition holds both academic and practical value.

First, this paper summarizes several classic face recognition algorithms based on convolutional neural networks, analyzes and discusses their network structures and recognition performance, and outlines their advantages and limitations. Secondly, addressing the difficulty of learning identity transformations in deep neural networks, we further explore residual network models, analyze their prominent advantages in learning identity transformations, and select ResNet34 as the backbone network for this experimental study. Finally, to enhance the network's recognition performance, we introduce the concept of attention mechanisms. Drawing parallels from human observation patterns, we discuss the principles of how attention mechanisms function in neural networks. We also incorporate a channel-based attention structure called the SE block into the original network to further improve its effectiveness.

In the final experiments, we use face data from 10 volunteers as the training dataset. We successfully construct a ResNet34 network based on an attention mechanism and conduct comparative experiments with a ResNet34 network without the attention mechanism. We plot the change curve of the test set's accuracy. The experiments yield the following conclusions: 1) The attention-based network model achieves good recognition performance, with the test set's recognition accuracy reaching approximately 96.1%. 2) The SE block exhibits significant improvement when added to any part of the residual network, with the optimal position being after the residual branch and before the branch aggregation. 3) The attention mechanism offers good improvement for different backbone networks, demonstrating its generalizability.

Keywords: Face Recognition · Deep Learning · ResNet · Attention Mechanisms

L. Sun and Y. Chen (Eds.): CWSN 2024, CCIS 2341, pp. 181–204, 2025.
https://doi.org/10.1007/978-981-96-2186-6_15

1   Introduction

1.1   Research Background and Significance

In recent years, the field of artificial intelligence has witnessed explosive growth, especially in the areas of multimodal research [8], crowdsensing [5,15], and large-scale models [10], sparking a surge of enthusiasm. This has led to AI-based applications becoming more deeply and widely integrated into people's lives, even influencing our way of life. However, it has also inevitably posed certain security risks, such as the generation of risky images (e.g., malicious photos of sensitive individuals) by generative models. Therefore, some traditional computer vision problems, such as face recognition [6] (used to determine if an image generated by a large model contains sensitive individuals), have regained research value. This article will focus on face recognition technology and explore its potential in face recognition applications. Face features possess consistency, uniqueness, and non-replicability, providing stable and excellent conditions for identifying personal information. Therefore, face recognition is widely used in various fields of our lives, such as traffic management, identity registration, case detection, intelligent robots, and so on.

Based on different application scenarios, face recognition can be classified into static and dynamic face recognition. Static face recognition scenarios are generally single and stable, while dynamic face recognition, compared to easier-to-implement static recognition, is more prone to various interference factors due to the complexity and non-restrictiveness of its recognition scenarios, such as facial occlusion [19], pose differences, light differences, low resolution, and so on. In addition, there are many other influencing factors affecting the efficiency and accuracy of face recognition technology applications, including significant differences in facial features across age groups [18], and the significant impact of hardware limitations on the application effects deployed on terminals [16], and so on.

In summary, we can understand that although the current development of face recognition techno

1.2   Research Status at Home and Abroad

In 1888, the concept of "face recognition" was first proposed in a paper titled "Personal Identification and Descriptions" published in Nature. Over the past 100 years, the development of face recognition technology has undergone three stages: semi-mechanical recognition, human-computer interaction recognition, and fully automated recognition [17]. Many ingenious and classic face recognition algorithms have also been created, some traditional methods including Principal Component Analysis [7], Laplacian Eigenmaps [13], Locality Preserving Projections [14], Sparse Representation [9], etc. In recent years, with the development of neural network algorithms and the advent of the big data era, more accurate and efficient algorithms have sprung up, and face recognition technology has achieved tremendous development, becoming one of the most valuable and promising research areas in computer vision.

After 2006, deep learning began to emerge more and more in front of the general public, and applications based on deep learning have gradually become widespread. In the ILSVRC in 2012, the deep learning network AlexNet not only achieved excellent results in the field of image recognition, but its performance in the field of image recognition also far exceeded other computer vision algorithms. Since then, more and more universities, research institutions, and companies have begun to pay attention to the application of deep learning in computer vision. After the success of AlexNet, researchers have also developed more and more network architectures, such as VGG network, GoogleNet, and InceptionNet. These networks have achieved impressive results in the field of image recognition, and they have also begun to be widely used in face recognition-related applications. After applying these advanced networks, the accuracy of face recognition has also been significantly improved, from initially less than 60% to finally even surpassing the accuracy of human recognition. The progress of face recognition technology is closely related to the continuous improvement of convolutional neural network technology.

1.3   Research Content

The research content of this paper is the methodology study on face recognition based on attention mechanisms, proposing a face recognition method that combines attention mechanisms on the basis of the residual neural network model, ResNet. The attention mentioned here refers to deterministic attention focused on the channel domain, also known as soft attention.

The specific research contents are described as follows:

Firstly, an introduction is given to convolutional neural network image recognition models, and the reasons for choosing convolutional neural networks as the recognition model are analyzed through a comparative analysis with traditional neural network models. Since the number of parameters requiring iterative optimization in convolutional neural networks is far less than that of ordinary neural networks, it is concluded that convolutional neural networks have the advantages of low computational complexity and high efficiency in the field of image recognition. Then, several classical convolutional neural network models are comparatively analyzed, leading to the conclusion that the accuracy of network recognition increases with the depth of the network. However, it is also pointed out that when the network depth reaches a certain level, the network recognition effect may decrease instead of increasing.

Addressing the problem mentioned above, where the recognition accuracy is difficult to further improve in overly deep network structures, the possible causes are analyzed. The conclusion is that when the network structure is overly deep, it is more prone to gradient vanishing and gradient explosion, making it more difficult to learn identity transformations in deep neural networks. Therefore, a neural network model based on residual networks is adopted. By analyzing the working principle of residual blocks in neural networks, it is concluded that the residual structure can ensure efficient learning of identity transformations while increasing the network depth.

The aforementioned network models assign equal weights to each feature of the image. To further improve the network recognition rate, this paper aims to enable the network to make trade-offs in learning image features, that is, to incorporate an attention mechanism into the original model. This paper proposes adding a channel-focused attention structure, Squeeze-Net, to the original network model. Related research shows that adding SE blocks to any layer of the network can improve the recognition effect. Experimental results show that the network model with the added attention mechanism indeed achieves a significant improvement in recognition accuracy.

1.4   The Organization of This Paper

Section 1: Introduction. This chapter begins with a brief introduction to the origin and development of face recognition technology, discussing its application value in daily life. Subsequently, it analyzes the current development status of face recognition research domestically and internationally. Finally, it provides a macro introduction to the main research content of this paper.

Section 2: Introduction to Convolutional Neural Network Face Recognition Methods. This chapter introduces the working principles of convolutional neural networks and analyzes why convolutional neural network algorithms are chosen. It then introduces some traditional convolutional neural network structures and analyzes their structural characteristics and recognition effects.

Section 3: Research on Face Recognition Methods Based on Attention Mechanisms. This chapter first analyzes the working principles of residual network blocks and then introduces the structure of the residual neural network, ResNet, chosen in this paper. Secondly, it focuses on introducing the working mechanism and advantages of attention mechanisms in computer vision. Finally, this chapter proposes a method of adding an attention network structure, the SE block, to the original residual network.

Section 4: Experimental Results and Analysis. This chapter first introduces the source and preprocessing methods of the experimental data used in this paper. It then analyzes how various hyperparameters in the network structure of this experiment are determined. Finally, it analyzes and discusses the experimental results, concluding that adding an attention mechanism significantly improves network performance.

Section 5: Conclusion. This chapter first summarizes the research conclusions of the article. It also analyzes the shortcomings of the experiment, such as the over-simplicity of the training dataset scenarios and the lack of generalizability of the experimental results. Subsequently, it provides a reasonable outlook for the future development prospects of face recognition technology.

2 Convolutional Neural Network Face Recognition Method

2.1 Convolutional Neural Networks

Convolutional Neural Networks (CNNs) are a class of feedforward neural networks that are widely applied in computer vision and natural language processing fields. Characterized by convolution operations, CNNs' primary structures include convolutional layers, pooling layers, and fully connected layers. They solve the loss function through forward propagation and optimize network parameters through backpropagation algorithms to reduce network losses. Additionally, compared to other neural network structures, the existence of receptive fields in CNNs enables parameter sharing. This feature not only significantly reduces computational costs but also allows CNNs to fully utilize local subtle features for locally invariant classification of input features.

Let's elaborate on why this paper selects Convolutional Neural Networks through an example.

Assuming the input feature map of layer L-1 has dimensions of (W) $64 \times 64 \times 3$. In a Convolutional Neural Network, let's assume layer L employs 6 convolutional kernels (filters) of dimension 5×5 (F), with zero padding (P) and a stride (S) of 1. According to the formula for calculating the output feature map's dimensions:

$$W_{\text{output}} = \left\lfloor \frac{W_{\text{input}} + 2P - F}{S} + 1 \right\rfloor \tag{1}$$

We can obtain that the dimension of the feature map output from layer L is $60 \times 60 \times 6$.

As mentioned above, if we consider an equivalent fully connected neural network, the number of neurons in layer L-1 should be $64 \times 64 \times 3 = 12288$. And the number of neurons in layer L is 21600. According to the calculation formula for the linear transformation part of a fully connected neural network:

$$z^{[L]} = W^{[L]} \times a^{[L-1]} + b^{[L]} \tag{2}$$

From this, we can deduce that the dimension of the parameters $W^{[L]}$ in the fully connected network's L-th layer is 21600×12288, and the dimension of the parameters $b^{[L]}$ is 21600×1. Therefore, the total number of parameters in the L-th layer of the fully connected network is $21600 \times 12288 + 21600 = 265,442,440$. In contrast, the number of parameters in the convolutional neural network is $5 \times 5 \times 6 + 6 = 156$. It is evident that the number of parameters in the convolutional neural network is far less than that of the fully connected neural network, making the computational cost of the convolutional neural network smaller and its computational efficiency superior.

There are two reasons why convolutional neural networks can significantly reduce the scale of parameters: sparse connectivity and parameter sharing. To understand sparse connectivity in convolutional neural networks, let's first look at the process of convolution operation (Fig. 1):

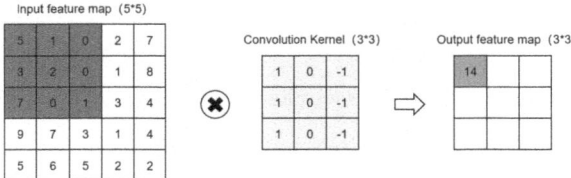

Fig. 1. Convolution operation

We can observe that the feature values marked in green in the output feature map are only related to the 3 × 3 region marked in blue in the input feature map, while the remaining feature values in the input will not affect the output in the green region. This is the concept of sparse connectivity in convolutional neural networks.

Another reason for the reduction in the scale of parameters in convolutional neural networks is parameter sharing. The input feature map shares the f × f parameters in the convolution kernel. Due to the local feature invariance in convolutional neural networks, parameter sharing not only reduces the scale of parameters but also ensures the recognition effect of the network model. We can intuitively have an approximate understanding of the local feature invariance of convolution. We can regard the convolution kernel as a square feature extractor, and a slight offset of 1–2 pixels in the image will not cause significant changes in the extraction results, thus ensuring the recognition effect of the network.

2.2   Classical Convolutional Neural Networks

Convolutional neural networks (CNNs) are currently widely used in computer vision, natural language processing, and other fields. Decades have passed since the emergence of CNNs, during which time many classic neural network models have emerged. In this chapter, we will focus on introducing three network structures: LeNet-5, AlexNet, and VGG16. Additionally, we will provide an overview of their network architectures and recognition performance.

LeNet5. LeNet [4] is one of the earliest convolutional neural network models. The predecessor of LeNet-5, LeNet, was originally designed to recognize digits on stamps. It employed stochastic gradient descent for parameter optimization, which has been adopted by subsequent deep learning algorithms. LeNet-5, which evolved from LeNet, not only inherited the previous learning pattern but also introduced pooling layers to optimize the model and reduce the computational complexity. Experiments have shown that LeNet-5 achieved tremendous success in handwritten digit recognition, and its emergence largely laid the foundation for subsequent convolutional neural network structures.

The network structure of LeNet-5 is illustrated in the Fig. 2. The entire network consists of 7 layers, including 2 convolutional layers, 2 pooling layers, and 3 fully connected layers. The network has approximately 60,000 parameters. When outputting the results, the network originally used Gaussian connections, but nowadays, softmax classifiers are more commonly used. Although the depth of LeNet-5 may not seem remarkable today, its structure comprehensively includes the basic components of contemporary convolutional neural networks, making it a seminal work in the field of convolutional neural networks.

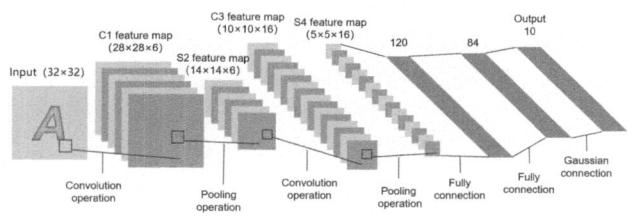

Fig. 2. The network architecture of LeNet-5 [4]

AlexNet. AlexNet [3] has five convolutional layers, three fully-connected layers, and 1,000 classification units, totaling approximately 60 million parameters. Compared to the aforementioned LeNet-5, AlexNet has a deeper network architecture and more neurons, allowing it to recognize more complex and higher-dimensional image features.

AlexNet has three innovative aspects in its network design: 1) It innovatively uses a convolutional stack structure of "convolution-convolution-pooling" in the network architecture for image feature extraction. 2) It employs techniques like dropout and data augmentation to address the issue of overfitting. 3) It replaces the original activation function Sigmoid with the ReLU function, which has better training performance. These three aspects have been widely used in subsequent convolutional neural network architectures (Fig. 3).

VGG16. VGG16 [11] model improves upon AlexNet by replacing the larger convolutional kernels in the original AlexNet with several consecutive convolutional layers with 3×3 kernels. The advantages of this approach are as follows:

1. A deeper network structure is able to learn more complex function transformations, thus improving the network's recognition performance.
2. It has fewer parameters, reducing computational costs. For example, three consecutive 3×3 convolutional layers have a total of 27 parameters, while a single 7×7 convolutional kernel has 49 parameters.
3. Using smaller convolutional kernels is more conducive to preserving image feature information, reducing the probability of underfitting.

The network architecture of VGG16 is shown in Fig. 4.

Number of parameters
AlexNet
FLOPS
4M
Fully connected layer 1000
4M
16M
Fully connected layer 4096 / ReLU
16M
37M
Fully connected layer4096 / ReLU
37M
Max Pooling 3×3s2
442K
Convolution 3×3s1, 256 / ReLU
74M
1.3M
Convolution 3×3s1, 384 / ReLU
112M
884K
Convolution 3×3s1, 384 / ReLU
149M
Max Pooling 3×3s2
Normalization Layer
307K
Convolution 5×5s1, 256 / ReLU
223M
Max Pooling 3×3s2
Normalization Layer
35K
Convolution 11×11s4, 96 / ReLU
105M

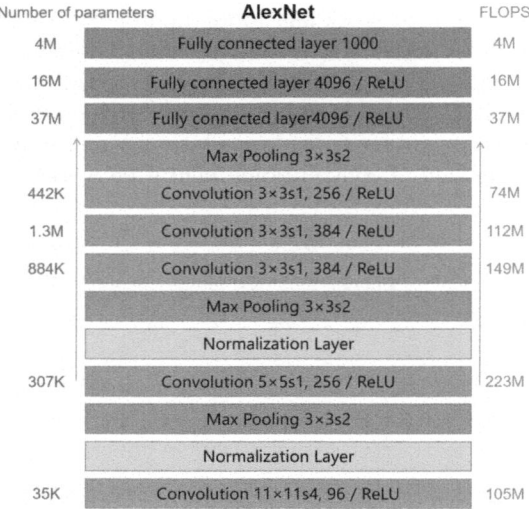

Fig. 3. The Network Architecture of AlexNet [3]

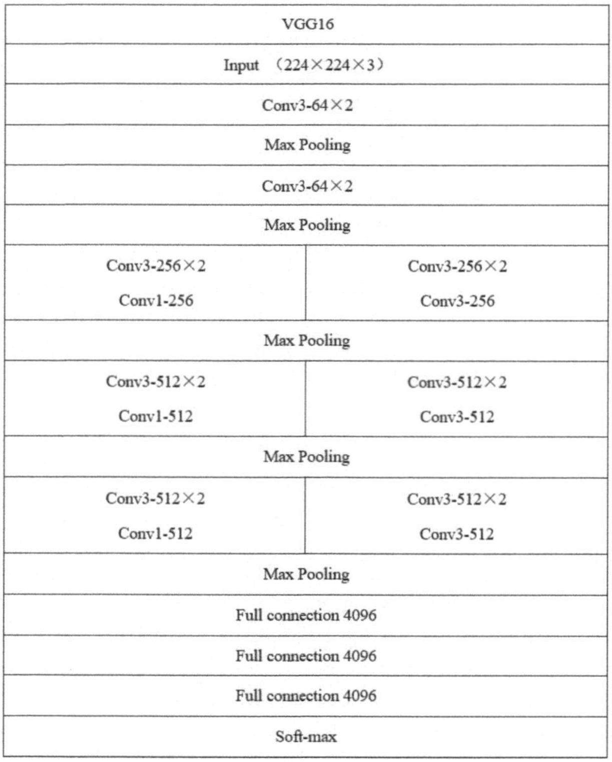

VGG16
Input （224×224×3）
Conv3-64×2
Max Pooling
Conv3-64×2
Max Pooling
Conv3-256×2
Conv1-256
Conv3-256×2
Conv3-256
Max Pooling
Conv3-512×2
Conv1-512
Conv3-512×2
Conv3-512
Max Pooling
Conv3-512×2
Conv1-512
Conv3-512×2
Conv3-512
Max Pooling
Full connection 4096
Full connection 4096
Full connection 4096
Soft-max

Fig. 4. The Network Architecture of VGG16 [11]

3   Research on Face Recognition Methods Based on Attention Mechanism

In this section, we will focus on the convolutional neural network model based on the attention mechanism adopted in this experiment. Firstly, we need to select an appropriate convolutional network and address the problem of difficult learning of identity transformations in deep networks mentioned in the previous chapter. Then, we will introduce the attention mechanism in the field of computer vision and analyze its advantages in feature extraction. Finally, we will attempt to incorporate an attention mechanism module into our chosen neural network to enhance the network's recognition performance.

3.1   Construction of Convolutional Neural Network Model

To better introduce the function and principles of ResNet [1], let's first understand the concept of skip connection. Skip connection refers to a type of connection in residual neural networks that enables the activation values of a certain layer to be passed to deeper layers of the network. It is precisely because of the existence of skip connections that ResNet can train very deep network structures. Now let's analyze the role of skip connections in residual neural networks through Fig. 5 with illustrations.

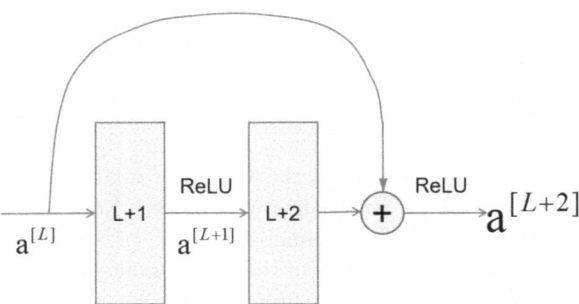

Fig. 5. Skip connections

Assuming there is an L-layer network, with the ReLU function as the activation function, and the activation value output from the Lth layer is $a^{[L]}$. We want to increase the number of layers in the network to achieve better recognition performance, so we add two layers as shown in Fig. 5 to the original network, with the ReLU function as the activation function for these layers as well. After observation, the formula for calculating the activation value output from the (L+2)th layer with skip connection is as follows:

$$a^{[L+2]} = \mathrm{ReLU}\left(z^{[L+2]} + a^{[L]}\right) \tag{3}$$

$$z^{[L+2]} = w^{[L+2]}a^{[L+1]} + b^{[L+2]} \tag{4}$$

where $w^{[L+2]}$ and $b^{[L+2]}$ are the parameters of the (L+2)th layer. By analyzing the above equation, we can see that if $w^{[L+2]}$ and $b^{[L+2]}$ are very small, $z^{[L+2]}$ will tend towards 0, and in this case, $a^{[L+2]}$ will be equal to ReLU($a^{[L]}$). Let's further analyze the specific formula of the ReLU activation function:

$$RELU(z) = \begin{cases} z & \text{if } z \geq 0 \\ 0 & \text{if } z < 0 \end{cases} \tag{5}$$

By observing the formula of ReLU, we can deduce that since the network employs the ReLU function, $a^{[L]}$ must be greater than or equal to 0, hence ReLU($a^{[L]}$) = $a^{[L]}$. This allows us to discover that skip connections enable the network to easily learn identity transformations. Correspondingly, if the added layers do learn something useful, the overall network performance will also improve. The existence of residual structures ensures that as we attempt to expand the network scale and enhance its learning capacity, the learning of identity transformations is not affected by the increasing depth of the network, which significantly enhances the depth limit of the network model to a certain extent. This is the role of skip connections in residual neural networks.

The network structure shown in Fig. 5, which incorporates skip connections, is referred to as a residual block. ResNet is constructed by stacking these residual blocks together. This experiment took into account both the network training cost and recognition performance, ultimately selecting the 34-layer residual network structure, ResNet34. In ResNet34, a skip connection is established every two layers of the network, forming a residual block. The overall structure can be broadly viewed as consisting of 5 network layers. The specific network structure is outlined in Fig. 6:   The specific composition of each network structure layer is as follows:

Convolution 1: The composition of the Convolution 1 layer consists of only one global convolutional layer, which has a relatively broad convolution operation. The convolution kernel has a dimension of $7 \times 7 \times 64$ and a convolution step size of 2. In this layer, the features of the input image are initially extracted.

Convolution 2_x: In this layer, we first perform maximum pooling with a stride of 2 on the feature map input from the previous layer to compress data and parameters. This is followed by three consecutive residual block structures. Each residual block in this network structure layer consists of two convolutional layers, each with a convolution kernel size of $3 \times 3 \times 64$. The output size of this network structure layer is a feature map of $28 \times 28 \times 64$.

Convolution 3_x: Convolution 3_x consists of four consecutive residual blocks, and two of the network layers in the residual block perform convolution with a kernel size of $3 \times 3 \times 128$, resulting in a feature map of $28 \times 28 \times 128$. We can see that after this layer, the length and width of the feature map are halved and the number of channels is doubled for each subsequent network structure layer.

Convolution 4_x: Convolution 4_x includes 6 consecutive residual blocks, each of which has a convolution kernel size of $3 \times 3 \times 256$, resulting in a feature map with a final output dimension of $14 \times 14 \times 256$.

Network Layer	Output Size	Residual Network 34
Conv 1	112×112	7×7, 64, step 2
Conv 2_x	56×56	3×3 Max pooling, step 2
		$\begin{bmatrix} 3 \times 3 & 64 \\ 3 \times 3 & 64 \end{bmatrix} \times 3$
Conv 3_x	28×28	$\begin{bmatrix} 3 \times 3 & 128 \\ 3 \times 3 & 128 \end{bmatrix} \times 4$
Conv 4_x	14×14	$\begin{bmatrix} 3 \times 3 & 256 \\ 3 \times 3 & 256 \end{bmatrix} \times 6$
Conv 5_x	7×7	$\begin{bmatrix} 3 \times 3 & 512 \\ 3 \times 3 & 512 \end{bmatrix} \times 3$
	1×1	Pooling, 1000d full connection, soft-max
FLOPS		3.6×10^9

Fig. 6. The Network Architecture of Resnet

Convolution 5_x: Convolution 5_x consists of three consecutive residual blocks, with a convolution kernel size of $3 \times 3 \times 512$ for each layer. In this layer, the number of feature map channels in the network is further expanded to 512, with each channel outputting a feature map size of 7×7 After going through the five network structure layers described above, the output $7 \times 7 \times 512$ feature map is subjected to a global average pooling operation to obtain a $1 \times 1 \times 512$ one-dimensional vector, which is equivalent to 512 neural units. Then, a fully connected layer is used to classify the output through the softmax function to obtain the final desired output.

The number of floating-point operations performed by the above process per second is approximately 3.6×10^9. The ResNet34 network and the VGG16 network are similar in recognition speed, but the ResNet34 network clearly has deeper network layers and the ability to learn more features of the input image.

3.2 Attention Mechanism

When humans observe an image, our brains tend to selectively process the information perceived by our eyes. For example, in the Fig. 7, human attention is often focused more on the eagle in the picture, while ignoring the information about the sky in the background. This is a manifestation of the role of attention in actual observation.

In general neural network training, the network treats all features of the input image equivalently. This not only increases the computational burden but also makes it possible for some non-essential features to overshadow important ones, interfering with the network model's recognition of objects. Therefore, we hope that when our network recognizes images, it can also make choices about the

Fig. 7. Eagle

input features, ignoring some information that is irrelevant to the recognition target. This is because, based on our simple intuition, when we glance over an image, it is often difficult to form a deep impression; however, focusing on specific parts can allow us to pay attention to some important information. The same applies to neural networks. Take the above image as an example, obviously, we hope that the neural network can recognize that this is a picture of an eagle. However, since the sky occupies more pixels in the image, without making choices, the network may mistakenly identify it as a picture of the sky.

The advantages of the attention mechanism in face recognition projects are also obvious. The network model with the attention mechanism will pay more attention to distinctive key points such as eyebrows, eyes, noses, and mouth corners during training, while ignoring other irrelevant information including the background. This greatly enhances the distinction of feature information, reduces the risk of misjudgment, and improves the effect of the face recognition model.

In contemporary computer vision, the attention mechanism is often implemented through masking. Specifically, it involves highlighting the areas of the image that require attention through re-encoding, allowing the network to learn the features that need to be focused on through training, thus achieving the attention mechanism in the network. This idea has led to the birth of two different attention mechanisms: soft attention and hard attention. Soft attention is deterministic attention, with attention domains including spatial domain, channel domain, and mixed domain. Since the parameters in soft attention are differentiable, they can be directly generated through network training. However, hard attention is not differentiable and is mainly implemented through reinforcement learning.

3.3   Study on Attention Mechanism in Convolutional Neural Networks

The attention module selected in this experiment is the champion of the 2017 ILSVR competition, SENet [2] Squeeze-and-Excitation Networks. The SE structure is an attention implementation module for the channel domain, which focuses on the learning of channel features by assigning different weights to each channel of the input feature map, reducing the impact of less relevant channel features on the output. The weight parameters of each channel are obtained by the network through self-learning, and like other parameters in the network, they are iteratively optimized by the network's final loss function and optimizer. The structure of the SE module is shown in the Fig. 8.

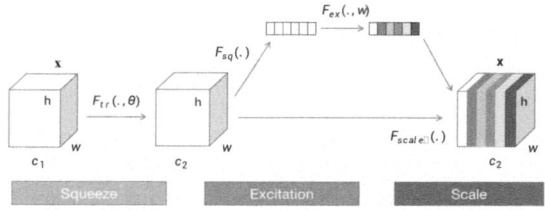

Fig. 8. The structure of the SE module [2]

As we can see from the Fig. 8, the internal operation of the SE structure mainly includes three steps, namely Squeeze, Excitation, and Scale. The F_{tr} in the figure refers to the conventional convolution operation. In the Squeeze operation, the feature map with dimensions $W \times H \times C$ from the upper network is compressed into a feature vector with dimensions $1 \times 1 \times C$, which is achieved through global average pooling in the network. In this step, each channel is compressed into 1 dimension, which to some extent can be considered as representing the global receptive field of each channel's real number, which will play an important role in subsequent tasks. The specific formula for the F_{sq} operation in the figure is as described in the formula 6.

$$s = F_{sq}(c_2) = \frac{1}{H \times W} \sum_{i=1}^{H} \sum_{j=1}^{W} c_2(i, j), z \in R^C \tag{6}$$

The subsequent Excitation operation is similar to a two-layer fully connected network, where the network automatically learns the weights of each channel through the parameter w, explicitly establishing the correlation between channels at a macro level. In Excitation, the network incorporates the $1 \times 1 \times C$ one-dimensional vector generated after the Squeeze operation into a fully connected layer, and is activated through the ReLU function after linear transformation. In the second fully connected layer, we need to predict the weight coefficients of each channel in the feature map. Therefore, in this layer, we choose to use the Sigmoid function as the activation function, and finally output the weight coefficients of each channel. The r in the fully connected layer is the attenuation coefficient, which exists to reduce the number of neurons and reduce the computational scale. The F_{ex} change formula in this process is as follows:

$$F_{ex}(z, W) = \sigma(g(z, W)) = sigmoid(W_2 ReLU(W_1 z)) \tag{7}$$

The dimensional spaces of W1 and W2 are respectively:

$$W_1 \in R^{\frac{C}{r} \times C}, W_2 \in R^{C \times \frac{C}{r}} \tag{8}$$

Finally, in the Scale operation, we multiply each channel with the C 0–1 weight coefficients output in Excitation, which achieves a certain degree of trade-off between different channel features and obtains the feature map after the hybrid attention mechanism.

$$\bar{x} \cdot c = Fscale(c, s) = s \cdot c \tag{9}$$

In this paper, we will add an SE module after each residual branch and before the aggregation in the original network to achieve the effect of hybrid attention mechanism in the network. We will discuss the improvement of the network model recognition performance after adding attention mechanism in the next section.

4   Experimental Results and Analysis

4.1   Selection and Preprocessing of the Dataset

The experimental data used in this experiment was provided by volunteers. The face data of the volunteers was captured by a camera, and the face information was captured and cropped using the Haar face detector from the OpenCV library. The captured images were then recorded into different folders. Subsequently, two lists, imgs and labs, were created. The imgs list was used to store the face data, while labs represented the corresponding labels. As the imgs list read in the face data, labels were assigned to the images based on their respective file paths. Finally, the zip function was used to combine the images with their corresponding labels into tuples, resulting in the final dataset. A total of 10,000 face images from 10 volunteers were collected in this experiment, with 1,000 images per volunteer. These data were randomly split into a training set and a testing set in a 7:3 ratio (Fig. 9).

To meet the requirements of face recognition under various complex conditions, we processed the experimental data to varying degrees. Firstly, we asked the volunteers participating in the experiment to perform a series of continuous pose and expression changes during the face data collection process, which enriched the facial features and improved the ability of the training model to recognize faces under different poses. Secondly, we also recorded a batch of

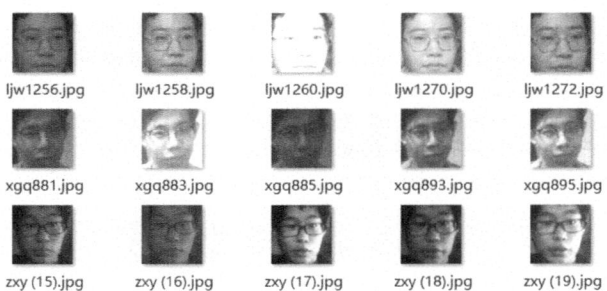

Fig. 9. Training face data

image data of volunteers wearing masks during the face data collection, simulating facial features under occlusion conditions and enhancing the model's scene adaptability. Then, we wrote a reshape function to randomly crop and flip some images to avoid overfitting during network training. Finally, we wrote a relight function that randomly reassigned values to each pixel of the recorded images based on their original values, randomly changing the image brightness to simulate facial features under different lighting conditions, enabling the training model to handle extreme scenarios such as overexposure and overly dark scenes.

By preprocessing the experimental samples, we effectively reduced the risk of overfitting and improved the robustness of the model to a certain extent, enabling the trained model to excel in face recognition tasks under different environments.

4.2   Selection of Hyperparameters

In convolutional neural networks, there exist a large number of parameters. Among them, the parameters that the network needs to learn, and which are the focus of this paper, are the parameters w in each convolutional kernel and the bias parameters b. Their final values determine the final output of the neural network model. However, there are also various other parameters in the network, whose values are subjectively determined by the experimenter and can influence the learning results and efficiency of the parameters w and b. These parameters are called hyperparameters, including the network's learning rate, the number of gradient descent iterations, the activation function, etc. In this section, we will focus on introducing two hyperparameters that are most relevant to our research objectives and explain how we determined these hyperparameters. These two hyperparameters are the network learning rate and the reduction ratio r in the SE structure.

Learning Rate. The learning rate is a hyperparameter of considerable importance in all supervised learning networks. The assignment of the learning rate determines whether the target loss function can converge and the speed of convergence. An appropriate learning rate can enable the network's loss function to converge in the shortest time while ensuring the accuracy of the network.

Let's use the gradient descent algorithm as an example to describe the effect of the learning rate in supervised learning. In gradient descent, the iteration formula for each parameter is as follows, where the parameter α represents the learning rate, which can also be understood as the step size of gradient descent.

$$\theta_j = \theta_j - \alpha \frac{\Delta J(\theta)}{\Delta \theta_j} \tag{10}$$

In the gradient descent algorithm exemplified in this paper, the value of the hyperparameter α should not be too small or too large. A small value can lead to slow convergence of parameters, while a large value may cause the parameters to bounce repeatedly around the convergence point, as shown in the Fig. 10. Therefore, the selection of the learning rate must be within an appropriate range.

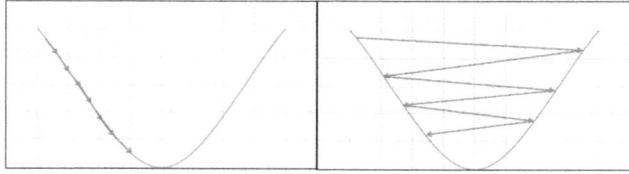

Fig. 10. The Impact of Learning Rate on the Convergence Process of Functions

Currently, the commonly used learning rate setting standard in various studies is to initially assign a relatively large value to the learning rate to accelerate the convergence speed when the network begins learning. As the number of iterations increases, the learning rate is gradually reduced to prevent oscillation of the learning function around the convergence point. After summarizing and analyzing, we can further break down the problem of selecting the learning rate into choosing the initial learning rate and how to perform learning rate decay.

In this paper, for the problem of selecting the initial learning rate, we refer to the method proposed in Leslie N. Smith's paper [12]. In this paper's approach, the experimental data is divided into several batches. After each batch of data training is completed, the network parameters are reset, and the final loss function after that batch's training is recorded. We also vary the learning rate with each change in training batch, ultimately obtaining a one-to-one mapping between the loss function and the learning rate. The final mapping result has already been derived in that paper, and the mapping curve is shown in Fig. 11.

In the figure, it is evident that the initial learning rate that minimizes the loss function is 0.1, which is also the initial learning rate chosen by most experiments. Therefore, in this experiment, we also assign the initial value of the learning rate as 0.1.

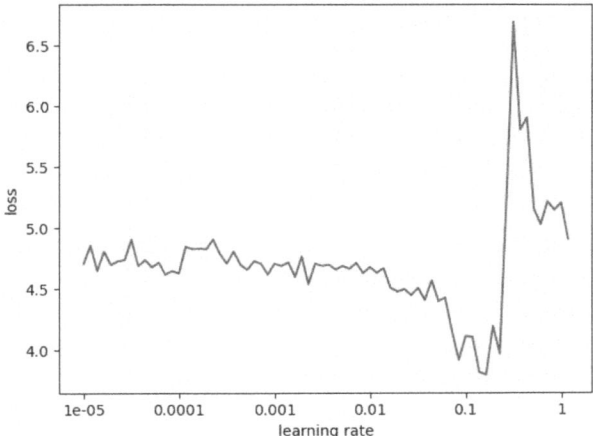

Fig. 11. The Curve of Loss Function Varying with the Initial Learning Rate

Regarding the issue of learning rate decay, it can be further divided into two methods: unlimited decay and interval decay. In our experiments, we choose interval decay. This involves setting a range for the decay rate (in this experiment, the range is 0.001–0.1) and allowing the learning rate to vary within this range as the training data increases. Here, we choose a cosine decay. With this approach, the issue of learning rate decay in convolutional network training is also resolved.

Decay Parameter. As shown in Fig. 8, it is evident that in the first fully connected layer of the Excitation operation, the number of channel units is reduced from C to C/r, where r is the reduction parameter in the SE (Squeeze-and-Excitation) structure. The role of the hyperparameter r is to simplify the network structure and reduce the number of parameters required for learning the channel weight coefficients. Clearly, the choice of the hyperparameter r will directly affect the effectiveness of the SE module and the amount of parameter computations.

In our experiments, we will refer to the experimental results from the original paper to select the hyperparameters. The original paper presents the Top-1 and Top-5 error rates corresponding to different reduction factors as well as the number of parameters in the SE module. From the experimental data, we observe that the impact of the reduction factor on the network error rate is not significant, and a larger reduction factor obviously results in a smaller number of parameters. Therefore, considering both maintaining network performance and minimizing computational cost, we ultimately select a reduction parameter of 16.

4.3   Analysis of the Enhancement Effect of Attention Mechanism

The general idea of this experiment is to utilize the same dataset to train a ResNet34 network with an SE (Squeeze-and-Excitation) module and a ResNet34 network without an SE module, respectively. By comparing and analyzing the recognition accuracy of the two networks upon convergence, we aim to evaluate the improvement effect of introducing the attention mechanism on the network.

1. Randomly shuffle the 10,000 face images used in the experiment and divide them into 100 batches (epochs).
2. Train the networks in batches using the experimental data, and record the recognition accuracy of the test set after each batch of training is completed.
3. Plot the variation curves of recognition accuracy for the two networks for further analysis.

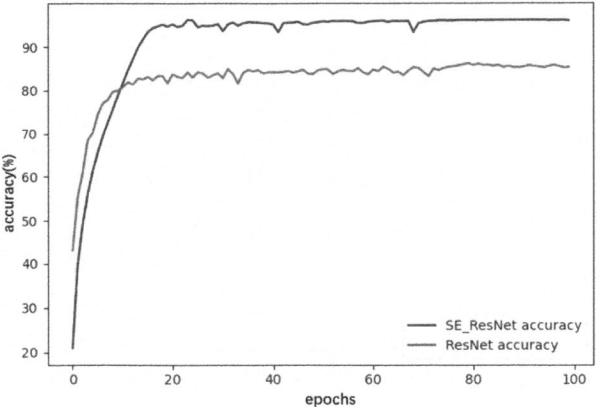

Fig. 12. Comparison of Recognition Effects of Residual Networks

After analyzing the curves in Fig. 12, this paper draws the following conclusions:

At the beginning of the training, the accuracy of the conventional ResNet34 network was significantly higher than that of the ResNet34 network with the SE module. Moreover, the conventional ResNet34 network converged earlier. Upon initial analysis, this situation may have occurred due to the introduction of more parameters, leading to an increase in the amount of learning. However, the final converged recognition accuracy of the conventional ResNet34 network was not high, only around 85.7%. In contrast, the recognition accuracy of the model with the SE module increased significantly, and the final converged accuracy on the test set reached 96.1%, representing an approximate 10-percentage-point improvement. It can be seen that the introduction of the attention mechanism significantly enhances the network's recognition performance.

4.4   Research on the Insertion Position of SE Blocks

In the original paper, the authors of the SENet development team pointed out various ways of inserting SE blocks into ResNet networks. Depending on the position of insertion, we categorize SE residual blocks into several different network structures, including the standard SE structure, SE-PRE structure, SE-POST structure, and SE-Identity structure. The specific network structures are illustrated in the Fig. 13.

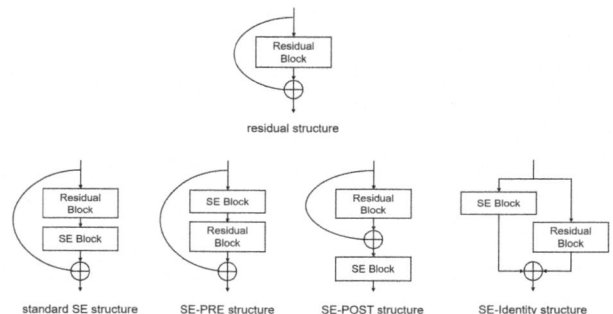

Fig. 13. Placement of SE Modules at Different Positions in the Residual Structure

This paper constructed SE_ResNet34 network models based on the above four structures. Then, experiments were conducted using the same dataset on these four different network structures, and the final converged network accuracies are as shown in Table 1:

Table 1. Accuracy under different network structure

Network structure	Accuracy
Standard SE	96.21%
SE-PRE	95.89%
SE-POST	92.53%
SE-Identity	91.89%

Based on the analysis of Table 1, the following conclusions can be drawn in this paper: the accuracy rates of the standard SE structure and the SE-PRE structure are almost identical, while the SE-POST structure and the SE-Identity structure relatively perform worse in terms of recognition accuracy. This aligns with the experimental results in the original paper (it should be noted that the original experiment drew conclusions based on the analysis of Top_1 Error and Top_5 Error). Therefore, it is concluded that in the residual network structure, the optimal insertion position for the SE block is after the residual branch and before the convergence of the branches. Based on this, it is deemed appropriate to select the standard SE structure or the SE-PRE structure as the experimental network in this paper.

4.5 SE Module Performance in Different Backbone Networks

To further explore the effectiveness of SE modules on different networks based on previous research, we also selected VGG16 as the backbone model for experimentation. In the analysis of the VGG16 model in Sect. 2.2.3 of this paper, we learned that the VGG16 model consists of 5 layers (with each pooling layer as a boundary). We added an SE module after each pooling layer and then conducted comparative experiments using the same dataset to analyze the improvement effect of the SE module on the VGG16 network model. Figure 14 shows the accuracy curves of the training set before and after introducing the SE module to the VGG16 model.

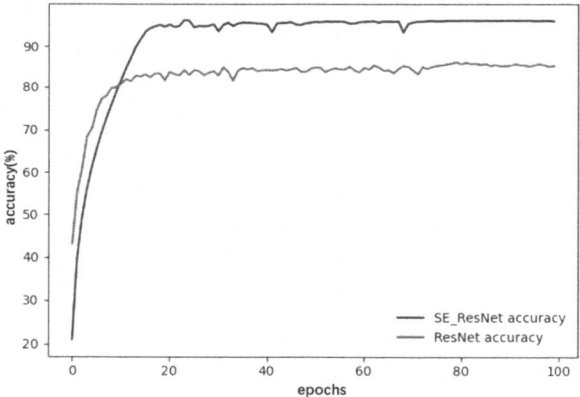

Fig. 14. SE-VGG16 recognition effect comparison

The experimental results show that the accuracy of the VGG16 model on the test set after convergence is approximately 85.63%, while the accuracy of the test set after adding the SE module is about 93.71%. Figure 15 depicts the accuracy curves of the test set during training for different backbone SENets, with the orange line representing the SE_ResNet34 network and the green line representing the SE_VGG16 network.

By analyzing the curves in Figs. 14 and 15, we can observe that the SE module significantly improves the recognition performance of the VGG16 network. In fact, numerous studies have shown that the SE module effectively enhances different backbone networks. Therefore, regardless of which network model is

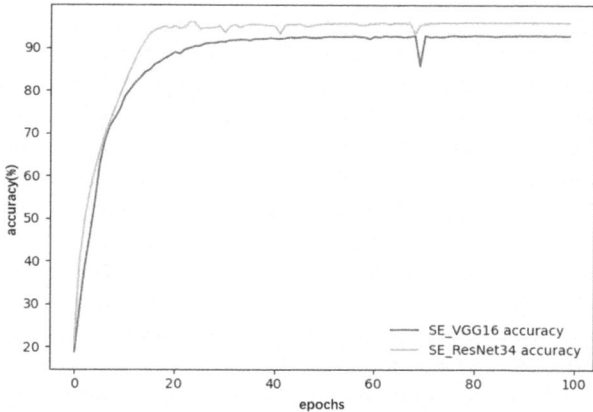

Fig. 15. SE-Net recognition effect of different backbone networks

used in the face recognition algorithm, the SE module can be utilized to optimize the network structure and enhance recognition performance. It is evident that the SE module possesses good universality for different networks.

5   Conclusion

5.1   Article Summary

At the beginning of the article, we first introduced the origin of the concept of face recognition and explained the practical application and scientific significance of this topic. Then we detailed the current research status and application of face recognition technology both domestically and internationally, leading to the introduction of traditional face recognition methods and modern face recognition technology based on deep learning. Subsequently, we focused on face recognition algorithms based on convolutional neural networks, introduced in detail the network architecture and algorithmic process of convolutional neural networks for face recognition, and analyzed the characteristics and limitations of classical convolutional networks. Aiming at the problems discovered in our previous work, starting from the network structure and feature weights, this paper proposed a residual neural network with a hybrid attention mechanism as the network structure for this experiment, and obtained good feedback results in the final experiment.

In summary, the key points of this experiment are as follows:

First, this paper selected several representative and constructive convolutional neural network models in the field of computer vision, collected and summarized academic materials related to these networks, and analyzed and summarized the structural characteristics and innovations of each network. These characteristics are widely used in today's convolutional neural networks. Therefore, by analyzing these traditional network structures, we can further understand the common characteristics and advantages of convolutional neural network structures, as well as their deficiencies in facing some specific problems.

Second, to address the difficulty in learning identity changes in deep networks, we chose to utilize a residual neural network structure through research. Then we introduced the skip connection structure, and by analyzing the specific formulas of operations and activation functions in skip connections, we explained how the learning ability of the residual network structure remains superior in deep networks. Furthermore, to enable the network to ignore other irrelevant features and focus on face feature recognition in complex environments, we proposed the idea of hybrid attention mechanisms in the experimental network and introduced the SE structure, an attention module based on the channel domain.

Finally, based on the above-mentioned concepts, we conducted experiments on the efficiency of face recognition models. The experimental data came from 10 volunteers, totaling 10,000 face images, which were randomly divided into a training set and a test set in a 7:3 ratio. The experimental networks were ResNet34 and ResNet34 with an SE structure, both of which were constructed using PyTorch in a Python environment. The network with the hybrid attention mechanism was trained on the same dataset, and the value of the loss function after each iteration and the final results were continuously recorded. In these experiments, experimental variables were strictly controlled, and the experimental conclusions were drawn by comparing the recognition performance of the network before and after integrating the attention mechanism.

The conclusions of this experiment are as follows:

1. The network with a hybrid attention mechanism achieves a significant improvement in face recognition efficiency.
2. The attention module can be added to any position in the network structure, but the improvement efficiency varies.
3. The attention module has strong universality and can improve the performance of networks with any structure.

5.2   Future Outlook

This paper proposes a network recognition algorithm that integrates a hybrid attention mechanism into a residual neural network, which demonstrates relatively superior recognition rates compared to traditional network models in handling face recognition problems. However, to address more complex recognition issues and capture more facial features, there are still many aspects of this experimental project that can be improved. Currently, the author believes that the following directions are worthy of further in-depth research:

1. The experimental data used in this experiment were provided by volunteers around the author, which lacks sufficient generalizability in terms of the number of identified individuals and the variety of facial features. Additionally, the processing of the experimental data, which only includes the occlusion

of masks, is insufficient to mimic all occlusion scenarios in real life. Therefore, in the later stages of the experiment, we can expand the network training dataset by including faces with other characteristics (such as faces of
European or other ethnic groups), modify the data processing approach, and
simulate facial features under more diverse conditions.

2. The number of network layers used in the experiment is relatively small.
   Currently, the residual network alone has already evolved into structures with
   50, 108, or even deeper layers, and other deep learning algorithms also utilize
   networks with more layers. A deeper network means that it can learn more
   facial features, which translates to better recognition performance under more
   complex conditions. In future experiments, we can conduct experiments with
   hybrid attention mechanisms on deeper and more diverse networks.

3. The SE module adopted in this experiment is not the only attention structure
   available. For instance, there are also lightweight attention modules like the
   ECA [20] module. Furthermore, the SE module is an attention structure based
   on the channel domain, while there are also attention algorithms based on
   the spatial domain and mixed domains. The application or combination of
   these attention mechanisms in convolutional networks represents a promising
   direction for future research.

Acknowledgement. This work is supported in part by National Key R&D Program
of China under Grant Nos. 2022YFB3103700 and 2022YFB3103702, and National Natural Science Foundation of China under Grant Nos. 62272193 and 62102161, and CCF-
Baidu Open Fund (No. 2021PP15002000)

References

1. He, K., Zhang, X., Ren, S., Sun, J.: Deep residual learning for image recognition. In:
   Proceedings of the IEEE Conference on Computer Vision and Pattern Recognition,
   pp. 770–778 (2016)
2. Hu, J., Shen, L., Sun, G.: Squeeze-and-excitation networks. In: Proceedings of the
   IEEE Conference on Computer Vision and Pattern Recognition, pp. 7132–7141
   (2018)
3. Krizhevsky, A., Sutskever, I., Hinton, G.E.: ImageNet classification with deep convolutional neural networks. In: Advances in Neural Information Processing Systems, vol. 25 (2012)
4. LeCun, Y., Bottou, L., Bengio, Y., Haffner, P.: Gradient-based learning applied to
   document recognition. Proc. IEEE **86**(11), 2278–2324 (1998)
5. Li, H., Zhiwen, Yu., Luo, Y., Cui, H., Guo, B.: ContinuousSensing: a task allocation
   algorithm for human-robot collaborative mobile crowdsensing with task migration.
   CCF Trans. Pervasive Comput. Inter. **2024**, 1–16 (2024)
6. Liu, Y., Chen, J., Li, Y., Wu, T., Wen, H.: Joint face normalization and representation learning for face recognition. Pattern Anal. Appl. **27**(2), 1–15 (2024)
7. Mahmood, N.H., Ariffin, I., Omar, C., Jaafar, N.S.: MATLAB implementation of
   face identification using principal component analysis. Adv. Mater. Res. **433**(2012),
   5402–5408 (2012)

8. Rafi, S., Das, R.: Topic-guided abstractive multimodal summarization with multimodal output. Neural Comput. Appl. **2023**, 1–16 (2023)

9. Ren, Y., Wang, Z., Chen, Y., Shan, X., Zhao, W.: Sparsity preserving discriminative learning with applications to face recognition. J. Electr. Imaging **25**(1), 013005–013005 (2016)

10. Scheschenja, M., Viniol, S., Bastian, M.B., Wessendorf, J., Konig, A.M., Mahnken, A.H.: Feasibility of GPT-3 and GPT-4 for in-depth patient education prior to interventional radiological procedures: a comparative analysis. Cardiovasc. Interv. Radiol. **47**(2), 245–250 (2024)

11. Simonyan, K., Zisserman, A.: Very deep convolutional networks for large-scale image recognition. arXiv preprint: arXiv:1409.1556 (2014)

12. Smith, L.N.: Cyclical learning rates for training neural networks. In: 2017 IEEE Winter Conference on Applications of Computer Vision (WACV). IEEE, pp. 464–472 (2017)

13. Yan, H., Yang, J.: Joint Laplacian feature weights learning. Pattern Recogn. **47**(3), 1425–1432 (2014)

14. Yang, B., Li, Q.Z.: Local binary pattern-based discriminant graph construction for dimensionality reduction with application to face recognition. Multimedia Tools Appl. **78**(16), 22445–22462 (2019)

15. Zhang, D., Xiong, H., Wang, L., Chen, G.: CrowdRecruiter: selecting participants for piggyback crowdsensing under probabilistic coverage constraint. In: Proceedings of the 2014 ACM International Joint Conference on Pervasive and Ubiquitous Computing, pp. 703–714 (2014)

16. 傅山, 王嘉义, 宁华, and 魏凡星. 基于人工智能的人脸识别技术与评估体系研究. 信息通信技术与政策 **47**(4), 71 (2021)

17. 刘茹莹. 浅谈人脸识别技术的发展. 信息记录材料 **21**(4), 21–22 (2020)

18. 孙文斌, 王荣, 孙连烛, 林源松., et al.: 基于深度学习的跨年龄人脸识别. Laser Optoelectr. Progress **59**(2), 0215001–0215001 (2022)

19. 徐遐龄, 刘涛, 田国辉, 于文娟, 肖大军, and 梁陕鹏. 有遮挡环境下的人脸识别方法综述. J. Comput. Eng. Appl. **57**, 17 (2021)

20. 车思韬, 郭荣佐, 李卓阳, and 杨军. 注意力机制结合残差收缩网络对遥感图像分类. Appl. Res. Comput./Jisuanji Yingyong Yanjiu **39**, 8 (2022)

Lightweight and Efficient Top-Down Human Pose Estimation Algorithm Research

Xiaofang Mu[1], Minghui Song[1(✉)] [iD], Hong Shi[1], Mingxing Hou[1], Shuxian Guo[1], and Wu Xiaotong[2]

[1] College of Computer Science Taiyuan Normal University, Taiyuan 030000, China
s437267115@163.com
[2] Insight Academy of Canada, Scarborough, Canada

Abstract. To address the challenge of enhancing the performance of human pose estimation algorithms while reducing floating-point computation, this paper proposes an efficient top-down lightweight human pose estimation model called Efficient RTMPose, which is built on RTMPose. Firstly, we propose MBLConv and apply it to EfficientNet as the backbone network of RTMPose to reduce the number of parameters and computational load. MBLConv comprises a series of convolutions and the Large Selective Kernel (LSK) mechanism, allowing for the dynamic adjustment of the receptive field of the feature extraction backbone. This allows the model to have a larger receptive field, enhancing its capability for human keypoint detection tasks. Next, we propose the tAPE-GAU, which integrates time Absolute Position Encoding (tAPE) into the Gate Attention Unit (GAU). By leveraging both global and local spatial information, tAPE-GAU maintains low parameter and computational complexity while enhancing the network's performance and robustness. This paper conducts experimental validation using MBLConv and tAPE-GAU on the MPII and COCO2017 datasets. The results demonstrate significant improvements in accuracy, parameter efficiency, and computational load compared to traditional models.

Keywords: Human pose estimation · Lightweight networks · Attention mechanisms · Absolute position encoding

1 Introduction

The human pose estimation algorithm has achieved excellent performance on the public benchmark set. However, its huge amount of computation and parameters is heavily dependent on efficient computing equipment, preventing deployment on edge devices to achieve real-time results. On the other hand, lightweight models often fail to meet the performance requirements for industrial applications. This paper investigates how to enhance performance while maintaining low computational requirements.

This work was supported by Shanxi Province Basic Research Program (202303021211187), Science and Technology Innovation Program for Higher Education Institutions in Shanxi Province (2022L403).

Although BlazePose [1] and optimized versions of MoveNet [2] have achieved real-time performance, they still fall short of meeting performance requirements. Existing efficient human pose estimation networks typically employ two approaches. One approach is to choose lightweight classification networks such as MobileNet [3], Efficient-Net [4], and ShuffleNet [5] to minimize redundancy in matrix-vector multiplication operations within convolutions. The other approach involves regression to determine keypoint information and reduce computational load. However, both of these methods often result in a decrease in network performance. Thus, the challenge of enhancing performance while maintaining low parameter counts arises.

In this paper, we present a novel structure called MBLConv, which incorporates spatial attention through the use of the Large Selective Kernel (LSK) [6] module. This allows for dynamic adjustment of the receptive field of the feature extraction backbone, enabling more effective processing of diverse backgrounds for detected objects. Additionally, the utilization of larger convolutional kernels enhances the network's receptive field, making it more suitable for our human keypoint detection task. We apply this module to EfficientNet [4] as the backbone network for RTMPose. Compared to the original model that utilizes CSPNext [7], our approach effectively reduces both the parameter count and computational load of the model.

Transformer [8] has demonstrated outstanding performance in numerous deep learning applications. When applied to time series data, Transformers require effective position encoding to capture the sequence of the data. In this paper, we propose tAPE-GAU, which incorporates time Absolute Position Encoding (tAPE) [9] into the Gated Attention Unit (GAU) [10]. This injects temporal positional information into the input embedding vectors, enabling the model to comprehend the order of tokens in the sequence. It further utilizes global information to better represent keypoints, enhancing the model's generalization ability. Experimental results show that this module significantly improves model performance while maintaining the same parameter count and computational load.

In summary, the primary contributions of this paper are as follows:

- We propose a novel structure, MBLConv, and apply it to EfficientNet as the backbone network for RTMPose. This significantly reduces the number of parameters and computational load of the model while maintaining accuracy.
- We propose tAPE-GAU, which introduces time Absolute Position Encoding (tAPE) into the Gated Attention Unit (GAU). This enables the model to better utilize global information for keypoint representation. By maintaining the same parameter count and computational load, tAPE-GAU significantly improves model performance.
- We propose Efficient RTMPose and experimentally evaluated on both the COCO2017 and MPII datasets. It demonstrates the ability to improve model performance while reducing computational complexity.

2   Related Works

Human Pose Estimation Framework: The objective of this task is to detect, locate, and connect the coordinates of key points on the human body in an image, forming a skeletal representation of the human body. In recent years, the performance of human pose estimation algorithms has continuously improved. However, maintaining high performance often comes with high parameter counts and computational costs, making these models unsuitable for deployment on edge devices. This limitation restricts their ability to effectively enhance our daily lives. To address this issue, Yu proposed an improved and efficient network called Lite-HRNet [11]. This network replaces the high-cost 1×1 convolution in the Shuffle Block with a conditional channel weighting unit. It calculates weights across channels and resolutions, effectively reducing computational costs;HRNet-DEKR [12] utilizes a direct regression approach for keypoint coordinates. It extracts features and conducts regression separately for each keypoint, thus achieving decoupling between keypoints;Li proposed a regression-based method known as Simple Coordinate Classification (SimCC) [13], which conducts coordinate classification independently for vertical and horizontal coordinates to generate the final predictions.These methods effectively improve model efficiency but at the cost of performance. Our work aims to design a model that achieves both high efficiency and high performance to meet the needs of industrial applications.

Vision Transformers: The Transformer model [8], a classic algorithm in the field of Natural Language Processing (NLP), has also achieved notable success in practical visual computation. Squeeze-and-Excitation (SE) [14] is a channel attention module that adaptively recalibrates feature responses along channel directions by explicitly modeling interdependencies between channels; Spatial attention modules, such as GCNet [15] and SGE [16] enhance the network's capacity to model contextual information through spatial masks; Woo combined the advantages of spatial and channel attention mechanisms to propose CBAM [17]. Li designed a building block called the Selective Kernel (SK) unit [18], which can capture objects at different scales, enabling neurons to adaptively adjust their receptive field sizes based on the input. The LSK module is similar to the SK unit block, which adaptively aggregates feature information along the channel dimension, the LSK module aggregates feature information along the spatial dimension. We utilized the LSK module to develop MBLConv and integrated it into EfficientNet, improving its capacity to extract human keypoint features.

Positional Encoding: The self-attention mechanism in Transformers [8] is insensitive to positional information, as it disregards the order of elements in the input sequence. Even if the positions of two elements in the sequence are swapped, the encoded result remains unaffected. To address the temporal issue, Dosovitskiy [19] proposed absolute positional encoding, while Chu [20] introduced dynamically generated conditional position encodings (CPE). Since these positional encodings are predefined and independent of input tokens, they can easily generalize to input sequences longer than those observed during training. On the other hand, tAPE considers the input embedding dimensions and length by incorporating the embedding dimension parameters into the frequency terms of the sine and cosine functions. This allows for easy integration into the Transformer module. By incorporating this positional encoding into the gating mechanism, we effectively enhanced the model's accuracy without escalating computational expenses.

Gating Mechanism: The Gated Recurrent Unit (GRU) [21] includes two gating mechanisms: the update gate and the reset gate. These mechanisms enable the GRU network to selectively remember or ignore information when processing sequential data, thereby better capturing long-term dependencies within sequences.The Gated Linear Unit (GLU) [22] divides the input vector into two equal parts. One part is used for gating, while the other part is weighted using the gating mechanism to retain important information and discard irrelevant information. Compared to GRU, GLU has fewer parameters; The Gated Attention Unit (GAU) combines attention mechanisms with gating mechanisms to better handle long sequences with higher computational efficiency and improve model performance. Our tAPE-GAU further enhances GAU by introducing time Absolute Position Encoding. This enhancement improves model performance while maintaining similar efficiency.

3   Method

3.1   Efficient RTMPose

This paper proposes Efficient RTMPose based on RTMPose [23]. The overall structure is shown in Fig. 1. The backbone network selected for feature extraction is MBL-EfficientNet. The Large Selective Kernel mechanism offers a larger receptive field, effectively enhancing the ability to extract features of human keypoints, compared to the original model using CSPNext-m [7], our model shows a 0.3% decrease in accuracy on the MPII dataset, but with a 58% reduction in the number of parameters and a 77% reduction in computational cost. Subsequently, a convolutional layer, a fully connected layer, and a gated attention module (tAPE-GAU) are applied. By introducing absolute temporal positional encoding, which further considers both global and local positional information, the model's performance improved by 1.1% without compromising its efficiency. Finally, the output is fed into SimCC [13], which converts the keypoint position prediction task into two classification tasks for the x-axis and y-axis coordinates, predicting the horizontal and vertical positions of the keypoints. We pruned SimCC by removing its expensive upsampling layers, significantly reducing the model's parameter count and computational cost with minimal loss in accuracy.

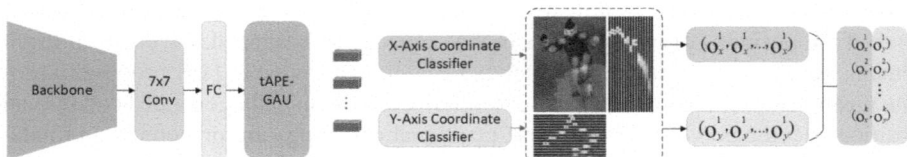

Fig. 1. The overall structure of Efficient RTMPose first involves passing through MBL-EfficientNet and a convolutional layer with a kernel size of 7×7. This is followed by a fully connected layer and a gated attention module, tAPE-GAU, which is used to optimize the representation of K keypoints. Finally, 2D human pose estimation is decomposed into two classification problems along the x-axis and y-axis, with the feature points being localized horizontally and vertically in each direction.

3.2 MBL-EfficientNet

During the training of the pose estimation network, we observed that the recognition accuracy of wrist and ankle joints was relatively low, leading to a degradation in the overall performance of the network. Since these joints are considered small targets in practical scenarios, we aimed to enhance their accuracy by expanding the receptive field.

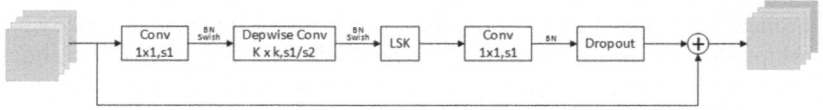

Fig. 2. The MBLConv structure mainly consists of two standard 1×1 convolutions with Batch Normalization (BN) and Swish activation functions, a $k \times k$ Depth-Wise convolution, an LSK module, and a Dropout layer.

This paper proposes a new structure-MBLConv, with its specific architecture illustrated in Fig. 2. By using the LSK module to introduce spatial attention, the receptive field of the feature extraction backbone can be dynamically adjusted. This allows for more effective handling of various extensive backgrounds and enhances the detection of human keypoints. We applied this structure to EfficientNet, resulting in MBL-EfficientNet, and conducted experiments on the MPII dataset. The accuracy of wrist joints increased by 1.4%, knee joints by 2.7%, and ankle joints by 3.0%, while the accuracy of other joints remaining mostly unchanged. Overall, accuracy improved by 1.1%, as shown in Table 4.

Large Selective Kernel

The LSK module employs a spatial selection mechanism based on large Depth-Wise convolution kernels, effectively weighting and spatially integrating them. On this basis, it dynamically adjusts the weights of each convolution, thereby achieving adaptive regulation of each convolution kernel and adjusting the receptive field of each target in the space as needed. The detailed calculation formula is as follows:

$$k_{i-1} \leq k_i; d_1 = 1, d_{i-1} < d_i \leq RF_{i-1} \tag{1}$$

$$RF_1 = k_1, RF_i = d_i(k_i - 1) + RF_{i-1} \tag{2}$$

where k represents the size of the convolution kernel, d denotes the dilation rate, and RF indicates the size of the receptive field.

The core module, LSK, consists of a series of large kernel convolutions and a spatial kernel selection mechanism. The specific structure is shown in Fig. 3. During the forward propagation process, this module weights the input feature map through a series of convolution operations, using Sigmoid weights to adjust the attention of different parts. The final output feature map is the result of the input feature map multiplied by the attention weights.

First, a spatial selection mechanism is used to select features from large convolution kernels of different scales. The features from convolution kernels with different receptive fields are then concatenated:

$$\widetilde{U} = [\widetilde{U}_1; ...; \widetilde{U}_i] \tag{3}$$

Then, average pooling and max pooling operations are applied to $\widetilde{U}$ to extract spatial relationships, denoted as $\mathcal{P}_{avg}$ and $\mathcal{P}_{max}$, respectively. The spatial pooling features are concatenated using a convolutional layer, converting the two-channel pooling features into N spatial attention feature maps:

$$\widehat{SA} = \mathcal{F}^{2 \rightarrow N}([\mathcal{P}_{avg}(\widetilde{U}); \mathcal{P}_{max}(\widetilde{U})]) \tag{4}$$

where $\widehat{SA}$ represents the spatial attention feature maps. Subsequently, the Sigmoid activation function is applied to each spatial attention feature map $\widehat{SA}_i$, yielding independent spatial selection masks corresponding to each large convolution kernel. Next, the features from the decoupled large convolution kernel sequence are weighted with their corresponding spatial selection masks. These are then fused using an $\mathcal{F}(\cdot)$ convolutional layer to obtain the attention feature $\mathcal{S}$:

$$\mathcal{S} = \mathcal{F}(\sum_{i-1}^{N}(\sigma(\widehat{SA}_i) \cdot \widetilde{U}_i)) \tag{5}$$

where σ represents the Sigmoid function. Finally, the output of the LSK module is obtained by performing element-wise multiplication between the input feature $\mathcal{X}$ and the attention feature $\mathcal{S}$:

$$\mathcal{Y} = \mathcal{X} \cdot \mathcal{S} \tag{6}$$

We utilized this module in conjunction with a series of 1×1 convolutions for upscaling and downscaling to create MBLConv. By repeatedly stacking this structure, we constructed LSK-EfficientNet as our backbone network, enabling it to perform the human pose estimation task more effectively.

LSK-EfficientNet utilizes a simple yet efficient compound coefficient to scale CNNs in a more structured manner. Unlike traditional methods that arbitrarily scale network dimensions such as width, depth, and resolution, this approach uniformly scales network dimensions using a series of fixed-scale coefficients (Table 1).

3.3 tAPE-GAU

Since the Gated Attention Unit (GAU) is a self-attention mechanism that is insensitive to position and sequence information, we propose the tAPE-GAU module. This enhancement aims to improve the model's performance by better incorporating temporal and positional information. By introducing time Absolute Position Encoding (tAPE)

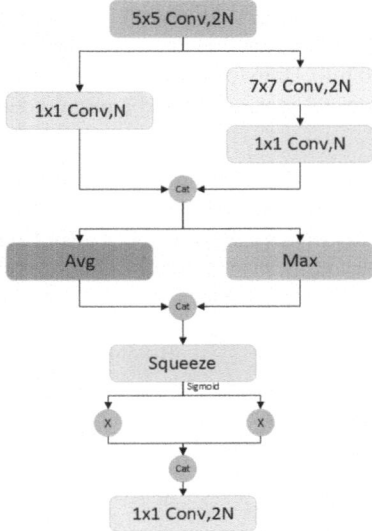

Fig. 3. LSK Module Structure Diagram. Where 1×1Conv, 3×3Conv, 5×5Conv, 7×7Conv represent convolution operations with kernel sizes of 1, 3, 5, and 7, respectively, N represents the number of channels, Cat refers to the concatenation function in Torch, Avg and Max represent average pooling and max pooling operations, and Squeeze denotes the dimensionality reduction operation.

into GAU, we inject temporal position information into the input embedding vectors. This enables the model to comprehend the token sequence's order, empowering it to utilize global information more effectively for improved keypoint representation.

The Gated Attention Unit (GAU) is more efficient and performs better compared to a standard Transformer. Specifically, GAU combines the Gated Linear Unit (GLU) and self-attention mechanisms:

$$O = (\phi_u(XW_u) \odot A \cdot \phi_v(XW_v))W_o \quad \in \mathbb{R}^{T\times d} \tag{7}$$

where $\odot$ represents element-wise multiplication; ϕ is an element-wise activation function; and $A \in \mathbb{R}^{T\times T}$ contains the token-token attention weights. The attention mechanism is implemented using the following method, as shown in Eq. 8:

$$A = \frac{1}{n}relu^2(\frac{Q(X)K(Z)^T}{\sqrt{S}}), Z = \phi_Z(XW_Z) \tag{8}$$

where $W_z = \mathbb{R}^{d\times s}, s$ represents the size of the attention head, and in this paper, we set $s = 128$, Q, K are simple affine transformations, $relu^2$ indicates applying the $relu$ activation function followed by squaring, $1/n$ is a normalization factor used to mitigate the effect of sequence length.

In Eq. 8, if A is an identity matrix, then GAU degenerates into GLU [22]. If U is an all-ones matrix, then GAU degenerates into self-attention.

Time Absolute Position Encoding (tAPE) combines the sequence length and input embedding dimensions in absolute position encoding. This method is simple and effective, can be easily integrated into Transformer modules, and can be used for downstream tasks such as prediction, external regression, and anomaly detection.

Table 1. LSK-EfficientNet Structure Table The LSK-EfficientNet architecture consists of a total of 9 stages. The first stage consists of a standard convolutional layer with a kernel size of 3×3 and a stride of 2. Stages 2 to 8 consist of repeated stacks of the MBLConv structure. Stage 9 consists of a standard 1×1 convolutional layer, an average pooling layer, and a fully connected layer. All convolutional layers include batch normalization (BN) and the Swish activation function.

Stage	Operator	Resolution	Channels	Layers
1	Conv3 × 3	224 × 224	32	1
2	MBLConv1,k3 × 3	112 × 112	16	1
3	MBLConv6,k3 × 3	112 × 112	24	2
4	MBLConv6,k5 × 5	56 × 56	40	2
5	MBLConv6,k3 × 3	28 × 28	80	3
6	MBLConv6,k5 × 5	14 × 14	112	3
7	MBLConv6,k5 × 5	14 × 14	192	4
8	MBLConv6,k3 × 3	7 × 7	320	1
9	Conv1 × 1&Pooling&FC	7 × 7	1280	1

There are several options for absolute position encoding, including fixed encoding using sine and cosine functions of different frequencies, known as Vanilla APE, and learnable encoding through trainable parameters [18]. By using sine and cosine functions for positional encoding, the model's embedding dimension at the i-th timestep position can be represented by the following Eq. 9:

$$p_i(2k) = \sin i\omega_k \quad p_i(2k+1) = \cos i\omega_k \quad \omega_k = 10000^{-\frac{2k}{d_{model}}} \tag{9}$$

where $k \in [0, \frac{d_{model}}{2}]$, d_{model} represents the embedding dimension, ω_k is the frequency term, indicating the frequencies of the sine and cosine functions used to generate the embedding vectors, and position embedding $p_i \in \mathbb{R}^{d_{model}}$, The variation of ω_k ensures that no positions smaller than 10^4 are assigned similar embeddings. However, tAPE considers both the input embedding dimensions and the sequence length, merging the embedding dimension parameter into the frequency term of the sine and cosine functions:

$$\omega_k^{new} = \frac{\omega_k \times d_{model}}{L} \tag{10}$$

where L represents the length of the sequence. tAPE provides a balance between these two properties in its encoding, mitigating the various anomalies that arise as the embedding dimension d_model increases, due to the vectors being sampled from low-frequency sine functions.

Our gated attention module, tAPE-GAU, incorporates time absolute position encoding into the self-attention mechanism, enabling it to consider both sequence and positional information. This optimization enhances the representation of human keypoints, improving the robustness and generalization capability of the algorithm. Experimental results demonstrate that the gated attention module, tAPE-GAU, achieved a 1.2% improvement in accuracy on the MPII dataset while maintaining the same computational complexity.

4   Experiments

4.1   Experimental Environment and Evaluation Indicators

The experimental platform for this study utilized an AMD Ryzen 9 5900X processor and a GeForce RTX 3090 GPU. The Python version employed was 3.8.18. We employed the PyTorch 1.13.1 deep learning framework, utilizing the AdamW optimizer (Adam with decoupled weight decay). The initial learning rate was set to 0.004, and we employed the Flat-Cosine learning rate schedule with a weight decay of 0.05. The experiments in this paper were conducted using the COCO2017 [24] and MPII [25] human keypoint datasets.

COCO is the most popular benchmark for 2D human pose estimation. COCO2017 comprises over 200,000 images with 250,000 annotated human instances, each containing annotations for 17 key points. This paper follows the standard split of train2017 and val2017, containing 118,000 and 5,000 images for training and validation, respectively. Additionally, 20,000 images are reserved for testing. This paper employs the standard mean Average Precision (mAP) as the evaluation metric for the COCO dataset. In this experiment, we exclusively evaluate the performance of models trained solely on the COCO dataset, without combining training with other datasets. The input image size is set to 256×192.

The MPII Human Pose dataset serves as a benchmark for human pose estimation. It comprises approximately 25,000 images with annotations for around 40,000 human instances, each annotated with 16 keypoint locations. The evaluation metric is the $PCKh$ score, which represents the head-normalized probability of correctly detected keypoints. The experiments on the MPII dataset utilize the $PCKh@0.5$ ($\alpha = 0.5$) metric as the evaluation criterion, and the input image size is uniformly set to 256×256.

4.2   Analysis of Results

To demonstrate the effectiveness of our proposed method, we compare it with HigherHRNet [26], DEKR [12], EfficientHRNet [27], AlphaPose [28], SimpleBaseline [29], and RTMPose-m [23] on the COCO2017 dataset, as shown in Table 2:

On the COCO2017 dataset, This algorithm significantly reduces computational load while maintaining high performance. utilizing the MBL-EfficientNet-b0 network resulted in only a 2.4% decrease in accuracy, while reducing parameters by 58% and lowering computational complexity by 79%. When employing the MBL-EfficientNet-b3 network, accuracy increased by 1.7%, accompanied by a 47% reduction in computational complexity. In comparison to SimpleBaseline, the number of parameters decreased by 81.6% and computational complexity decreased by 97%, while accuracy remained largely unchanged.

Through the visualization results in Fig. 4, our algorithm demonstrates more accurate predictions of human keypoints and skeletons in comparison to the original RTM-Pose algorithm, particularly in scenarios involving human interaction, occlusion, and blur. This indicates that Efficient RTMPose exhibits better robustness and generalization capabilities in complex environments.

Table 2. Method Comparison on the COCO2017 Validation Set

Methods	Backbone	mAP	Params	GFlops
HigherHRNet [26]	HRNet-W32	66.4	28.6 M	47.9
HigherHRNet [26]	HRNet-W48	68.4	63.8 M	154.3
DEKR [12]	HRNet-W32	67.9	29.6 M	45.4
DEKR [12]	HRNet-W48	69.6	65.7 M	141.5
EfficientHRNet [27]	EfficientHRNet-H1	59.2	16.0 M	28.4
EfficientHRNet [27]	EfficientHRNet-H2	52.9	10.3 M	15.4
AlphaPose [28]	ResNet 50	69.7		5.91
SimpleBaseline [29]	VGG-19	73.7	68.6 M	35.6
RTMPose-m [23]	CSPNext-m	71	13.6M	1.93
RTMPose [23]	EffieientNet-b0	65.6	5.7 M	0.4
Ours	MBL-EffieientNet-b0	68.6	5.7 M	0.4
Ours	MBL-EffieientNet-b3	72.7	12.6 M	1

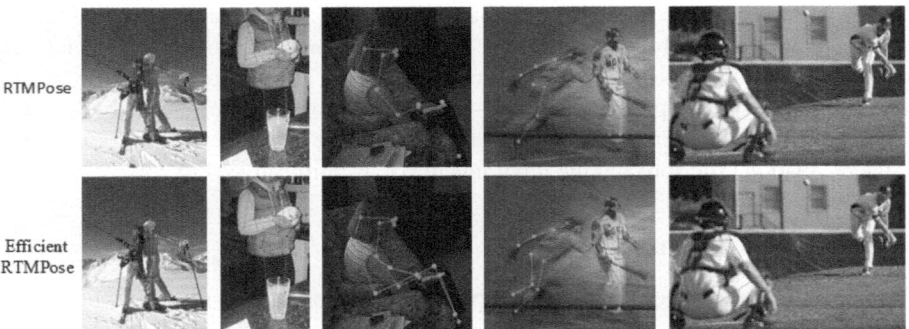

Fig. 4. Visualization comparison between RTMPose and Efficient RTMPose.

4.3   Control Experiments

To demonstrate the effectiveness of using MBL-EfficientNet as the backbone network, along with the MBLConv and tAPE-GAU modules, we conducted experiments by replacing the backbone network with CSPDarkNet [30], MobileNetv2 [31], and the initial CSPNext [7] on the MPII dataset for training. The results are summarized in Table 3. After considering both the number of parameters and computational load, we selected EfficientNet as our backbone network.

After considering parameters, computational complexity, and accuracy comprehensively, we opted to use EfficientNet as the backbone network. Subsequently, we conducted ablation experiments by separately integrating MBLConv and tAPE-GAU into RTMPose. The backbone network was divided into MBL-EfficientNet-b0 and MBL-EfficientNet-b3, denoted as "b0" and "b3" in Table 4:

Table 3. Backbone Ablation Experiment Results on the MPII Dataset

Backbone	PCKh@0.5	Params	GFlops
CSPNext-m [30]	89	13.59 M	2.57
CSPDarkNet [30]	87.8	13.66 M	2.73
MobileNetv2 [31]	86.2	3.93 M	0.48
EffieientNet-b0 [4]	87.6	5.06 M	0.59

Table 4. Ablation Experiment Results on the MPII Dataset

MBL-EffieientNet-b0Methods	Backbone	MBLConv	tAPE-GAU	PCKh@0.5	Params	GFlops
RTMPose [23]	b0			87.6	5.06 M	0.59
RTMPose+MBLConv	b0	✓		88.7	5.71 M	0.58
RTMPose+tAPE-GAU	b0		✓	88.8	5.71 M	0.59
RTMPose+MBLConv+tAPE-GAU	b0	✓	✓	89	5.71 M	0.59
RTMPose	b3			89.4	12.16 M	1.38
RTMPose+MBLConv	b3	✓		89.7	12.60 M	1.38
RTMPose+tAPE-GAU	b3		✓	89.9	12.60 M	1.38
RTMPose+MBLConv+tAPE-GAU	b3	✓	✓	90.1	12.60M	1.38

From Table 4, it is evident that integrating MBLConv and tAPE-GAU into the model leads to significant performance improvements while keeping the computational complexity of the model unchanged. The performance enhancement is most pronounced when both MBLConv and tAPE-GAU are simultaneously applied to the model.

5   Conclusions

This paper focuses on researching how human pose estimation algorithms can improve their performance while maintaining lightweight characteristics. Building upon RTM-Pose, we propose Efficient RTMPose. The first contribution is the introduction of the MBLConv module, which incorporates the Large Selective Kernel (LSK module). We apply MBLConv to EfficientNet as our backbone network, significantly reducing computational complexity while enhancing its ability to extract features for human keypoint detection tasks. Furthermore, we introduce the gated attention module, tAPE-GAU, and apply it to RTMPose. This optimization further enhances the task of keypoint representation while maintaining the efficiency of the model. The advantages of our algorithm lie in its lightweight architecture, robustness, and generalization ability. It offers a novel solution to the challenges posed by tasks such as pose estimation, which often involve significant parameterization and computational complexity.

References

1. Bazarevsky, V., Grishchenko, I., Raveendran, K., Zhu, T., Zhang, F., Grundmann, M.: Blazepose: on-device real-time body pose tracking. arXiv preprint: arXiv:2006.10204 (2020)
2. Votel, R., Li, N.: Next-generation pose detection with movenet and tensorflow. js. TensorFlow Blog **4**, 4 (2021)
3. Howard, A.G., et al.: MobileNets: efficient convolutional neural networks for mobile vision applications. arXiv preprint: arXiv:1704.04861 (2017)
4. Tan, M., Le, Q.: EfficientNet: Rethinking model scaling for convolutional neural networks. In: International Conference on Machine Learning, pp. 6105–6114. PMLR (2019)
5. Zhang, X., Zhou, X., Lin, M., Sun, J.: ShuffleNet: an extremely efficient convolutional neural network for mobile devices. In: Proceedings of the IEEE Conference on Computer Vision and Pattern Recognition, pp. 6848–6856 (2018)
6. Li, Y., Hou, Q., Zheng, Z., Cheng, M.M., Yang, J., Li, X.: Large selective kernel network for remote sensing object detection. In: Proceedings of the IEEE/CVF International Conference on Computer Vision, pp. 16794–16805 (2023)
7. Wang, C.Y., Liao, H.Y.M., Wu, Y.H., Chen, P.Y., Hsieh, J.W., Yeh, I.H.: CSPNet: a new backbone that can enhance learning capability of CNN. In: Proceedings of the IEEE/CVF Conference on Computer Vision and Pattern Recognition Workshops, pp. 390–391 (2020)
8. Vaswani, A., et al.: Attention is all you need. In: Advances in Neural Information Processing Systems, vol. 30 (2017)
9. Foumani, N.M., Tan, C.W., Webb, G.I., Salehi, M.: Improving position encoding of transformers for multivariate time series classification. Data Min. Knowl. Disc. **38**(1), 22–48 (2024)
10. Hua, W., Dai, Z., Liu, H., Le, Q.: Transformer quality in linear time. In: International Conference on Machine Learning, pp. 9099–9117. PMLR (2022)
11. Yu, C., et al.: Lite-HRNet: a lightweight high-resolution network. In: Proceedings of the IEEE/CVF Conference on Computer Vision and Pattern Recognition, pp. 10440–10450 (2021)
12. Geng, Z., Sun, K., Xiao, B., Zhang, Z., Wang, J.: Bottom-up human pose estimation via disentangled keypoint regression. In: Proceedings of the IEEE/CVF Conference on Computer Vision and Pattern Recognition, pp. 14676–14686 (2021)
13. Li, Y., et al.: SimCC: a simple coordinate classification perspective for human pose estimation. In: European Conference on Computer Vision, pp. 89–106. Springer (2022)
14. Hu, J., Shen, L., Sun, G.: Squeeze-and-excitation networks. In: Proceedings of the IEEE Conference on Computer Vision and Pattern Recognition, pp. 7132–7141 (2018)
15. Cao, Y., Xu, J., Lin, S., Wei, F., Hu, H.: GcNet: non-local networks meet squeeze-excitation networks and beyond. In: Proceedings of the IEEE/CVF International Conference on Computer Vision Workshops (2019)

16. Li, Y., Li, X., Yang, J.: Spatial group-wise enhance: enhancing semantic feature learning in CNN. In: Proceedings of the Asian Conference on Computer Vision, pp. 687–702 (2022)

17. Woo, S., Park, J., Lee, J.Y., Kweon, I.S.: CBAM: convolutional block attention module. In: Proceedings of the European Conference on Computer Vision (ECCV), pp. 3–19 (2018)

18. Li, X., Wang, W., Hu, X., Yang, J.: Selective kernel networks. In: Proceedings of the IEEE/CVF Conference on Computer Vision and Pattern Recognition, pp. 510–519 (2019)

19. Dosovitskiy, A., et al.: An image is worth 16x16 words: transformers for image recognition at scale. arXiv preprint: arXiv:2010.11929 (2020)

20. Chu, X., Tian, Z., Zhang, B., Wang, X., Shen, C.: Conditional positional encodings for vision transformers. arXiv preprint: arXiv:2102.10882 (2021)

21. Cho, K., et al.: Learning phrase representations using RNN encoder-decoder for statistical machine translation. arXiv preprint: arXiv:1406.1078 (2014)

22. Dauphin, Y.N., Fan, A., Auli, M., Grangier, D.: Language modeling with gated convolutional networks. In: International Conference on Machine Learning, pp. 933–941. PMLR (2017)

23. Jiang, T., Lu, P., Zhang, L., Ma, N., Han, R., Lyu, C., Li, Y., Chen, K.: RTMPose: real-time multi-person pose estimation based on MMPose. arXiv preprint: arXiv:2303.07399 (2023)

24. Lin, T.-Y., et al.: Microsoft COCO: common objects in context. In: Fleet, D., Pajdla, T., Schiele, B., Tuytelaars, T. (eds.) ECCV 2014. LNCS, vol. 8693, pp. 740–755. Springer, Cham (2014). https://doi.org/10.1007/978-3-319-10602-1_48

25. Andriluka, M., Pishchulin, L., Gehler, P., Schiele, B.: 2D human pose estimation: New benchmark and state of the art analysis. In: Proceedings of the IEEE Conference on Computer Vision and Pattern Recognition, pp. 3686–3693 (2014)

26. Cheng, B., Xiao, B., Wang, J., Shi, H., Huang, T.S., Zhang, L.: HigherhrNet: scale-aware representation learning for bottom-up human pose estimation. In: Proceedings of the IEEE/CVF Conference on Computer Vision and Pattern Recognition, pp. 5386–5395 (2020)

27. Neff, C., Sheth, A., Furgurson, S., Middleton, J., Tabkhi, H.: EfficienthrNet: efficient and scalable high-resolution networks for real-time multi-person 2D human pose estimation. J. Real-Time Image Proc. **18**(4), 1037–1049 (2021)

28. Fang, H.S., et al.: AlphaPose: whole-body regional multi-person pose estimation and tracking in real-time. IEEE Trans. Pattern Anal. Mach. Intell. (2022)

29. Xiao, B., Wu, H., Wei, Y.: Simple baselines for human pose estimation and tracking. In: Proceedings of the European Conference on Computer Vision (ECCV), pp. 466–481 (2018)

30. Bochkovskiy, A., Wang, C.Y., Liao, H.Y.M.: YOLOv4: optimal speed and accuracy of object detection. arXiv preprint: arXiv:2004.10934 (2020)

31. Sandler, M., Howard, A., Zhu, M., Zhmoginov, A., Chen, L.C.: MobileNetV2: inverted residuals and linear bottlenecks. In: Proceedings of the IEEE Conference on Computer Vision and Pattern Recognition, pp. 4510–4520 (2018)

Research on Transformer Tracking with Temporal Context and Bounding Box Refinement Module

Xiaofang Mu[1], Zijian Wang[1(✉)] [iD], Hong Shi[1], Mingxing Hou[1], Yiming Wu[1], Shuxian Guo[1], and Xiaotong Wu[2]

[1] College of Computer Science, Taiyuan Normal University, Taiyuan 030000, China
WangZJ@stu.tynu.edu.cn
[2] Insight Academy of Canada, Scarborough, Canada

Abstract. Siamese network-based algorithms have progressively supplanted traditional methods in single-object tracking, offering superior accuracy and real-time performance. Nonetheless, in these tracking algorithms, the temporal context between consecutive frames remains underutilized. This leads to a drift in bounding boxes when similar objects emerge and obscure the original target, thereby adversely affecting tracking performance. To tackle this challenge, we propose a single-object tracking algorithm that amalgamates temporal context and bounding box refinement within the Siamese network framework. Building upon the TransT algorithm, our approach integrates time-adaptive convolution during the feature extraction stage of target tracking to enhance the utilization of temporal context. We introduce Alpha-Refine as a bounding box refinement module to acquire more precise target contour information. The efficacy of our algorithm compared to TransT is substantiated through extensive experiments. Results on challenging datasets, including GOT-10k, TrackingNet, and OTB100, notably excel in tests on the large-scale datasets GOT-10k and TrackingNet benchmarks. Our tracker runs at approximatively 36 fps on GPU.

Keywords: single-object tracking · Siamese network-based · temporal context · Alpha-Refine

1 Introduction

As a cornerstone of computer vision, single-object tracking entails identifying a target in the initial frame of a video. SiamFC [1] pioneered the integration of dual-branch Siamese networks into target tracking tasks. Here, a shared backbone network extracts features for the target template and search frames separately, framing the tracking task as a similarity matching problem between these features. Generally, Siamese network-based target tracking methods comprise three fundamental components: feature extraction, feature fusion, and tracking head [7, 18]. TransT [6], on the other hand, replaces

---

This work was supported by Shanxi Province Basic Research Program (202303021211187), Science and Technology Innovation Program for Higher Education Institutions in Shanxi Province (2022L403).

the correlation operation in SiamFC with attention and adopts a stacked Transformer structure instead of traditional convolutional structures to enhance information interaction between template and search features. This approach performs comparably to the state-of-the-art SiamR-CNN [28] at the time, but achieves nearly 10 times the speed of SiamR-CNN.

The TransT [6] model currently stands out for effectively integrating the Siamese network framework with the attention mechanism found in Transformers. Previous experiments have revealed a common challenge among Siamese network-based models, including TransT: they often mislocate the bounding box to a similar object rather than the intended target when confronted with occlusion by visually similar objects. As depicted in Fig. 1, TransT experiences bounding box drift when similar objects occlude the target in datasets like OTB [31], resulting in inaccurate tracking. Similarly, algorithms such as Ocean [35] encounter analogous issues, where predictions can be swayed by surrounding contextual information in complex scenarios. This shortfall can be attributed to these frameworks overlooking the strong inherent correlation between consecutive frames, specifically the temporal context.

In this study, drawing inspiration from the insights gleaned from TCTrack [4], our objective is to address the previously mentioned challenges by integrating temporal context between consecutive frames into the TransT [6] model. This strategy capitalizes on the temporal cues inherent in tracking videos. To accomplish this, we introduce temporal adaptive convolutions [17] at the feature extraction stage, wherein features are extracted using convolutional weights dynamically adjusted based on the preceding frame. Moreover, to augment the tracker's efficacy in capturing target edge details, we introduce Alpha-Refine [32] as a bounding box refinement module. This module incurs a minimal computational overhead while effectively enhancing the precision of the tracker's output, leading to more precise tracking bounding boxes and a notable improvement in tracking performance. Our principal contributions can be summarized as follows.

- At the feature extraction level of TransT, we introduced temporal context, specifically temporal adaptive convolutions, to effectively prevent the generation of incorrect tracking results when similar targets occlude the tracked target.
- We introduced Alpha-Refine as a bounding box refinement module to regress bounding boxes more accurately, thereby effectively enhancing the tracker's performance.
- We validated the effectiveness of our algorithm through extensive experiments and analysis. Our approach achieved superior performance on three benchmark datasets: GOT-10k, TrackingNet, and OTB100.

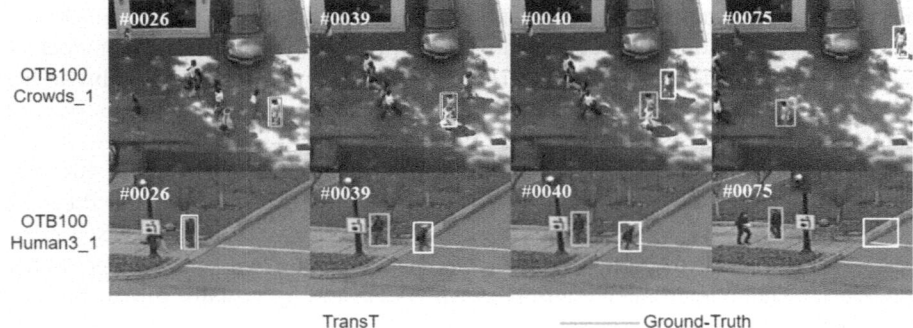

Fig. 1. The challenges encountered by TransT on the OTB dataset.

2   Related Works

Transformer Tracking. The introduction of DETR [5] has led to successful applications of Transformers in the field of object detection. Transformers, utilizing attention mechanisms, can effectively capture global information [27]. Some models have already applied Transformer architectures to visual tracking [6, 29]. In TransT, replacing the correlation operation in Siamese networks with attention significantly enhances the tracking performance of the tracker and effectively mitigates challenges like occlusion. In this work, we continue to use TransT and leverage attention-based modules designed for ego-context augment (ECA) and cross-feature augment(CFA) modules. These modules effectively integrate features from both the template and search regions, thereby improving better target localization and bounding box regression.

Temporal Context. Previous research has primarily focused on leveraging temporal information within tracking scenes to improve tracking performance [8, 20, 21]. Currently, most deep learning-based temporal tracking methods involve dynamic template integration with Transformers [29], template memory updating [12, 14, 33], graph networks [13], weighted sums [34], among others. These methods update template features explicitly or implicitly based on predefined parameters and utilize discrete temporal information during tracking by considering the transformed template features. While these approaches have somewhat improved tracking performance, they do not fully exploit the temporal context between consecutive frames. In this work, we introduce temporal adaptive convolutions [4, 17] at the feature extraction stage to better utilize the temporal context across consecutive frames.

Bounding Box Refinement Module. Most existing trackers adopt a multi-stage tracking strategy to achieve accurate results. These methods typically first roughly locate the target and then refine the results from the previous stage using a refinement module. For instance, networks such as SiamRPN [6] utilize stacked RPN [25] as refinement modules, which further enhance the tracker's discriminative capability and accuracy. However, such an approach requires the refinement module to be trained end-to-end with the previous Siamese tracker, which lacks flexibility in combining with other trackers.

Alpha-Refine [32] effectively addresses the inflexibility issue of previous refinement modules by utilizing pixel-wise correlation [30], a corner prediction head, and an auxiliary mask head as core components. Validation of algorithms such as ATOM [9], DiMP [2] confirms the effectiveness of the AR module, which is crucial as it requires no training and is plug-and-play. In summary, this paper introduces Alpha-Refine as a bounding box refinement module, enabling the model to output more accurate bounding boxes and thereby improving the tracker's performance.

3   Method

The workflow of our algorithm is illustrated in Fig. 2 and can be divided into four modules: the online feature extraction network, feature fusion network, prediction heads, and bounding box refinement module. The feature extraction module utilizes TAda-Conv [17] to incorporate the temporal context and extract features for both the template and search regions. These features are then inputted into the feature fusion network for enhancement and fusion. The prediction heads perform binary classification and bounding box regression on the enhanced features to generate initial tracking results. Finally, the target is passed through the Refine module to obtain more accurate target bounding boxes than the original predictions. This paper provides a detailed explanation of each component of the model, with a specific focus on two crucial parts: TAdaConv and Alpha-Refine [32]. Illustrations and discussions will be provided.

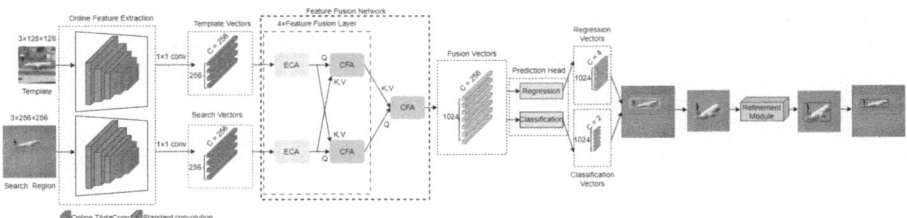

Fig. 2. Overview of our framework. The main work is divided into the following three parts, i.e., TAdaConv for online feature extraction shown in Fig. 3. The module used for feature fusion in TransT is shown in Fig. 4. Alpha-Refine is used for optimizing the bounding box, as shown in Fig. 5.

3.1   Feature Extraction Using TAdaConv

Inspired by TCTrack [4], which first integrated the TAdaConv [17] module into the feature extraction stage of tracking tasks, this paper incorporates temporal adaptive convolution into the feature extraction stage of the TransT [6] tracker to address the overlooked temporal context information in this framework. We replaced the last two convolutional layers of ResNet with TAdaConv. The structure of TAdaConv is shown in Fig. 3. Formally, given the input features of the online TAdaConv at a certain stage X_t in frame t, the online TAdaConv $\tilde{x}_t$ can be obtained as the output.

$$\tilde{X}_t = W_t * X_t + b_t \tag{1}$$

We utilize the concept of temporal adaptive convolution, where the symbol $*$ represents the convolution operation, X_t represents convolution temporal weights, b_t represents convolution bias. For standard convolutional layers, learnable weights and bias parameters are utilized and shared across the entire sequence of tracking. In online convolutional layers, parameters are computed based on learnable parameters (W_b and b_b) that change with each frame, and calibration factors, i.e., $W_t = W_b \cdot \alpha_t^w$ and $b_t = b_b \cdot \alpha_t^b$. Specifically, the weights and bias parameters of the convolutional kernel are adjusted based on the calibration factor of the current frame to accommodate the dynamic nature of time-series data. The introduced TAdaConv processes only one frame at a time, thus considering only past temporal information. By retaining a time context queue $\hat{X} \in \mathbb{R}^{L \times C}$ of L frame descriptors, the time context queue $\hat{X} \in \mathbb{R}^C$, we can still preserve information about past frames in the time context.

$$\hat{X} = Cat(\hat{X}_t, \hat{X}_{t-1}, \ldots, \hat{X}_{t-L+1}) \tag{2}$$

In the above equation, 'Cat' denotes concatenation. We use Global Average Pooling (GAP) to process the upcoming frame features to obtain frame descriptors. Then, two convolution operations are performed on the time context queue $\hat{X}$ to generate calibration factors $\alpha_t^w = \mathcal{F}_w(\hat{X}) + 1$ and $\alpha_t^b = \mathcal{F}_b(\hat{X}) + 1$, where the convolution operation is represented by $\mathcal{F}_i$. Specifically, the weights of these convolution operations are initialized to 0, meaning that during the initialization phase, the calibration factors and convolution parameters are equal to the basic convolution parameters. For the initial time $t \leq L - 1$, as there is not enough historical information, we use the descriptor of the first frame $\hat{X}_1$ for padding. Finally, given the backbone data considering the time context in the feature extraction process, we obtain the similarity mapping R_t for the t-th frame.

$$R_t = \varphi_{tada}(Z) \star \varphi_{tada}(X_t) \tag{3}$$

Here, Z represents the template, and $\star$ represents depth correlation [18]. Then, F_t is obtained through a convolutional layer, i.e., $F_t = \mathcal{F}(R_t)$.

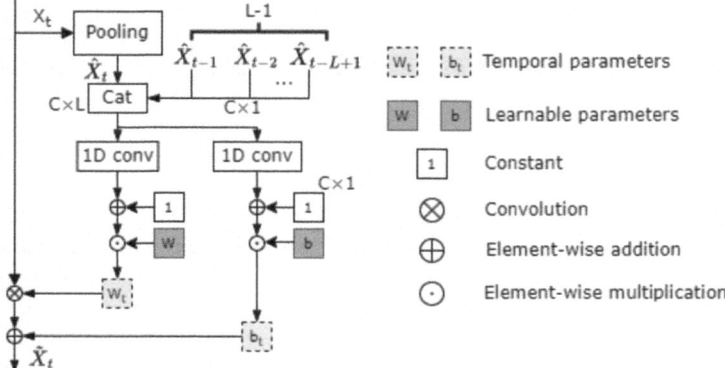

Fig. 3. The structural diagram of TAdaConv. The temporal calibration factor, generated from the feature sequence, has a count of L.

3.2 Bounding Box Refinement Module

When encountering certain challenging scenarios such as low-resolution or low-contrast frames, the bounding box regressor of the tracker may fail to provide accurate bounding boxes. Inspired by multi-stage tracking strategies, we address this issue by introducing a bounding box refinement module in this paper. Alpha-Refine [32] is a plug-and-play module with strong regression capabilities, efficiently refining the output of local trackers. Due to its flexibility and effectiveness, we adopt Alpha-Refine as the bounding box refinement module in our framework. Figure 4 illustrates the overall architecture of the Alpha-Refine module. This module adopts a Siamese network structure, comprising reference and test branches as two input branches. These branches share the same backbone network parameters, and the features extracted by the backbone network are fused (we continue to use the correlation module for fusion, i.e., the original paper employs pixel-wise correlation [30]). The fused features are then processed through convolutions to obtain the prediction head. The advantage of the Alpha-Refine module lies in its use of a smaller search space, approximately twice the size of the object, compared to ordinary trackers, which helps suppress background clutter, better localize the target, and reduce computational costs. We no longer use simple correlation operations like sliding windows in the fusion module. Instead, we represent the template K and search region S as features and perform pixel-wise correlation. Firstly, we represent $K \in \mathbb{R}^{C \times H_O \times W_O}$ and $S \in \mathbb{R}^{C \times H \times W}$ as features of the template and search region, respectively. Pixel-wise correlation decomposes K into $H_O W_O$ small kernels $K_j \in \mathbb{R}^{C \times 1 \times 1}$, and then computes correlation for each of them, resulting in a correlation map $C \in \mathbb{R}^{H_O W_O \times H \times W}$, which can be described by the following formula.

$$C = \{C_j \mid C_j = K_j * S\}_{j \in \{1,\ldots,H_O \times W_O\}} \tag{4}$$

This equation uses $*$ to represent naive correlation[1], which ensures that each correlation map encodes information from the local region on the target while avoiding excessive blurring of features from the correlation window.

3.3 Feature Fusion Network

Multi-head Attention Mechanism. Attention is a key component of the feature fusion network in the TransT [6] model. Given queries Q, keys K and values V, the attention function is the scaled dot-product attention, defined as Eq. (5):

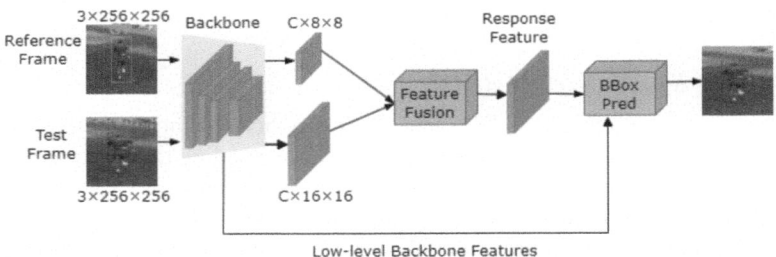

Fig. 4. The structure of Alpha-Refine module.

$$Attention(Q, K, V) = softmax(\frac{QK^T}{\sqrt{d_k}})V \tag{5}$$

d_k is the key dimension. As described in [27], extending the attention mechanism to multiple heads allows the mechanism to consider various distributions of attention, enabling the model to focus on different aspects of information. The mechanism for multi-head attention is defined as Eq. (6). For more detailed information on attention, please refer to the cited reference [27].

$$MultiHead(Q, K, V) = Concat(H_1, \ldots, H_{n_h})W^O \tag{6}$$

$$H_i = Attention(QW_i^Q, KW_i^K, VW_i^V) \tag{7}$$

where $W_i^Q \in \mathbb{R}^{d_m \times d_k}$, $W_i^K \in \mathbb{R}^{d_m \times d_k}$, and $W^O \in \mathbb{R}^{n_h d_v \times d_m}$ are parameter matrices. In this work, we will continue to use $n_h = 8$, $d_m = 256$, and $d_k = d_v = d_m/n_h = 32$ as default values.

Ego-Context Augment (ECA). The structure of ECA is shown on the left side of Fig. 5. ECA employs the multi-head self-attention mechanism in a residual form to adaptively integrate information from various positions in the feature map. As mentioned in Eq. (5), the attention mechanism lacks the ability to differentiate information based on the positions of input feature sequences. Therefore, a spatial positional encoding process is introduced to the input $X \in \mathbb{R}^{d \times N_x}$. The spatial positional encoding is generated using sine functions [5]. Hence, the mechanism of ECA can be summarized as follows:

$$X_{EC} = X + MultiHead(X + P_x, X + P_x, X) \tag{8}$$

where $P_x \in \mathbb{R}^{d \times N_x}$ represents the spatial positional encoding, and $X_{EC} \in \mathbb{R}^{d \times N_x}$ is the output of ECA.

Cross-Feature Augment (CFA). The structure of CFA is shown on the right side of Fig. 5. CFA utilizes the multi-head cross-attention mechanism in a residual form to fuse the feature vectors of two inputs. Similar to ECA, CFA also includes spatial positional encoding. Additionally, the FFN module enhances the model's fitting capability by incorporating two linear transformations that create a fully connected feed-forward network with a ReLU activation function in between.

$$FFN(x) = max(0, xW_1 + b_1)W_2 + b_2 \tag{9}$$

where the symbol W represents the weight matrix, and b represents the bias vector. Subscripts indicate different layers. Therefore, the mechanism of CFA can be summarized as follows:

$$X_{CF} = \widetilde{X}_{CF} + FFN(\widetilde{X}_{CF})$$

$$\widetilde{X}_{CF} = X_q + MultiHead(X_q + P_q, X_{kv} + P_{kv}, X_{kv}) \tag{10}$$

where $X_q \in \mathbb{R}^{d \times N_q}$ represents the input of the application module's branch, $P_q \in \mathbb{R}^{d \times N_q}$ represents the spatial positional encoding corresponding to X_q. $X_{kv} \in \mathbb{R}^{d \times N_{kv}}$ is the input of the other branch, and $P_{kv} \in \mathbb{R}^{d \times N_{kv}}$ is the output of CFA. According to Eq. (10),CFA calculates the attention map based on the multiple element-wise products between X_{kv} and X_q. It then reweights X_{KV} based on the attention map and adds it to X_q, enhancing the representation capability of the feature map.

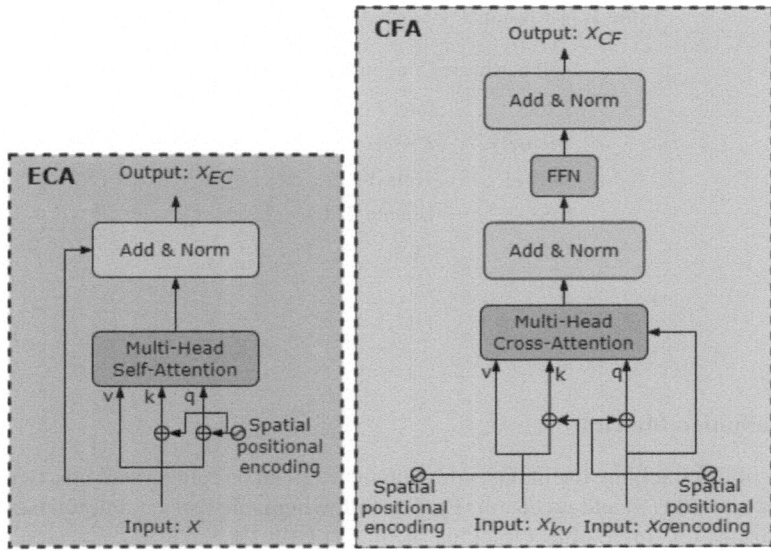

Fig. 5. On the left side is the ECA module, and on the right side is the CFA module. The ECA module is based on multi-head self-attention. The CFA module is based on multi-head cross-attention. Spatial position encoding are used to encode position information. ECA enhances the contextual information of the input and CFA adaptively fuses the feature from two branches.

4 Experiments

4.1 Implementation Environment

The algorithm is implemented using the PyTorch framework, and the specific hardware devices and software environment are shown in Table 1. The algorithm continues to train using four publicly available datasets (GOT-10k [16], LaSOT [11], COCO [22], TrackingNet [24]), as used in the TransT [6] algorithm. The parameters of the backbone network are initialized with a pre-trained ResNet-50 [15] model on ImageNet [26]. The training is set for a total of 500 epochs using the AdamW optimizer, with a learning rate of 1e-5 for the backbone network and 1e-4 for other parameters, and a weight decay of 1e-4. The training is performed on two Tesla T4 GPUs, with a batch size of 16, and the learning rate is reduced by a factor of 10 after the 300th epoch.

Table 1. Hardware Devices and Software Environment.

soft hardware	Configuration details
CPU	Intel Xeon Gold 5218
Memory	256GB
GPU	Tesla T4
OS	Ubuntu 22.04
Cuda	11.4
Python	3.7
Pytorch	1.12.1

4.2   Evaluation Metrics

In single-object tracking, the main evaluation metrics can be categorized into two major types: success rate (S) and precision (P). The following table lists commonly used evaluation metrics for single-object tracking methods (Table 2).

Table 2. Evaluation Metrics for Single-Object Tracking.

category	principle	Evaluation Metrics	dataset
S	The Intersection over Union ratio between the tracking result and the ground truth	AO(average overlap)	GOT-10k
		SR(success rate)	GOT-10k
		AUC(area under the curve)	TrackingNet
P	The pixel distance between the tracking result and the ground truth	Precision plot	TrackingNet
		Precision	TrackingNet
		Normalized precision	TrackingNet

(1) **Success Rate,** Success rate is defined as the pixel-level intersection over union (IoU) between the predicted bounding box and the ground truth bounding box. It reflects the performance of the tracker in estimating the target size.

$$S = I_{oU}(p, g) = \frac{p \cap g}{p \cup g} \tag{11}$$

In Eq. (11), I_{oU} represents the intersection over union, p represents the predicted bounding box, g represents the ground truth bounding box. The Average Overlap (AO) can reflect the performance of the method on the entire test set.

$$O_A = \sum_{t=0}^{n} \frac{S}{n} \tag{12}$$

In Eq. (12), O_A represents the Average Overlap. The overlap rate can indicate whether the method successfully tracks the target object in the current frame. Setting a threshold for the overlap rate (e.g., 0.5) indicates successful tracking if the rate exceeds that threshold in a frame. Therefore, the method's performance can be evaluated by the success rate (SR) at a specific threshold. Commonly used metrics include SR0.5 and SR0.75, which represent the proportions of frames in a video sequence where the overlap rate S is greater than 0.5 and 0.75, respectively. The Area Under the Curve (AUC) can be used to assess the performance of a method, with a higher AUC value indicating better performance.

(2) **Precision**, The precision is the Euclidean distance between the predicted bounding box's center position and the ground truth bounding box's center position. It reflects the performance of the tracker in locating the target.

$$P = \sqrt{\|(p_x, p_y) - (g_x, g_y)\|} \tag{13}$$

In Eq. (13), (p_x, p_y) represents the center coordinates of the predicted bounding box, (g_x, g_y) represents the center coordinates of the ground truth bounding box. Precision is the proportion of frames within a specific threshold, denoted as precision (P). On the x-axis, the threshold value T is plotted, and on the y-axis, the proportion of frames in the video sequence that satisfy the condition P > T is plotted. This allows for the plotting of a precision curve.

$$P_{norm} = \|W\left((p_x, p_y) - (g_x, g_y)\right)\| \tag{14}$$

In Eq. (14),

$$W = diag(g_x, g_y) \tag{15}$$

In Eq. (15), diag() represents the operation of constructing a diagonal matrix.

4.3 Evaluation on TrackingNet, GOT-10k and OTB100 Datasets

To validate the effectiveness of the tracking algorithm, we chose to compare it against the algorithms used in the TransT paper as well as TransT itself, on three well-known benchmark datasets: GOT-10k [16], TrackingNet [24], and OTB100 [31]. The OTB100 dataset comprises 100 video sequences, encompassing 11 tracking challenges, including motion blur, lighting variation, and target deformation. As shown in Fig. 6, our algorithm achieved an improved success rate compared to the baseline model TransT [6]. Our algorithm utilizes temporal context information, which enhances performance when encountering specific challenges, as illustrated in Fig. 6 when addressing in-plane rotations. Regarding precision, our algorithm also significantly improved when addressing specific challenges, as shown in Fig. 7, such as motion blur and scale variation, surpassing the performance of the baseline model.

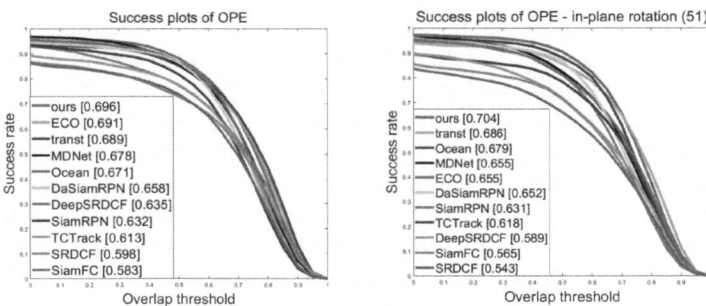

Fig. 6. The left figure illustrates the success rate of various algorithms on the OTB dataset, while the right figure depicts the success rate of a specific challenge (in-plane rotation) on the OTB dataset.

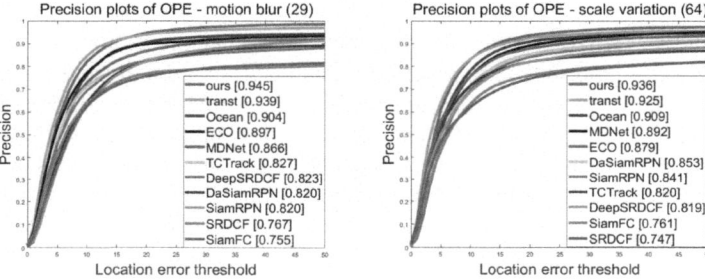

Fig. 7. Precision of multiple algorithms on two specific challenges (motion blur, scale variation) in the OTB dataset.

GOT-10k [16]. The GOT-10k dataset, released by the Chinese Academy of Sciences, consists of 10,000 training sequences and 180 testing sequences. We compared our algorithm with 10 excellent algorithms, including the baseline model TransT [6]. The experimental results are presented in Table 3, showing that our algorithm achieves a 0.9% improvement in AO, 0.8% improvement in $SR_{0.5}$, and 1.3% improvement in $SR_{0.75}$ compared to the baseline algorithm TransT. Thanks to the refinement carried out by the Alpha-Refine module in terms of bounding box regression, our algorithm achieves a higher overlap between predicted bounding boxes and ground truth boxes. This demonstrates that our algorithm performs better when encountering objects with special motion patterns.

TrackingNet [24]. TrackingNet is a large-scale tracking dataset that consists of 511 sequences for testing, covering diverse target classes. Table 3 presents the comparison results of our algorithm with ten excellent tracking algorithms, including TransT [6]. Our algorithm achieves an 82.6% AUC, 87.7% Precision (P), and 81.2% Precision (P_{Norm}) on TrackingNet. These results show a 1.2% improvement in AUC compared to the baseline algorithm TransT.

Table 3. The comparative results of multiple algorithms on the GOT-10k and TrackingNet datasets.

Method	GOT-10k [16]			TrackingNet [24]		
	AO	$SR_{0.5}$	$SR_{0.75}$	AUC	P_{Norm}	P
Ours	**73.2**	**83.2**	**70.2**	**82.6**	**87.7**	**81.2**
TransT [6]	72.3	82.4	68.9	81.4	86.7	80.3
TransT-GOT [6]	67.1	76.8	60.9	–	–	–
SiamR-CNN [28]	64.9	72.8	59.7	81.2	85.4	80.0
Ocean [35]	61.1	72.1	47.3	–	–	–
KYS [3]	63.6	75.1	51.5	74.0	80.0	68.8
DCFST [36]	63.8	75.3	49.8	75.2	80.9	70.0
PrDiMP [10]	63.4	73.8	54.3	75.8	81.6	70.4
D3S [23]	59.7	67.6	46.2	72.8	76.8	66.4
SiamRPN++ [18]	51.7	61.6	32.5	73.3	80.0	69.4
ATOM [9]	55.6	63.4	40.2	70.3	77.1	64.8
SiamFC [1]	34.8	35.3	9.8	57.1	66.3	53.3

4.4 Visualization Analysis

In order to visually demonstrate the differences between our algorithm and other algorithms, two video sequences were selected from the OTB [31] dataset. The tracking results of our algorithm and three other algorithms, including the baseline model TransT [6], were overlaid on the images to clearly visualize the variations between the algorithms. ECO and Ocean are representative and high-performing algorithms in the field of related filtering combined with convolution and Siamese network methods, while TransT serves as the benchmark algorithm for our approach. As shown in Fig. 8, the bounding boxes represented in red indicate our algorithm, the dashed black boxes represent the TransT [2] algorithm, the dashed green boxes represent the ECO [19] algorithm, and the dashed blue boxes represent the Ocean [35] algorithm.

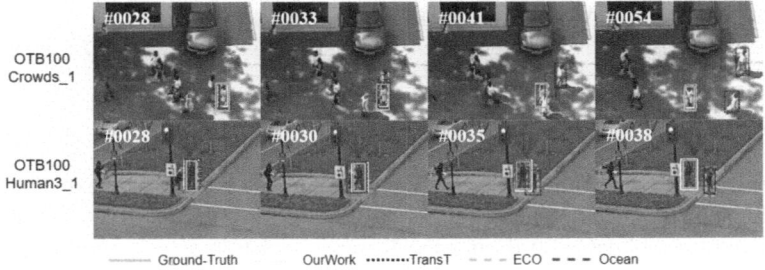

Fig. 8. Our algorithm compared with several trackers in the visual analysis of the OTB dataset.

In the $Crows_1$ sequence, when the tracked target encounters similar objects passing by and experiences slight occlusion, the baseline algorithm TransT [6] and the Ocean [35] algorithm lose track of the target's position due to interference from the similar objects. In comparison, our algorithm maintains the correct bounding box from frame 26 to 54 without drifting. In the $Human3_1$ sequence, when a similar object rapidly passes in front of the tracked target and causes occlusion, all algorithms except ours and the baseline algorithm TransT lose track in frame 35. This can be attributed to the effective utilization of global information by our algorithm's attention mechanism. In frame 38, the TransT algorithm also experiences drifting in the bounding box. This is because our algorithm utilizes temporal context information and adjusts the bounding box based on the information from previous frames. This reduces interference from the surrounding environment and results in precise bounding boxes.

4.5   Ablation Study and Analysis

To validate the effectiveness of our experiments, we conducted detailed ablation experiments on the GOT-10k [16] dataset using a server equipped with two Tesla T4 GPUs. The experimental results, as depicted in Table 5, demonstrate the effectiveness of integrating the temporal context module (TAdaConv) during the feature extraction phase. Compared to the baseline algorithm TransT [6], AO improved by 0.5%, $SR_{0.5}$ improved by 0.4%, and $SR_{0.75}$ improved by 0.7%. This clearly indicates the effectiveness of incorporating temporal context information. By recording the target's previous positional information, we can effectively address issues such as tracker disengagement when faced with certain challenges. Additionally, the incorporation of the refinement module (Alpha-Refine [32]) enables more precise adjustments to the final bounding box, leading to an overall performance improvement of the tracker (Table 4).

Table 4. Ablation results of each module

Module	AO	$SR_{0.5}$	$SR_{0.75}$
TransT	72.3	82.4	68.9
TransT+TAdaConv	72.8	82.8	69.6
TransT+AlphaRefine	72.5	82.9	69.4
TransT+TAdaConv+AlphaRefine	**73.2**	**83.2**	**70.2**

5   Conclusions

This paper extends the TransT model by incorporating temporal context information and a bounding box refinement module. The algorithm introduces Temporal Adaptive Convolution (TAdaConv) during the feature extraction stage to utilize temporal context information, enhancing spatial features by dynamically calibrating convolutional weights based on the previous frame. Additionally, we integrate the Alpha-Refine refinement module into the tracker to significantly improve the quality of bounding box estimation and thus enhance tracking performance. Visual analysis of experiments demonstrates that our algorithm effectively addresses tracking loss issues when similar objects appear and occlude the target. Our algorithm has been validated to achieve higher performance compared to the baseline TransT model on datasets such as GOT-10k, TrackingNet, and OTB100. In the future, we will continue to optimize the network structure to ensure real-time tracking speed while maintaining tracking performance and apply it to drone tracking applications.

References

1. Bertinetto, L., Valmadre, J., Henriques, J.F., Vedaldi, A., Torr, P.H.S.: Fully-convolutional Siamese networks for object tracking. In: Hua, G., Jégou, H. (eds.) ECCV 2016. LNCS, vol. 9914, pp. 850–865. Springer, Cham (2016). https://doi.org/10.1007/978-3-319-48881-3_56
2. Bhat, G., Danelljan, M., Gool, L.V., Timofte, R.: Learning discriminative model prediction for tracking. In: Proceedings of the IEEE/CVF International Conference on Computer Vision, pp. 6182–6191 (2019)
3. Bhat, G., Danelljan, M., Van Gool, L., Timofte, R.: Know your surroundings: exploiting scene information for object tracking. In: Vedaldi, A., Bischof, H., Brox, T., Frahm, J.-M. (eds.) ECCV 2020. LNCS, vol. 12368, pp. 205–221. Springer, Cham (2020). https://doi.org/10.1007/978-3-030-58592-1_13
4. Cao, Z., Huang, Z., Pan, L., Zhang, S., Liu, Z., Fu, C.: TCTrack: temporal contexts for aerial tracking. In: Proceedings of the IEEE/CVF Conference on Computer Vision and Pattern Recognition, pp. 14798–14808 (2022)
5. Carion, N., Massa, F., Synnaeve, G., Usunier, N., Kirillov, A., Zagoruyko, S.: End-to-end object detection with transformers. In: European Conference on Computer Vision, pp. 213–229. Springer (2020)
6. Chen, X., Yan, B., Zhu, J., Wang, D., Yang, X., Lu, H.: Transformer tracking. In: Proceedings of the IEEE/CVF Conference on Computer Vision and Pattern Recognition, pp. 8126–8135 (2021)
7. Chen, Z., Zhong, B., Li, G., Zhang, S., Ji, R.: Siamese box adaptive network for visual tracking. In: Proceedings of the IEEE/CVF Conference on Computer Vision and Pattern Recognition, pp. 6668–6677 (2020)
8. Dai, K., Wang, D., Lu, H., Sun, C., Li, J.: Visual tracking via adaptive spatially-regularized correlation filters. In: Proceedings of the IEEE/CVF Conference on Computer Vision and Pattern Recognition, pp. 4670–4679 (2019)
9. Danelljan, M., Bhat, G., Khan, F.S., Felsberg, M.: Atom: Accurate tracking by overlap maximization. In: Proceedings of the IEEE/CVF Conference on Computer Vision and Pattern Recognition, pp. 4660–4669 (2019)
10. Danelljan, M., Gool, L.V., Timofte, R.: Probabilistic regression for visual tracking. In: Proceedings of the IEEE/CVF Conference on Computer Vision and Pattern Recognition, pp. 7183–7192 (2020)
11. Fan, H., et al.: LaSOT: a high-quality benchmark for large-scale single object tracking. In: Proceedings of the IEEE/CVF Conference on Computer Vision and Pattern Recognition, pp. 5374–5383 (2019)
12. Fu, Z., Liu, Q., Fu, Z., Wang, Y.: STMTrack: template-free visual tracking with space-time memory networks. In: Proceedings of the IEEE/CVF Conference on Computer Vision and Pattern Recognition, pp. 13774–13783 (2021)
13. Gao, J., Zhang, T., Xu, C.: Graph convolutional tracking. In: Proceedings of the IEEE/CVF Conference on Computer Vision and Pattern Recognition, pp. 4649–4659 (2019)

14. Guo, Q., Feng, W., Zhou, C., Huang, R., Wan, L., Wang, S.: Learning dynamic Siamese network for visual object tracking. In: Proceedings of the IEEE International Conference on Computer Vision, pp. 1763–1771 (2017)
15. He, K., Zhang, X., Ren, S., Sun, J.: Deep residual learning for image recognition. In: Proceedings of the IEEE Conference on Computer Vision and Pattern Recognition, pp. 770–778 (2016)
16. Huang, L., Zhao, X., Huang, K.: GOT-10k: a large high-diversity benchmark for generic object tracking in the wild. IEEE Trans. Pattern Anal. Mach. Intell. **43**(5), 1562–1577 (2019)
17. Huang, Z., et al.: Tada! temporally-adaptive convolutions for video understanding. arXiv preprint: arXiv:2110.06178 (2021)
18. Li, B., Wu, W., Wang, Q., Zhang, F., Xing, J., Yan, J.: SiamRPN++: evolution of Siamese visual tracking with very deep networks. In: Proceedings of the IEEE/CVF Conference on Computer Vision and Pattern Recognition, pp. 4282–4291 (2019)
19. Li, B., Yan, J., Wu, W., Zhu, Z., Hu, X.: High performance visual tracking with Siamese region proposal network. In: Proceedings of the IEEE Conference on Computer Vision and Pattern Recognition, pp. 8971–8980 (2018)
20. Li, F., Tian, C., Zuo, W., Zhang, L., Yang, M.H.: Learning spatial-temporal regularized correlation filters for visual tracking. In: Proceedings of the IEEE Conference on Computer Vision and Pattern Recognition, pp. 4904–4913 (2018)
21. Li, Y., Fu, C., Ding, F., Huang, Z., Lu, G.: AutoTrack: towards high-performance visual tracking for UAV with automatic Spatio-temporal regularization. In: Proceedings of the IEEE/CVF Conference on Computer Vision and Pattern Recognition, pp. 11923–11932 (2020)
22. Lin, T.Y., et al.: Microsoft COCO: common objects in context. In: Fleet, D., Pajdla, T., Schiele, B., Tuytelaars, T. (eds.) ECCV 2014. LNCS, vol. 8693, pp. 740–755. Springer, Cham (2014). https://doi.org/10.1007/978-3-319-10602-1_48
23. Lukezic, A., Matas, J., Kristan, M.: D3S-a discriminative single shot segmentation tracker. In: Proceedings of the IEEE/CVF Conference on Computer Vision and Pattern Recognition, pp. 7133–7142 (2020)
24. Muller, M., Bibi, A., Giancola, S., Alsubaihi, S., Ghanem, B.: TrackingNet: a large-scale dataset and benchmark for object tracking in the wild. In: Proceedings of the European Conference on Computer Vision (ECCV), pp. 300–317 (2018)
25. Ren, S., He, K., Girshick, R., Sun, J.: Faster R-CNN: towards real-time object detection with region proposal networks. In: Advances in Neural Information Processing Systems, vol. 28 (2015)
26. Russakovsky, O., et al.: ImageNet large scale visual recognition challenge. Int. J. Comput. Vision **115**, 211–252 (2015)
27. Vaswani, A., et al.: Attention is all you need. In: Advances in Neural Information Processing Systems, vol. 30 (2017)
28. Voigtlaender, P., Luiten, J., Torr, P.H., Leibe, B.: Siam R-CNN: visual tracking by re-detection. In: Proceedings of the IEEE/CVF Conference on Computer Vision and Pattern Recognition, pp. 6578–6588 (2020)
29. Wang, N., Zhou, W., Wang, J., Li, H.: Transformer meets tracker: Exploiting temporal context for robust visual tracking. In: Proceedings of the IEEE/CVF Conference on Computer Vision and Pattern Recognition, pp. 1571–1580 (2021)
30. Wang, Z., Xu, J., Liu, L., Zhu, F., Shao, L.: RANet: ranking attention network for fast video object segmentation. In: Proceedings of the IEEE/CVF International Conference on Computer Vision, pp. 3978–3987 (2019)
31. Wu, Y., Lim, J., Yang, M.H.: Online object tracking: a benchmark. In: Proceedings of the IEEE Conference on Computer Vision and Pattern Recognition, pp. 2411–2418 (2013)

32. Yan, B., Zhang, X., Wang, D., Lu, H., Yang, X.: Alpha-refine: boosting tracking performance by precise bounding box estimation. In: Proceedings of the IEEE/CVF Conference on Computer Vision and Pattern Recognition, pp. 5289–5298 (2021)
33. Yang, T., Chan, A.B.: Learning dynamic memory networks for object tracking. In: Proceedings of the European Conference on Computer Vision (ECCV), pp. 152–167 (2018)
34. Zhang, L., Gonzalez-Garcia, A., Weijer, J.V.D., Danelljan, M., Khan, F.S.: Learning the model update for Siamese trackers. In: Proceedings of the IEEE/CVF International Conference on Computer Vision, pp. 4010–4019 (2019)
35. Zhang, Z., Peng, H., Fu, J., Li, B., Hu, W.: Ocean: object-aware anchor-free tracking. In: Vedaldi, A., Bischof, H., Brox, T., Frahm, J.-M. (eds.) ECCV 2020. LNCS, vol. 12366, pp. 771–787. Springer, Cham (2020). https://doi.org/10.1007/978-3-030-58589-1_46
36. Zheng, L., Tang, M., Chen, Y., Wang, J., Lu, H.: Learning feature embeddings for discriminant model based tracking. In: Vedaldi, A., Bischof, H., Brox, T., Frahm, J.-M. (eds.) ECCV 2020. LNCS, vol. 12360, pp. 759–775. Springer, Cham (2020). https://doi.org/10.1007/978-3-030-58555-6_45

VibECG: Non-contact Electrocardiogram Monitoring Based on mmWave Sensing

Qi Lin$^{(\boxtimes)}$, Langcheng Zhao, Anfu Zhou, and Huadong Ma

School of Computer Science, Beijing University of Posts and Telecommunications, Haidian, Beijing 100080, China
{linky,zhaolangcheng,zhouanfu,mhd}@bupt.edu.cn

Abstract. In this study, we propose VibECG, an innovative non-contact method for capturing electrocardiogram (ECG) recordings using mmWave radar technology. VibECG addresses the discomfort and inconvenience of traditional adhesive electrodes by contactlessly capturing minute chest vibrations and transforming them into high-fidelity ECG waveforms using advanced signal processing and conditional Generative Adversarial Nets (cGAN). Practical results show that VibECG-generated ECGs have a high correlation (Pearson correlation coefficient of 0.85) with ground truth, surpassing existing methods. This reliable system extends mmWave sensing applications and explores potential for long-term unobtrusive ECG monitoring.

Keywords: mmWave radar · cGAN · non-contact ECG monitoring

1 Introduction

Electrocardiography (ECG) is a crucial clinical method for monitoring human cardiac health and diagnosing cardiovascular diseases. By attaching electrodes to the skin of the subject, an ECG machine can record changes in cardiac electrical activity, including depolarization and repolarization of the atria and ventricles [1]. ECGs are used for monitoring vital signs of patients in wards and for detecting conditions such as arrhythmias and myocardial infarction in clinics [2]. Beyond the clinical setting, daily ECG monitoring outside the clinic plays a significant role in the screening, diagnosis, and treatment of episodic diseases. However, existing medical devices still rely on adhesive electrodes, causing skin discomfort and inconvenience during ECG monitoring.

With the advancement of smart health technologies, ECG devices are evolving towards miniaturization and intelligence. The emergence of patch-type heart monitoring devices has introduced portable dynamic ECG recorders and single-lead ECG devices. Single-lead ECG patch monitoring, requiring only a bandage-sized device, can provide longer ECG records, aiding in the detection of episodic arrhythmia events or hidden cardiac problems [1], but still faces issues of discomfort and allergies due to long-term attachment. Recent popular smartwatch

ECG monitoring technologies, despite their high accessibility, require user inter-action with the watch electrodes for ECG measurement, thus only allowing for brief monitoring (about 30 s) but not continuous.

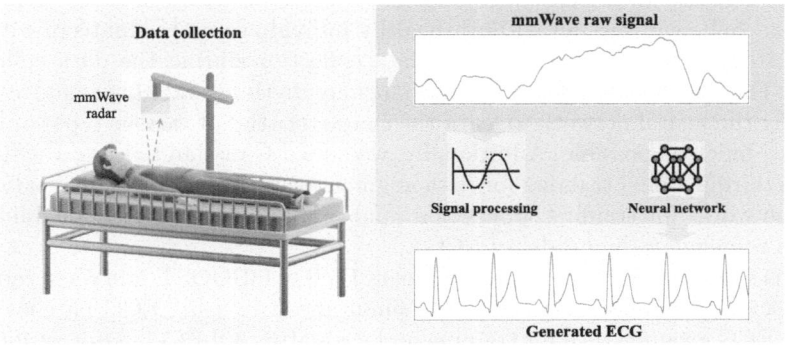

Fig. 1. VibECG system interaction scenario.

In light of the current situation, this paper introduces VibECG, a method and system for capturing ECG records without physical contact with the human body. The application scenario and system process, as shown in Fig. 1, involve capturing chest micro-motions with mmWave radar, then reconstructing the ECG through signal processing and generative neural network models, enabling unobtrusive continuous ECG monitoring in home settings for early disease screening and warning. To realize VibECG, this study primarily addresses two challenges.

Challenge 1: Extracting Fine-Grained Cardiac Activity from mmWave. Non-contact cardiac activity monitoring can utilize devices like radar and Wi-Fi to detect chest micro-motions. These devices emit signals towards the human chest, and the reflected signals contain cardiac activity information use-ful for heart rate monitoring. Early non-contact cardiac monitoring technologies mainly achieved heart rate monitoring, obtaining average heart rates over a period through spectral signal processing methods. However, due to algorith-mic and sensor limitations, these methods could only estimate rough heart rates and were unable to extract minute cardiac events within a single heartbeat [3]. Recent studies have converted raw wireless signals collected by devices into ECG waveforms that better reflect the fine-grained activities of the heart, but fidelity still needs improvement. The main reasons include simultaneous physiological activities like breathing during cardiac beats, other movements during monitor-ing, and environmental noise within the radar's detection range. To overcome this challenge, we applied acceleration filtering to the mmWave raw signals after phase extraction during the signal processing stage. Acceleration filtering helps to isolate the rapid changes associated with heartbeats from slower movements like breathing and other body motions, thereby enhancing the accuracy of the cardiac activity detection.

Challenge 2: Improving Generative Model so as to Enable ECG Synthesis from mmWave. Most work has focused only on normal sinus rhythms, and the generation of ECGs for abnormal cardiac activities has not been ideal. For this challenge, we invited both healthy individuals and volunteers with frequent arrhythmias to participate in data collection during the data collection phase. The dataset included both normal sinus rhythms and abnormal rhythms, allowing the neural network to learn the characteristics of various types of heartbeats as much as possible. Additionally, we added Gaussian noise to the filtered signals during model training for data augmentation. We used conditional generative networks for training, prediction, and evaluation, ultimately enabling our system to generate high-fidelity ECGs.

This study used the Texas Instruments IWR1443BOOST mmWave radar [4] to collect raw mmWave signals, while simultaneously using ECG patches [5] to collect ECG ground truth for training and evaluating VibECG. After verification and evaluation, VibECG demonstrated excellent ECG generation performance, with an average Pearson correlation coefficient (PCC) of 0.8525 between the ECG reconstructed from mmWave signals and the ground truth, improving by 7.4% compared to prior methods. For ECG segment with arrhythmia, the PCC can still achieve 0.8358.

In summary, the **contributions** of this work include:

- We applied acceleration filtering to the phase-extracted mmWave signals, effectively filtering out interference other than cardiac activity, facilitating the extraction of finer-grained cardiac activity features.
- Using processed mmWave data and ECG ground truth as conditions, we achieved cross-domain mapping from cardiac mechanical activity to ECG waveforms using a conditional GAN model.
- During model training, we enhanced the data by adding Gaussian noise to the filtered signals, resulting in positive improvements in several evaluation metrics compared to the original performance of the cGAN.

2   Related Work

2.1   Breathing and Heartbeat Monitoring

In the field of wireless sensing, millimeter waves have been widely applied. Beyond scenarios such as autonomous driving and smart homes, millimeter waves have recently made their way into the health sector. The mmVital system, proposed in [6], utilizes 60 GHz millimeter wave signals directed at the human body and analyzes the reflected signal strength (RSS) to estimate breathing and heart rates. It is primarily used for sleep monitoring, including sleep posture recognition and the detection of central sleep apnea and hypoventilation events. [7] explored the potential of using millimeter wave gas spectroscopy (MMWGS) for analyzing the breathing of patients with chronic obstructive pulmonary disease (COPD) [8]. Due to its high sensitivity, specificity, and selectivity, MMWGS technology is considered an ideal tool for medical diagnosis, especially in compact, low-cost systems used in hospitals. These works demonstrate the effectiveness, reliability, and potential future development of millimeter wave applications in the health and medical field. However, there are certain limitations in monitoring and analyzing more granular vital signs. Therefore, building on related work, this paper explores the capability of millimeter waves to recover ECGs for monitoring fine-grained cardiac activities during various stages of the cardiac cycle.

2.2   Conditional Generative Adversarial Nets

Conditional Generative Adversarial Nets (cGAN) were first introduced in [9] as an extension of traditional Generative Adversarial Nets (GANs). cGANs incorporate additional conditional information, such as labels or text descriptions, into the generator and discriminator, making the generated images or data more precise and diverse. cGANs have shown promising application potential in various fields, including image and text-to-image synthesis. Based on cGAN, [10] implemented an image-to-image translation method known as pix2pix. Through conditional adversarial networks, this method can transform input images into output images of different styles, such as converting daytime photos into nighttime scenes or sketches into detailed pictures. This work showcases the powerful application capabilities of cGANs in image processing and computer vision. Similarly, millimeter wave signals and ECG waveforms can be analogously considered as a type of image. By adapting the input, output, conditional information, and network architecture of cGAN to our data characteristics, we can utilize cGAN to translate millimeter waves into ECGs.

3   System Design

3.1   Overview

When monitoring the subject's ECG, the entire system consists of three main components: the mmWave radar device, the signal processing module, and the cGAN module. These components are responsible for cardiac activity sensing, cardiac information extraction, and cross-domain ECG mapping, respectively.

The mmWave radar continuously transmits frequency-modulated signals to the human chest and receives the reflected signals affected by chest vibrations. These signals undergo a series of transformations to obtain raw signals containing cardiac activity information. Subsequently, the signals need further processing to extract the phase changes over time and filter out information or noise unrelated to cardiac activity. To enhance the system's ability to generate ECGs, we augment the training dataset by adding Gaussian noise, which is then input into cGAN for training, prediction, and evaluation. This process ultimately enables the model to generate high-fidelity ECG waveforms, achieving the core functionality of the VibECG system, which is to reconstruct ECGs from mmWave signals. The overall interaction flow of the system's various modules is shown in Fig. 2.

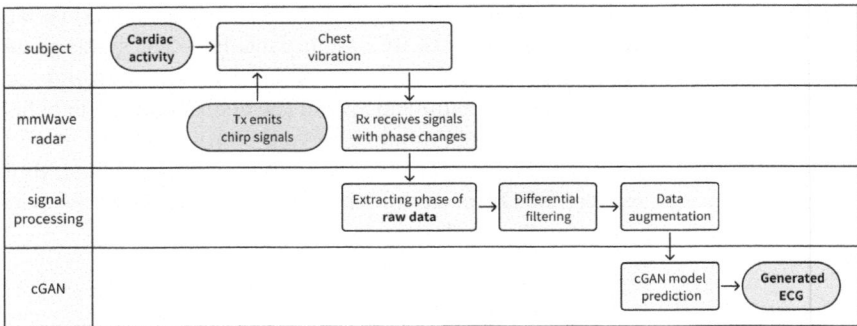

Fig. 2. Overview of the whole system design.

3.2 Preprocessing and Acceleration Filtering

When collecting raw data, we use the mmWave radar to emit mmWave signals to the subject and receive the echo signals. The received echo signals then undergo signal preprocessing, where beamforming is used to focus on the heart region of the echo, extracting the cardiac mechanical activity data hidden within the echo signals. In this section, we describe the specific process of signal preprocessing in conjunction with the technical principles of the mmWave radar.

The radar is equipped with 2 transmitting antennas and 4 receiving antennas. The transmitting antennas alternately emit signals using time-division multiplexing. Based on the radar's antenna arrangement and positional relationships, a virtual antenna array is constructed for beamforming. Specifically, the multi-antenna arrangement of the mmWave radar is specially designed with fixed relative positions between antennas. Beamforming can utilize the relative position information between multiple antennas to map the sensed information into three-dimensional space and extract the radar signal components at specific three-dimensional coordinates (x, y, z):

$$\text{Map}(x, y, z) = \sum_{i=1}^{8} \exp\left(-\frac{j2\pi}{\lambda}\left[x_i \cdot x + y_i \cdot y\right]\right) \cdot \text{Bin}(z) \tag{1}$$

where i represents the antenna channel (2 transmitters and 4 receivers provide 8 antenna channels), x_i and y_i represent the corresponding coordinates of the i-th channel in space, and $\text{Bin}(z)$ represents the signal component at distance z. Subsequently, frequency domain filtering is used to locate and extract cardiac activity information from the beamformed signals, including the amplitude and frequency offset of the heartbeats. Based on the located cardiac activity information, a specific coordinate beam signal is determined.

First, the $\text{Map}(x, y, z)$ is converted to phase signals, and the power spectral density (PSD) of the radar signal at each three-dimensional coordinate is calculated, denoted as $\text{PSD}(x, y, z, f)$, representing the power of the signal component at coordinate (x, y, z) with frequency f, where f is in units of beats per minute (bpm). This frequency is the phase change frequency, which corresponds to the frequency of minute displacements of the chest cavity. We then calculate the sum of the power spectral density in the heart rate band (40–200 bpm) for each coordinate, denoted as $F_{\text{heart}}(x, y, z)$, representing the energy of the cardiac signal:

$$F_{\text{heart}}(x, y, z) = \sum_{f=40}^{200} \text{PSD}(x, y, z, f) \tag{2}$$

The higher the $F_{\text{heart}}(x, y, z)$ value, the closer the signal at that coordinate is to the heart's position. To determine the coordinate of the heart's position, we select the coordinate with the maximum $F_{\text{heart}}(x, y, z)$ value for subsequent signal processing.

$$(x_0, y_0, z_0) = \arg \max_{(x,y,z)} \left(F_{\text{heart}}(x, y, z) \right) \tag{3}$$

After determining the specific coordinates, we extract the phase information at the heart's position, so as to convert the complex signal into its phase representation, which better represent the chest vibration. After phase extraction, we use a differential filter to perform acceleration filtering on the phase signal of each channel, calculating the signal's derivative to highlight its cardiac characteristics. This filtering method is more effective than traditional band-pass filtering.

The effects of each intermediate step in the signal processing process are shown in Fig. 3. The first row shows the raw mmWave signal at the heart's position, the second row shows the extracted phase changes, and the third row shows the results after acceleration filtering, clearly identifying the cardiac cycle and heart rate.

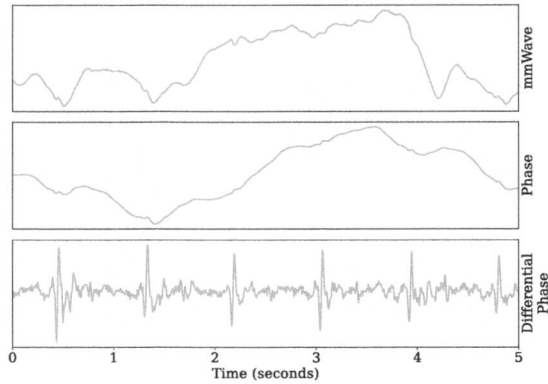

Fig. 3. Results of signal processing at various stages.

3.3   Data Augmentation

To further enhance the system's performance in generating ECG signals from mmWave radar data, we apply Gaussian noise to the acceleration-filtered mmWave signals in the training set for data augmentation. By introducing Gaussian noise to the training data, the model learns to make accurate predictions even in the presence of noise. This approach makes the model more robust to noise in the input data, thereby improving its performance in real-world applications [11]. Additionally, adding Gaussian noise increases the diversity of the training data, thus reducing the risk of overfitting [12]. In summary, by incorporating Gaussian noise during the subsequent training process, we can significantly improve the model's robustness and generalization ability, leading to better ECG generation performance in practical applications.

3.4   cGAN

The processed mmWave signals are input into the neural network module of this system to complete the conversion from millimeter waves to electrocardiograms (ECG). We design a conditional Generative Adversarial Nets (cGAN) model [9] to generate ECGs from mmWave. A cGAN consists of two main components: the generator and the discriminator. The generator's task is to generate realistic data based on the input random noise and conditional information, while the discriminator is responsible for distinguishing between real and generated data. Through this adversarial training, the generator gradually improves the quality of the generated data, and the discriminator continuously enhances its discrimination ability. In cGANs, conditional information is introduced into both the generator and the discriminator to guide the generation and discrimination processes. This conditional information can be class labels, text descriptions, or other relevant features. By introducing conditional information, cGANs can generate data with specific attributes, achieving more precise and targeted generation.

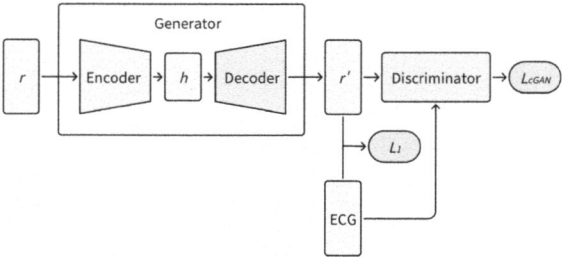

Fig. 4. Architecture of cGAN model.

The structure of cGAN model designed in this paper includes a U-Net-based generator and a discriminator, as shown in Fig. 4. The generator adopts a U-Net structure, consisting of multiple downsampling (UNetDown) and upsampling (UNetUp) modules. The input to the generator is the mmWave signal, and the output is the generated ECG signal. Detailed structure of the generator is shown in Fig. 5a. The first layer of the generator is a downsampling module, receiving an input with 1 channel and outputting 128 channels. The subsequent downsampling modules gradually increase the number of channels to 256 and 512, with Dropout added in the last downsampling module to prevent overfitting. The upsampling modules gradually restore the size of the feature maps, reducing the number of channels from 512 to 256 and 128, with skip connections added in each upsampling module to retain high-resolution features. Finally, the generator outputs the signal through an upsampling layer and a convolutional layer.

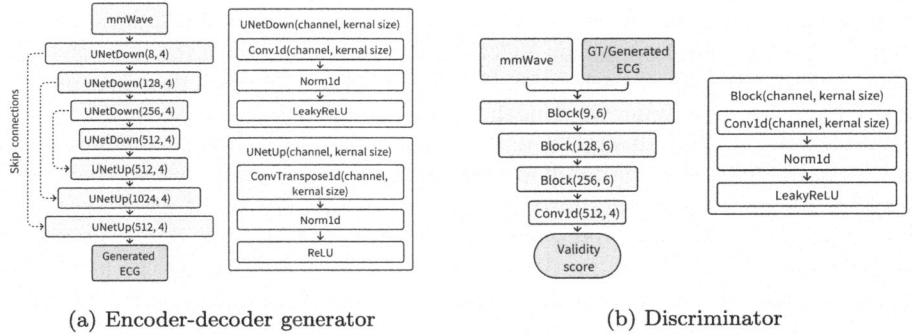

(a) Encoder-decoder generator   (b) Discriminator

Fig. 5. Structures of cGAN components.

The discriminator's task is to distinguish between real and generated data. To achieve this, the discriminator receives concatenated inputs of real and generated data and extracts features through a series of convolutional layers, ultimately outputting a probability value representing the authenticity of the input data. Specifically, the input to the discriminator is the mmWave signal and the generated ECG signal. The structure of the discriminator is shown in Fig. 5b. The first layer of the discriminator is a convolutional layer, receiving an input with 9 channels (8 mmWave channels and 1 ECG channel) and outputting 128 channels without normalization. The subsequent convolutional layers gradually increase the number of channels to 256 and 512, with the last convolutional layer outputting a single-channel probability value. Through this design, the discriminator can effectively extract features from the input signals and distinguish between real and generated signals.

The loss function calculation includes generator loss and discriminator loss. The generator loss consists of the GAN loss and sample loss, where the GAN loss measures the authenticity of the generated signal, and sample loss measures the difference between the generated signal and the real signal.

Through the above design, we implement a cGAN model for cross-domain ECG conversion, which can utilize conditional mmWave to generate ECG with specific cardiac cycle characteristics.

4 Evaluation

4.1 Experiment Setup

In our experiments, we used the TI IWR1443BOOST mmWave radar [4], and adopted a configuration with 2 Tx and 4 Rx, forming an 8-channel virtual antennas. The radar sampling frequency was set to 250 Hz with TI DCA1000EVM data transmission card. Simultaneously, to record the ground truth ECG, we used CarePulse [5] ECG patches synchronously at a sampling frequency of 125 Hz. We segmented all data into 5-second segments, with the mmWave data having a length of 1250 samples and the ECG data having a length of 625 samples. To align the data lengths of each channel, we performed interpolation resampling on the ECG data, unifying the length to 1250 samples.

We invited 11 volunteers to participate in the experiment, including 10 healthy individuals and 1 individual with premature ventricular beats. Each volunteer remained in a supine position, and approximately 1 h of mmWave data and single-lead ECG data were recorded synchronously. During data collection, the hardware module of the mmWave radar was positioned facing the left chest area of the subject's heart at a distance of 20–60 cm. Our dataset includes both normal sinus rhythm data and arrhythmia data, with a total duration of 11 h.

4.2 Showcase and Overall Performance

The overall effectiveness of the system is primarily reflected in the waveform morphology of the generated ECG and the Pearson correlation coefficient (PCC) with the ECG ground truth. An ECG signal typically includes several main waveform components, such as the P wave, QRS complex, and T wave, which represent different stages of cardiac electrical activity. Figure 6 compares the waveform of a 5-second segment of the ECG ground truth with the ECG generated by our system. The figure annotates various parts of the ECG waveform within a cardiac cycle. The P wave represents atrial depolarization, i.e., atrial contraction. It usually appears as a small positive wave but can also be biphasic. The QRS complex represents ventricular depolarization, i.e., ventricular contraction. Within the QRS complex, the Q wave is a small negative wave, the R wave is a large positive wave, and the S wave is a negative wave. The T wave represents ventricular repolarization, i.e., ventricular relaxation, and typically appears as a medium-sized positive wave [1,2]. As shown in the figure, the ECG waveform generated by our system from mmWave signals accurately corresponds to ground truth. It can reflect the characteristics of heartbeats just like a real ECG, providing valuable information for monitoring cardiac health [13].

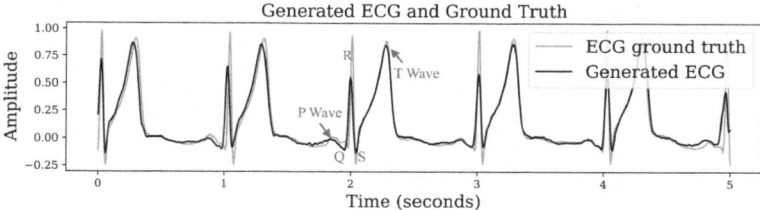

Fig. 6. Generated ECG compared to the ground truth.

The overall performance of the system can be evaluated based on the Pearson correlation coefficient (PCC) between the generated ECG and the ground truth. The PCC ranges from –1 to 1, and a PCC greater than 0.8 indicates a strong correlation [14,15], implying high reliability of the generated ECG. Table 1 compares the PCC and root mean square error (RMSE) of the ECG generated by our system with that of the baseline method. VibECG can generate ECG signals with a PCC of 0.8525 and an RMSE of only 0.1462. In addition, for ECG segment with arrhythmia, the PCC can still achieve 0.8358. This performance not only surpasses the contactless ECG baseline but also meets the strong correlation standard, demonstrating high reliability. The advancement of VibECG compared with prior work can be summarized as, *(i)* custom-designed preprocessing and acceleration filtering as we introduced in Sect. 3.2, which eliminates ambient noise and extract cardiac signal. Such cardiac signal make the machine learning model better fitting than original chest displacement signal in [16]. *(ii)* The Gaussian augmented cGAN model as mentioned in Sect. 3.4, which provides better transformation capability than conventional CNN in the baseline.

Table 1. Comparison of PCC and RMSE values for different methods

Method	PCC	RMSE
VibECG	0.8525	0.1462
Conventional CNN	0.7938	0.7706

4.3 Errors of R-R Interval, T Wave, and Heart Rate

Section 4.2 introduced the R-R interval and T wave, both of which hold significant importance in the cardiac cycle. We calculated the millisecond-level errors for these three time indicators and compared them with the method using conventional CNN. As shown in Table 2, the timing errors of VibECG are much lower than those of the baseline method. Specifically, VibECG achieves an R-R interval error of 13.1 ms, a T wave error of 21.6 ms, and a heart rate error of 1.1 bpm.

Table 2. Timing errors of R-R, T wave, and heart rate (HR) error

Method	R-R interval (ms)	T wave (ms)	HR error (bpm)
VibECG	13.1	21.6	1.1
Conventional CNN	76.4	94.0	8.6

4.4   PCC Under Different Data Augmentation Scales

As mentioned in Sect. 3.3, to improve the robustness and generalization ability of the model, we added Gaussian noise to the training dataset for data augmentation. To evaluate the effectiveness of this method and determine the optimal noise scale, we designed experiments to test the changes in PCC performance under different noise scales. By keeping other variables constant but adding Gaussian noise with different variances during training, we tested the PCC of the ECG generated by the corresponding trained models. The experimental results are shown in Fig. 7. It can be seen that adding an appropriate scale of noise to the training data indeed improves the PCC, with the best effect observed at a noise variance of 0.1. This result validates the effectiveness of the data augmentation design in VibECG and provides a basis for selecting specific noise parameters.

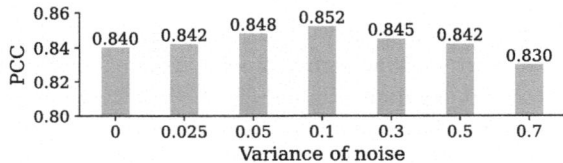

Fig. 7. Variation of PCC under different noise scales.

5   Discussion

Recent works [17,18] have improved non-contact cardiac monitoring technologies, but VibECG has taken a step further. Compared to mmECG proposed by Xu et al. [18], we have reconstructed high-fidelity ECG waveforms that capture the details of the P, QRS, and T wave features, whereas mmECG only segmented the heart's contraction and relaxation cycles. The encoder-decoder model based on transformer and temporal convolutional network (TCN) proposed by Chen et al. [17] adopts a sequence-to-sequence (Seq2seq) inference method, where each sampling point of the signal requires a separate inference, resulting in higher demand of computility. In contrast, our cGAN model is more lightweight.

In addition, the robustness of the system is very important in practical application scenarios. Non-ideal postures can degrade signal quality, potentially affecting system performance. To address this, Zhao et al. [19] offers a solution by using the cardiac quality filter to ensure signal quality. Additionally, Xu et al. [20] suggests that clothing material has minimal impact on cardiac activity monitoring.

6 Conclusion

In this study, we proposed VibECG, an innovative non-contact method for ECG monitoring using mmWave radar. With the VibECG system, we can effectively capture minute chest vibrations and transform these vibration signals into high-fidelity ECG waveforms through advanced signal processing and cGAN. The work presented in this paper explores the potential for long-term continuous unobtrusive ECG monitoring.

References

1. Noseworthy, P.A., et al.: Effect of longer-term ambulatory cardiac monitoring vs conventional follow-up on detection of atrial fibrillation in patients with cryptogenic stroke: the loop study. JAMA **320**(12), 1171–1182 (2018)
2. Moody, G.B., Mark, R.G.: The impact of the MIT-BIH arrhythmia database. IEEE Eng. Med. Biol. Mag. **20**(3), 45–50 (2001)
3. Turakhia, M.P., et al.: Diagnostic utility of a novel leadless arrhythmia monitoring device. Am. J. Cardiol. **112**(5), 520–524 (2013)
4. Instruments, T.: DCA1000EVM. https://www.ti.com/tool/DCA1000EVM. Accessed 15 Jan 2024 (2024)
5. Carepulse: Carepulse Patch. https://index.carepulse.cn/home/index.html. Accessed 15 Jan 2024 (2024)
6. Yang, Z., Pathak, P.H., Zeng, Y., Liran, X., Mohapatra, P.: Vital sign and sleep monitoring using millimeter wave. ACM Trans. Sens. Netw. (TOSN) **13**(2), 1–32 (2017)
7. Rothbart, N., Stanley, V., Koczulla, R., Jarosch, I., Holz, O., Schmalz, K., Hübers, H.-W.: Millimeter-wave gas spectroscopy for breath analysis of COPD patients in comparison to GC-MS. J. Breath Res. **16**(4), 046001 (2022)
8. Raherison, C., Girodet, P.-O.: Epidemiology of COPD. Eur. Respir. Rev. **18**(114), 213–221 (2009)
9. Mirza, M., Osindero, S.: Conditional generative adversarial nets. arXiv preprint: arXiv:1411.1784 (2014)
10. Isola, P., Zhu, J.-Y., Zhou, T., Efros, A.A.: Image-to-image translation with conditional adversarial networks. In: Proceedings of the IEEE Conference on Computer Vision and Pattern Recognition, pp. 1125-1134 (2017)
11. Perez, L.,Wang, J.: The effectiveness of data augmentation in image classification using deep learning. arXiv preprint: arXiv:1712.04621 (2017)
12. Shorten, C., Khoshgoftaar, T.M.: A survey on image data augmentation for deep learning. J. Big Data **6**(1), 1–48 (2019)
13. Wang, L., et al.: Continuous and contactless monitoring of cardiac activity using millimeter-wave radar. IEEE Trans. Biomed. Eng. **67**(7), 2157–2164 (2020)
14. Randazzo, V., et al.: Article from PubMed central. J. Name (2023). Accessed 8 June 2024
15. Hinkle, D.E., Wiersma, W., Jurs, S.G.: The use of pearson correlation coefficient in linearity assessment of calibration curves for analytical methods. J. Chem. Educ. **80**(2), 169–171 (2003)
16. Toda, D., Anzai, R., Ichige, K., Saito, R., Ueki, D.: ECG signal reconstruction using FMCW radar and convolutional neural network. In: 2021 20th International Symposium on Communications and Information Technologies (ISCIT), pp. 176-181. IEEE (2021)

17. Chen, J., Zhang, D., Wu, Z., Zhou, F., Sun, Q., Chen, Y.: Contactless electro-cardiogram monitoring with millimeter wave radar. IEEE Trans. Mob. Comput. **23**(1), 270–285 (2022)
18. Xu, X., et al.: mmECG: monitoring human cardiac cycle in driving environments leveraging millimeter wave. In: IEEE INFOCOM 2022-IEEE Conference on Computer Communications, pp. 90-99. IEEE (2022)
19. Zhao, L., et al.: mmArrhythmia: contactless arrhythmia detection via mmWave sensing. Proc. ACM Inter., Mob., Wearable Ubiquit. Technol. **8**(1), 1–25 (2024)
20. Xu, C., et al.: CardiacwWave: a mmWave-based scheme of non-contact and high-definition heart activity computing. Proc. ACM Inter., Mob., Wearable Ubiquit. Technol. **5**(3), 1–26 (2021)

Human Activity Recognition Based on Fine-Grained Capture Spatiotemporal Features of Body RFID Skeleton

Meng Liu(ID), Yihong Chen(✉)(ID), and Yilin Zhao(ID)

The Internet of Things Perception and Big Data Analysis Key Laboratory of Nanchong City, China West Normal University, Nanchong 637002, China
cyhswpi@126.com

Abstract. Skeleton-based human activity recognition has become one of the research hotspots in the field of pattern recognition. However, existing methods have limitations in achieving fine-grained capture of human activity spatiotemporal features, such as (1) being unable to distinguish which neighboring nodes are important to the current node; (2) Unable to capture local temporal features. In this article, we utilize RFID, which has the advantages of privacy protection, identifiability, and battery free maintenance, to perceive human activities. We design a body RFID skeleton graph to express human activities and propose a body RFID skeleton spatiotemporal graph convolutional network (BRS-GCN) to capture the spatiotemporal features of the body RFID skeleton graph at a fine-grained level, thereby achieving human activity recognition. The recognition performance advantage of BRS-GCN compared to existing HARs has been verified through experiments.

Keywords: Human activity recognition · Body RFID skeleton · GCN · Multi-head graph attention network · Multi-scale time convolution

1 Introduction

Human Activity Recognition (HAR) is a technology that identifies and classifies human activities through sensor data. It has important applications in multiple fields, including health monitoring, smart homes, security systems, sports analysis, and human-computer interaction [1–9].

Skeleton-based human activity recognition is a technology that utilizes the position information of body skeleton joints to identify and classify human activities. Compared with traditional video-based or sensor-based methods, skeleton-based methods have advantages such as small data volume, high computational efficiency, and minimal environmental impact. At present, skeleton-based human activity recognition mainly uses ordinary cameras or depth cameras [10] to obtain video data of human activities. Next, by detecting the body skeleton nodes in

L. Sun and Y. Chen (Eds.): CWSN 2024, CCIS 2341, pp. 247–257, 2025.
https://doi.org/10.1007/978-981-96-2186-6_19

the video, the skeleton data of human activities is obtained. Then, using classification models to extract spatiotemporal features from skeleton data, human activity recognition can be achieved. However, this video-based HAR method faces issues such as privacy leakage, line of sight limitations, and lighting effects. Radio frequency identification (RFID) is a wireless communication technology that uses radio signals to identify target objects and obtain corresponding information [11]. It has significant advantages such as identifiability, privacy protection, battery-free maintenance, beyond line of sight, and unaffected by light. This article combines skeleton data to comprehensively perceive the key features of human motion and the outstanding advantages of RFID, and provides a body RFID skeleton for fully perceiving key features of human activity.

Human activities are reflected in the changes of the body skeleton in temporal and spatial. Therefore, how to capture the spatiotemporal features of human activities on skeleton data is the main problem that skeleton-based HAR needs to solve. Existing research utilizes Graph Convolutional Networks (GCNs) [12] for spatial features and Long Short Term Memory Networks (LSTMs) [13] for temporal features in human activities. However, there are two issues: (1) GCNs assign the same weights to the current node and its neighbors, which prevents the model from distinguishing the importance of each neighboring node. But in the process of human activity, the contribution of each node to the overall activity is different. GCNs cannot model the importance between nodes, therefore it cannot capture more abundant spatial features in the body skeleton at a fine-grained level. (2) LSTMs can capture temporal features with long-term dependencies in body skeletal sequences, they cannot capture action features at different time scales in a fine-grained manner, and their ability to capture local temporal details and overall trends of actions is weak. At the same time, LSTMs have a large number of parameters, long model training time, and high requirements for computing resources.

In response to the above issues, this article combines an RFID skeleton activity graph that fully express human activities and proposes a body RFID skeleton spatiotemporal graph convolutional network for human activity recognition. The contribution proposed in this article:

(1) We utilize RFID to perceive human activities and collect activity data, proposing an RFID skeleton activity graph to express the spatiotemporal features of human activities.
(2) We propose a body RFID skeleton spatiotemporal graph convolutional network to capture human activity spatiotemporal features at a fine-grained level and achieve human activity recognition.

The second part of this article summarizes the existing HAR and focuses on analyzing the advantages of RFID-based HAR and the problems of existing skeleton-based HAR models. The third part provides a detailed analysis of the principle of RFID sensing human activities, explains how to construct an RFID skeleton activity graph, and proposes a human activity recognition model based on RFID skeleton activity graph. The fourth part verified the effectiveness and high accuracy of our proposed model through experiments. The fifth part is a summary of our work.

2 Related Works

In recent years, human activity recognition has been widely applied in the field of health monitoring, which can significantly improve the quality and efficiency of healthcare. For example, in elderly and patient monitoring, HAR technology can monitor the daily activities of the elderly and patients in real-time, providing important health information and warning signals. Real time monitoring of the exercise status of elderly individuals is achieved through the use of built-in accelerometers and gyroscopes in wearable devices such as smartwatches and fitness trackers in fall detection. Once a fall is detected, the system can immediately send an alert to family members or medical service providers, providing timely assistance. The HAR model identifies changes in daily activities such as walking, sitting, and standing time by monitoring the activity patterns of elderly and patients over a long period of time. By analyzing these data, changes in their health status can be evaluated, helping doctors make diagnostic and treatment decisions.

Traditional human activity recognition is usually based on machine vision methods, which are limited by line of sight and light effects, and also pose a threat to user privacy and security [14]. With the development of sensors, wireless sensors have also been used in HAR, but these methods have the disadvantages of difficult battery maintenance and strong intrusion sensitivity [15]. These issues have caused controversy among existing HAR schemes based on machine vision and sensors. As researchers deepen their understanding of wireless signals, some wireless communication technologies such as WIFI are applied to human activity recognition, effectively overcoming the related problems of existing schemes and achieving good results. However, they themselves do not have the features of target object labeling and cannot solve the problem of target object identity recognition [16]. RFID, with its tag aware features, can effectively solve the three core key issues in the field of the Internet of Things: identity recognition, location localization, and state perception of target objects, standing out among existing human activity recognition solutions. RFID-based HAR includes both unbound-RFID HAR and bound-RFID HAR.

The types of activities recognized by unbound-RFID based HAR are limited and cannot recognize complex activities. There is edge ambiguity, which makes it difficult to perceive human activities in a fine-grained manner. Moreover, the orientation between the human body and the tag can seriously affect the ability to perceive activities. Compared with sensor-based HAR, bound-RFID has outstanding advantages such as battery-free maintenance, lightweight, and low intrusion. At the same time, the identifiable advantages of RFID can be utilized to identify active individuals and active parts. Therefore, this article studies the HAR of bound-RFID with privacy protection, easy identification of active individuals, low intrusion sensitivity, and battery-free maintenance. Early research on HAR based on bound-RFID was relatively limited, and most of it used traditional machine learning methods such as SVM and DTW as recognition methods. These HARs have limited modeling capabilities for complex activities, cannot effectively capture the spatiotemporal features of activities, and are difficult to model nonlinear problems.

Some researchers use deep learning to study skeleton-based HAR [17]. GCNs and LSTMs can capture the spatiotemporal features of complex human activities in skeleton-based human activity data, improving the performance of skeleton-based HAR. However, traditional GCNs do not consider the importance of the correlation between nodes, and the weights assigned to each pair of nodes are the same. In the process of information aggregation, the current node's attention to each adjacent node is the same, which makes the model unable to reflect the true importance differences between nodes. In real human activities, the importance of each skeleton node is different. We should pay attention to important skeleton nodes at a fine-grained level in order to obtain more accurate and authentic activity information. LSTMs provide a distinct advantage for modeling time series with long-term dependencies. However, in real-life human activities, there is both long-term and short-term temporal information. Although LSTMs have dynamic receptive fields, in order to effectively capture long-term dependencies, there is a certain requirement for the length of the input sequence. However, real activities involve short-term actions, and the real and effective data sequences are limited. LSTMs lack the ability to model short-term actions. Therefore, to address these issues, this study combines Graph Attention Networks (GAT) with multi-scale temporal convolutional networks to propose a body RFID skeleton spatiotemporal graph convolutional network. This model uses a multi-head attention mechanism to automatically learn the correlation strength (attention weight) between nodes, thereby distinguishing the importance of nodes. Different attention heads can also enable models to comprehensively understand human movements from multiple different perspectives, which is helpful for distinguishing subtle differences in movements. Multi-scale time convolution extracts temporal features at different time scales, which can capture both long-term temporal information and local temporal details. Meanwhile, multi-scale time convolution has fewer gating units and fewer parameter quantities than LSTM. On a large number of human activity datasets, multi-scale time convolution consumes less training time and resources, and has lower computational costs.

3   Models and Methods

3.1   Construction of RFID Skeleton Activity Graph

This article designs a tag deployment scheme based on the features of skeletal movement and changes in bones at joints in human activities. RFID tags are deployed at the main joints of the human body to obtain key information about human activities. This article designs a body RFID skeleton as shown in Fig. 1. Each subject is bound with 16 RFID flexible passive tags, which are mostly deployed at the main joints of the human body. This can effectively monitor the movement of the corresponding deployment positions, which we refer to as node tags. Next, we set the identifier of node tags based on their deployment location. As shown in Fig. 1, node tags numbered 0, 1, 8, and 9 identify the human torso, node tags numbered 2–7 identify the human arms, and node tags numbered 10–15 identify the human legs.

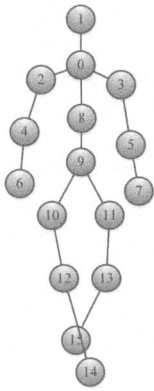

Fig. 1. Body RFID skeleton.

When the RFID system successfully reads a tag, the data acquisition system will obtain a tag response record u, which includes five values: electronic product code (EPC), timestamp (Timestamp), Doppler frequency (DF), received signal strength (RSSI), and phase. The EPC value is the number m of the skeleton node, which is labeled m ($m \in [0, 15]$), the DF value represents the speed and direction of human activity movement, the RSSI value represents the significant displacement of human activity, and the Phase value represents the small displacement of human activity. Therefore, DF, RSSI, and Phase together form a set of tag response feature data used to express human activities. We assume that the average duration of a human activity is 5 s, during which the tag generates the most h sets of tag response feature data. Due to the RFID system's ability to retrieve tag response records in chronological order when reading tags, the data collection system can also express changes in human activity over time.

This article proposes to represent a human pose in human activities using a body RFID skeleton, and each human activity is represented by h continuously changing human poses. Specifically, the t-th ($t \in [0, h\text{-}1]$) group tag response feature data of all 16 node labels is used to construct the t-th body RFID skeleton. There is also a sequential time relationship between the h body RFID skeletons, that is, they form a sequence of body RFID skeletons. Each RFID skeleton structure of the human body fully expresses the spatial features of human activities. Therefore, we jointly construct an RFID skeleton activity graph that can comprehensively express human activities from h body RFID skeletons.

3.2   Body RFID Skeleton Spatiotemporal Graph Convolution Network: BRS-GCN

We propose the Body RFID Skeleton Spatiotemporal Graph Convolutional Network (BRS-GCN) for the body RFID skeleton activity graph. Its structure is shown in Fig. 2(a). Our model first learns the multi-scale temporal features of the body RFID skeleton activity graph, and then learns the deep spatial features of the activity graph. BRS-GCN consists of RFID Skeleton Activity Graph Batch Layer, MSTC, Multiple RFID Skeleton Activity Graph Attention Layers, Pool, and FC for Activity Prediction. Firstly, the batch processing layer of the RFID skeleton activity graph will perform batch processing operations on B_S RFID skeleton activity graphs. For batch processing operations, we renumbered the nodes in multiple RFID skeleton activity graphs and constructed an adjacency matrix representing the connection relationships between nodes in multiple RFID skeleton activity graphs. Secondly, the multi-scale time convolutional layer (MSTC) learns the multi-scale time features of multiple RFID skeleton activity graphs. Thirdly, the attention layers of multiple RFID skeleton activity graphs adaptively assign attention weights to each pair of adjacent nodes, making the aggregated feature information more abundant. Furthermore, the pooling layer (Pool) adopts average pooling and maximum pooling to extract representative feature data, and reduces the dimensionality of the final feature data used for classification. Finally, two fully connected layers (FC) and a Softmax classifier for activity prediction were concatenated to map activity features to the probability space representing the activity itself, thus achieving activity classification.

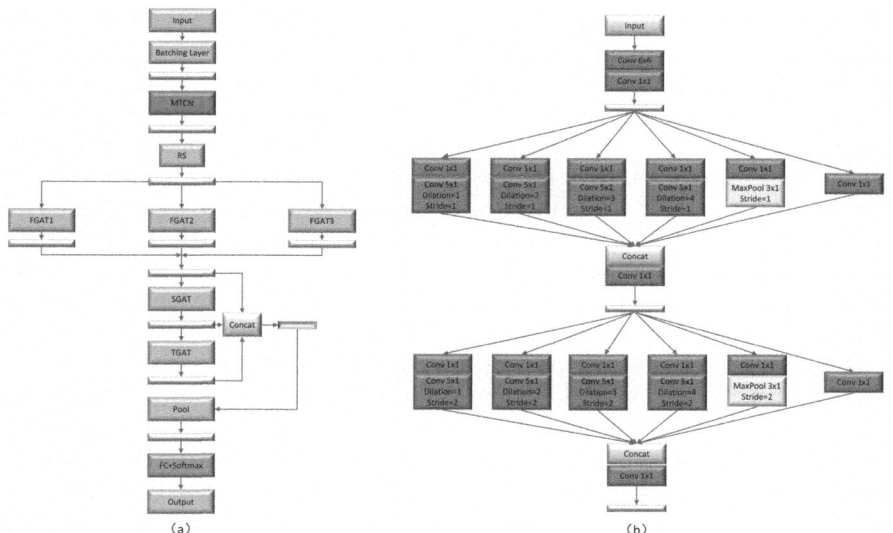

Fig. 2. (a) BRS-GCN structure. (b) MSTC structure.

Multi-scale Time Convolutional Layer (MSTC): Take the node feature matrix $S(S \in R^{16B_S \times h})$ from the batch processed multiple RFID skeleton activity graphs $G(G = <S, A>)$ as input for the multi-scale time convolutional layer. The MSTC is shown in Fig. 2(b). MSTC mainly consists of three layers: The first layer is to enhance the channel dimension and reduce the time dimension. The second and third layers are both multi-scale time convolutions. Then there are MaxPool operations and 1×1 convolutions that implement residual connections. Concatenate the outputs of six branches and use one convolution to increase the channel dimension. The difference between multi-scale time convolutions in the second and third layers lies in the inconsistent step size of the convolution kernels. Small step convolution kernels can capture local time details and fast actions, while large step convolution kernels can extract overall motion trends and long-term time dependencies.

Multiple RFID Skeleton Activity Graph Attention Layers: The node feature matrix after time feature extraction is: $S'(S' \in R^{16B_S \times C \times T})$, where C represents the number of channels, and T represents the time dimension. Before inputting to the spatial feature extraction module, it is necessary to perform a deformation operation to transform it into a two-dimensional matrix: $H(H = [h_1, h_2, ..., h_i, ..., h_{16B_S}] \in R^{16B_S \times N_C}, I \in [1, 16B_S], h_i \in R^{N_C}$, where $N_C = C \times T$. Then input multiple RFID skeleton activity graphs: $G(G = <H, A>)$ into the spatial feature extraction module. We use a multi-head attention network to extract spatial features from RFID skeleton activity graphs. The specific implementation details are as follows: For each attention head k, in order to calculate the attention weights between nodes, first we need to perform a linear transformation on the feature vectors of neighboring nodes for $<i, j>$, and obtain the transformed feature vectors: $h_i^{(k)} = W^{(k)} h_i$, $h_j^{(k)} = W^{(k)} h_j$. Then, we can calculate the attention coefficients between nodes i and j:

$$e_{ij}^{(k)} = a^{(k)\top} [h_i^{(k)} \parallel h_j^{(k)}] = a^{(k)\top} [W^{(k)} h_i \parallel W^{(k)} h_j], \tag{1}$$

where $\parallel$ represents the concatenation operation, $W^{(k)}$ is the weight parameter matrix of the linear transformation in the k-th attention head, and $a^{(k)}$ is the attention weight vector in the k-th attention head. Node j represents the first-order neighborhood of node i. In order to make the attention coefficient easy to compare among all neighboring nodes of node i, we use $softmax()$ to normalize it and obtain result β_{ij}^k. Finally, we use the normalized attention weights to update the feature representation of node i, and concatenate the updated feature representations of all attention heads to obtain the final feature vector h_i' of node i. The calculation formula is as follows:

$$h_i' = \sigma \left(\mathop{\parallel}_{k=1}^{K} \left(\sum_{j \in N_{(i)}} \beta_{ij}^{(k)} h_j^{(k)} \right) \right). \tag{2}$$

Pooling Layer (Pool) and Fully Connected Layer (FC): Pooling operations use average pooling and maximum pooling. Both types of pooling involve pooling each RFID skeleton activity graph from multiple RFID skeleton activity graphs into a single node. The pooled feature data is V. Then, the pooled feature V is input into a two-layer fully connected network to obtain the final feature F. Next, we use the Softmax function to transform the final feature F into a probability distribution vector P belonging to each activity. Finally, we use the cross entropy loss function to calculate the loss between the predicted value P and the true label L, and then use the Adam optimizer to update the model parameters to obtain the optimal model and model parameters.

4   Experiments

4.1   Human Activity Dataset

We propose a new bound-RFID human activity recognition method that combines the motion perception ability of the skeleton with the advantages of RFID. This experiment used the Impinj R420 reader, Larid S9028PCR antenna, and Impinj M4E tag. The existing bound-RFID HAR methods have the problems of few activity categories and low accuracy. We have developed a data collection system based on the LLRP protocol and obtained the most diverse activity dataset. We attach 16 RFID tags to the body skeleton nodes (Fig. 1). The data collection system stores the label response records of each activity sample in order, forming the CWNU-RDA dataset. Each record includes EPC, timestamp, Doppler frequency, RSSI, and phase. The dataset and the 21 human activities are available at https://github.com/cwnu-iot/BRS-GCN.git.

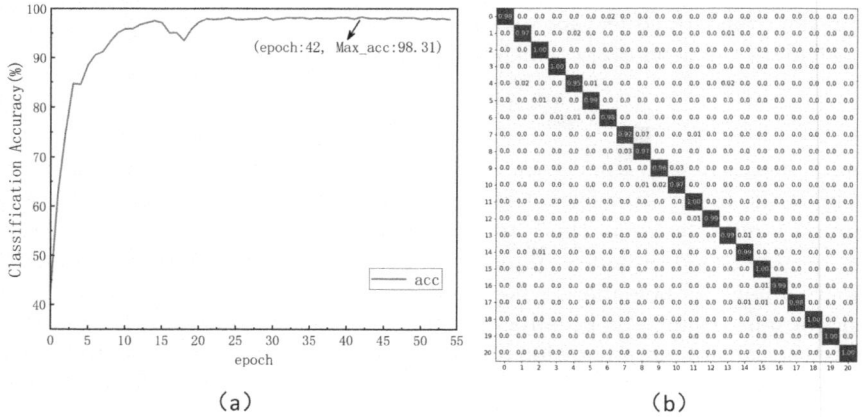

(a)   (b)

Fig. 3. (a) The trend of classification accuracy with increasing epoch. (b) BRS-GCN confusion matrix.

To make the experimental environment acceptable for people of various heights, the antenna height was set to 2 m. To increase the antenna's reading range and cover the nearest tags, we set the angle between the antenna plane and the support pole to 35°. At this angle, the vertex of the antenna's reading range is precisely parallel to the ground and 2 m above. In this arrangement, the potential measurement blind zone occurs only 0.73 m in front of the antenna.

We have recruited 15 volunteers with a ratio of male to female volunteers of 8:6, heights ranging from 1.55 to 1.85 m, and ages ranging from 18 to 30 years old. Each volunteer performed each human activity 40 times, and the responses recorded by all tags comprised the activity samples for each human activity. The duration of the human activity is the time required to obtain these activity samples, which we reasonably set at 5 s. After all 15 volunteers completed 21 activities, we collected 12,700 activity samples.

4.2   Analysis of Identification Results

During training, the human activity dataset was divided into a training set, validation set, and test set in an 8:0.5:1.5 ratio. As shown in Fig. 3 (a), the model was trained for 55 epochs, with an initial learning rate of 0.003, reduced by 0.1 every 20 epochs. A batch size of 256, initial node vector size of 192, and feature dimension of 512 were used. The Multi-Scale Time Convolutional Layer (MSTC) had channel counts of 16, 36, and 48, respectively. The CrossEntropy Loss function and Adam optimizer were employed to update the model parameters. The model achieved its highest recognition accuracy of 98.31% at epoch 42, with accuracy stabilizing after 40 epochs.

When the model achieves its maximum recognition accuracy of 98.31%, Fig. 3(b) displays the model's recognition accuracy for each activity. The figure shows that the model achieved 100% accuracy in recognizing 7 specific activities and over 90% accuracy for most others, demonstrating the model's effectiveness. However, activities with high similarity, such as "stride with swinging arms" and "steps with swing arms", had slightly lower recognition rates, indicating that activity similarity negatively impacts classification accuracy. Despite this, the model maintained over 95% accuracy for similar activities, proving its reliability and precision.

Table 1. Classification model comparison experiment results.

	Classification accuracy (%)	Parameter size (MB)
GCN [12]	73.09	2.74
LSTM [13]	93.45	14.53
ST-GCN [18]	97.24	11.82
CTR-GCN [19]	97.55	5.74
BRS-GCN (Ours)	**98.31**	6.17

In addition, we evaluated the recognition performance of several deep learning and skeleton-based human activity recognition models [12,13,18,19] on the

CWNU-RDA dataset. These models struggled to identify important neighboring nodes and capture local temporal features, leading to lower classification accuracy and higher model complexity. In contrast, the proposed BRS-GCN achieved the highest classification accuracy with fewer parameters. Comparative results are shown in Table 1.

5 Conclusion

In this article, we use RFID to perceive human activities, design a body RFID skeleton to study the expression of human activities, and propose a body RFID skeleton spatiotemporal graph convolutional network (BRS-GCN) for skeleton-based human activity recognition. The experimental results indicate that BRS-GCN can capture the spatiotemporal features of human activities at a fine-grained level, thereby accurately identifying human activities, and has stronger expressive power than other networks. For RFID-based systems, multipath effects can have negative impacts on the accuracy of human activity recognition, such as signal interference and distortion, increased noise in received signals, etc. To this end, we will adopt data fusion technology in subsequent research, supplementing RFID signals by combining data from other types of sensors (such as visual sensors) to improve the accuracy of activity recognition.

Acknowledgments. This work is supported by the National Natural Science Foundation of China (no. 62171390, no. 61871330), and supported by the Natural Science Foundation of Sichuan Province (no. 23NSFSC1767).

References

1. Mallick, R., Yebda, T., Benois-Pineau, J., Zemmari, A., Pech, M., Amieva, H.: Detection of risky situations for frail adults with hybrid neural networks on multimodal health data. IEEE Multimed. **29**(1), 7–17 (2022). https://doi.org/10.1109/MMUL.2022.3147381
2. Huynh-The, T., Hua, C.-H., Tu, N.A., Kim, D.-S.: Physical activity recognition with statistical-deep fusion model using multiple sensory data for smart health. IEEE Internet Things J. **8**(3), 1533–1543 (2021). https://doi.org/10.1109/JIOT.2020.3013272
3. Phukan, N., Mohine, S., Mondal, A., Manikandan, M.S., Pachori, R.B.: Convolutional neural network-based human activity recognition for edge fitness and context-aware health monitoring devices. IEEE Sens. J. **22**(22), 21816–21826 (2022). https://doi.org/10.1109/JSEN.2022.3206916
4. Ding, M., Ding, Y., Wei, L., Xu, Y., Cao, Y.: Individual surveillance around parked aircraft at nighttime: thermal infrared vision-based human action recognition. IEEE Trans. Syst. Man Cybern.: Syst. **53**(2), 1084–1094 (2023). https://doi.org/10.1109/TSMC.2022.3192017
5. Imran, H.A.: Khail-net: a shallow convolutional neural network for recognizing sports activities using wearable inertial sensors. IEEE Sens. Lett. **6**(9), 1–4 (2022). https://doi.org/10.1109/LSENS.2022.3197396

6. Huang, H., Wu, D., Liang, Z., Sun, F., Dong, M.: Virtual interaction and manipulation control of a hexacopter through hand gesture recognition from a data glove. Robotica **40**(12), 4375–4387 (2022). https://doi.org/10.1017/S0263574722000972

7. Fan, Y.C., Wen, C.Y.: Real-time human activity recognition for vr simulators with body area networks. In: 2023 International Conference on Consumer Electronics - Taiwan (ICCE-Taiwan), PingTung, Taiwan, pp. 145–146 (2023). https://doi.org/10.1109/ICCE-Taiwan58799.2023.10226881

8. Huang, W., Zhang, L., Wu, H., Min, F., Song, A.: Channel-equalization-HAR: a light-weight convolutional neural network for wearable sensor based human activity recognition. IEEE Trans. Mob. Comput. **22**(9), 5064–5077 (2023). https://doi.org/10.1109/TMC.2022.3174816

9. Leng, Y., Chen, C.C., Sun, Q., Huang, J., Zhu, Y.: Energy-efficient video processing for virtual reality. In: 2019 ACM/IEEE 46th Annual International Symposium on Computer Architecture (ISCA), Phoenix, AZ, USA, pp. 91–103 (2019). https://doi.org/10.1145/3307650.3322264

10. Bagate, A., Shah, M.: Human activity recognition using RGB-D sensors. In: 2019 International Conference on Intelligent Computing and Control Systems (ICCS), Madurai, India, pp. 902–905 (2019). https://doi.org/10.1109/ICCS45141.2019.9065460

11. Su, J., Liu, A.X., Sheng, Z., Chen, Y.: A partitioning approach to RFID identification. IEEE/ACM Trans. Netw. **28**(5), 2160–2173 (2020). https://doi.org/10.1109/TNET.2020.3004852

12. Kipf, T.N., Welling, M.: Semi-supervised classification with graph convolutional networks. arXiv preprint (2016). https://doi.org/10.48550/arXiv.1609.02907

13. Hochreiter, S., Schmidhuber, J.: Long short-term memory. Neural Comput. **9**(8), 1735–1780 (1997). https://doi.org/10.1162/neco.1997.9.8.1735

14. Vishnu, C., Datla, R., Roy, D., Babu, S., Mohan, C.K.: Human fall detection in surveillance videos using fall motion vector modeling. IEEE Sens. J. **21**(15), 17162–17170 (2021). https://doi.org/10.1109/JSEN.2021.3082180

15. Nho, Y.-H., Ryu, S., Kwon, D.-S.: UI-GAN: generative adversarial network-based anomaly detection using user initial information for wearable devices. IEEE Sens. J. **21**(8), 9949–9958 (2021). https://doi.org/10.1109/JSEN.2021.3054394

16. Wang, H., Zhang, D., Wang, Y., Ma, J., Wang, Y., Li, S.: RT-fall: a real-time and contactless fall detection system with commodity WiFi devices. IEEE Trans. Mob. Comput. **16**(2), 511–526 (2017). https://doi.org/10.1109/TMC.2016.2557795

17. Dai, C., Liu, X., Xu, H., Yang, L.T., Deen, M.J.: Hybrid deep model for human behavior understanding on industrial internet of video things. IEEE Trans. Industr. Inf. **18**(10), 7000–7008 (2022). https://doi.org/10.1109/TII.2021.3058276

18. Yan, S., Xiong, Y., Lin, D.: Spatial temporal graph convolutional networks for skeleton-based action recognition. In: AAAI, vol. 32, no. 1 (2018). https://doi.org/10.1609/aaai.v32i1.12328

19. Chen, Y., Zhang, Z., Yuan, C., Li, B., Deng, Y., Hu, W.: Channel-wise topology refinement graph convolution for skeleton-based action recognition. In: Proceedings of the IEEE/CVF International Conference on Computer Vision (ICCV), pp. 13359-13368 (2021). https://doi.org/10.48550/arXiv.2107.12213

ChewSense: Real-Time Detection of Chewing Counts and Food Types with Reverse Signals from Headphones

Chenyu Bao[1], Qingbin Li[1], Fangming Tian[1], Qiance Zang[1], and Feng Hong[1,2]($\boxtimes$)

[1] College of Information Science and Engineering, Ocean University of China, Songling Road, Qingdao 266100, Shandong, China
{baochenyu,liqingbin,tfm,zangqiance}@stu.ouc.edu.cn, hongfeng@ouc.edu.cn
[2] Sanya Oceanographic Institution, Ocean University of China, Zhenxing Road, Sanya 572024, Hainan, China

Abstract. The eating detection system can track dietary information, aiding in the cultivation of healthy eating habits. However, previous research has primarily focused on detecting eating periods without finely identifying users' chew count, nor promptly alerting users to insufficient chewing. We propose a real-time dietary detection system called ChewSense, which utilizes earphones to capture intraoral reverse signals, thereby identifying chew counts and the types of food consumed in a single mouthful. ChewSense segments eating signals into chewing segments and validates the authenticity of these segments through pre- and post-action verification. Through a six-month experiment involving 10 volunteers, results demonstrate that ChewSense can accurately identify chew counts and food types, with average accuracies reaching 84.58% and 82.90%, respectively.

Keywords: Eating · Chewing · Earphone Reverse Signals

1 Introduction

Poor dietary habits can lead to obesity issues [1]. The purpose of dietary records is to document information such as when people eat and what they consume. By analyzing dietary records, doctors can indirectly assess whether people have healthy eating habits. Traditional dietary records rely on self-reporting tools such as food frequency questionnaires (FFQs), 24-h recalls, and food diaries. Unfortunately, these methods are often susceptible to user forgetfulness [2,3]. Consequently, numerous studies are turning to wearable sensors to objectively automate dietary records, effectively circumventing the limitations of self-reporting methods.

C. Bao, Q. Li, F. Tian and Q. Zang—Contributing authors.

© The Author(s), under exclusive license to Springer Nature Singapore Pte Ltd. 2025
L. Sun and Y. Chen (Eds.): CWSN 2024, CCIS 2341, pp. 258–268, 2025.
https://doi.org/10.1007/978-981-96-2186-6_20

Fig. 1. User scenario of ChewSense: When a user wears a commercial headphone and eats, ChewSense conducts chew counts and food type recognition for each mouthful, providing reminders if the chew count for a mouthful is too low.

In this article, we introduce an eating detection system called ChewSense, whose user scenario is illustrated in Fig. 1. When users wear commercial earphones and consume food, ChewSense utilizes the earphones' reverse signals for real-time chew counting and food type recognition, providing feedback to users in a visual format. ChewSense promptly alerts users to chew more when it detects a low chew count for a mouthful.

Unlike previous research, ChewSense utilizes bone conduction signals to detect chewing. As people chew food, bone-conducted sound propagates within the oral cavity and is received by commercial headphones as Earphone Reversed Signals (ERS) [4], which are clearer compared to signals propagated through air. Furthermore, unlike most other studies that only detect eating periods, ChewSense is capable of finely segmenting each eating signal, continuously monitoring chewing instances in real-time, and providing feedback to help users develop the habit of chewing more.

Building a real-time system that detects, counts, and provides feedback to users for each chew faces two major challenges: (1) Traditional signal studies, which typically emphasize post-collection analysis, lack real-time capabilities. However, ChewSense requires the real-time and accurate detection of chewing counts from recorded signals, providing timely feedback to users after each chewing instance. To address this issue, we first resample the signals and employ an energy-based segmentation method to extract potential chewing segments. (2) During eating, users may perform actions such as coughing, which could be incorrectly identified as chewing. To tackle this problem, we utilize convolutional neural networks for action classification and validate the authenticity of chewing segments using the time series of key actions.

The main contributions of this paper are summarized as follows:

- We have successfully designed and implemented ChewSense. It utilizes off-the-shelf commercial earphone devices to real-time identify the types of food consumed and the number of chews for each mouthful using Earphone Reverse Signals (ERS). Most importantly, when users have a low chew count, ChewSense promptly reminds them, helping them develop healthy eating habits.
- We devised a motion segmentation algorithm to promptly segment potential chewing segments from complex eating signals. Additionally, by validating the temporal sequence before and after key actions, we improved the reliability of the system.
- Through a six-month experiment involving ten volunteers, Chew-Sense achieved an average absolute error of 3.66 in chew counting, with an accuracy of 84.58%. As for food type recognition, it achieved an accuracy of 82.90%.

2   Related Work

Research on detecting eating activities can be categorized into four types based on sensing modalities: proximity sensing, inertial sensing, optical sensing, and acoustic sensing.

Proximity Sensing. This approach determines the distance between an object and the emitter by measuring the time it takes for emitted light to return to the sensor. For example, Chun et al. introduced a necklace called NeckSense for detecting eating events [5]. Jaw movement during chewing is detected by the sensor, allowing perception of eating actions. Experimental results showed that the device achieved an accuracy of 78.2% and a recall rate of 72.5% in detecting eating events in daily life environments. However, this method is susceptible to interference from walking behaviors due to their similar frequency and amplitude characteristics.

Inertial Sensing. This method typically utilizes mature commercial devices to track large movements associated with eating, thereby inferring people's eating periods. For instance, Dong et al. strapped a smartphone to the forearm and used its IMU to measure eating periods [6]. They found significant arm movements before and after eating, allowing the determination of eating times with an accuracy of 81%. Other studies mostly employ data from inertial sensors in smartwatches or modified devices to identify eating activities [7,8]. However, this method is susceptible to interference from body movements during speech.

Optical Sensing. This research utilizes changes in light source intensity during the eating process. For example, Zhang et al. developed a necklace called NeckSense, where the ambient light sensor reading on the necklace decreases when the user lowers their head to feed, thus detecting feeding actions [9]. Additionally, Taniguchi and Kazuhiro found that changes in ear canal shape during chewing cause differences in reflected light, enabling estimation of eating periods [10]. A drawback of such approaches is that the intensity of ambient light sources can affect detection results.

Acoustic Sensing. This method senses eating activities by collecting sounds emitted during chewing. For instance, Bi et al. proposed the wearable device Auracle, where they designed and assembled the hardware of Auracle to detect eating activities in free-living environments using a contact microphone placed behind the ear [11]. Rahman et al. developed BodyBeat, placing modified piezoelectric microphones on the neck to identify chewing and swallowing sounds, categorizing activities as eating or drinking [12]. However, most studies of this kind either collect signals of chewing sounds and environmental noises propagated through air, which are not clear enough, or require custom-made sensing devices rather than existing commercial ones, increasing the difficulty of acquiring sensing devices.

3   System Overview

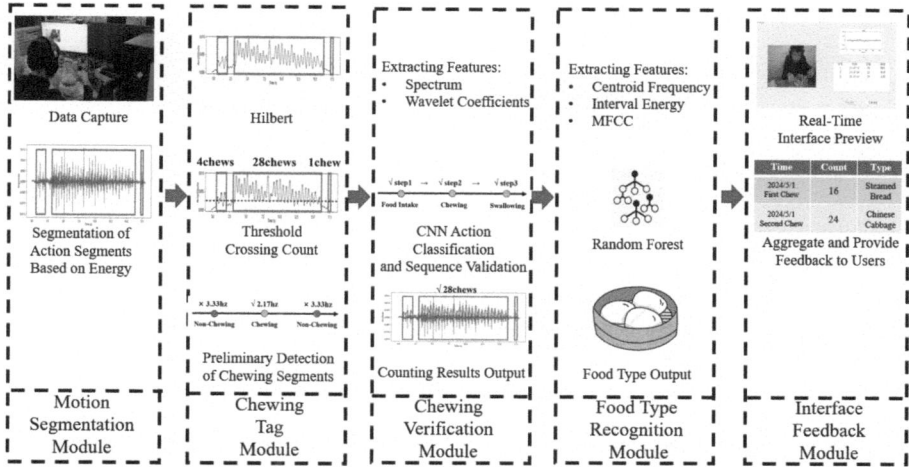

Fig. 2. System overview of ChewSense

ChewSense consists of five modules, as shown in Fig. 2. The motion segmentation module is responsible for coordinating the hardware to capture the overall signal of the user's eating activity. It resamples the signal and uses the short-time power values of sliding windows to determine whether the current window is in a non-silent state. This module records and merges consecutive active windows to obtain active motion segments in the signal.

The chewing tag module processes motion segments using Hilbert transform and then preliminarily identifies potential chewing segments using a threshold-crossing counting method.

The chewing verification module computes features such as the spectrum and wavelet coefficients of the signal. It initially classifies all motion segments using a CNN and then further verifies each chewing segment by checking whether the preceding action is feeding and the subsequent action is swallowing. By analyzing the time sequence between actions, it further filters out misidentified chewing segments and outputs the chewing count results.

The food type recognition module calculates signal features for segments confirmed as chewing and performs food type recognition using a pre-trained random forest model.

Finally, the interface feedback module aggregates chewing count and food type recognition results for each bite and provides real-time feedback to the user.

3.1   Motion Segmentation Module

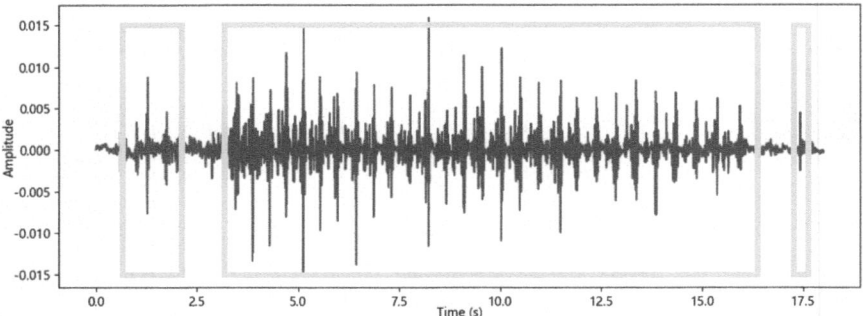

Fig. 3. A user's single mouthful eating signal is segmented into three active action segments.

The motion segmentation module aims to collect real-time user data and segment out action sequences potentially related to eating. Due to the real-time calculation requirement of ChewSense for chewing counts per mouthful, we downsample the signal from 44100 Hz to 4000 Hz to reduce computational overhead. Subsequently, we employ time windows of 0.6 s in size with a step size of 0.3 s to detect active actions, labeling windows with short-term power values exceeding a certain threshold as active windows. In the preliminary dataset collected, we compute the average short-term power values for four types of actions-silence, food intake, chewing, and swallowing-as 0.009, 0.136, 0.799, and 0.246, respectively, within the time windows. We set the threshold to four times the short-time power value of silence actions: sufficient to distinguish silence windows from others. For adjacent non-silent windows, we merge them to obtain several active action segments. As depicted in Fig. 3, this illustrates a single mouthful eating signal from a user. Due to the presence of silent windows, this signal is segmented into three active action segments with time spans of 1.2 s, 12.9 s, and 0.3 s, respectively.

3.2   Chewing Tag Module

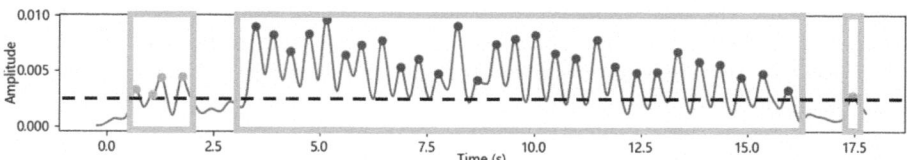

Fig. 4. The envelope plot of a single mouthful eating signal. The number of peaks crossing the threshold is counted for each action segment to further calculate the motion frequency.

The chew tagging module is utilized for preliminary assessment of which motion segments may constitute chewing. We employ Hilbert transformation to extract the envelope of the signal. Since chewing signals typically manifest as dense and continuous peaks, we are inspired by the study of Chun et al. [13] and utilize the threshold crossing frequency method to tag chewing motions. Specifically, we define an amplitude threshold for the envelope and calculate the frequency at which the signal crosses this threshold to assess potential chewing motions. If the computed motion frequency aligns with the chewing frequency (which mainly falls between 0.94 Hz and 2.17 Hz [14]), the signal segment is labeled as chewing; otherwise, it is labeled as non-chewing.

As depicted in Fig. 4, the envelope plot extracted from a typical user's single mouthful eating signal reveals three distinct segments highlighted by red boxes, representing the actions of food intake, chewing, and swallowing, respectively. Upon analyzing similar datasets, we found that setting the envelope amplitude threshold to 0.0025 (illustrated by the black dashed line in the figure) enables the extraction of the majority of characteristic peaks corresponding to chewing actions, yielding optimal results for validating chewing segments. The green, red, and orange peaks represent the number of peak points crossing the threshold in different action segments, which are 4, 28, and 1, respectively. The time spans of these three action segments are 1.2 s, 12.9 s, and 0.3 s, respectively. By dividing the number of peak points by the time span of each action segment, we obtained action frequencies of 3.33 Hz, 2.17 Hz, and 3.33 Hz, respectively. Comparing these frequencies with the chewing frequency, we found that only the frequency of the second action segment aligns with the chewing frequency, thus it is labeled as chewing.

3.3   Chewing Verification Module

The chewing verification module aims to further validate the accuracy of the chewing segments detected by the previous module, as determining chewing segments solely based on the frequency at which the signal crosses the threshold may not be accurate. As shown in Fig. 5, it displays the time-domain plot and envelope diagram of a user's coughing signal. In the figure, the red boxes represent the motion segments merged from active windows, while the black dashed line represents the threshold set to 0.0025 in the threshold-crossing counting method. The frequency characteristics of crossing the threshold in this signal are similar to the chewing frequency of the human body, which may lead to misidentification as chewing segments.

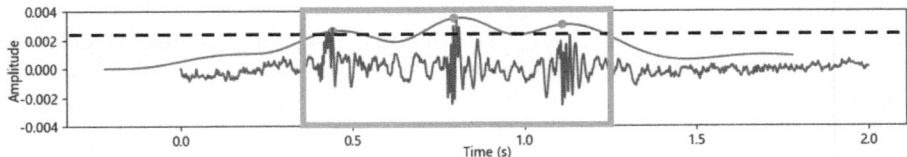

Fig. 5. A user's coughing signal may be misidentified as a chewing signal when using the threshold-crossing frequency method.

Upon analyzing the entire eating process, we found that the chewing action is always accompanied by actions of food intake into the mouth before and swallowing food afterward, and these three actions strictly follow a time sequence. Therefore, by examining the time sequence between actions, we can further verify whether the detected chewing signal segments are genuinely valid.

We employ a convolutional neural network (CNN) as the core structure of the feature learning network. Since most tasks in ChewSense involve real-time processing, CNNs are chosen due to their higher computational efficiency compared to other models. For each motion segment, we compute spectral and wavelet coefficient features and classify the motion segment into specific categories: feeding entry, swallowing, or other. After classifying each action segment, we examine whether the preceding and subsequent actions of each chewing segment match the expected sequence. If they do not match, the segment is discarded.

3.4   Food Type Recognition Module

The food type recognition module, after the preliminary validation by the chewing tag module and the final validation by the chewing verification module, determines which segments represent chewing actions. For these chewing segments, we calculate the following signal features: including 11 MFCC coefficients, centroid frequency, and energy in the range of 200 to 3000 Hz. Subsequently, we employ a random forest classifier to classify food types.

3.5   Interface Feedback Module

The final module of ChewSense is used to consolidate detection results and output them to the user interface. When the system detects that the user's chew count is too low, this module alerts the user through the reminder function within the program interface.

4   System Evaluation

4.1   Experiment Setup

We invited 10 volunteers to wear headphones and have lunch, eating according to their own habits. These 10 volunteers had varied eating styles: some chewed slowly and thoroughly, some ate quickly, and others had the habit of watching their phones while eating. They represented the majority of eating styles people have during meals. We collected reverse sound signals using ATH M30x headphones, with a sampling rate of 44100 Hz. Utilizing the audio and video recording features of ChewSense, we were able to replay the videos and label the signal source files, marking the eating times, types of food, and number of chews. In total, we collected 1072 min of eating data.

4.2   Chew Count Accuracy

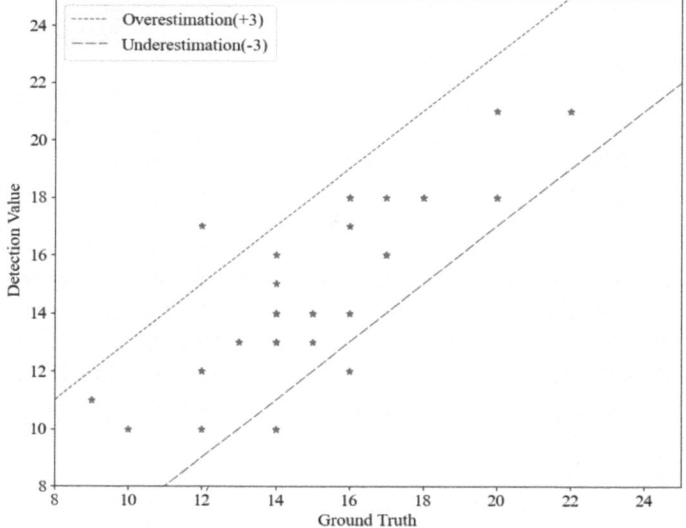

Fig. 6. Scatter plot of ground truth values vs. detected count of chewing for each mouthful during a meal for volunteer A.

To evaluate the accuracy of our chewing count method, we compared the chewing counts detected by ChewSense with the annotated counts in the recorded videos. Figure 6 displays the scatter plot of detected and ground truth values for each chewing segment of volunteer A during a meal. We observe that the count errors for most chewing segments range from −3 to 3, and the distribution of count errors per mouthful is relatively uniform.

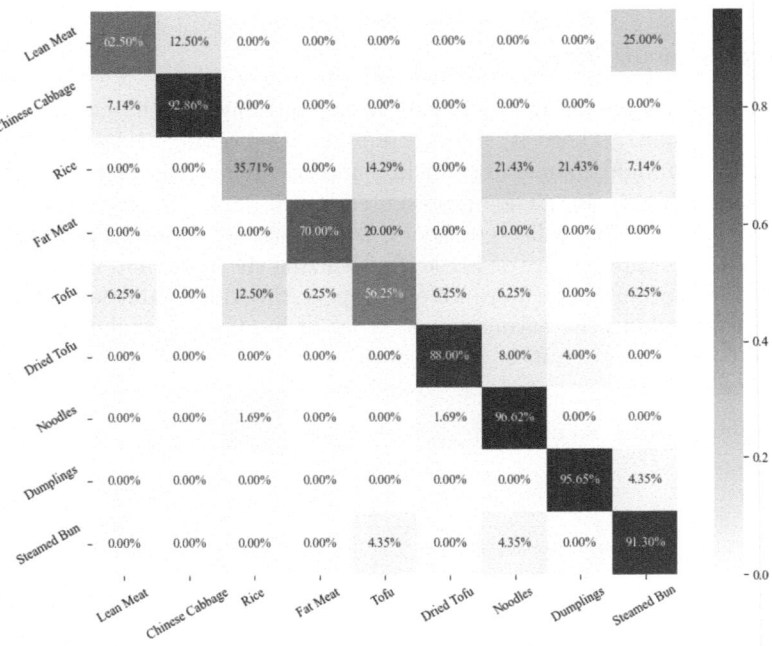

Fig. 7. Confusion matrix for food type recognition.

Figure 8 displays the accuracy and absolute error of chewing counts for the 10 volunteers. The accuracy of chewing counts for all volunteers was 84.58%, with an average absolute error of 3.66. Volunteer A had an accuracy of 90.12% and an average absolute error of 1.44. Among the ten volunteers, the accuracy of volunteer A was significantly higher than others, mainly because the threshold in the chewing tag module was designed based on the characteristics of volunteer A. The same algorithm applied to different individuals may result in differences.

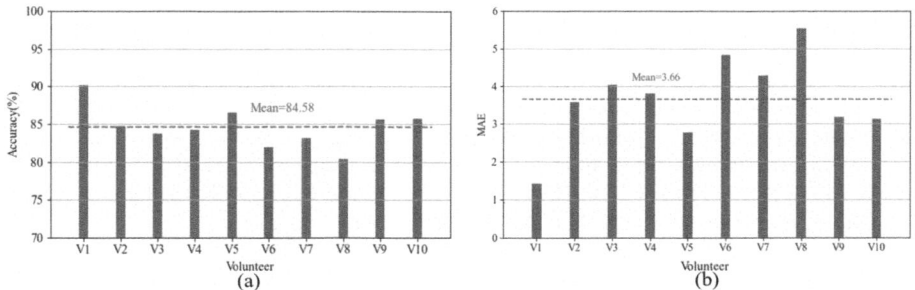

Fig. 8. (a) The accuracy and (b) the average absolute error of chewing counts for the 10 volunteers.

4.3 Food Type Identification Accuracy

In the dataset, Volunteer A had a total of 192 chewing segments. We trained a model using random forest and validated the accuracy of the model in identifying food types using leave-one-out cross-validation method. The confusion matrix for volunteer A's food types is shown in Fig. 7, with an overall accuracy of 82.90% and a recall rate of 82.12%. The results indicate that: firstly, the recognition rate of rice is relatively low and it is easily confused with staple foods such as noodles and dumplings. This may be because rice easily absorbs water and can change texture with soup. Secondly, the recognition rates for lean meat, fat meat, and tofu are relatively low. Lean meat is often recognized as steamed buns, and fat meat is often recognized as tofu, which may be related to their similar textures. Lastly, Chinese cabbage is relatively easy to distinguish because it has a higher moisture content, producing crisp and distinctive sound characteristics during chewing.

5 Conclusion

This paper introduces ChewSense, a novel dietary detection system capable of identifying the chew count and food types for each mouthful consumed by individuals using earphone reverse signals. In the implementation of the system, we segmented chewing segments in the eating signals and validated the authenticity of these segments using pre-action and post-action verification. Experimental results demonstrate that ChewSense accurately identifies chew counts and food types with accuracies of 84.58% and 82.90%, respectively. Moreover, ChewSense provides timely feedback to users when their chew count is too low. We hope that ChewSense can help individuals develop healthy eating habits.

Acknowledgments. This work has been supported by National Natural Science Foundation of China (Grant No. 41976185) and the graduate education quality improvement program of Sanya Oceanographic Institution, Ocean University of China (Grant No. SOIYK009).

References

1. Flegal, K.M., Graubard, B.I., Williamson, D.F., Gail, M.H.: Excess deaths associated with underweight, overweight, and obesity. JAMA **293**(15), 1861–1867 (2005)
2. Alshurafa, N., et al.: Counting bites with bits: expert workshop addressing calorie and macronutrient intake monitoring. J. Med. Internet Res. **21**(12), 14904 (2019)
3. Heitmann, B.L., Lissner, L.: Dietary underreporting by obese individuals-is it specific or non-specific? BMJ **311**(7011), 986–989 (1995)
4. Prakash, J., Yang, Z., Wei, Y.-L., Hassanieh, H., Choudhury, R.R.: EarSense: earphones as a teeth activity sensor. In: Proceedings of the 26th Annual International Conference on Mobile Computing and Networking, pp. 1–13 (2020)
5. Chun, K.S., Bhattacharya, S., Thomaz, E.: Detecting eating episodes by tracking jawbone movements with a non-contact wearable sensor. Proc. ACM Interact. Mob. Wearable Ubiquit. Technol. **2**(1), 1–21 (2018)
6. Dong, Y., Scisco, J., Wilson, M., Muth, E., Hoover, A.: Detecting periods of eating during free-living by tracking wrist motion. IEEE J. Biomed. Health Inform. **18**(4), 1253–1260 (2013)
7. Thomaz, E., Essa, I., Abowd, G.D.: A practical approach for recognizing eating moments with wrist-mounted inertial sensing. In: Proceedings of the 2015 ACM International Joint Conference on Pervasive and Ubiquitous Computing, pp. 1029–1040 (2015)
8. Nakamura, Y., Nakaoka, R., Matsuda, Y., Yasumoto, K.: eat2pic: an eating-painting interactive system to nudge users into making healthier diet choices. Proc. ACM Interact. Mob. Wearable Ubiquit. Technol. **7**(1), 1–23 (2023)
9. Zhang, S., et al.: NeckSense: a multi-sensor necklace for detecting eating activities in free-living conditions. Proc. ACM Interact. Mob. Wearable Ubiquit. Technol. **4**(2), 1–26 (2020)
10. Taniguchi, K., Chiaki, H., Kurosawa, M., Nishikawa, A.: A novel earphone type sensor for measuring mealtime: consideration of the method to distinguish between running and meals. Sensors **17**(2), 252 (2017)
11. Bi, S., et al.: Auracle: detecting eating episodes with an ear-mounted sensor. Proc. ACM Interact. Mob. Wearable Ubiquit. Technol. **2**(3), 1–27 (2018)
12. Rahman, T., et al.: BodyBeat: a mobile system for sensing non-speech body sounds. In: MobiSys, vol. 14, pp. 2–594 (2014)
13. Chun, K.S., Bhattacharya, S., Thomaz, E.: Detecting eating episodes by tracking jawbone movements with a non-contact wearable sensor. Proc. ACM Interact. Mob. Wearable Ubiquit. Technol. **2**(1), 1–21 (2018)
14. Po, J., Kieser, J., Gallo, L.M., Tésenyi, A., Herbison, P., Farella, M.: Time-frequency analysis of chewing activity in the natural environment. J. Dent. Res. **90**(10), 1206–1210 (2011)

Simulated Annealing-Based Routing Optimization Algorithm for LEO Satellite-Assisted UAV Networks

Yang Shen and Xiaojun Zhu[✉]

College of Computer Science and Technology,
Nanjing University of Aeronautics and Astronautics, Nanjing, China
{shenyang,xzhu}@nuaa.edu.cn

Abstract. Unmanned Aerial Vehicles (UAVs) are critical to the military and have enormous potential for expansion, but they are vulnerable to jamming on the battlefield, reducing the quality of communication links and operational effectiveness. Low-Earth orbit (LEO) satellites can be used as auxiliary communication nodes to enhance the communication stability of UAV networks in a complex electromagnetic environment. Therefore, in this paper, we establish a model of a LEO satellite-assisted UAV network in a spectrum denial environment. We propose a routing optimization algorithm based on simulated annealing to improve communication quality through route planning and a reasonable allocation of network bandwidth resources. Numerical results verify the efficiency of the proposed algorithm, and the advantages of LEO satellite-assisted UAV networks in terms of data transmission are also analyzed.

Keywords: UAV · LEO satellite · Spectrum denial · Jamming · Routing · Simulated annealing

1 Introduction

Various industries have widely used UAVs due to their high flexibility, quick response, and strong environmental adaptability. In the military field, UAVs can perform tasks such as tactical reconnaissance, situational awareness, and long-range strikes. In the Russo-Ukrainian War, UAVs were instrumental in electronic warfare, target indication, and precise strikes. However, UAVs on the battlefield will inevitably be threatened by malicious jamming attacks. Jamming will degrade the quality of communication links, impacting intelligence gathering and combat operations.

Cognitive radio technology is currently one of the main strategies for dealing with jamming [1]. UAVs dynamically sense the radio environment and adjust communication parameters according to changes in the environment. Another strategy is trajectory planning, which optimizes UAV flight paths based on geographic information and real-time environmental data, avoiding known or potential interference areas [2]. UAV swarms can discard non-communicative

L. Sun and Y. Chen (Eds.): CWSN 2024, CCIS 2341, pp. 269–279, 2025.
https://doi.org/10.1007/978-981-96-2186-6_21

nodes, allowing the remaining nodes to quickly restore the network through their autonomy and collaborative capabilities [3]. In addition to the above solutions, dynamically adjusting the transmission power to increase signal coverage and anti-jamming capabilities is also one of the most common means of dealing with jamming [4].

The rapid advancement of LEO satellites has opened up new prospects for UAV development. LEO satellites offer several advantages over typical communication satellites, including less transmission latency, stronger anti-jamming capabilities, and more reliable communication stability. The coordinated operation of LEO satellites and UAVs has numerous application possibilities, including disaster area rescue communication [5], Internet of Things data gathering (IOT) [6], edge computing [7], and more. Nevertheless, there is currently limited research on the use of LEO satellites to facilitate communication among clusters of UAVs in a spectrum denial environment.

In this paper, we establish a model of a UAV network assisted by a LEO satellite under spectrum denial. Next, we improve communication quality through route planning and allocation of network bandwidth resources. Our goal is to maximize data stream satisfaction, the concept and calculation method of which are given in Sect. 3. To this end, we design a routing optimization algorithm based on simulated annealing that can calculate approximate solutions relatively quickly in large-scale networks. The simulation results verify the effectiveness of our approach.

2   Related Works

Existing works on anti-jamming for UAVs mainly focus on cognitive radio technology, trajectory planning, and power control. For example, Mei *et al.* [1] suggested a cognitive radio-based interference coordination method that optimizes resource block allocation and power control through UAV sensing capabilities. Yin *et al.* [8] proposed an anti-jamming communication technique based on multi-agent layered Q-learning (MALQL) to jointly optimize the channel and power allocation. In [9], Mou *et al.* designed a path-planning algorithm based on graph convolutional neural networks. The UAV continuously monitors its surroundings and the locations of other UAVs, swiftly adjusting its position to reestablish communication after any damage. The preceding investigations face certain practical implementation limitations. 1) Finding an available frequency band in an area with a lot of interference may be difficult because of the limited spectrum resources. 2) Moving the UAV to restore network connectivity may conflict with the original mission, which will have a negative impact on the combat plan. 3) Heavy interference constrains the amplitude and range of power adjustment, preventing it from providing adequate anti-jamming capacity.

In regard to the cooperation of satellites and UAVs, Deb *et al.* [10] proposed the use of UAV base stations to establish network connections in disaster-stricken areas. They designed a delay-aware routing algorithm based on Q-learning to route data to the nearest access point through multiple hops of neighboring

UAVs. When UAVs are outside the reach of transmission, communication is established using LEO satellites. Jia *et al.* [11] employed a LEO satellite network to assist UAVs in gathering remote Internet of Things data. For latency-tolerant data, UAVs collect, store, and carry it, and then fly to the destination station. For latency-sensitive data, UAVs collect the data and then transmit it to the ground station via the satellite link. For the scenario of LEO satellites assisting UAVs in performing reconnaissance missions, Han *et al.* [12] designed a trajectory optimization method based on reinforcement learning to improve data transmission performance.

To the best of our knowledge, there are very few existing studies that explore the topic of LEO satellite-assisted UAV network communications under spectrum denial, despite its critical importance to the military. Furthermore, existing studies often assume that each UAV can communicate directly with satellites, which is not feasible in practice. In military operations, UAVs usually adopt a large-scale cluster combat strategy, and the cost of deploying satellite modules for all UAVs is too high. It is more appropriate to selectively install satellite communication modules on some UAVs.

3   Problem Formulation

As shown in Fig. 1, UAVs carry out reconnaissance missions on the battlefield following a predetermined path, and there is frequent data interaction between them. We divide UAVs into two categories: master UAVs and slave UAVs. Master UAVs are equipped with satellite communication modules and can communicate directly with the LEO satellite. Slave UAVs rely on master UAVs to communicate with the LEO satellite. Because UAVs have a limited transmission distance, they can only communicate directly with neighboring nodes within their communication range. The source node forwards data to the destination node via a multi-hop route. When UAVs fly through an interference region, some communication links are interrupted, and the original routes become invalid. One common approach is to find an alternative route to bypass the interference area. Nevertheless, interference reduces the communication resources of the network, so numerous data streams could compete for communication resources on the same link. Moreover, if the interference area is large enough to completely cut off the UAV network, there will be no available routes. Another approach is to use the LEO satellite as a relay node, which has the downside of significantly increasing latency. For each data stream, a choice must be made between a route with and without a satellite link.

We use h to denote the flight altitude of UAVs, $w_i = (x_i, y_i, h)$ to represent the coordinates of the UAV u_i, and $w_{jam} = (x_{jam}, y_{jam}, 0)$ to represent the coordinates of the interference source on the ground. Since there are few blocking objects in the air, the communication channels between UAVs are line-of-sight. We use orthogonal frequency division multiple access technology (OFDMA) to avoid transmission interference between UAVs. We calculate the channel gain from UAV u_i to UAV u_j of the free-space model as:

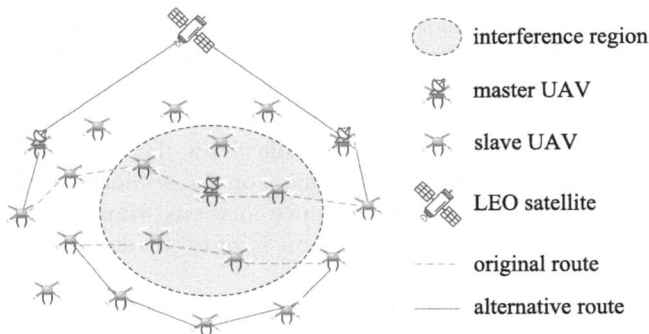

Fig. 1. LEO satellite-assisted UAV network under spectrum denial

$$G_{ij} = \frac{\beta_0}{||w_i - w_j||^2}, \tag{1}$$

where β_0 is the channel gain per unit distance. The channel gain from the interference source to u_j is:

$$I_j = \frac{\beta_0}{||w_{jam} - w_j||^2} \tag{2}$$

Hence, we calculate the signal-to-noise ratio as:

$$\text{SINR}_{ij} = \frac{G_{ij}P_i}{\sigma^2 + I_j P_{jam}}, \tag{3}$$

where P_i is the transmission power of u_i, P_{jam} is the transmission power of the interference source, and σ^2 is the power of environmental noise. If SINR_{ij} is greater than the predefined signal-to-noise ratio threshold SINR_{th}, a communication link can be established from u_i to u_j. Therefore, the maximum transmission range from u_i to u_j is:

$$d_{ij}^{th} = \left[\frac{\beta_0 P_i}{\text{SINR}^{th} (\sigma^2 + I_j P_{jam})} \right]^{1/2} \tag{4}$$

Data can be transferred from u_i to u_j when the distance is less than d_{ij}^{th}. For a given channel bandwidth B, the maximum data rate from u_i to u_j can be calculated as:

$$C_{ij} = B \cdot \log_2(1 + \text{SINR}_{ij}) \tag{5}$$

We consider a set of UAVs $U = \{u_1, u_2, \cdots, u_R\}$ and a LEO satellite ls in the network. The network is represented as a directed graph $G = (V, E)$, where $V = U \cup \{ls\}$, and an edge $(i,j) \in E$ if node i can transfer data to node j. We assume that there is a set of data streams $F = \{F_1, F_2, \ldots, F_k\}$ in the network. Table 1 lists the key notations used in this paper. It should be noted that the network bandwidth $C(i,j)$ is the maximum data rate calculated by Eq. 5. The end-to-end delay is the sum of the delays at all links in the route.

Table 1. Key Notations

Symbol	Description
$T(i,j)$	The delay of link (i,j)
$C(i,j)$	The network bandwidth of link (i,j)
si	The source node of Fi
ti	The destination node of Fi
Di	The maximum delay that Fi can accept
Ri	The network bandwidth requirement of Fi
hi	The end-to-end delay of Fi
fi	The network bandwidth allocated to Fi

To measure the quality of the route of Fi, we define routing satisfaction S_i as the evaluation index, which consists of two parts: delay satisfaction $S(h_i)$ and network bandwidth satisfaction $S(f_i)$. We calculate $S(h_i)$ as:

$$S(h_i) = \begin{cases} 1, & 0 \leq h_i \leq D_i \\ \exp\left(\frac{D_i - h_i}{2D_i}\right), & h_i > D_i \end{cases} \tag{6}$$

The network bandwidth satisfaction $S(f_i)$ is:

$$S(f_i) = \left(\frac{f_i}{R_i}\right)^{1/2} \tag{7}$$

Considering that data streams have different priorities for latency and bandwidth, we use λ_i to adjust the weights, with the range of λ_i being between 0 and 1. Therefore, the routing satisfaction S_i is calculated as:

$$S_i = \lambda_i S(h_i) + (1 - \lambda_i) S(f_i) \tag{8}$$

Our goal is to maximize the total routing satisfaction:

$$\max \sum_{1 \leq i \leq k} S_i \tag{9}$$

4 Algorithm Design

4.1 Mathematical Programming Formulation and Exact Algorithms

In this section, we first give the constraints of the problem. Let $x_i(u,v)$ be the binary indicator variable such that $x_i(u,v) = 1$ if the route of F_i passes through the link (u,v). The problem is formulated as

$$\max_{f_i,(u,v)\in E} \sum_{1\leq i\leq k} S_i$$

$$\text{s.t.} \quad x_i(u,v) \in \{0,1\}, \quad \forall i=1,2,\ldots,k \tag{10}$$

$$\sum_{v:(s_i,v)\in E} x_i(s_i,v) = 1, \quad \forall i=1,2,\ldots,k \tag{11}$$

$$\sum_{v:(v,t_i)\in E} x_i(v,t_i) = 1, \quad \forall i=1,2,\ldots,k \tag{12}$$

$$\sum_{v:(u,v)\in E} x_i(u,v) \leq 1, \quad \forall u \in V, \forall i=1,2,\ldots,k \tag{13}$$

$$\sum_{q:(u,q)\in E} x_i(u,q) = \sum_{q:(q,u)\in E} x_i(q,u), \quad \forall u \neq s_i, t_i, \forall i=1,2,\ldots,k \tag{14}$$

$$\sum_{i=1}^{k} x_i(u,v) \cdot f_i \leq C(u,v), \quad \forall (u,v) \in E \tag{15}$$

$$f_i \geq 0, \quad \forall i=1,2,\ldots,k \tag{16}$$

$$f_i \leq R_i, \quad \forall i=1,2,\ldots,k \tag{17}$$

Equations (11)–(14) denote that each data stream can only choose one path for transmission. Equation (11) indicates that the source node of each data stream must connect to one neighbor node to transmit data. Equation (12) indicates that the destination node must connect to one neighbor node to receive data. Equations (13) and (14) indicate that intermediate nodes must satisfy flow conservation, and they can only select one node as the next hop. Equations (15)–(17) are constraints on network bandwidth.

This problem can be solved using any mathematical planning optimizer, such as CPLEX and Gurobi, which can handle small problem sizes. This provides us with an exact algorithm for the routing optimization problem, typically utilized for assessing heuristic algorithms. Note that in the worst case, it runs in exponential time due to the hardness of the problem.

4.2   Simulated Annealing-Based Routing Optimization Algorithm

The exact algorithms only apply to small-scale networks due to their large running times. We thus propose a simulated annealing-based routing optimization (SA-ROP) algorithm to quickly obtain approximate solutions for large-scale networks.

Simulated annealing (SA) is a probabilistic optimization algorithm inspired by the process of annealing in metallurgy, where materials are heated and then slowly cooled to remove defects and optimize their structure. In optimization, SA explores the solution space by occasionally accepting worse solutions to escape local optima, similar to how heating allows atoms to move freely before settling into a lower energy state as the material cools. As the algorithm progresses, the probability of accepting worse solutions decreases, allowing the system to stabilize at an approximate optimal solution.

Algorithm 1. Simulated Annealing-Based Routing Optimization Algorithm

---

Input: Initial temperature T_0, final temperature T_{end}, cooling rate q, maximum iterations L

Output: Approximate optimal solution to the problem P_{best}, objective function value $S(P_{best})$

1: $P_{base} = \{p_1, p_2, \ldots, p_k\}$ ⟵ Generate initial solution of the problem
2: T ⟵ T_0
3: k ⟵ 1
4: **while** $T > T_{end}$ and $k \leq L$ **do**
5:      Generate new solution P_{temp} using Algorithm 2
6:      ΔS ⟵ $S(P_{temp}) - S(P_{base})$
7:      **if** $\Delta S > 0$ or $e^{\Delta S/T} \geq \text{rand}(0,1)$ **then**
8:          P_{base} ⟵ P_{temp}
9:      **end if**
10:     k ⟵ $k + 1$
11:     **if** $k > L$ **then**
12:        T ⟵ $q \cdot T$
13:        k ⟵ 1
14:     **end if**
15: **end while**
16: P_{base} ⟵ P_{best}

The pseudocode of SA-ROP is presented in Algorithm 1. Firstly, we randomly generate a path p_i for each data stream F_i and allocate network bandwidth to form the initial solution $P_{base} = \{p_1, p_2, \ldots, p_k\}$. The scheme for allocating network bandwidth is as follows: if multiple data streams traverse an edge and can simultaneously meet their bandwidth requirements, then each data stream receives bandwidth equal to its own demand; if not, the bandwidth allocation is proportionate to their respective demands. In each iteration, a new solution P_{temp} is generated. Algorithm 2 presents the process of generating a new solution. A path p_m is randomly selected from P_{base}. For p_m, we identify all nodes that meet the following conditions: 1) the source node s_m of p_m can reach the node; 2) the node can reach the destination node t_m of p_m; and 3) the node is not on p_m. We randomly select a node n from these nodes, then find the path P_{n1} with the shortest delay from s_m to n and the path P_{n2} with the shortest delay from n to t_m. The new path, p'_m, is formed by concatenating P_{n1} and P_{n2}. Next, we reallocate the network bandwidth for the data streams, resulting in a new solution P_{temp}. If P_{temp} has a higher total routing satisfaction, it is accepted; otherwise, the Metropolis criterion is used to determine whether to accept P_{temp}.

Algorithm 2. Generate New Solution

Input: Current solution P_{base}
Output: New solution P_{temp}

1: $P_{temp} \longleftarrow P_{base}$
2: Randomly select a path p_m from P_{temp}, s_m and t_m are source and destination nodes of p_m
3: $N \longleftarrow \{n \mid n$ is reachable from s_m and can reach t_m, and $n \notin p_m\}$
4: Randomly select a node $n \in N$
5: Find the path p_{n1} with the shortest delay from s_m to n
6: Find the path p_{n2} with the shortest delay from n to t_m
7: $p'_m \longleftarrow p_{n1} + p_{n2}$
8: Replace p_m with p'_m in P_{temp}
9: Reallocate network bandwidth

---

5 Simulation Evaluation

In this section, we evaluate the performance of SA-ROP in a number of randomly generated networks. All experiments are conducted on the Windows 11 operating system with Intel(R) Core(TM) i7-11800H @ 2.30 GHz CPU and 16 GB memory.

5.1 Simulation Setup

The simulation parameters are as follows: UAVs fly at an altitude of 100 m. The channel gain per unit distance is $\beta_0 = -60$ dB. The UAV transmit power is $P_i = 6$ W, and the interference source transmit power is $P_{jam} = 20$ W. The environmental noise power is assumed to be $\sigma^2 = -169$ dBm/Hz. The signal-to-noise ratio threshold is $\text{SINR}_{th} = 1$. The channel bandwidth is $B = 5$ MHz. The delay between UAVs is 10 ms. The delay and maximum data rate between master UAVs and the LEO satellite are 200 ms and 50 Mbps, respectively. We set the size of the scenario to 800 m × 800 m and the location of the ground interference source as the center of the area. The task requirements create uncertainty in the formation shape of the UAVs, so we randomly distribute them in the area, provided that the distance between adjacent UAVs is not less than 50 m. The data streams are also randomly generated.

5.2 Performance Analysis

We initially investigate the impact of the LEO satellite on the communication performance of UAV networks, using transmission success rate and total routing satisfaction as performance metrics. The transmission success rate refers to the proportion of data streams that can find a transmission path. In detail, a LEO satellite is involved in the network, and the number of UAVs changes from 30 to 70. We randomly generate data streams for each network under low and high traffic load conditions, repeat them 10 times, and then calculate the average transmission success rate and total routing satisfaction. Low-traffic load means

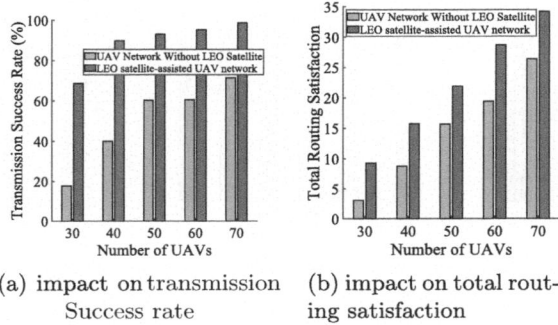

(a) impact on transmission   (b) impact on total rout-
Success rate   ing satisfaction

Fig. 2. Impact of LEO satellite on UAV networks of different sizes

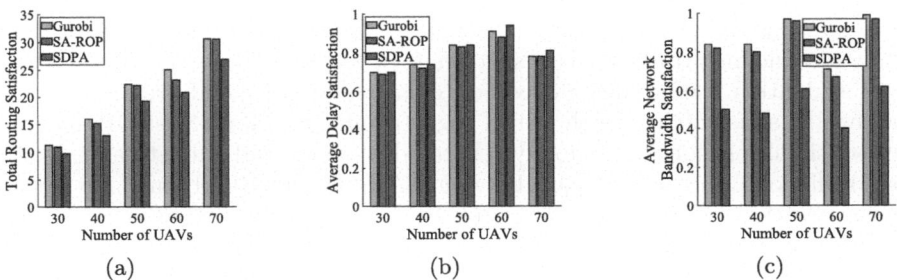

(a)   (b)   (c)

Fig. 3. (a) Total route satisfaction, (b) average delay satisfaction, and (c) average network bandwidth satisfaction of different algorithms under low-traffic load.

the number of data streams is 50% of the number of UAVs, while high-traffic load means the number of data streams is 100% of the number of UAVs. Figure 2 displays the performance results of various random networks. As expected, the LEO satellite always helps the UAV network achieve better communication performance across different network scales. Particularly in smaller networks, the LEO satellite significantly enhances the robustness of the UAV network. This is because the network is divided into several disconnected subnets by interference regions, which can only be crossed by the satellite. As the UAV network expands, new routes may be found to bypass the interference regions from the network edges, but some data streams will inevitably fail to find viable routes without the aid of the LEO satellite.

To effectively evaluate the performance of SA-ROP, the optimal solution obtained by Gurobi is used as an optimal benchmark. Since Gurobi may run for a long time, we restrict the running time to 5 min and report the best-found solution if it does not terminate. The shortest delay path algorithm (SDPA) is also used for comparison. In SDPA, we find the path with the shortest delay for all data streams, then use an optimizer to allocate network bandwidth. Both SA-ROP and SDPA can find a solution within a few seconds.

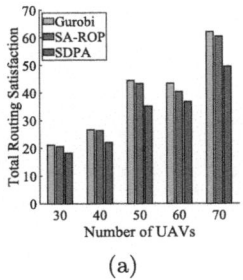 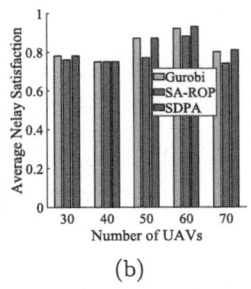 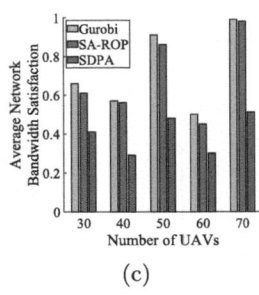

(a)   (b)   (c)

Fig. 4. (a) Total route satisfaction, (b) average delay satisfaction, and (c) average network bandwidth satisfaction of different algorithms under high-traffic load.

Figure 3 and Fig. 4 show the performance comparison of different algorithms under low and high traffic loads, respectively. In addition to total routing satisfaction, evaluation metrics include average delay satisfaction and average network bandwidth satisfaction. As shown in Fig. 3(a) and Fig. 4(a), SA-ROP achieves near-optimal solutions in randomly generated networks and data streams. Under low-traffic load, the average gaps between SA-ROP and Gurobi in three performance metrics are 3.34%, 1.72%, and 3.17%, respectively. Under high-traffic load, the average gaps between SA-ROP and Gurobi in three performance metrics are 3.14%, 5.18%, and 5.17%, respectively. While SDPA has the highest average delay satisfaction, its average network bandwidth satisfaction lags far behind the other two algorithms. SA-ROP average network bandwidth satisfaction is, on average, 67.52% higher than SDPA. This is because SDPA only seeks the shortest delay path, causing multiple data streams to compete for network bandwidth on the same link. In contrast, SA-ROP balances between delay and network bandwidth, avoiding congestion caused by using a common node for multiple data streams. SA-ROP effectively balances the load by arranging the transmission of data streams with low delay requirements via high-bandwidth LEO satellite paths. Particularly, as shown in Figs. 3(c) and 4(c), high-traffic load significantly reduces the average network bandwidth satisfaction of all three algorithms. Therefore, reasonable allocation of network bandwidth resources is key to improving overall network performance. The proposed SA-ROP is proven to achieve near-optimal solutions with low time complexity, making it suitable for practical large-scale systems.

6   Conclusion

In this paper, we focus on the communication challenge faced by large-scale UAV clusters in a spectrum-denied environment. In a spectrum-denied environment, we use an LEO satellite as an auxiliary communication node and develop a model of a LEO satellite-assisted UAV network. To improve the communication performance of the network, we propose a routing algorithm based on simulated annealing to optimize network bandwidth allocation and routing planning.

An approximate solution is produced by a number of iterations in a short time. Simulation results demonstrate the efficacy and superiority of the proposed algorithm.

Acknowledgments. This work was supported by the National Natural Science Foundation of China (62372230).

References

1. Mei, W., Zhang, R.: UAV-sensing-assisted cellular interference coordination: a cognitive radio approach. IEEE Wirel. Commun. Lett. **9**(6), 799–803 (2020)
2. Gao, Y., Wu, Y., Cui, Z., Yang, W., Li, N.: Anti-jamming trajectory and power design for cognitive UAV communications. In: International Wireless Communications and Mobile Computing (IWCMC), pp. 1370–1375 (2021)
3. Chen, M., Wang, H., Chang, C.-Y., Wei, X.: SIDR: a swarm intelligence-based damage-resilient mechanism for UAV swarm networks. IEEE Access **8**, 77 089–77 105 (2020)
4. Ma, N., et al.: Reinforcement learning-based dynamic anti-jamming power control in UAV networks: an effective jamming signal strength based approach. IEEE Commun. Lett. **26**(10), 2355–2359 (2022)
5. Mohamed, E.M., Alnakhli, M., Fouda, M.M.: Joint UAV trajectory planning and LEO-sat selection in SAGIN. IEEE Open J. Commun. Soc. (2024)
6. Ma, T., et al.: UAV-LEO integrated backbone: A ubiquitous data collection approach for B5G internet of remote things networks. IEEE J. Sel. Areas Commun. **39**(11), 34911–3505 (2021)
7. Lakew, D.S., Tran, A.-T., Dao, N.-N., Cho, S.: Intelligent self-optimization for task offloading in LEO-MEC-assisted energy-harvesting-UAV systems. IEEE Trans. Netw. Sci. Eng. (2024)
8. Yin, Z., Lin, Y., Zhang, Y., Qian, Y., Shu, F., Li, J.: Collaborative multiagent reinforcement learning aided resource allocation for UAV anti-jamming communication. IEEE Internet Things J. **9**(23), 23 995–24 008 (2022)
9. Mou, Z., Gao, F., Liu, J., Wu, Q.: Resilient UAV swarm communications with graph convolutional neural network. IEEE J. Sel. Areas Commun. **40**(1), 393–411 (2021)
10. Deb, P.K., Mukherjee, A., Misra, S.: XiA: send-it-anyway Q-routing for 6G-enabled UAV-LEO communications. IEEE Trans. Netw. Sci. Eng. **8**(4), 2722–2731 (2021)
11. Jia, Z., Sheng, M., Li, J., Niyato, D., Han, Z.: Leo-satellite-assisted UAV: joint trajectory and data collection for internet of remote things in 6G aerial access networks. IEEE Internet Things J. **8**(12), 9814–9826 (2020)
12. Han, C., et al.: Satellite-assisted UAV trajectory control in hostile jamming environments. IEEE Trans. Veh. Technol. **71**(4), 3760–3775 (2021)

SimilarBP: Leveraging Similar Samples for Few-Shot PPG-Based Blood Pressure Measurement

Yixuan Song$^{(\boxtimes)}$ ⓘ, Dong Zhao ⓘ, Qi Wang ⓘ, and Zhou Fang ⓘ

Beijing University of Posts and Telecommunications, Beijing, China
{songyixuan,dzhao,wang_qi,fz20001119}@bupt.edu.cn

Abstract. Arterial blood pressure (ABP) monitoring plays a vital role in the prevention of cardiovascular diseases. However, conventional cuff-based devices are unsuitable for continuous monitoring due to their lack of portability and comfort. Photoplethysmography (PPG) sensors have been explored in recent studies for ABP measurement, nevertheless, achieving a balance between accuracy and user burden remains a difficulty. This study proposes a deep learning-based ABP monitoring system SimilarBP that combines the strengths of personalized and user-independent models, aiming to achieve high ABP measurement accuracy with few-shot personal data. SimilarBP pre-trains a user-independent model on a large dataset, then fine-tunes it using few-shot personal data, along with similar samples from the large dataset. Challenges include identifying similar samples and reducing the impact of incorrect ABP labels. To address these challenges, this study proposes an individualized contrastive learning model (ICLM) for identifying similar samples and an ABP label correction algorithm (ALCA) for correcting ABP labels. SimilarBP is validated on a public dataset and a real-world volunteer dataset. Evaluation results demonstrate that SimilarBP meets the AAMI standard.

Keywords: Blood pressure · PPG sensing · Contrastive learning · Label correction

1 Introduction

Arterial blood pressure (ABP) is a critical indicator for assessing cardiovascular system function. Long-term hypertension can lead to serious health issues such as heart disease, stroke, renal failure, visual impairment, and peripheral arterial disease. Therefore, continuous ABP monitoring is crucial for preventing these conditions. However, the widely used cuff-based ABP monitoring devices are not suitable for continuous ABP monitoring due to portability and comfort.

Nowadays, many researchers have studied the use of Photoplethysmography (PPG) sensors on the wearable devices to achieve ABP monitoring. However,

ⓒ The Author(s), under exclusive license to Springer Nature Singapore Pte Ltd. 2025
L. Sun and Y. Chen (Eds.): CWSN 2024, CCIS 2341, pp. 280–291, 2025.
https://doi.org/10.1007/978-981-96-2186-6_22

existing methods struggle to balance the accuracy and usage burden. For example, i) Pulse Transit Time (PTT) [1,2] based methods achieve high ABP measurement accuracy, but require the user to calibrate the model and to touch the extra ECG electrode with other hands. ii) User-independent Deep learning methods [3–6] utilize large datasets to achieve zero-shot ABP measurement, but sacrificing accuracy due to individual differences that are hard to obtain from PPG data, such as vascular elasticity, skin properties, and blood viscosity. iii) Personalized Deep learning methods [7–9] achieve high ABP measurement accuracy, but require extensive personal data (at least 10 samples) for training.

To address these issues, we aim to design a deep learning-based ABP monitoring system that combines the advantages of both personalized and user-independent methods. Our system is developed based on a large number of exploratory experiments. We collected wrist PPG data that was temporally synchronized with ABP data from 1,006 individuals in a hospital setting, as depicted in Fig. 1.

Our analysis reveals: i) Sometimes different people have the same PPG features, but their SBPs are different. ii) Sometimes different people have the same SBP, but their PPG features differ (as illustrated in Fig. 2). The observations suggest that the relationship between PPG features and blood pressure may be consistent among individuals with similar physiological features, including but not limited to vascular elasticity, skin properties, and blood viscosity. Therefore, our system first pre-trains a user-independent model, then fine-tunes it using the target user's few-shot sample data along with samples showing similar physiological features in large datasets.

However, as shown in Fig. 3, we found that the PPG features have large fluctuations within a 30-second period, while the cuff-based ABP monitor can only provide ABP data within one pressurization cycle (about 40 s). This discrepancy leads to a multi-value mapping problem between the PPG features and the ABP labels, resulting in incorrect ABP labels. This issue impairs the model's ability to correctly learn the relationship between the PPG features and blood pressure.

Given these findings, our system faces two unique challenges:

i) *Identifying Similar Samples for Personalization.* Our goal is to effectively train personalized models using data from similar individuals in a large dataset. However, directly measuring physiological features and individual differences using only PPG features or personal information poses a challenge. To tackle this challenge, we develop a contrastive learning model that can identify individuals with similar ABP and PPG patterns.

ii) *Reducing the Impact of Incorrect Labels When Fine-Tuning with Few-Shot Data.* Our goal is to fine-tune models using few-shot data with precise labels. However, existing works [1,2,8,10,11] using cuff-based devices for ABP label acquisition often leads to ABP labels that are not synchronized with continuous PPG data, resulting in label incorrectness. To overcome this, we propose an algorithm that models the relationship between short-term ABP variations and PPG features, enabling the correction of incorrect labels using as few as three accurate labels.

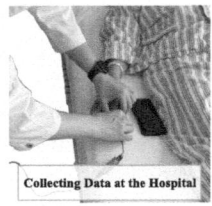

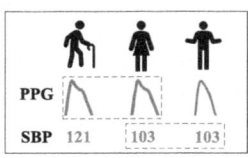

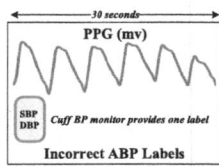

Fig. 1. Hospital-based exper- **Fig. 2.** Individual Differ- **Fig. 3.** Incorrect ABP Labels.
iments.   ences.

The contributions of this study can be summarized as follows:

i) We design a system, SimilarBP, that combines the advantages of personalized and user-independent models models to achieve more accurate ABP
measurement.
ii) We design an Individualized Contrastive Learning Model (ICLM) to learn
the individual differences from the large dataset by constructing pairs of
positive and negative samples.
iii) We design an ABP Label Correction Algorithm (ALCA) for PPG data by
modeling the relationship between short-term ABP variations and PPG features.

2   Related Work

PPG is a non-invasive measurement technique that reflects cardiovascular status
by measuring changes in blood volume. The exploration of PPG-based blood
pressure measurement methods can be categorized as follows.

PTT-Based Methods. The PTT-based method estimates ABP by measuring
the time a pulse wave takes to travel from the heart to other body parts, as
demonstrated in [1,2]. This method typically requires two sensors, such as ECG
and PPG, and relies on user assistance for calibration and maintaining sensor
contact during the measurement process. Despite its clinical significance, the
PTT-based method faces limitations in capturing the complex nonlinear relationship between PPG signals and ABP.

User-Independent Deep Learning Methods. User-independent methods
employ large datasets for zero-shot ABP measurement [3–6,10]. However, due
to the difficulty in directly extracting physiological features—such as vascular
elasticity, skin properties, and blood viscosity—from PPG data, these models
often fail to capture individual differences. Consequently, the accuracy of these
models at an individual level is not optimal.

Personalized Deep Learning Methods. In contrast to user-independent
approaches, personalized ABP models are pre-trained on large datasets and

subsequently fine-tuned with individual data [7–9]. Although these models can effectively adapt to individual differences, they require the collection of a substantial amount of personal calibration data for fine-tuning, typically at least 10 samples, which poses a significant burden on the user.

3   System Overview

The ABP monitoring system SimilarBP (Fig. 4) consists of two stages:

Pre-training. First, a feature extractor is designed to extract PPG and ABP features from a large dataset, such as the Blumio dataset. Subsequently, the Individualized Contrastive Learning Model (ICLM) maximizes/minimizes the PPG and ABP features of inter-group/intra-group samples to obtain different clusters of individuals.

Personalized Fine-Tuning. First, the target user's data labels are corrected using the ABP Label Correction Algorithm (ALCA). Then, features are obtained through the pre-trained ICLM. After that, the k-nearest neighbors (KNN) algorithm [12] is used to identify the cluster that is most similar to the target user's features. Finally, the personalized ABP measurement model is fine-tuned by leveraging the target user's few-shot samples along with data from the most similar cluster.

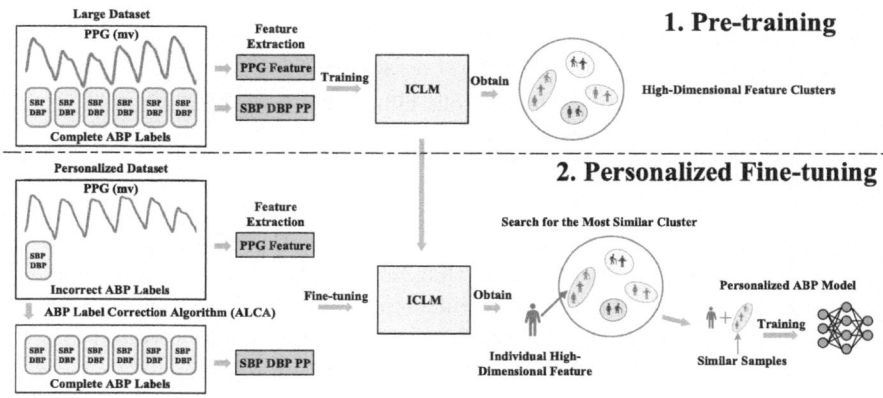

Fig. 4. System overview of SimilarBP.

4   Method

4.1   Feature Extraction

Preprocessing. We employ a sliding window (size of w_{size}) with a stride of w_{stride} to split PPG segment into cardiac cycles. Specifically, we employ the Automatic Multiscale-based Peak Detection (AMPD) algorithm [13] to find the local minimum points to extract cardiac cycles from the PPG segment (Fig. 5).

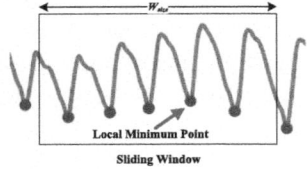

Fig. 5. Cardiac cycles extraction.   **Fig. 6.** PPG features in a cardiac cycle.

Table 1. Details of five PPG features

Features	Descriptions
DC	Related to the volume of blood in blood vessels that are not involved in the heartbeat
Amp	Related to stroke volume
H_{dn}	Related to peripheral resistance
T_d	Describes the diastolic filling time
T_s	Describes the systolic ejection time

PPG Features. After preprocessing PPG data, we extract five common features $F = \{DC, Amp, H_{dn}, T_s, T_d\}$ (Fig. 6) that are widely utilized in existing ABP measurement works, i.e., Direct Current component (DC), Amplitude (Amp), Height of dicrotic notch (H_{dn}), Systolic time (T_s) and Diastolic time (T_d). The details of the above features are shown in Table 1.

ABP Features. We utilize Systolic Blood Pressure (SBP), Diastolic Blood Pressure (DBP), and Pulse Pressure (PP) to represent the ABP features, i.e., $Z = \{SBP, DBP, PP\}$.

4.2   Individualized Contrastive Learning Model (ICLM)

As outlined in Sect. 1, our goal is to train personalized models using data from similar individuals. However, directly capturing individual differences using solely PPG features or personal information presents a significant challenge. To address this, we design the Individualized Contrastive Learning Model (ICLM) to learn these individual differences in an unsupervised manner.

Positive Pair Construction. We hope that people within the same cluster (having similar ABP distribution and PPG features) are close to each other. Therefore, for a sample of individual u collected at time t, i.e., $s_u^t = (F_u^t, Z_u^t)$, the positive sample s^+ is the sample of individual u with ABP features difference less than ε. Where ε is 5 because the ABP differences less than 5 mmHg can meet the requirement of AAMI standard [14].

Negative Pair Construction. We aim to ensure that individuals from different clusters remain distant from one another in the feature space. Therefore, samples from different individuals with an ABP feature difference of less than 5mmHg are considered negative samples s^-.

Loss Function. For a sample $s \in B$ (the sample set of a training batch), the loss function is formulated as follows:

$$\mathcal{L}_f = \sum_{s^+ \in S_p} \frac{exp(sim(s, s^+)/\tau)}{\sum_{s' \in S_n \cup S_p} exp(sim(s, s')/\tau)} \tag{1}$$

The positive sample set for sample s in the batch is denoted as $S_p \subset B$, and the negative sample set as $S_n \subset B$. τ is the temperature parameter, and $sim(a, b) = a^T b / \|a\| \|b\|$ represents the cosine similarity between a and b.

4.3   ABP Label Correction Algorithm (ALCA)

We explore the factors that could lead to the change of ABP within 2 min in a resting state. We assume that factors such as vascular resistance changes, emotional stress, physical activity, diet, water, and sugar intake undergo little change in the resting state. After the correlation analysis of ABP features and PPG features on the Blumio dataset, considering the average of all individuals, we find that there is a significant correlation between the change of PP/DBP and the change of T_d within 2 min, as shown in Table 2.

Table 2. Correlation between ABP features and PPG features

Features	Pearson Correlation
ΔDBP VS ΔT_d	−0.65
ΔPP VS ΔT_d	0.63

Based on this finding, the following equation group is established for correcting ABP labels on an individual basis:

$$\begin{cases} \Delta DBP = k_1 \Delta T_d + b_1, \\ \Delta PP = k_2 \Delta T_d + b_2 \end{cases} \tag{2}$$

k_1 and k_2 are the scaling parameters describing the linear relationship between ΔT_d and ΔDBP, and ΔT_d and ΔPP, respectively. b_1 and b_2 are the bias parameters. The differences in these four parameters represent individual variations.

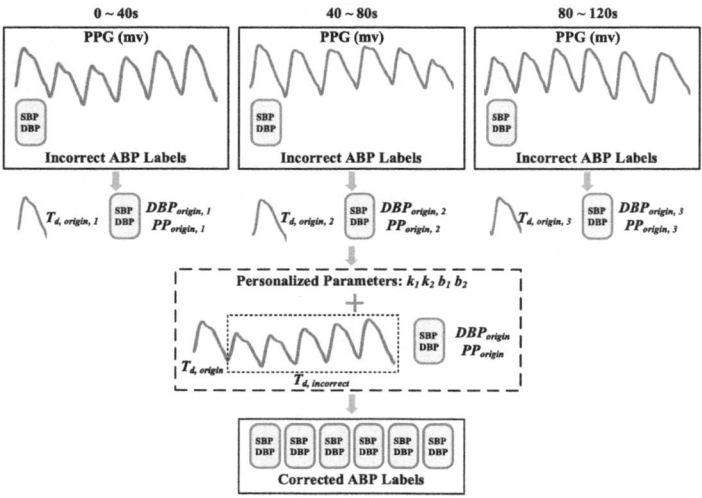

Fig. 7. ABP Label Correction Algorithm (ALCA).

At least three sets of ground truth data from a cuff-based ABP monitor, collected without interruption, are required to solve for the personalized parameters k_1, b_1, k_2, and b_2. Therefore, we collect ABP data three times, each time obtaining an ABP label (DBP_{origin}, SBP_{origin}, PP_{origin}) and continuous PPG data. The first period $T_{d,origin}$ of PPG data is considered the most relevant to the ABP label. Using the three sets of data, we calculate the personalized parameters k_1, b_1, k_2, and b_2. Then, by utilizing the PPG features $T_{d,incorrect}$ associated with the incorrect ABP labels, we compute the correct ABP labels using Eq. (3). The complete correction process is detailed in Fig. 7.

$$\begin{cases} DBP_{correct} = k_1(DT_{incorrect} - DT_{origin}) + b_1 + DBP_{origin}, \\ PP_{correct} = k_2(DT_{incorrect} - DT_{origin}) + b_2 + PP_{origin}, \\ SBP_{correct} = DBP_{correct} + PP_{correct} \end{cases} \quad (3)$$

4.4   Personalized ABP Model

Searching for the Most Similar Cluster. Using ICLM, we successfully cluster PPG features from a large dataset (called the set of clusters C). Individuals with similar physiological features were grouped together. The target user's personalized data, after being corrected by ALCA, also acquire individual PPG features through the pre-trained ICLM. We use the KNN algorithm [12] to find the cluster C_i that is most similar to the target user's features i.

Fine-Tuning. The target user's few-shot sample data and the most similar cluster data are used to fine-tune the personalized ABP model. Due to the limited amount of personalized data, we choose a simple deep learning model with four linear layers. The first layer maps the five input features to 256 dimensions, followed by intermediate layers with 128 and 64 dimensions. The final layer outputs the SBP and DBP values.

5   Experiment

In this section, we validate the performance of SimilarBP through extensive experiments, focusing on two main questions: i) What is the impact of ICLM and ALCA on the performance of ABP measurement? ii) How effective is ICLM in clustering PPG features?

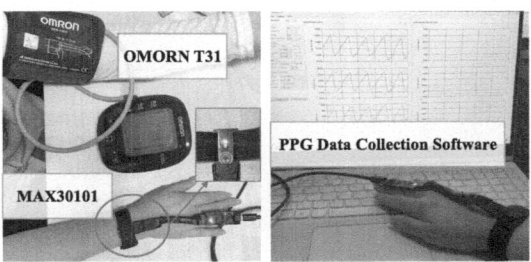

Fig. 8. Data collection equipment.

5.1   Experimental Setup

Datasets. We choose to adopt the Blumio dataset [15] because it contains continuous ABP waveforms, which helps to avoid issues with incorrect ABP labels. Specifically, for our pre-training dataset, we select individuals with recording times exceeding 7 min. Those with recording times of less than 7 min, totaling 68 individuals, are designated for the personalized dataset.

To better validate the performance of SimilarBP in real-world scenarios, we recruit 100 volunteers and collect a personalized dataset (as shown in Fig. 8). This dataset includes ABP data (using OMORN T31 [16]) and wrist-PPG data (with MAX30101 [17]) from 57 males and 43 females ($17 \leq$ Age ≤ 84, $150 \leq$ Height ≤ 187 cm, $38 \leq$ Weight ≤ 85 kg).

Evaluation Metrics. The Association for the Advancement of Medical Instrumentation (AAMI) standard [14] is adopted to evaluate the performance of SimilarBP, i.e., the Mean Error (ME) of the measurement results of the ABP monitoring device should be within the range of ± 5 mmHg, and the Standard Deviation (STD) of all measurement results should not exceed 8 mmHg.

5.2   Overall Performance

As shown in Table 3, `SimilarBP` meets the AAMI standard in both Blumio dataset and volunteers dataset, i.e., $ME \leq 5$ mmHg and $STD \leq 8$ mmHg.

Table 3. Experiment Results

Dataset	Experiment Type	ABP	ME	STD	$\|ME\| \leq 5$	$\|STD\| \leq 8$
Blumio (68 individuals)	SimilarBP	SBP	2.08	3.85	63 (/68)	65 (/68)
		DBP	0.98	3.21	64 (/68)	68 (/68)
	SimilarBP (w.o. ICLM)	SBP	5.96	7.89	35 (/68)	38 (/68)
		DBP	5.63	8.16	39 (/68)	32 (/68)
Volunteers (100 individuals)	SimilarBP	SBP	2.33	3.95	94 (/100)	92 (/100)
		DBP	1.24	3.28	97 (/100)	94 (/100)
	SimilarBP (w.o. ALCA)	SBP	3.79	5.69	86 (/100)	81 (/100)
		DBP	2.29	4.84	90 (/100)	85 (/100)

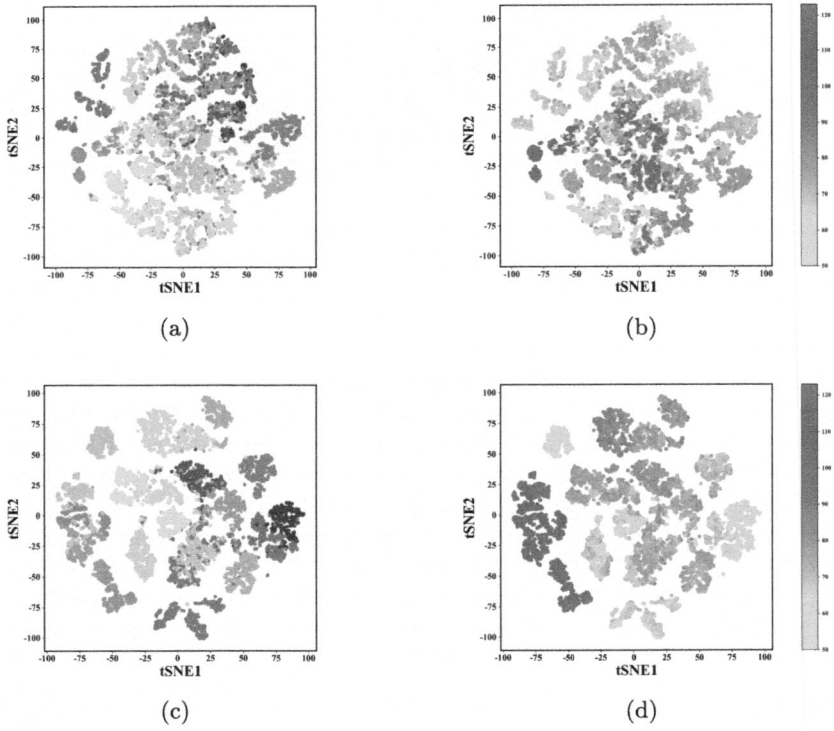

Fig. 9. PPG features before and after applying ICLM. (a–b) Original features, (c–d) Features after ICLM. Different individuals (a, c) and DBP (b, d) are distinguished by color.

For individual differences, over 93% of individuals meet the standard, demonstrating the effectiveness of `SimilarBP` for ABP measurement. The ME of `SimilarBP` (w.o. ICLM) increases to (SBP: 3.96, DBP: 2.63), and STD (SBP: 4.80, DBP: 4.16), performing worse compared to `SimilarBP` using ICLM, which indicates that ICLM has a positive impact on model performance. In the Volunteer dataset, the prediction accuracy of `SimilarBP` significantly improves compared to `SimilarBP` (w.o. ALCA), achieving ME (SBP: 2.33, DBP: 1.24) and STD (SBP: 3.95, DBP: 3.28), which indicates that the corrected ABP labels improved the model's accuracy. For individual differences, over 92% of volunteers meet the standard, demonstrating the effectiveness of `SimilarBP` in real-world ABP monitoring scenarios.

5.3 Understanding the Performance of `SimilarBP`

We use the t-SNE method [18] to visualize PPG features in two dimensions to assess the clustering effect of ICLM on the large dataset. We compare: i) the original PPG features (Fig. 9(a–b)) and ii) the PPG features after ICLM processing (Fig. 9(c–d)). In Fig. 9(a, c), different colors distinguish between different individuals, while in Fig. 9(b, d), different colors distinguish between different DBP values. By comparing the PPG features before and after the application of ICLM, it is evident that ICLM enables the PPG features in Fig. 9(c) to form distinct clusters more clearly. More importantly, each cluster corresponds to distinct ABP variations as shown in Fig. 9(d), further illustrating the effectiveness of these features in the ABP regression model.

6 Conclusion

This study proposes a deep learning-based ABP monitoring system `SimilarBP`, which achieves high ABP monitoring performance with few-shot labeled data. We validate the performance of our system on both public datasets and a real-world volunteer dataset. Experimental results show that `SimilarBP` achieves ME (SBP: 2.08, DBP: 0.98) and STD (SBP: 3.85, DBP: 3.21) on the Blumio dataset, and ME (SBP: 2.33, DBP: 1.24) and STD (SBP: 3.95, DBP: 3.28) on the real-world volunteer dataset, both meeting the AAMI standard. Ablation experiment results also demonstrate the effectiveness of `SimilarBP` in ABP measurement with our two innovative designs: I) Individualized Contrastive Learning Model (ICLM), and ii) ABP Label Correction Algorithm (ALCA).

Despite its promising results, `SimilarBP` has two limitations: i) It does not measure ABP under motion as the training datasets used were collected under static conditions. Future work should include data collected under dynamic conditions. ii) It requires three user calibrations due to our label correction method, limiting its zero-shot capabilities. Future efforts will focus on reducing calibration needs or developing methods using fewer calibration points.

Acknowledgments. The work was supported by the Beijing Natural Science Foundation (L223002).

References

1. Carek, A.M., Conant, J., Joshi, A., Kang, H., Inan, O.T.: Seismowatch: wearable cuffless blood pressure monitoring using pulse transit time. Proc. ACM Interact. Mob. Wearable Ubiquit. Technol. **1**(3), 1–16 (2017)
2. Wang, E.J., et al.: Seismo: blood pressure monitoring using built-in smartphone accelerometer and camera. In: Proceedings of the 2018 CHI Conference on Human Factors in Computing Systems, pp. 1–9 (2018)
3. Yao, P., et al.: Multi-dimensional feature combination method for continuous blood pressure measurement based on wrist PPG sensor. IEEE J. Biomed. Health Inform. **26**(8), 3708–3719 (2022)
4. Hsiao, C.-Y., Han, C.-F., Lee, R.-G., Hsiao, C.-C., Lin, R.: Feasibility study of dual-PPG sensors for blood velocity and pressure estimation. In: 2018 IEEE International Conference on Systems, Man, and Cybernetics (SMC), pp. 4065–4070. IEEE (2018)
5. Aguet, C., et al.: Blood pressure monitoring during anesthesia induction using PPG morphology features and machine learning. PLoS ONE **18**(2), e0279419 (2023)
6. Natarajan, K., et al.: Photoplethysmography fast upstroke time intervals can be useful features for cuff-less measurement of blood pressure changes in humans. IEEE Trans. Biomed. Eng. **69**(1), 53–62 (2021)
7. Schlesinger, O., Vigderhouse, N., Eytan, D., Moshe, Y.: Blood pressure estimation from PPG signals using convolutional neural networks and Siamese network. In: ICASSP 2020 - 2020 IEEE International Conference on Acoustics, Speech and Signal Processing (ICASSP), pp. 1135–1139 (2020)
8. Leitner, J., Chiang, P.-H., Dey, S.: Personalized blood pressure estimation using photoplethysmography: a transfer learning approach. IEEE J. Biomed. Health Inform. **26**(1), 218–228 (2022)
9. Fan, F., Gu, Y., Shen, J., Dong, F., Chen, Y.: FewShotBP: towards personalized ubiquitous continuous blood pressure measurement. Proc. ACM Interact. Mob. Wearable Ubiquit. Technol. **7**(3) (2023)
10. Cao, Y., Chen, H., Li, F., Wang, Y.: Crisp-BP: continuous wrist PPG-based blood pressure measurement. In: Proceedings of the 27th Annual International Conference on Mobile Computing and Networking, pp. 378–391 (2021)
11. Wang, W., Mohseni, P., Kilgore, K.L., Najafizadeh, L.: Cuff-less blood pressure estimation from photoplethysmography via visibility graph and transfer learning. IEEE J. Biomed. Health Inform. **26**(5), 2075–2085 (2021)
12. Cover, T., Hart, P.: Nearest neighbor pattern classification. IEEE Trans. Inf. Theory **13**(1), 21–27 (1967)
13. Scholkmann, F., Boss, J., Wolf, M.: An efficient algorithm for automatic peak detection in noisy periodic and quasi-periodic signals. Algorithms **5**(4), 588–603 (2012)
14. Stergiou, G.S., et al.: A universal standard for the validation of blood pressure measuring devices: association for the advancement of medical instrumentation/European society of hypertension/international organization for standardization (AAMI/ESH/ISO) collaboration statement. Hypertension **71**(3), 368–374 (2018)
15. Gomes, E., Liao, C., Shay, O., Bikhchandani, N.: A dataset of synchronized signals from wearable cardiovascular monitoring sensors (2021)
16. Omron T31 (2024). https://www.omronhealthcare.com.cn/product/info/1/T31.html

17. Ma, C., et al.: STP: self-supervised transfer learning based on transformer for noninvasive blood pressure estimation using photoplethysmography. Expert Syst. Appl. **249**, 123809 (2024)
18. van der Maaten, L., Hinton, G.: Visualizing data using t-SNE. J. Mach. Learn. Res. **9**(Nov), 2579–2605 (2008)

Author Index

B

Bao, Chenyu   I-258
Ben, Yuwei   II-96

C

Chai, Baobao   I-76
Chai, Xiaolin   I-168
Chen, Yihong   I-247
Chen, Zhuoying   II-158

D

Dai, Haipeng   I-16
Ding, Yuxuan   II-40
Ding, Zhi   I-64
Dong, Chao   I-16, II-29
Dong, Fang   I-104
Dong, Pingping   II-74
Dong, Wei   I-64
Dong, Yu   II-110
Du, Junzhao   II-14

E

Ejaz, Muhammad Asim   II-184

F

Fan, Yu   II-40
Fan, Zequn   I-40
Fang, Zhou   I-280
Fei, Haiqiang   I-52, I-92

G

Gao, Yi   I-64
Gong, Hang   II-195
Gu, Yuxiang   II-206
Guo, Hao   II-135
Guo, Shuxian   I-205, I-218
Guo, Zhongwen   II-170

H

Han, Jianmin   II-121
Han, Jinsong   I-143
Hao, Shasha   II-3
Hong, Feng   I-258
Hou, Mingxing   I-205, I-218
Hu, Gangqiang   II-121
Hu, Ruilin   I-130
Huang, Tianyu   I-104
Huang, Xinming   II-195
Huang, Yao   I-76

J

Jia, Xu   I-27
Jiang, Nan   I-3
Jiang, Yan   II-96

K

Kong, Boyu   I-64

L

Li, Bing   II-121, II-206
Li, Borui   I-118
Li, Jinru   I-40
Li, Qi   II-195
Li, Qingbin   I-258
Li, Wei   II-96
Li, Wenhao   I-52
Li, Yidi   II-135
Li, Ziyi   I-3
Liang, Wei   II-228
Lijie, Xu   I-27
Lin, Qi   I-234
Lingyun, Jiang   I-27
Liu, Changyuan   II-14
Liu, Hui   II-14
Liu, Jianwei   I-143
Liu, Jinhui   II-170
Liu, Liang   II-40
Liu, Meng   I-247
Liu, Mengyang   I-104

Liu, Peng II-63
Liu, Qiang II-96
Liu, Sizhou II-135
Liu, Taoying II-96
Liu, Wenbin I-181
Liu, Yingjian II-170
Liu, Yongji I-92
Liu, Yuzhao I-155
Lodhi, Muhammad Ali II-184, II-217
Lou, Zhaoyang I-168
Lu, Jianfeng II-121
Lu, Li I-130
Lu, Songtao I-118
Lv, Jiamei I-64

M
Ma, Chao II-158
Ma, Huadong I-234, II-40
Ma, Huahong II-206
Ma, Ming II-195
Mahmood, Khalid II-217
Mo, Ziying II-74
Mu, Xiaofang I-205, I-218

P
Pan, Qingxian I-40
Peng, Jing II-195

Q
Qi, Peng II-3, II-110
Qu, Yuben I-16
Qureshi, Khalid Ibrahim II-184, II-217

R
Ren, Zheng I-130

S
Saijun, Yang I-27
Shang, Ce I-168
Shen, Yang I-269
Shi, Hong I-205, I-218
Shou, ShenWei II-147
Song, Chao I-130
Song, Minghui I-205
Song, Wenfan I-143
Song, Yixuan I-280
Sun, Jinyao II-29
Sun, Limin I-92
Sun, Yan I-168

T
Tao, Dan II-3, II-110
Tian, Fangming I-258
Tian, Haodong I-104
Tian, Shizhao I-92
Tu, Qiang II-53

W
Wang, Chuqing II-228
Wang, En I-181
Wang, Guijuan I-76
Wang, Haitao II-53
Wang, Hui II-147
Wang, Jinfa I-52
Wang, Lei II-184, II-217
Wang, Qi I-280, II-63
Wang, Qian II-74
Wang, Qingshan II-63
Wang, Ruoyu II-170
Wang, Shuai I-118
Wang, Weilong I-118
Wang, Zijian I-218
Wei, Kai I-40
Weifeng, Lu I-27
Wu, Hejun II-53
Wu, Honghai II-206
Wu, Xiaotong I-218
Wu, Yiming I-218

X
Xiang, Hui II-14
Xiaotong, Wu I-205
Xie, Pengjin II-40
Xing, Ling II-206
Xu, Guoqing I-181
Xu, Zhao-Dong I-118

Y
Yang, Chenxu II-135
Yang, Yarun II-63
Yao, Muyan II-3, II-110
Yu, Jiguo I-76
Yu, Song I-40
Yu, Zesheng I-3
Yu, Zhongyuan I-76

Z

Zang, Qiance I-258
Zeng, Xiaowei II-121
Zha, Zonghai II-170
Zhang, Hongfei II-135
Zhang, Hongliang I-76
Zhang, Jing I-3, II-74
Zhang, Kairan II-135
Zhang, Lei II-29
Zhang, Lianming II-74
Zhang, Ruyan I-16
Zhang, Shugan II-195
Zhang, Xiaofeng I-52
Zhang, Yuejing I-3

Zhao, Dong I-280
Zhao, Langcheng I-234
Zhao, Yilin I-247
Zheng, Chunyang I-52
Zheng, Meng II-228
Zhou, Anfu I-234
Zhou, Ruiting I-104
Zhou, Xiaolei I-118
Zhu, HongSong I-52
Zhu, Hongsong I-92
Zhu, Weiping II-158
Zhu, Xiaojun I-16, I-269, II-29
Zou, Yunguo II-158
Zou, Zefeng I-3

The manufacturer's authorised representative in the EU is Springer
Nature Customer Service Centre GmbH, Europaplatz 3, 69115 Heidelberg,
Germany. If you have any concerns regarding our products, please
contact ProductSafety@springernature.com

Printed and bound by CPI Group (UK) Ltd, Croydon, CR0 4YY
29/04/2026
02099537-0003